William Black

The Monarch of Mincing Lane

William Black

The Monarch of Mincing Lane

ISBN/EAN: 9783743407800

Manufactured in Europe, USA, Canada, Australia, Japa

Cover: Foto ©ninafisch / pixelio.de

Manufactured and distributed by brebook publishing software (www.brebook.com)

William Black

The Monarch of Mincing Lane

THE MONARCH OF MINCING LANE.

NEW YORK:
JOHN B. ALDEN, PUBLISHER,
1883.

THE MONARCH OF MINCING LANE:

CHAPTER I.

TOWARDS the lower end of Park Lane there are a number of small, narrow, round-fronted houses—*bijou residences* they are called by the auctioneers—which look as if their balconies had been squeezed out of them by absolute pressure. At a window overlooking one of those miniature balconies stood, on the forenoon of a certain day in February, two young people, who did not seem to be in an amiable frame of mind. They looked out in a silent and absent way, on the strange glare of wintry sunshine that lay over the familiar scene before them; but they did not seem to notice the peculiar effect it produced. At this moment, indeed, Hyde Park was transfigured; and any one less intent upon personal affairs could not fail to have been struck by its appearance. Above the tall houses of Knightsbridge and Kensington Gore, that lay in a faintly blue shadow, there was, instead of the sun, a confused mass of shifting golden mist; and this strong centre of light shone over the broad slopes of the park, which were intensely green with melted hoar frost, and sent a pale radiance to gleam whitely on the ranges of buildings lying west of the Marble Arch. Down in front of Park Lane the leafless trees stood dark and clear in this bewildering light, and you could see through them the arm and shield of the Achilles statue; while around the Serpentine the masses of elms were of a pale blue, and that again became a dusky purple among the close trees of Kensington Gardens. The strong, shifting yellow glare seemed to be the light of the coming spring fighting with the retreating fog of the winter; the atmosphere had grown warm and moist, and the grass was glittering with the gleaming drops of the melted rime; while down by Apsley House a man was wheeling along a barrowful of primroses and violets imbedded in moss, and you could buy a pennyworth of the sweet new life that was beginning to throb and swell in the clear country air far out beyond the town.

The elder of these two persons was a young man of about twenty-four, whom you would at first sight have taken for a Spaniard. But with his dark complexion, his black moustache, and somewhat haughty bearing, he showed an English height of stature and breadth of shoulder, and exhibited an unmistakably English bluntness and directness of manner. He was handsome rather than good looking—well formed, strong, with a clear dark eye, a square, intellectual forehead, and a profusion of dark and wavy hair. There was strength in his appearance rather than grace; and there was at times perceptible in the reticence of his manhood a trace of wilfulness in speech or gesture that was clearly juvenile, and spoke of a somewhat uncurbed youth. He was dressed fashionably, but rather negligently, and had a riding switch in his hand.

When two young people stare persistently at nothing, look morose, and keep near each other without uttering a word, they are lovers and have fallen out.

His companion, who had now sat down at the opposite side of the window, had apparently, like himself been out riding. She still wore her habit, and her hat lay beside his on the table behind them. In fact, they had just returned from a canter in the Row, where, it is presumable, the quarrel had arisen.

She was certainly not much his junior; and there was a mature womanly grace and ease about her figure and manner. She was not lovely. Men might have said of her. " Handsome sort of woman;" women would have said of her, " Plain —decidedly plain." But strong men, and intellectual men, have fallen in love with plain women; and, indeed, those women who figure in history as having enchained and fascinated, beyond power of protest or resistance, the greatest men of their time have almost invariably been plain; nor has it always happened that they have possessed compensations for their want of personal beauty in the way of wit, ability, or special accomplishments. But since ever history began to be minute, we know that the mistresses of great statesmen and the loves of great poets have been, as a rule, the reverse of beautiful; and in our own times, in our own small circles, there are few of us who have not met some plain commonplace sort of woman who somehow exercises a nameless fascination over all the men around her, and, in the poor competition of the drawing-room, wins easy victories over the heads of far more beautiful women. Perhaps Miss Thormanby, who now sat twisting a corner of her glove, did not possess this power of general fascination; but she had certainly taken captive the man who stood beside her, and who so frequently rebelled, in a savage and bitter way, against his slavery. Yet he did not wish to break the chains that bound him. Had he so resolved, he had a powerful and resolute will that would have sent him into Lopez's army or into the Australian bush for half a dozen years, and so completed his freedom. But to a young man, however dissatisfied he may be with the woman with whom ill-luck has made him fall in love, there is something very sad and hopeless in relinquishing all the future he had constructed for them both. He has a vague idea that he will never again love a woman as he loves this one. If he destroys the beautiful world that love has painted for him in the distance, it will never, he thinks, be possible to build it up again. Thus he would rather struggle on with those weaknesses of character which he perceives in his companion, and strive to improve her and raise her to that higher standard of womanhood which is his ideal. That he should ever undertake such a task, shows what a peculiar film love may cast over the eyes of the clearest-headed men.

Mary Thormanby had a handsome figure and a good presence. Her features were rather irregular; her complexion pale, and a trifle dull; her eyes large, gray, and fine; her hair flaxen. Her face generally was cold, and seemed to want flexibility; while her aquiline nose, her thin lips, and a certain gait she had, gave one a notion that she was unimpressionable, resolute, and proud. If such was the expression of her general appearance, her manner speedily contradicted it; for nothing could exceed the almost unnecessary complaisance of her bearing, especially to strangers. She had a trick of making friends with one in a few seconds; and she seemed to bring herself, by the exercise of a swift, keen, intellectual sympathy, immediately *en rapport* with the person addressed. It was then that her eyes grew full of light and intelligence, and banished the apparent coldness of her face. Her teeth, too, it should be mentioned, were beautifully white and regular; and when, with this access of sympathy brightening the big gray eyes, she chose to smile and disclose the nut-white teeth, the transformation of her face was perfect, and you would regard her thenceforth as quite a different creature from the impassive, reserved woman who had entered the room with the cold dignity of an empress.

"You are romantic, and I am not—that is all," she said, at last, to her companion, Philip Drem.

There was a touch of indifference, or resignation in her voice, as though she had ceased to care any longer about the matter in dispute.

"Yes," he answered, bitterly, "I suppose I am romantic; I fancied that women were instinctively truthful and sincere."

"You carry *your* sincerity to the verge of rudeness," she said, calmly.

"Perhaps."

There was an interval of dead silence, only broken by the rumbling of the carriages down below as they rolled past towards Piccadilly, or, conversely, up to Oxford street. The glare of yellow sunlight still hung over Kensington, and fell on the wet, green slopes of the Park and on the white fronts of the houses in the north. At length she was provoked into speaking, and said, sharply,—

"The fact is, you have been a spoiled boy all your life, and you not only expect to have everything you want, but you expect that every one will be to you just what you want them to be."

"That is asking no sacrifice from you," he said, with what was remarkably like a sneer; "you can be anything to anybody. You can persuade the greatest stranger that you have been of his or her way of thinking all your life. You are too clever to be sincere. You persuade yourself that all this pretence is kindness to the people whom you meet; but it is only an intellectual feat you are proud of, and you forget that it is deception as well. Why, the way in which you flattered and cajoled that hideous old woman, O'Mallory——"

"Lady O'Mallory was a friend of my parents in Ireland," said Miss Thormanby, not caring to take any notice of what he had said about herself, "and I ought to do my best to please her for their sakes. If you have no respect for me, at least respect those older than yourself——"

"Respect the O'Mallory!" he cried, with a laugh.

"I say you are merely a spoiled boy. It is the same now as when we first began to know you down in Surrey. Then there was nobody in the house—nobody in the world—but Master Philip. No one was thought of but Master Philip; and even when your papa came down from town, he had no authority in his own house. Master Philip strolled about with his gun and amused himself; and luncheon, and dinner, and visitors were alike expected to wait on Master Philip. A foolish stepmother was the worst of the lot; and looked upon herself as only too happy if her darling boy would accept the daintiest bit of everything at table. She was delighted to wait upon him herself; and would have gone out shooting with him to load his gun, I daresay, if she only knew how. Then Master Philip goes to Cambridge, and is nearly expelled for throwing a man into the river and kicking his hat in after him. But all at once Master Philip gets into some political clique, begins to study diligently, takes his degree, and comes up to London a fierce Radical. Nothing will do for him but that every man and woman he meets must be honest—that is to say, rude and vulgar—and you are contemptible if you do not nourish great schemes for the future of street scavengers, and costermongers, and such people. To tell you the truth, Philip, I begin to feel your latest hobby a little tiresome. If politics only mean that you are to become suspicious of your friends and disagreeable in your manner, I prefer letting them alone. When I have been privileged to meet representatives of the classes about whom you are so anxious, I have generally found them ready to get half a crown by begging rather than by work—others very ready to pocket a spoon or a brooch when they have been mending the water-pipes or painting the house—others systematically cheating you in the addition of their bills; and I really don't see why one should so trouble one's self about their political privileges and position. They won't thank you for your disinterested efforts—which seem to me to consist chiefly in insulting your friends; and so I wish you would assume some other character."

"You have the nimblest wit of any woman I know," he said, provoked into a grim smile.

"You are quite aware that you are fencing with the question, and that politics have remarkably little to do with your habit of making believe. Why do I protest against your constant hypocrisy-if I must speak plainly? I want to show you the absurdity of all this pretense, that answers no end whatever. I want you to be honest. And you indignantly deny that you are guilty of anything but common courtesy; and then the next minute you meet some hideous old fool of a woman——"

"That is Lady O'Mallory, I presume," she interjected.

"Or some man to whom you have been scarcely introduced, and you talk to the one as if she were your only friend, and to the other as if you were engaged to him. You ought to have more self-respect than to play the hypocrite in order to amuse these people——"

"Really, Philip, your Radical politics are teaching you charming language. However, plain-speaking, as you suggest, must be such a novelty to me, that I ought to welcome it. I wish, though, you would be a little more consistent in your censures. You say I ought to be more honest; I should appear to be what I am; I should show everybody what I think. Yet you yourself are constantly charging me with having degraded views of life—with caring for nothing beyond amusement, dress, and the talk of society. I have no grand aspirations; I only live for my own gratification; I am selfish and so on, and so on, and so on. If my true nature is so very bad, and mean, and petty, and contemptible, is it not better that I should conceal it? If I am so selfish, ought I not to pretend to take an interest in other people and their affairs? Being so poor, and commonplace, and unsympathetic a creature, surely my hypocrisy becomes a virtue; and I wish that you too, would become so much of a hypocrite as to lessen your rudeness and treat me with a little of the respect which you would show to any stranger."

With that she drew herself up to her full height, and walked across the room to the table on which her hat and riding whip lay.

Philip shrugged his shoulders.

"I wish you would treat me with a little of the profuse affection you show to *every* stranger!" he muttered. But she did not hear him.

Then she took her hat and whip into her hand, gathered up her dress with the other, and, with her pale clear-cut English face looking pitiless and proud, said coldly,—

"I must change my dress for luncheon; uncle and aunt will be home presently. Will you stay?"

"No thank you."

"Do you dine with us this evening then?"

' I scarcely remember whether I promised or not. But since you are in so amiable a mood, perhaps I had better dine at the club. I hope you won't refuse to shake hands with me."

In this way they bade each other good-bye; he went downstairs, and out into the street.

"Why can't I leave her alone," he said to himself, as he walked down to Piccadilly, "and let her be as God made her? If I could get her to assume sincerity, it would still be an as-

sumption. It would only be adding another to her *roles;* and
I should see through the piece of acting. As it is she has many
good qualities; and sometimes exhibits a flash of sincerity that
blinds one like lightning, so sudden and startling it is. Perhaps
it is startling, because it is unexpected."

There was a hard smile on his face, begotten of this thought,
as he walked into his club in St. James's Street, went into the
reading-room, and looked at the second edition of the "Times."
He did not see anything of the type before him; or, at least,
he had no sort of notion what the words meant. He was regarding mechanically a telegram which told of another despairing
effort of Austria to pacify her incorrigible Czechs, but he was
thinking of Mary Normanby and her uncle and aunt.

"She knows well why the old Major and his vulgar wife
are so delighted to see me at dinner. She knows well what
the proposal about a quiet little rubber after dinner means;
and she knows that though the Major and I pay in threepenny
points, it is guinea points that have to be paid afterwards. She
understands the Major's little joke which always put her and
me as partners, while he and mother Delaney settle down to
the plucking of their conscious victim. What an amiable young
man they must consider me, thus to sit and lose sovereigns for
the sake of playing with their niece! And Mary knows that I
see their coarse and obvious game; and I have caught her clear
gray eyes glancing furtively at me at times, and I have seen a
quick blush of shame covering her cheeks, as that awful old
woman loudly claimed two by honors when Mary herself had
played ace and queen. Yet they are content to play the open
trick night after night; and it is only Mary who is sometimes
driven by shame to protest against it. 'Bless me!' says the
old fat woman, with a giggle of wonder, 'what a bad memory I
have! Sure I thought I played the quane!'"

He became aware at this moment that some one else wanted
to look down the column of latest intelligence; so he moved
an inch or two to one side, and recalled himself so far as to
glance at the news. One of the paragraphs was as follows:

"ST. NAZAIRE, Feb. 8.—*The brig* 'Georgiette,' *from Mar-
tinique to St. Nazaire, reports the total loss, in longitude* 18° 10,' *of
the ship* 'Westmoreland,' *Captain Seaford, from Jamaica to London. The* 'Westmoreland' *was caught in a heavy gale and
foundered with all hands on board.*"

"So that is the end of poor old Tom Seaford," said Philip

Drem, as he slowly left the room, "the kindly fellow with the dark blue eyes and the curly brown hair, who used to take me on his knee, and empty his pockets of all sorts of wonderful toys, and sing those famous old ballads. I must go along to my father, and ask what he is going to do for Tom's widow and child. He must do something for them; for I fancy he treated poor old Seaford very hardly when he was alive."

The club-porter called a Hansom; the young man stepped inside, and bade the cabman drive to Mincing Lane.

CHAPTER II

When Shanghai first became the El Dorado of English commerce, and boys at school were taught to long for ten years' penal servitude in China, as a sort of purgatory whence they should reach the modern heaven of unlimited wealth, Richard Drem went out to this land of promise, and found it amazingly fruitful. His constitution could stand any amount of heat—a fact which his fellow-clerks used to say promised well for his comfort in the next world. He was never guilty of any extravagance or folly; he was found to be an adept in bargaining with the natives who are the greatest liars in the world, for he encountered them with their own weapons; and so pertinaciously did he stick to business that his becoming a partner, his setting up a firm for himself, and his gradually extending his commercial relations, and forming agencies in all parts of the world, were steps of a career which followed each other with amazing swiftness. But while Richard Drem was yet making his way, there arrived in Shanghai a Spaniard named Estariz, with his only daughter. What had tempted this old man, who was apparently poor and friendless, to seek his living in this remote climate, no one knows; nor can one well understand how Richard Drem first conceived the notion of marrying a girl who was penniless. There is reason to believe that the Senorita Anna was led to sacrifice herself, in order to gain for her unsuspecting father a stituation in the house of which Richard Drem was now a junior partner. At all events, they were married; and the young and handsome Spanish girl died in giving birth to a son. When Richard Drem, having founded the great firm of Drem & Co., in Yokohama, Canton, Melbourne, and Calcutta, returned to London, Philip was a small boy of six or seven years of age.

Richard Drem was now a very important man. He was the luminous head of all the Drem family; and he was content to earn the pleasure of bestowing alms on his poor relations if only they would keep at a distance, and not disgrace him before his London friends. Sometimes the unconscious perversity of human nature made him rebel against the charity he gave, and the adulation he reaped; and I believe that at such times he almost wished himself without a farthing in order to spite these pests of claimants.

All his relations were not equally poor. There were the Seafords, for example, a Devonshire family, who were his cousins. It was shortly after his return to England that Richard Drem discovered that his cousin, Tom Seaford, who had always been a roving and merry-hearted fellow, rather wild and given to all manner of mad pranks, had some years before completed the list of his offences by marrying a young Devonshire girl, the daughter of a fisherman, or some other obscure person. Mr. Drem took it upon him to lecture Tom. His cousin, never very cautious in his language, not only spoke up for his wife, but added some phrases about Richard Drem which the latter never forgot or forgave. From that moment Tom Seaford became the object of Richard Drem's bitterest enmity, which soon showed itself in stirring up disturbances between Tom and his father a weak old man, who was at last induced to forbid his son to come near the house. The rest of the story we need not enter into at present.

On this February afternoon Mr. Drem was seated in his private room, on the first floor of the Mincing Lane offices. He was a short, broad-built man, with a red, irregularly-shaped face, and a mass of short, thick, white hair, that seemed to stand on end as it rose straight from his forehead. He was dressed in black, and he wore a snow-white neckcloth.

Downstairs, as the early twilight made the long mahogany desked apartment looked dusky and gray, there was profound silence, broken only by a cough or the scratching of a pen. The tea, sugar, coffee, cotton, jute, and other brokers (who are the floats that tell the commercial angler when his bait has taken) had ceased to rush in frantically with bids; the business of the day was practically over; and a gentle state of coma had fallen over most of the clerks. The young gentleman nearest the door, whose papa had paid £500 to have him placed on that tall stool, and whose business it was to answer inquiries, pay sugar duties, and carry checks to the shipbrokers, was pretending to add up the figures of certain landing accounts, but was in reality busy in trying to sketch the face of a popular actress on his blotting paper. He was thus engaged when the door of the office was gently opened, and a small, slight woman, dressed in black, with a young girl by her side, entered.

She inquired timidly whether Mr. Drem were within. The young gentleman was striving desperately to recall the likeness of the actress, which an unlucky touch at the end of the nose had somehow spoiled. The small woman with the gentle face, the singularly dark blue eyes, and prematurely gray hair, again asked in a timid way, if she could see Mr. Drem. The young gentleman threw down the pen, turned round, blushed violently when he saw or fancied he saw two ladies waiting on him, and then in a hasty manner, said, "Certainly," opened the small door, and showed them upstairs.

They had no sooner gone up stairs than it suddenly occurred to the young gentleman that he had been guilty of the serious crime of sending some one upstairs unannounced; and he returned to his desk with a qualm at his heart. Down came the head clerk from the other end of the office.

"Who are these people?" he asked, coldly.

"I don't know, sir," stammered the youth. "I forgot——"

"Then don't forget yourself so far again."

As he was going away he caught sight of the actress's profile on the blotting paper. He said nothing; but he quietly took up the sheet, tore it into fragments, threw them in the fire, and then gravely walked back to his desk. The young gentleman began to think that commerce was a despicable thing, and that his father should have sent him into the army or the Church.

Mr. Ewart, the head clerk, had no sooner returned to his desk than there came into the office Mr. Arthur Drem, Mr. Richard Drem's nephew, a small, lean young man, with fair hair and gray eyes. His desk was opposite that of Mr. Ewart; and, as he hung up his hat, he said to the head clerk:

"Seen the second edition of the *Times*?"

"No; Mr. Drem is not done with it yet."

"The 'Westmoreland' has gone down."

"The 'Westmoreland!'"

"Yes; every nail in her has gone to the bottom."

"Thank God!" said Mr. Ewart, piously.

"And every man, too."

"Ah! I am sorry for that. But the wreck is a great relief

to me in the present state of the market. Mr. Smith, be good enough to see what invoices you have by the 'Westmoreland,' and give me a note of the quantities."

Meanwhile the two strangers had gone upstairs, and paused irresolutely on the landing. One of them was a middle-aged woman, whose soft brown hair, visible underneath her black bonnet, was streaked with gray. She had a pretty, rather sad face, with deep blue eyes, a smooth forehead, and a fair complexion, somewhat tanned and freckled by the sun even now in winter. She was dressed plainly and neatly in black. The other was evidently her daughter, and showed her mother's prettiness transferred to the springtime of youth and health. She was too young to be admired as a handsome woman; for there was an evidently girlish timidity in her manner and in the soft light of her eyes. Dark-blue eyes they were—of that intense, almost violet, blue which is at once so rare and so beautiful. She had over her white forehead masses of wavy brown hair that had a gleam of gold in it; and the tender oval girlish face had a healthy pink glow, as bright, and yet as delicate, as the blush on a white sea-shell. It was a pretty face even in its soft immaturity—a pure, trustworthy face, that only wanted time to give it repose and calm. It was in the eyes that the girlishness of Lilian Seaford's daughter chiefly showed itself —a half-frightened, bird-like look that gave to the whole face an expression of innocence and youth, that spoke of the time when the soul is not yet familiar with the earth, and finds in all new things a wonder and a delight.

Mrs. Seaford tapped gently at the glass door in front of her.

"Come in," said a harsh and reedy voice.

She opened the door. Mr. Drem looked up from his desk with astonishment in his small eyes. When in that decorous office had two women, unannounced, ever presented themselves before him. He did not rise; he merely continued his stare, apparently waiting for them to state the object of such an unprecedented intrusion.

"I called, sir, to ask if you had heard anything yet of the 'Westmoreland,'" said the small woman with the timid voice and the gray hair.

"You've come to the wrong place," he said curtly, "you must go to the ship-brokers," With that he turned to his desk as much as to say: "Go to the ship-brokers, or to the devil, only don't bother me."

"I have been to the ship-brokers, sir," she said, meekly.

"And if they can't tell you anything about the ship, how do you think I can?" he asked, with another stare.

"I thought it possible you might have received some news," she said. "I came up from Devon six weeks ago to meet my husband; and I have waited to hear something about the ship, and I cannot hear anything."

Richard Drem now turned himself round in his chair.

"Are you then——"

"Captain Seaford is my husband, sir." She spoke in a low tone, as if fearing to offend the great merchant, whom she had been taught to fear.

He in turn regarded her from head to foot, glanced at her daughter, and then said, coldly,—

"Oh indeed. Pray sit down; and I will ask about the 'Westmoreland.'"

He whistled down a tube for Mr. Ewart, who forthwith presented himself.

"How is it that these—ladies—have been sent up in this way?"

"Mistake, sir, of Mr. Mowbray."

"Kick the young fool out of the place if he does it again—do you hear? What about this ship—this 'Westmoreland?' Have you heard anything of her? She is from Jamaica—eh, eh? From Jamaica, isn't she?"

"The 'Westmoreland' is——"

Somehow the man happening to glance at the woman whose eyes were fixed upon him, paused. There flashed upon him a suspicion as to the object of her visit.

"Well, well?" said Richard Drem, impatiently, apparently wishing the whole of them were where the 'Westmoreland' lay at that moment. "What is it? what is it? Have you heard of the 'Westmoreland?'"

The woman's frightened eyes had noticed his hesitation.

"You *have* heard," she said, advancing a step towards him. Where is—the ship?"

"Madam, the 'Westmoreland' is lost," he said.

"Lost! And my husband?"

"The telegram says all on board were drowned," said the man, knowing as he spoke, that his words were killing all the joy that might yet be possible to her in life.

"My husband dead!—dead!" she exclaimed, with white, scared face, and a strange look in her eyes, as if she were possessed—as if she were gazing out on the great sea striving to find something. "Oh! Lilian, he is never coming back to us any more!"

She threw her arms around her daughter's neck and hid her face from the light, while the young girl sobbed with a vague apprehensive grief over a misfortune which she was scarcely capable of comprehending.

Mr. Ewart slipped down the stairs unperceived; and Richard Drem came forward to his cousin's widow.

"I am very sorry," he said. "I didn't know, I hope you will bear up against it, now that it is past help, you know. He and I never got on well together; but we will let by-gones be by-gones if you like. And if I can be of any assistance to you——"

The woman looked up and confronted him. The white face was now full of scorn and the musical soft voice had grown harsh and cold.

"From you? We are to take money from you, that murdered him? Ah! you look surprised; but you know that it is true; you know that it is you who have killed him. What harm did he ever do you, that you lied and lied until you had him driven from his father's house?—what did he ever do to you that you pursued him with your hate and malice until he was cast off, until not one of his friends cared to know how my poor husband was fighting his way in the world? He had but two friends left, and now you have cut him off from us too, and we shall never see him any more. And now that you have done it—now that you have been successful—you offer us your pity and assistance! Lilian, come away—quickly; you are not safe so near that man who murdered your father, and my poor husband."

"Was the woman possessed?" asked Richard Drem of himself. There was a wild look in her eyes that had succeeded the appalling calm with which she had heard the tidings of her husband's death; and there was a violence in her manner strangely out of keeping with her slender physique and the timidity of her face.

While he stood there, astonished, bitterly annoyed and growing rapidly angry, the woman seized her daughter's hand, and half-dragged the girl out of the room. She shut the door behind her; and then the force of her indignation, that had so far sustained her, gave way utterly. She caught the girl to her, and smoothed back the rich brown hair from her forehead, and kissed her tearfully, with incoherent expressions of fondness.

"Let us go away from here, mamma," said Lilian Seaford. "The place frightens me. Let us go home."

"Home? We must never go home any more," said the poor woman, weeping bitterly, and thinking of the pleasant place in Devonshire where her young married life had been spent.

They went downstairs through the office, and into Mincing Lane. As the two strangers looked around in a sort of bewildered way, they knew they were alone in London.

CHAPTER II.

It was very seldom, indeed, that Mr. Philip honored his father's offices in Mincing Lane with a visit. Sometimes he drove down in a hansom, and condescended to take the advice of Mr. Ewart upon money matters. On these occasions he spoke but briefly to his pale-faced cousin, and never thought of going upstairs to see his father. Richard Drem was a man of business; and as the liberal allowance he gave his son was to be reckoned in figures just like anything else, the matter was transacted through the mediation of his head clerk.

Sometimes, too, Mr. Philip, after having indulged somewhat too freely in whist or pool with Mary Thormanby's uncle, was forced to appeal to Mr. Ewart for help out of his difficulties. This the clerk readily granted; and even ventured, in his grave, paternal way, to hint that the young gentleman should be a little more careful about his money, and a good deal less extravagant. So far as the advice helped him to pecuniary relief Mr. Philip took it, and was negligently thankful; but where it referred to entrenchment he laughed it off in his careless way, much to the envy and the chagrin of his cousin, Arthur, who bitterly complained of the habits of this spoiled child of fortune, and perhaps thought every £50 note which Philip received was so much taken out of the business, to which he, Arthur, secretly hoped to succeed. As for Philip Drem, he had no more notion than an infant of the value of money. He knew that a sovereign represented so many pair of gloves, or a handful of cigars, or a few cab-fares; but he had no idea that it mattered whether he kept it or lost it. This sublime indifference was very aggravating to Richard Drem, as may be well understood. There was no great affection existing between father and son; and Philip was never at any pains to conceal the estimation in which he held his parent's character.

It must be rather hard for a father to find himself being constantly called upon for checks, and knowing that the recipient of them values him only as a sort of banker; that his money can purchase for him neither the respect nor the love of his son. Richard Drem gave Mr. Philip plenty of money, because it was befitting that his son should have the means, as well as the education of a gentleman; but he occasionally rebelled against the young man's too open thanklessness; and accordingly the private life of the Drem family was sometimes marked by very pretty incidents. Mr. Drem, hot with wine and wrath, presiding at the dinner-table, and directing diverse insults at the head of his heir; the latter sitting dark and composed, with a look of haughty contempt upon his face; and Mrs. Drem, Mr. Drem's second wife, timidly interfering and begging Philip to mind.

"Mind?" the young man would say. "Why should I mind? I have got accustomed to these symptoms of uneasy digestion; and he will remember nothing of them in the morning."

When Mr. Philip did not visit the Mincing Lane offices on account of money, it was to call on a little lame lad whom he had induced Mr. Ewart to take in his employ. This lad, by name Alec Lawson, was the grandson of an old Scotchman, living at Hampstead, with whom Philip Drem had become accidentally acquainted. Philip had taken a liking to the lame boy, and had not only got him a good place and a fair salary in the office, but he also used to interfere in a somewhat arbitrary manner with Mr. Ewart's authority, and go down and carry off the lad for a day's holiday whenever the whim entered his head. So it was that these two had become something of companions; the handsome, careless, good-natured favorite of fortune finding much novelty, doubtless, in the fellowship of this lame lad, whose pale face, large forehead, prominent and strangely bright eyes, and clammy, white, blue-veined hands spoke of a highly sensitive and nervous temperament: while a certain, restless look about the large liquid eyes told of a spirit too ardent for the delicate frame in which it was enshrined. Alec Lawson looked more like a Chatterton or Keats than one of the well-fed, well-conditioned, well-dressed young gentlemen around him; and one can understand that his appearance in such an office, and among such collaborateurs, would not have been a likely thing but for the fiat of Mr. Philip's somewhat imperious will.

When Mr. Ewart came downstairs, after having announced the loss of the "Westmoreland," he told Mr. Arthur Drem who the strangers were who had gone upstairs to see his uncle. The boy Lawson overheard their names, and knew that they were old friends of Philip Drem, the latter having often spoken to him about the pretty little woman down in Devonshire, who was a captain's wife, and had an only daughter. By and by he saw them go out; and, as he was wondering whether Mr. Philip would now, after the lapse of many years, recognize his old friends, who should walk into the office but Philip Drem himself. Before he had time to push before him the little swinging door of the partition, the boy had gone over to him, and said, in an eager whisper,—

"Do you know who has just been here? Mrs. Seaford and her daughter."

"Here! What did they want?"

"I don't know. They have this moment gone out."

Without a word, Philip Drem turned and went hastily out of the office into Mincing Lane. The dusky thoroughfare was full of people, and at first a hurried glance up and down showed him no one at all answering to what he fancied the strangers ought to be like. He caught a glimpse, however, of two figures turning the corner into Great Tower Street, and these, after a moment's hesitation, he followed. He soon overtook them, and a glance or two he managed to get of their faces enabled him to identify them. He would not have recognized the young girl, so much had she grown and altered within the past few years; but the mother's face he remembered, even although the lines of gray were more frequent in the soft brown hair.

While he was yet debating how to accost them, they had gone along to the end of Tower Street, and were crossing Tower Hill, towards Trinity Square. They had just left the pavement, when a big hulking fellow, who was dragging along a little boy, cuffed the latter severely for having stumbled. The child set up a piteous cry, and the man was about to strike him again, when the young girl suddenly turned aside, put her hand on his arm, and said,—

"Oh! pray don't do that!"

There was more of wonder than entreaty in her frank young face. She seemed not to understand why he should strike the child, and was as little prepared for his response to her interference. He shook off her hand with a brutal oath, and looked as if he meant to strike instead. She shrank away from him with a peculiar look of amazement and dread, as if she were at a loss to know why her good intention had so provoked him. She had gone forward naturally to save the boy from being beaten ; and lo ! it was not a man, but a wild beast, that confronted her !

Seeing the frightened look of both the women, the scoundrel at once changed his tone, and began to beg for alms. He had eaten nothing for three days ; neither had the boy beside him. Wouldn't they have pity on the poor—they who had their warm houses, and their plenty of meat ? Then, as he saw they were gradually drawing away from him and nearing the pavement of Trinity Square, he altered his tone into a menace. They had no pity, then for the poor ? Weren't they ashamed to live on the fat of the land, and let other people starve ? Did they mean to give him nothing ?

With that the widow tremblingly pulled out her purse, and was about to open it, when Philip Drem thought it was high time to interfere. He walked up to them.

" Get out of the way !" he said to the man, as he interposed between them.

As the scoundrel seemed not only unwilling to go, but determined to resent this interruption, the next minute found him a couple of yards off, stumbling over some rough granite, whither he had been sent by a remarkably significant shove. Indeed, so very pertinent was the message which this brief hint conveyed, that the man thought it prudent to remain where he had been flung, consoling himself with a good deal of unnecessary blasphemy.

"Put your purse in your pocket, Mrs. Seaford," said Philip. " Don't you know me ? "

When she saw before her the son of the man whom she had just left, she drew back for a second ; but then the remembrance of Philip as a boy seemed to dissociate him from his father, and she said, hurriedly,—

" Yes, I know you, Mr. Philip ; but I do not wish to speak to any one. I wish to be alone with my poor girl."

" But," said Philip, hesitatingly and respectfully, " you are alone in London, are you not ? Let me see you safely to the place where you are staying. You do not know London——"

There was a despairing look in the woman's face as she answered,—

" No, we do not know London ; and yet we must make our home here now. Six weeks ago, according to an old plan of ours, I sold off all our things down in Devon, and came up to meet my—my husband. So we have waited, and now—now I cannot go back—I cannot go back! We must remain in London."

"And where are you staying now?" he asked.

"We lodge in that house over there," said the young girl —whom Philip had scarcely noticed before—as she indicated a house on the north side of Trinity Square.

"And you are quite alone?"

"Yes."

"You have no friends in London?"

"Not one," said Mrs. Seaford; but it was in a weary tone which seemed to say that the want of friends was no great loss.

"Then you must let me see about getting proper lodgings for you. You cannot remain in this dreary neighborhood—it would kill you."

"That would not be much of a misfortune, perhaps," said the widow.

"You must let me take you away from here," continued Philip, in his impetuous way. "I have a friend up at Hampstead who, I know, will be glad to receive you until you can get a more suitable place. What do you say? Suppose you go into the house and tell them you will send for your things tomorrow."

Seeing that the two strangers looked upon this proposal in a helpless and bewildered way, the young man coolly took the management of the affair into his own hands, and acted with a discretion beyond his years in giving the newly-made widow something to do, so as to distract her attention from her sorrow. He accompanied them into the house, saw the landlady, and bade her bring her bill.

"I have no bill," said the stout person, "as they've paid reg'lar enough. But I'm entitled to two weeks' notice."

"How much?"

"Height shillings a week."

Philip put his hand in his waistcoat-pocket and threw a sovereign on the table.

"Give the odd shillings to your servants."

"But you must not pay the money for me, Mr. Philip," said Mrs. Seaford, with more of wonder than resentment in her soft eyes.

"You will pay me afterwards," he said curtly (for he was not in the habit of being interfered with), "and meanwhile I am going out to get a vehicle to take you up to Hampstead. I may be a quarter of an hour. You can in that time get ready whatever you want to take with you."

With which he walked out of the house and round to Mincing Lane. His father's brougham was at the door, and Richard Drem was coming out when his son met him.

"I have a favor to ask from you, sir," remarked Mr. Philip, in his coldest and haughtiest manner.

Richard Drem stared. For his son to ask for a favor (even in so stiff a fashion) was sufficiently surprising.

"Well, well?"

"Would you mind driving home in a hansom, and lending me the brougham?"

"You can't be going to dinner at this hour—you are not dressed."

"I am going to pay a visit."

"Very well, take the brougham," said Richard Drem, as he turned into the office again to send a clerk for a cab.

Richard Drem was not displeased. He fancied his son was going to call at some house where a brougham would look better than a cab; and he was gratified to think that Philip, whose negligent habits often irritated him, was beginning to see the advantage of keeping up appearances.

"Perhaps," thought the father, "he is going to visit Sir James. Ah! if he would only go less after that girl Thormanby, and take up with Violet Kingscote, one would be inclined to give him a dozen broughams to himself. Yet he has no notion of respectability. When I offered to give him a hansom for his own use, he did not even thank me, and prefers to go about town in these dingy vehicles, paying half-crowns, and risking infection."

If Mr. Richard Drem had known that his fine carriage, with its pair of handsome horses, was then being driven round to Trinity Square, in order to take the widow and daughter of poor Tom Seaford to the new lodgings at Hampstead, he would not have been so willing to grant the favor asked of him by his son.

When Mrs. Seaford, accompanied by her daughter, came out of the house and saw waiting for her a brougham, with a coachman, and a pair of tall horses, she hesitated. But Mr. Philip took little heed of her hesitation; and so it was that, in a second or two, the three were in the carriage and on their way to Hampstead.

During that long drive the young widow's eyes were far away and wistful. She saw the people and shops go past the window in a sort of dream; and she scarcely spoke a word. Philip forbore to break in upon her sad reverie, and was thus led into talking with the young girl who sat opposite him. He had now leisure to see how fair she was. Your true lover never sees a beautiful woman without comparing her with his own particular mistress, and endeavoring to prove to his own satisfaction the immense superiority of the latter. But the man must have been an idiot who could have compared the face of Mary Thormanby with that of this young Devonshire girl, whose lovely golden-brown hair, dark blue eyes, and pretty mouth, were perfect in their way. The beautiful hair was taken back from a forehead that was as white, and smooth, though not so low, as that of Clytie; and the eyes, large and dark in hue, were shaded with long eyelashes. Philip confessed that Lilian Seaford was a good deal prettier than his mistress of the saucy eyes and the irregular, pale, fascinating face; but while the one had the attractions of a woman, the other had only the pretty *naivete* of a child. The violet eyes met his glances without fear and without scruple. There was no self-consciousness in her face. She spoke to him in her direct, simple fashion, as though he had been an old man, or an old woman, or anything rather than a handsome young gentleman of twenty-four. There was a timidity, but no trace of shyness in her manner. When his dark eyes met hers, she neither glanced downward nor betrayed any signs of embarrassment. Indeed, he saw that she was sometimes wholly oblivious of his presence, and that her face bore the expression of a strange trance-like forgetfulness and absence, which he was in after-times to study with curiosity and wonder. Were transmigration of souls possible, you could have believed that within the mask of this pretty young creature there lurked the spirit of a wood-pigeon, and that, after she had spent a few minutes in looking at you with a strange, bird-like, frightened observation and curiosity, she had flown right away into some other realm of perpetual summer, and sunshine, and blue sky.

So they drove on towards Hampstead, and Philip scarcely remembered that he had not dined. He would have devoted the afternoon, however, with more equanimity to this present freak of generosity had he left Mary Thornmanby in a more amiable mood. If he could but have snatched five minutes to go and beg her forgiveness how gladly he would have done so.

He was inwardly laughing at himself for his own weakness when the carriage was pulled up at the small green gate of the garden in front of James Lawson's house.

CHAPTER IV.

OLD James Lawson, who now sits, with shaggy white hair and keen eyes, over a book at his own fireside, was at one time a Kirkintillock weaver, when hand-loom weaving was a lucrative calling. "Jims," as his neighbors called him, was known as a man of great probity and of a very fierce temper. But his temper, instead of expending itself in his own home, sought relief in getting up bitter and vigorous opposition to anything or anybody out of doors. Needless to say, Jims was at once a Radical and a Seceder, and the prime of his manhood was spent in stirring times, when there was plenty of occasion for his angry invective and his fearless action. In 1843, when half the national Church of Scotland went out in secession, Jims was one of the most active and vigorous of the lay agitators who protested against patronage. He left himself without a shilling in getting up the rough rudiments of the great sustentation-fund for the relief of the ministers. Two years later came the Puseyite squabble, which was looked upon in Kirkintilloch as a demonstration of the Scarlet Woman, and denounced vehemently. Then came the anti-corn-law agitation, the railway mania and the panic of 1845, and the Chartist riots of 1848. Stirring times, indeed! And the short, thickset weaver, whose shaggy eyebrows were then black, and his sallow face powerful and dark, lighted up by two piercing eyes, was a terror to his more timid neighbors. Jims was bitter of speech, and the scorn and reproach he dealt out to those around him who were weak-kneed or trimmers caused many to dread contact with the village Cato. A man who could look upon the cholera visitation of 1849 as a judgment of God upon the people that had misdirected, thwarted and killed the national aspirations for liberty of the previous year, was not likely to stay his hand or tongue in censuring private delinquencies.

In the midst of his various activities, Jims was struck dumb by a family misfortune. His only daughter was betrayed, and went to Glasgow but to die of her shame, leaving behind her an infant, whom Mrs. Lawson adopted. Jims was heard to say that a man who could not rule his own household was unfit to pass a judgment on the conduct of his neighbors; and from that day he never opened his lips to speak harshly of any human being. Indeed, he was so overwhelmed with shame and grief that he could not lift up his head; and in the end he was driven to take refuge in London, bringing with him his wife and grandson, and the relics of his household gods. Times were now changed. Hand-loom weaving in the large towns was practically extinct. With what little money he had saved, Jims opened a hosiery shop in Tottenham Court Road; and so well did he succeed, and so thriftily did his wife manage his domestic affairs, that they had now been able to retire into this small cottage in Hampstead to pass the rest of their days in peace. Their grandson Alec—now a lad of fourteen—was also receiving £80 a year from Drem & Co., so that he was no charge to them.

It had been one of the whims of Mr. Philip to prosecute the acquaintance with old James Lawson which he had casually made. There was something very novel and striking to the young man, who had been brought up in the half-sceptical atmosphere of modern society—who had been taught to regard politics as a diversion for wealthy men of middle age, and as a game played between two parties—who had been accustomed to that tone of despair with which even many thoughtful men speak of the inability of mere legislation to cure the evils of this country—it was something novel and striking for him to find a man who not only believed that these evils were curable, but who firmly believed and maintained that the cure for them was withheld by the interested upper classes. Jims, in his way, was both a prophet and a politician. He mourned with the desolation of a Jeremiah over the condition of the poor; and he attacked the strongholds of the rich with a fine confidence in his means worthy of a Saint Simon. The prophet (and we have several at present) who merely bewails the present condition of things, and pours out his scorn and indignation over our institutions and ourselves, is liable to be much disturbed by the practical question, What do you want? But Jims could tell you at once what he wanted, and back up his demands by an array of facts and figures, which lost none of their weight as you looked at the rough and powerful face, the shaggy white hair, and piercing eyes.

Mr. Philip was in no danger of becoming a pupil of this

fierce old man. He dared to dispute many of Jims' facts; and
his smattering of college lore enabled him to see that Jims ve-
hement logic was very often faulty. But Philip Drem liked to
visit the old man to catch the infection of belief from him. It is
something in these days to have the conviction that a man may
achieve an actual good for his fellow-men by working at this or
that piece of legislation, or even by demonstrating the rotten-
ness of this or that portion of our political system. Philip came,
from time to time, to steal a little of that patriotic fire which
Jims kept perpetually burning on his domestic altar. But while
the old man would have had him set our whole constitution in
flames with it, as a rotten and effete thing, the young man only
took it as a sort of torch to lighten his way and give confidence
to his feet. You must look at his position before you see the
necessity for his getting these occasional flashes of inspiration.
Young, strong, handsome, rich, there was no necessity for his
doing anything beyond enjoying himself. But more important
than the natural wish for personal enjoyment possessed by
every healthy young man, was the universal example of the
people among whom he had been brought up, and with whom he
associated. The young men of his acquaintance dismissed
politics as a nuisance, and did not understand convictions about
anything beyond the condition of horses, the quality of cigars,
and the style of their feminine friends. The admirable theory
of leaving well alone was the obvious principle on which the
vast majority of the people around him fashioned their lives.
They were not responsible for the condition of affairs out-of-
doors; they did their best in their own spheres, and let political
men fight about parliamentary bills as they might. Even at
Cambridge, where he fell in with a political clique, and became
a theoretical Radical, there were vague philosophic notions
wandering hither and thither about the necessary results of
competition, the natural recovery of the lost balance, the virtue
of the stronger force, and so on. These and other influences,
to be detailed hereafter, were hard to withstand. That he did
withstand them at all was mainly owing to the impulse he received from James Lawson's fervent faith; but even in per-
mitting himself to be warmed into something like a belief, he
had to recognize the fact that Jims himself was far from being
infallible, and was on some points manifestly absurd.

Jims received the two strangers into his parlor with the
grave courtesy and dignity of a Highland chief. But he had
no sooner heard from Philip the peculiar circumstances under
which they had visited him, than he summoned Mrs. Lawson,

who was downstairs in the kitchen. When the homely, kind-faced Scotchwoman come up, Jims confided the widow and her daughter to her care, and bade her take them to her own room. He added in a whisper, as they were going out,—

"Leave them to themselves, gude wife, and don't you bother them wi' your consolations. See that you put a Bible in the room, and dootless they'll find help there."

When they had left, he turned with a sharp glance of inquiry to Philip.

"They're no Romans, are they?"

"I fancy not; although there are a good many Catholics in Devon. I don't suppose it matters much."

"Not to you o' this generation, perhaps," said Jims, with something like a frown. "And so there is another vessel wrecked. What was in her?"

"Rum, probably, and sugar, and what not."

"Hadn't your fayther enough o' rum and sugar and spices? I wonder, does he ever go down on his knees and ask God to give him another stomach?"

"Well I don't suppose he intended eating any of the raw produce of the 'Westmoreland.'"

"No; he wanted to hand the stuffs on to the people who adulterate them for the poor, himself levying a pretty blackmail on them as they passed. Don't you think it is a pretty trade, Mr. Philip—sitting at a desk and making hundreds of pounds by the scratching of a pen? What does your father do for the world? He can't make a shoe or a spoon, he can't help a blade of grass to grow; he produces nothing; but while other people are toiling and working and sweating, he sits at a table wi' a quill pen in his hand, and grasps more money in a day than a score of them could do in a year."

"You are in one of your unreasonable moods to-night, Mr. Lawson," said Philip, quietly. "I don't admire my father's trade, but I fancy it is a good deal more necessary than the making of shoes or spoons. One might make shoes and spoons at home; but when one has to import produce from abroad, there is expensive machinery needed, and people capable of running a great risk, for which they must be paid proportionately. But I suppose you are joking."

A prophet never jokes. The sense of humor is fatal to prophecy; and Jims, in every other way a thorough Scotchman, had not the faintest notion of humor.

"Unreasonable! Aye, as unreasonable as Micah was unreasonable," he grumbled, "when he said, 'Woe to them that devise iniquity, and work evil upon their beds—when morning is light they practise it, because it is the power o' their hand. They covet fields, and take them by violence; and houses, and take them away; so they oppress a man and his house, even a man and his heritage."

"I don't know whose fields my father has been coveting; and I think the heavier toll he lays upon the rum that passes through his hands, the better," said Philip. "But suppose you leave that aside, and tell me what we are to do for these two poor creatures upstairs. You have a couple of spare rooms, haven't you?"

"Yes."

"Let them to me for £50 a year, and allow Mrs. Seaford and her daughter to use them as long as they like. Will you?"

"Mr. Philip," said Jims, with a touch of pride, "if I am to be paid for offering the shelter of my roof to a widow and her child, it is time, I think, I should give up my talk about the things that are happening around us."

"If you put it in that way, yes. I would not seek to bribe Jonah from going up against Nineveh; but still I do not see why you should not let me make a mercantile transaction of it. The habit runs in my family, if it does not in yours."

"We are sufficiently beholden to you already," said Jims, "for what you have done for our Alec. I hope you will say nothing more about this. Let a poor man have the dignity of his own house, and the privilege of offering its security to those who need it. If these two women are, as you say, without any means, you may do your share in getting them work of some kind or other, such as suits the dainty stomachs of people brought up genteelly who find themselves in poverty."

"Well," said the younger man, with a laugh, and stretching out his legs before him, "when I undertook to find lodgings for them, I did not contemplate accepting the responsibility of finding them the means of existence. But, upon my life, I don't see what I could do better, by way of employment. I should have the pleasure of tangible results; and that is more than I am likely to get by writing pamphlets on the tenure of land, isn't it, Mr. Lawson?"

"Yes, when you write them the wrong way," growled Jims.

It is needless to say that Jims went in for wholesale confiscation. The land belonged to the state; and the state was bound to see that no fictitious theory of absolute ownership should be allowed to interfere with the rights of every subject to participation.

"But," Philip would mildly urge, "if a man invests his savings in land, as he might in consols, under the security granted by certain laws, and if the state resolve to abrogate these laws, is it not bound to give him compensation?"

"Why?" Jims would ask, with face and eyes aglow. "If the state—that is the whole of us—have made a blunder, in Heaven's name let us rectify it, whoever suffers. And the landowners have had the benefit of the blunder hitherto," he would add with bitter emphasis.

Whatever effect Jims' fierce theories had upon Mr. Philip, there can be no doubt about there having been a powerful alternative. If they did not give one new convictions, they shook up those one had in a far from Socratic manner; and many a time Philip was provoked into the malicious pleasure of advancing some very milk-and-watery theory of popular rights, merely to observe Jims' explosive scorn and anger. This was very wrong, doubtless; but perhaps we are ceasing to reverence old age as we ought to do. She-bears no longer interfere to teach our children respect for a bald head.

There was a timid tap at the door, and Lilian Seaford stood hesitatingly at the entrance to the room.

"Mamma wishes to be alone," she said "and so I have come downstairs."

"Quite right, quite right," said Jims, "come in and sit by the fire. Where is my gude wife?"

"She went to make some tea, I think," said the girl.

"Aye, aye. When women are in trouble, they are sure to fly to tea. Sit ye down in the armchair, and make yourself comfortable. You are young to meet wi' so sore a trial; but young hearts are light, and get ower these things. No," he added suddenly, seeing that tears had sprung into the girl's eyes, "dinna' think I blame you for't. If you live long enough, you'll have plenty of trouble without wishin' to multiply what you meet wi' now. Think as little of it as you can, my lassie—that is my advice to you; and dinna' blame yourself if you find your young heart gets more quickly over sorrow than their's who are older than you. You will see some day that life wasna given us to spend in vain lamentations and regret."

The girl sat and stared vacantly into the fire. The absence of her bonnet now revealed the plenteousness and beauty of her waving sunbrown hair, the rebellious folds of which were tightly banded down over the small, neat head; and the close-fitting dress showed her slight, lissom figure, which was singularly well-formed to be that of sixteen. Jims laid his hand tenderly and softly on the young girl's head, and said,—

"You maun be brave and bear up, my lassie, for you will have to help your mother and lighten her grief; and young shoulders were made to prop old arms. You maun show yourself a woman now, and make some return for all she has done and suffered for you. And here comes your tea, which I suppose will be as welcome to you as to your elders."

Mrs. Lawson, having already been to the lonely woman upstairs, now carried the tray into the room herself, and made a pretty display of biscuits, jam, marmalade, and other delicacies peculiar to the afternoon meal of small households. Alec also came in, having arrived from the city; and so they all sat down to the table, Lilian Seaford instinctively drawing near the motherly woman who had spoken so kindly to her.

The shadow of certain death—that most pathetic of all the sacrifices demanded by human fate—still hung over them: yet Philip and Jims managed to introduce some cheerfulness into their talk, by way of beguiling the thoughts of the sensitive young girl beside them. They asked her questions about Devonshire, about her first impression of London, about what she had seen since her arrival. But she had seen scarcely anything. She and her mother had remained pretty much in their lodgings, waiting for him who was never to sail into port again. On one occasion, however, Lilian and her mother had gone to see the Tower, and the young girl's recollections of the place seemed to be sufficiently sombre.

"I came away thinking of all the men and women who had been shut up within those great walls, and it made me very sad."

"But don't you think," said Philip, "that we pity those fine knights and ladies out of all reason? When they were beheaded, that was bad for them, doubtless; but their mere confinement was nothing so painful as much that was happening all around to people who were free. Cœur-de-Lion in his German prison hadn't half so bad a time of it as any ordinary nurserymaid who has to suffer from the tempers of four or five children. Poets bewailed his captivity, and whole nations offered him sympathy; and yet it seems to me that he was remarkably well off, compared with most other people."

"But he had been led to expect better," said Lilian. "If he had been born a nursery-maid, he would have put up with the children, and not thought it much of a hardship."

"I suppose," said Philip, with a laugh, "he would still have retained his own nature under these other circumstances, and become the terror of the servants' hall."

"Aye, aye," said Jims; "a brutal temper that gets a costermonger six months' hard labor for thrashing his wife wins glory for a king when he falls out with some of his neighbors, and gets all his people to back him in the quarrel. You put vice on a higher platform, and it becomes an heroic virtue."

"You fancy, then," said Philip, "that if Mary Queen of Scotts had been born a maid-of-all-work she would have fallen in love with an organ-grinder, and earned no more glory than a dismissal?"

But Jims, although a Presbyterian and a Radical, was also a Scotchman, and did not like this ugly parody of the relations existing between Mary and Rizzio. He dropped the question of the different lights which circumstance throws upon the same nature and the same action, and chose instead to speak to Lilian of what she ought to do in the event of her and her mother making Hampstead their permanent home. The girl exhibited a prudence and sense in replying to these remarks which one would scarcely have expected from her; and it was only at times that Philip observed her sudden withdrawal from the conversation, as she relapsed into a trance-like fixity of vision, which impressed him as something strange, new, almost terrible. The girl seemed to see nothing and hear nothing. The large violet-blue eyes were intently fixed upon some insignificant object; and then, after a few seconds, or even minutes, you saw her recover herself with an effort and a start, as if she were forcing herself awake. Then she looked round as if she had newly come into a strange room among strange people, and as if some concentration were necessary before she could take up the thread of their talk.

Philip sat there until nearly nine o'clock; and then he left. When he went outside, it was a clear starlit night, with the moon just beginning to show herself in the south; and as he had effectually done himself out of his dinner, he resolved to walk all the way down to Park Lane, there being nothing better for him to do.

When he arrived there, instead of going at once into his father's house—a large stone-built mansion near the Oxford Street end of the lane—he walked down to the front of the considerably smaller residence inhabited by Major Delaney, his wife, and niece. There was the drawing-room window, at which he had been standing that forenoon along with Mary

Thormanby, when the envious demon who dogs the footsteps of
lovers hurried them into bitter speech and an angry parting. A
dull red light came through the curtains inside the French window; and he heard the sound of music. It was Mary, who was
playing a march he knew well. He was familiar with every
chord in it; but now as he heard it from a distance, there was
less of stately measured triumph in it, and more of the sadness
and tenderness of parting. Perhaps she, too, was thinking of
him as she played—perhaps remembering her attitude of the
morning with some compunction, and wishing for a few words
of reconciliation and kindness, should he enter? The Major
and his wife scorned ceremony, where a rich young gentleman
was concerned. He had taken greater liberties with social custom in their house, without rebuke. Perhaps Mary would thank
him with her wonderful gray eyes, and give him a flower in
token of forgiveness.

What suddenly upset Mr. Philip's present mood it would be
hard to say. But he suddenly muttered something which had a
wicked sound, turned on his heel, and, with a bitter laugh at
his own folly, walked rapidly up the lane and entered his own
house.

Somewhat later that night Lilian Seaford was awoke by a
strange cry. Hastily starting up, she became aware that the
room was full of moonlight, that streamed in from the small
window; and this light showed her her mother, sitting in the
bed beside her, with an unearthly whiteness on her face and a
ghastly fixity in her eyes.

"There, there!" cried the woman, pointing to the window,
'don't you see it, Lilian? don't you see it?—the ship is heaving
over, and they are crying for help! Why does the wind howl
so? for nobody will hear. See, Lilian, see!—the waves—the
waves—the waves—and, oh! my God, he has gone down!"

"Mamma, mamma, what do you mean?" cried the frightened girl.

The woman's eyes gradually lost that wild intensity; she
began to tremble violently, and then she seemed to become
aware of her daughter's presence. With a great shudder of
fear, she drew the girl towards her, and burst into a flood of
tears as she held her close to her bosom.

CHAPTER V.

"Philip," said Mrs. Drem, in her insidious way, "shall I ask Mary Thormanby and her aunt and uncle to come on Thursday next? You know your papa doesn't like them; but if it would please you to have them here, I will send them a card."

Mrs. Drem was a small, pale, flaxen-haired woman, with the gentlest of voices, and a manner which she meant to be very captivating and pleasing. She was much younger than her husband, whose coarse bearing and captious temper she bore with a sweet equanimity. She had been a poor relative of a very good family when he married her; and when she was suddenly lifted into wealth and luxury, instead of becoming haughty to her neighbors and imperious to her servants, she strove to fulfil the duties of her station with a persistence that was almost touching. True, the marriage had not brought Mr. Drem into communication with all those families of whose friendship she had been accustomed to boast in her days of maidenhood; and her husband was cruel enough at times (when afire with port-wine and ill-temper) to say that she had told him a pack of lies about her grand friends, and that she was a deceitful hypocrite; but, once his wife, there was nothing she did not do to accomplish the full measure of her obligations.

Among other things, she set to work to spoil her stepson, until Master Philip was fairly nauseated into rebelling against her officious kindness. He was not nearly so grateful to her as he ought to have been for her servile humoring of his boyish whims; for her profuse and secret presents; or for the way in which she endeavored to smooth down the somewhat rough relations existing between father and son. Her kindness and Philip's ingratitude came to a head at Eastbourne, while Philip was still a boy. He was accustomed to walk along the beach with her every morning before breakfast; and it was their chief amusement, as they strolled along, to watch the curious odds and ends of things that the sea had washed up during the night —bits of lobster-baskets, empty night-lights, a cut lemon, a soda-water bottle, a leaf of the New Testament, or an old shoe. Philip, much to his surprise and delight, used sometimes to find more valuable things than those; and, of course, one estimates at twenty times its worth any stray bit of flotsom and jetsom so picked up. The frequency of the findings, however, provoked the boy's suspicions; and, on a certain morning, he caught one of the servants coming up from the beach just as Mrs. Drem and he were going down. He wondered what the man had been doing there, but said nothing. His stepmother and he had not proceeded far on their accustomed beat when he detected something gleaming out of the sand, and partly hidden by the seaweed.

"What is it, Philip?" says Mrs. Drem, with a pretty surprise.

He picks up the shining object, clears away the sand, and finds a spick-and-span new purse, of red morocco, with a fine brass rim.

"What a lucky boy you are!" exclaims Mrs. Drem, in her quiet, sweet voice. "Since we have come down here, you have found such a lot of things—a penknife, a silver dog-whistle, a sovereign, and what not; and now here is a purse!"

"Yes; isn't it strange that the sea should be so strong as to float these things in," says the boy. "But I think I can explain the mystery, for I happened to see this purse on your dressing-table yesterday afternoon."

Mrs. Drem crimsoned for a moment, like a "caught" schoolgirl; then she burst out laughing, and asked him if he was not very grateful to her. Philip's face showed that he was rather disgusted. As he was only a boy, one is not sure whether his disgust was occasioned by her cringing to him and fostering his weakness, or by the discovery that he had *not* really found the articles in question. At all events, that little circumstance did Master Philip a world of good. He got fairly ashamed of being spoiled; and resented his stepmother's efforts in that direction as if they were so many insults. They were always very good friends; but he seemed to regard her with a certain coldness and suspicion ever after the incident of the purse.

Mrs. Drem now waited for Mr. Philip to say whether she should send a card for her dinner-party to the people whom her husband disliked. What her own feelings in the matter were no one could say; for it was at all times a difficult matter to discover Mrs. Drem's likes and dislikes. In the sweetest manner she would have asked Satan to give her his arm down to dinner, had either Mr. Drem or Philip invited him to the house.

"Do as you please," he said, without lifting his eyes from his book or uncrossing his legs, as he sat at his study-fire. "I don't care."

"You don't care, my dear!" said Mrs. Drem, with surprise. "And if you don't care whether Miss Thormanby is asked, who should?"

"I have not seen Miss Thormanby for some days," he said, carelessly.

"A lover's quarrel, I suppose," remarked Mrs. Drem, with a sweet smile.

"Do you think we are babies? People don't take the trouble to quarrel nowadays; it would disturb one's appetite for lunch."

Mrs. Drem said no more, but went gently out of the room and betook herself to her desk. Her first act was to inscribe some names on a couple of gilt cards; and then she said to herself, smiling at her own thoughtfulness: "If it is a quarrel, poor Philip will thank me for bringing about a reconciliation. His father would rather have the quarrel continued, that Philip might be induced to marry Violet; but then he need not know anything about it. And Philip may not marry Mary Thormanby after all."

The gilt cards were put in envelopes, and addressed in Mrs. Drem's formal small handwriting, which she had carefully cultivated in the few months preceding her marriage. Thus it was that, among the guests who arrived at Mrs. Drem's house on Thursday evening, Major and Mrs. Delaney and Miss Thormanby were included.

They were not among the first arrivals. Long before Mr. Philip had begun to glance expectantly to the door every time it was opened and some name announced, Mrs. Drem's drawing-room had been pretty well filled by those groups of twos and threes that somehow get together in the awkward time preceding dinner. Tall men stood upright in the middle of the floor, sulky and silent; short men bore up at them with some feeble endeavor to win them into conversation, and were looked down upon with contemptuous silence; the ladies were all talking together on couches and chairs, while even the youngest of them disdained to think of flirting for a few resultless minutes. If there was anything like flirtation, it was on the part of a small bright young lady, who had a neat round English face, with jet-black hair brushed tightly down over her forehead, and who was engaging in lively talk two young gentlemen. This was Miss

Violet Kingscote; and one of her attendants was Mr. Philip, who responded to her sallies with a sort of grave, paternal forbearance.

Miss Kingscote was evidently being "cornered" in some playful argument or other; for she suddenly broke away, with a pretty gesture of her head, and said to her cousin,—

"I can forgive you, Cecil, for being a Radical, but not Philip, for he is tall enough to be a Conservative. You never find Radicals above five feet six, do you?"

Lord Cecil Sidmouth, the younger son of a well-known Conservative peer, and one of a band of young aristocratic Radicals who had formed themselves into a philosophico-political society (of which more hereafter), was in reality about five feet six, had a large protuberant forehead, red hair, an eyeglass, and gloves much too big for him. He took his eyeglass between his finger and thumb, and said,—

"Do you know, Violet, you are becoming abominably impertinent? You who represent the lofty school of politics, ought to be more courteous to your enemies. The weapons of personality are left to us. If I am only five feet six, and therefore a Radical, it is the fault of my ancestors, who were all Conservatives; and, if it comes to that, I think you yourself are the smallest creature in this room. I don't say you are the less valuable on that account; for I think it was a remark of our Radical poet Burns, when asked why God had made a certain young lady very small, that——"

"Oh, Philip, save me!" she cried. "I can tell when he is settling down into the long swinging canter of a Union speech——"

"I was going to pay you a compliment, you ungrateful creature!" said the grave, red-headed young lord, fixing his eyeglass again.

"And after what I said of you, it was very kind, Cecil; and I will never do so any more," she said, contritely.

Violet Kingscote's bright and pleasant face suddenly grew reserved and formal; for she had caught the gray eyes of Mary Thormanby regarding her, as the latter entered the room, accompanied by her uncle and aunt. The two girls had never spoken to each other; but such instinctive antagonisms are common among women, and are easily traceable in the alteration of a look.

Miss Thormanby did not show to her best advantage in thus entering a room and confronting a lot of strangers. When her features were frozen into rest in this way, you could see that they were obviously not beautiful, while there was a coldness about her expression which was somewhat forbidding. It was when she was in close and confidential conversation with one person, that her face lit up and showed its special charm. Nor was any man who had had this peculiar fascination revealed to him ever after able to see that she was plain. Hence it was that people who had only seen her as she walked about a room, could not be made to understand why their gentleman friends raved about Mary Thormanby; while girls were no less puzzled when they looked at the photograph of this lady who won so much enthusiasm, and declared that she was positively ugly. But the beauty that enslaves is not the beauty of a perfect outline : nor will it be ever understood until physiology and æsthetics agree to make the inquiry together.

When Philip had shaken hands with Major Delaney and his wife, he turned to their niece, and in a quite frank and courteous way said,—

"Suppose, Mary, we agree to forget all that passed the other day; will you?"

The big gray eyes regarded him for a second or two with a calm indifference as she said,—

"I need not pretend to forget when I cannot help remembering."

A flush crossed the young man's face and he turned away abruptly, almost rudely, from her. He went back to Miss Kingscote.

"What is the matter with you, Philip?" asked that young lady.

"Surprise," said he, with a bitter smile. "I have just learnt that there's something about which Miss Thormanby cannot make a pretence."

Miss Violet discreetly said nothing, but turned to Cecil and began asking questions about the naughty philosophical society, against which certain very respectable newspapers were protesting strongly.

At length dinner was announced; and Mrs. Drem, thinking she had sufficiently consulted Philip's wishes in inviting Mary Thormanby, and her relatives, had arranged as a sort of propitiation to Mr. Drem, that Philip should take in Violet Kingscote to dinner. So it was that these two came together; and that the pretty, dark-haired, matter of fact young English lady found herself talking to a somewhat absent and preoccupied companion. Occasionally, indeed, she had to remind him of his duty, and to recall him from scowling vaguely at a certain couple far down the table.

"I tell you, you are losing all your manners," she said, "since you have taken to politics. You used to care for nothing but to please people, and you even condescended to be agreeable to me. And seriously, Philip, you know you can do no good in what you and Cecil talk about; and why should you annoy yourself to no purpose? I know a good deal of politics. I know that, to gain political power, you have to flatter a lot of vulgar and rude people, and make them believe that you have no care at heart but to obey their stupid wishes. You must pander to their prejudices in order to get into Parliament; and there you become the slave of this faction or that, and are only a voting unit. You needn't laugh, Philip; women *do* read more of the newspapers than the 'births, deaths, and marriages;' and any one can tell what politics really mean at present. You may be a Radical in theory, but how *could* you consort with such people? You would not understand them; they would not understand you. Do you know who is the great Radical down in Wisborough?"

"Who?"

"Why, that dreadful man Tring. Do you know that he is both a dissenting peacher and the agent of a fire-insurance office?"

"What more natural? You see he is able to insure you at the same time against fire in both worlds."

"I will not have you say such things to me."

"And I will not have you say such things to me. Don't you understand the part you are playing, in trying to sap my patriotic resolutions? To me you represent the world, the flesh, and the Conservative party; and you bring all the battery of your seductive persuasion to bear upon a poor young man who has plenty of foes to fight from within. For how do I know that it *is* of any use? And how do I know that the opinions of all my best friends are wrong, and that the opposite opinions held by many people whom I dislike are right? Is not everybody born in England sufficiently ready to identify certain principles with the upholders of them, and judge of an opinion by the social position of those who advance it, that, you, with your sly logic and your pretty eyes, should step in to play the siren? If you and I were not such old friends—if we were not such good friends as to make falling in love and that sort of nonsense impossible between us—I should have to surrender all my best resolves to you. As it is, I defy you, Miss Violet."

"That's all very well," said his companion: "and I wouldn't care a bit what sort of opinions you had, if they did not alter you. But you are really, Philip, being drawn more and more away from us. You are not one of us, as you used to be. I think papa begins to regard you as rather a dangerous person; and I know he says that the Analytical Society should be put down by law. And Colonel Torcester, too."

"Now, Violet, what has the poor colonel ever done that he should be set up in judgment on the Analytical?"

"Colonel Torcester is a man who has travelled much and studied much," retorted Miss Violet, with some asperity.

"Yes; he has been all over Norway and Sweden, and written a book about his shooting there which is as full of lies as it can be. Then his book about the habits of pointers! Don't you think he must have borrowed most of his facts from the story of Mother Hubbard and her dog Toby?"

"I think," said Violet, laughing, "that you are very unkind to a gentleman who mentions your own Yellowfoot in terms of such high praise."

All this time her companion had been furtively looking down the table as he played with his knife and fork; and what he saw there did not seem to please him much. Mary Thornanby, conscious that he was looking at her, did her best to show off her fascinations to Philip's pale cousin, Arthur, who sat next to her. Had her only object been to captivate that remarkably matter of fact person, she would probably have relinquished her endeavor in disgust; but she knew that every time she smiled and showed her beautiful teeth, every glance of her big gray eyes directed to the unimpressionable Arthur, every pretended little confidence between them, told somewhat higher up the table. It was not the ordinary pangs of jealousy, however, that Philip suffered—it was a far less bitter and a far sadder feeling.

"She knows that I see all this," he said to himself, "and that I know her coquetry to be merely a pretence. She has no interest whatever in my cousin. She knows that I am in love with her, and that I despise myself for being in love with her; and she wishes me to see that she can dare me to break the bonds that hold us together."

"You are very silent, Philip," said Miss Kingscote. "Are you thinking of what I have been saying? Do you mean to come back to us?—to leave the friends of the mob and the hustings, and become again one of your people?"

"I was thinking of something quite different, Violet," he

said. "Tell me; do you think a man can continue to love a woman whom he despises?"

"He cannot love her at all if he despises her," said Violet.

"That is nonsense," he said, abruptly. "That is one of the parrot sayings that all the essayists on the affections repeat. It is like the superstition about a man's only being able to love once, and like the other superstition about love making one careless as to the defects in the character of the person you love. Why, it is only when you have a great regard for some one that you take the trouble to wish she were better—that you see where she is imperfect and would like to improve her. It is no concern of mine if Mrs. Delaney makes a fool of herself with her head-dress, or if Lady O'Mallory remarks that Milton's enchanting poem of 'Paradise and the Peri' was the best thing he ever wrote. But suppose you are deeply interested in some one— suppose you are fascinated by glimpses of a fine nature in some man or woman, and yet you see this nature perverting itself, and lending itself to mean deceptions and paltry tricks—suppose you see one you cannot help loving glorying in a sort of self-degradation, and sneering at you for thinking that he or she ought to be better."

"And could you love any one with such a disposition?" asked Miss Kingscote, turning towards him her bright dark eyes.

"That is the very fun of it," said Philip. "I think I do."

Now it was none of Violet Kingscote's business to interfere in this matter. She knew well to whom her companion referred. Everybody expected Philip to marry Mary Thormanby; and although Violet, with her wilful little prejudices and sharp eyes, had formed a considerable dislike to the lady of Philip's choice, she did not quite believe all the ill of her that her companion had just hinted. It was none of her business; and besides, Miss Kingscote was a practical young lady. She liked to have a pleasant time at dinner; and she certainly thought that the gentleman who sat next her was bound to study her pleasure instead of bothering her about his love affairs.

"You mean you have had a quarrel, Philip," she said; "and I don't know about these things. But I think men are more impatient with the women they love than with other women, merely because they know more of them. They have studied them more, and know their weaknesses; while other women come near them with a thin veil of courtesy and formality to hide them. Don't you know that boys always fancy their sister's are very deceitful—far more deceitful than other girls—merely because they know so much of them? But when they get to know other women, they begin to see that their sisters are no worse than the rest."

"Well, Miss Violet," said Philip, with a laugh, "your candor about your own sex is charming. But it is too bad of me to bore you with my sorrow. Suppose we talk of something else. And it has occurred to me that I have a great favor to ask of you. And first I will tell you a story."

With that he began and told her all about the loss of the "Westmoreland," and the fortunes of Tom Seaford's widow and daughter. Miss Thormanby grew less fascinating towards the unresponsive Arthur when she saw that Philip was so much engrossed as to pay her no attention. The babble around the table increased. Mary Thormanby's corpulent and vulgarly-dressed aunt kept rallying the small, sweet, patient Mrs. Drem; and Mrs. Drem conducted herself towards her jocose and bouncing neighbor with the sort of silent contempt with which a well-bred minnow might look on the gambols of a frolicsome tadpole. Pretty much the same state of affairs prevailed between the Major and Sir James Kingscote, the tall, gray-haired man, with the keen, hard face, who vainly tried to ignore the burly warrior, and devote his attention to one of those silent and depressing young ladies who fill up the blanks of all dinner-tables.

Mr. Drem had grown very red and very sulky. He kept an eye on the servants and on Mrs. Drem, and visited her with an occasional glance of impatient anger whenever the former seemed dilatory or negligent. A sprightly young married lady endeavored to engage the great merchant in conversation from time to time, and sometimes managed to elicit a sort of half comtemptuous growl, which may have resembled the kind of language in vogue in pre-Adamite times, when the "missing link" was only on the way towards articulate speech.

When Philip had finished his story, he begged of his companion to consider whether she could be instrumental in getting some fancy work, such as gentlewomen in poor circumstances affect, for Mrs. Seaford and her daughter.

"I will gladly do whatever I can, Philip," said Violet; "I will make out to-night a list of all the things I could possibly find use for——"

"My dear child," remonstrated Philip, "you yourself surely don't want as many lace handkerchiefs and things of that sort as will employ two persons. What I want you to do is to go to the people with whom you deal for these things, and tell them to give work to Mrs. Seaford. It will at the least be an occupation for them; and I suppose Captain Seaford's life was insured for a good sum which will help them considerably."

Miss Kingscote had barely time to promise her co-operation in this charitable work when the mysterious and sudden movement took place with which ladies manage to rise all at once from the dinner-table. As they were going out Philip noticed that Mary Thormanby wore a delicate little necklet, of Venetian workmanship, which he had brought her from Paris the summer before, and presented to her on one quiet afternoon, when she was particularly good and grateful.

He sat down at the table again, moody and silent; Lord Cecil Sidmouth came round to him, bringing his glass in his hand.

"I say, old man, what's the matter with you? I hear there is to be a jolly row about that paper of Mercier's; a man at the Reform last night was saying that Lord Campbell's Act should be made to apply to the Analytical discussions. And after all, it is such humbug to say that the law should hold the crime to be as criminal in a man as in a woman, when common sense, and all the natural relations of the sexes, show you it as nothing of the kind. But I sell you what should be done. I would punish a man who inveigled a married woman into running away with him by making him marry her. If she is such a woman as would run away with him, what more fearful punishment could you invent? With such a law in operation, you would never hear of another case."

Lord Cecil's project did not receive even the compliment of a criticism. Philip asked him whether he would not go into the drawing-room at once, instead of sitting and idling over wine; and into the drawing-room, a short time thereafter, they accordingly went.

Before we follow them, a word may be said about a brief conversation which took place between Mr. Drem and Sir James Kingscote. The former, as usual, had drunk a good deal of wine, and his face was even redder than it ordinarily was. He had got Sir James to withdraw a short distance from the table, and was engaged in filling up the intervals of his sipping brown sherry with some eager commerical talk.

The tall-whiskered baronet was not a very rich man. His family was an old one (Sir James was accustomed to say in his proud way that the only Kingscote who had done an action unworthy of the name was his ancestor who had condescended to accept the baronetcy in 1660), and had at one time been wealthy enough. Perhaps Charles II. fancied the baronetcy a sufficient return for all the property that old Roden Kingscote had lost in the service of royalty; but, at all events, the second baronet found himself the heir to a very crippled estate, and his five successors had not been able to improve the condition of affairs since then. Sir James, the present baronet, had been driven into railways, and now saw the company on which he had chiefly depended on the brink of bankruptcy, with their shares rapidly sinking from day to day. It was on the subject of these shares that Mr. Drem was now advising him in a fine oracular fashion. Success had given Mr. Drem the right to be familiar with the baronet, who was an unlucky poor devil, quite incapable of amassing a fortune. With conscious superiority, Richard Drem smiled in a calm patronizing way, and pointed out to his companion that there was no help for him.

"Told you so long ago, Sir James. You would have been a richer man by several thousand pounds to-day if you had sold out when I told you. Bless you, these things can only be managed by the initiated. You amateurs come in and think you can be precious clever. It's no use; you have no experience. You only lose your money. It wants determination, pluck, brains—brains, I say—to succeed in business. I suppose you'd sit a horse or shoot a partridge better than I could, because you've had lots of practice; but you should remember that you have had no practice when you came to dealing in shares and competing with men who have lived all their life by it."

"I am afraid what you say is very true, Mr. Drem," said Sir James, coldly, and staring absently at the same time at the tablecloth before him. "But I had very good advice when I bought these shares."

"Well, never mind, Sir James, you can't help it. Better men than you have make mistakes; and, after all, it's only a few thousands. Bless you, I don't mind saying that if you could persuade my son to marry your daughter, I'd buy every share you have in that company at a hundred pounds apiece. There!"

For an instant the face of the tall, gray-haired man flushed angrily; but presently he laughed.

"It is an odd sort of joke, Mr. Drem; but I suppose you think the best think I can do, now that the shares are getting bad, is to become the father that you see in the theatre-pieces, and sell my daughter. Poor little Vi would be quite complimented if she knew the price you bid for her."

There was really no sarcasm in his tone, for he had instantly dismissed as too absurd the idea of Mr. Drem's being in earnest.

" There's many a jest that comes true," remarked Mr. Drem, with a slow and vinous wink. " People have been too hasty in fancying that Philip was going to marry that girl Thormanby. There are other signs in the air——"

" I think you may trust to your son selecting a good wife, whoever he chooses," remarked Sir James, somewhat sharply. " He is a young man of more than ordinary ability; blunt a little in his manner, and all the better for it, for it shows he is honest and trustworthy. His impulsiveness may be carrying him too far in these political notions of his——"

" Ah, yes, isn't it a pity!" sighed Richard Drem. " He has no more regard for his position and opportunities than if he were a tradesman or a clerk without a farthing to bless himself with. And I have done my best to make him a gentleman, Heaven knows. He has had everything in the way of education you could think of, no expense spared; and now he turns round and declares himself a Radical, just as if he were the son of a cab-proprietor! Don't you see, Sir James, that if he was marrying into a good respectable family, he would have to give up these low and vulgar people he takes an interest in? And the honor of an alliance with your family——"

" We need not speak about that at present, Mr. Drem," interrupted Sir James with some severity. " Your joke was only a joke, I know; and Philip will probably select a very good wife for himself without our interference."

" But I have a right to interfere!" exclaimed Mr. Drem, hotly. " I say I have a right to interfere! It is on my money he must live when he marries—my money—mine!"

" Then God help him!" muttered Sir James to himself, as he discreetly turned the conversation in some other direction.

Meanwhile Philip, full of thoughts of the afternoon on which he had given Mary Thormanby the tiny necklet, went into the drawing-room. An elderly little married woman was singing; and, of course, she sang a song of blighted hopes, and nightingales, and withered roses, finishing up with an affirmation on the part of the lover that, after all the ills and sorrows of life were over, he would meet his sweetheart in heaven and make it all right there. It did occur to Lord Cecil—and he mentioned the matter to Violet—that the heroine of the song was probably a coquette, that there were probably half a dozen disappointed lovers in the position of the gentleman who expected to meet her in heaven, and that if they all met her there, there might be as much disturbance and jealousy and wretchedness as had occurred down here.

"My dear Cecil," said Violet, "your sarcasm is very clever, but it is quite lost upon me. You might as well be sewing diligently with a threadless needle. For I know all you boys, after laughing at what you call sentiment, are sure to rush madly into love."

"My dear Violet," said the red-haired young lord, scowling through his eyeglass, "I will not be called a boy. I have written a book; I once nearly proposed to an actress; I have shot a bear; I have designs upon a seat in Parliament; and I will not be called a boy."

But Philip sat apart and alone, and stared into the fire, and communed with himself in this wise:

"What if, after all, it be true that a man only loves once? What if I am wilfully throwing away my solitary chance in life, and earning for myself that perpetual regret that haunts so many people? Scarcely a man one meets who does not say he wishes he had married the girl he first loved, even although she was not very pretty, nor very rich, nor very well educated. He invariably fancies he loved her better than any of her successors; and he treasures some bit of ribbon, and speaks kindly of certain places that have tender memories for him. Are all these people laboring under a delusion? Is this my only chance, and must I cling to it at whatever cost?"

There is, unfortunately, no kindly Zadkiel to pierce the future for any man or maiden who is thus perplexed; and all Philip's endeavors to guess at what might happen to him thereafter were vain. He could not tell what was the value of the love that he was so sorely tempted to cast away; he did not even know that the doubt was conclusive evidence that it ought to be cast away. He had no data for comparison. Perhaps it was true that he might never love any woman even with the imperfect love that he bestowed on this one. Perhaps it was better to seize the present hour, with such gladness as it might bring, and let the future shift for itself. Above all, might not this imperfect love, in happier times, grow fuller and more beautiful as he and she got to know each other better?

At that moment he wanted to see what should happen to him in the next half dozen years. Had he known what would happen to him within the next six months—had he known that after the full and perfect love which he longed for had fallen towards him, there would remain only a shadow of blackness and despair—he need not have troubled so much about his conduct towards Mary Thormanby on that particular evening.

As it was, he went over to where she sat the first moment that he saw she was alone, and said,—

"This estrangement is a very stupid thing, Mary."

"It was none of my making," she replied; but there was relenting in her tone.

"Don't be stupid. Why did you put on that necklet to-night?"

"Because I wished to make you sorry. Have I succeeded?"

And all at once the pale face was lit up with that nameless grace and fascination that she could so easily express, and she bestowed on him one look of frank reconciliation and forgiveness. Even at this moment, as he surrendered himself once more to his thraldom, it was with a sort of inward sigh. He was again friends with the woman he loved, and yet he was not too overjoyed. For there is nothing in love-affairs surer than this—that, when a man has once mistrusted a woman and wished to break the bonds that bind them together, the doubt returns with a fatal facility. The pitcher may go to the well many times uninjured, but in the end it is broken.

CHAPTER VI.

MR PHILIP played the part of special providence towards Mrs. Seaford and her daughter with an audacity that knocked the breath out of any possible remonstrance. In his imperious fashion, he had always been accustomed to meddle with the movements of the Hampstead household, until even the irascible Jims had got into a habit of letting him have his way; and now the Seafords, mother and daughter, fell into submission also. He became their physician, ordering them out of doors on the fine afternoons; he became their employer, contracting for mysterious fancy work to be supplied to a number of problematic ladies whose names his ingenuity invented on the spot; and he became their lawyer and banker, taking the management of a sum of £500 which fell to the widow on a policy of life-insurance effected by her husband—about the only instance of prudence and foresight which poor Tom Seaford had ever exhibited.

Now, persons who have fallen heir to some such insurance money, gift, or bequest, know that in most cases the original sum gets considerably curtailed on various pretenses before it reaches the hand of the legatee. But Mr. Philip easily persuaded Mrs. Seaford to go with him to his father's lawyer; and this gentleman, singular to relate, was so honorable and praiseworthy a person, that the £500 evidently reached her quite intact.

"A man in his position," remarked Mr. Philip—telling a lie with the most unblushing confidence—"can't be expected to care about little trifling commissions. When he takes such an affair in hand, it is merely as a sort of compliment, you know, to people who have larger dealings with him."

"It is very kind of you, Mr. Drem," said Mrs. Seaford.

"Of him, you mean, Mrs. Seaford," replied Philip, in a matter of fact way. "But, you know, he has all my father's business."

These diverse duties called Mr. Philip to Hampstead very frequently indeed. Why neither he nor any of the small household saw anything imprudent in these constant visits—why no one of them fancied for a moment that it was possible some measure of affection might arise between the two young people thus thrown together—or, worse still, that the vague misery of love might smite the one down, leaving the other untouched—it may be difficult to explain here. But up at Hampstead there was no difficulty or trouble in the matter. They all knew that Philip was as good as engaged to a lady in his own sphere of life. He made no secret of his affection for her, and would tell in the frankest fashion his reasons for going away suddenly of an afternoon.

It was the obvious relations existing between Philip and Lilian Seaford, however, that set the matter at rest, and blinded them to any possible danger lying ahead. He treated her as if she were merely a child. There was between them none of the formality and cautious self-defence with which young people who *might* marry arm themselves. Philip spoke bluntly to her. He pointed out her mistakes in French with the judicial accuracy of a schoolmaster; he criticised her dress, and reprimanded her when he thought it was too tight at the waist. He told her what books she ought to read, and which of them she ought to admire. In short, he thrust his opinions upon her in the tyrannical fashion he used to everybody around him; and the young girl submitted very meekly.

But all this time, when he was really exercising the functions of a parent to her, he was studying her with the deepest interest. Never before had he seen revealed to him so clearly and openly the workings of a pure and childlike nature, which had, nevertheless, peculiarities much more decided than mere innocence. The perfect frankness and confidence that reigned between them—unbroken and unshadowed by any thought of change in their present relations—helped him, of course, in this close observation, until he came to know her almost as he knew his own soul. He could read in her eyes, which she turned fearlessly towards him, the current of her every thought; and he began almost to reverence, as a revelation, the sight of this beautiful mental attitude of hers, which was full of wonder and delight over the world. All things were new to her; she looked at the blue sky, or the glamor of the sunlight as though she had never seen either before. The joy that life gave her was mirrored, from moment to moment, in her face; and the passage of time only provoked a shifting of lights without shadows. There was a divine optimism, too, in her notions of the men and women around her, which was very curious, and perhaps a trifle sad. She saw the world as it might have been; and she did not know how different it was from her dream. Philip never forgot having seen this beautiful, bird-like nature, that seemed to have dropped down from heaven into the mire and smoke of the City, confronted by the brutal lounger in Trinity Square; he never forgot the confused, frightened stare, the wonder of surprise with which she seemed to meet, but not to understand, the rude repulse given to her gentle interference. That incident she, too, never forgot. She spoke of it sometimes as a sort of puzzle: and I think when the innocent child read some story or other, the only notion of the villain of the plot she could form, was to make him something like the man she had seen opposite the Tower.

Very strange, also, to Philip were those unconscious trances of hers, in which she seemed to lose all knowledge of the people and things around her. It was not only in the house that these fits of reverie took place, for sometimes out of doors she would be found by her companions to have stolen away, without word or sign, into some other world. There was no trace of melancholy on her face then; no regret or shadow of sadness. The reverie was a quite happy one; and though she recalled herself with a start and a look of wonder, there was a strange pleasure in her eyes, as though she had been holding happy converse with unseen beings.

"We have abolished the devil, and we are becoming impertinent to the angels," Philip used to say to himself. "And yet who are they with whom she has been talking?"

No one, of course, but a young man, would be guilty of the pretty conceit of arguing the existence of angels, because a young girl in her absent moods must be talking with somebody; yet Philip was puzzled by these strange trances, and knew that, while all the beautiful workings of her mind lay bare and open to him, there was one direction in which she escaped him. Beyond that bar he could not go; and when he was on the point of saying that no human being ever knew another human being so closely and well as he knew her, lo! she had vanished and fled out of his sight into the blue, and he wondered that he did not hear the sound of invisible wings.

On the morning on which Mr. Philip went up to see about the final disposal of the £500, he found Lilian and Mrs. Lawson about to go out for a walk together over the Heath.

"I must go with you, to take care of you," said he; "and we will talk over business matters when we get back."

So he turned away from the door with them. It was a pleasant, mild morning in early March, with plenty of bright sunlight and a strong breeze blowing fresh and grateful from the south. James Lawson's cottage lay down at the east end of the heath, so that his Sunday rest was not broken in upon by the revellers who frequented the higher portions of the common. Indeed it was only from the top windows of the cottage that you could catch a glimpse of Highgate; and, when you left the house, you had to climb up the East Heath-road before you had anything like a view.

As they went up this road, the horizon gradually widened, until they could see, far up in the north, the white houses and the gray church spire shining in the sun. The strong south wind had swept along all the smoke of the City until it lay in a great bronze colored cloud behind the gleaming houses of Highgate, while over their head the sky was of a keen blue, and the warm spring light fell on the green slopes of the common, and the unsightly red gashes of the brick fields down in the hollow. You should have seen how the brisk breeze had brought a tingling color into the young girl's cheeks, and how the sunlight played hide-and-seek among her rich brown hair, throwing clear shadows across the warm color of her face, or down on the perfect whiteness of her neck.

Yet what was there to mention about this commonplace stroll, on an ordinarily bright forenoon, to scenes which were sufficiently familiar to all of them? Years afterwards we may look back upon some such insignificant morning, and find its every incident transfigured and made memorable by tender or tragic association. The lover walks with his mistress, and he does not see how fair the country is, for looking at her eyes. But when she has gone away, and he returns to the old place where they used to walk together, he finds the landscape imbued with the mournful recollections of these happy times, and it is very beautiful as well as sad to him. Then he paid no attention to the tree under which they sat, to the stile at which they parted; but now both are sacred to him, and his eyes are full of tears as he looks at them. Perhaps he goes down to the brook where they used to wander in the evenings; there are forget-me-nots there, but they grow for others now.

And if these three unconscious creatures who cheerfully wandered up the East Heath road, and past Wellwalk, thinking of the brightness of the morning, if they thought of anything, had known with what terrible associations these commonplace localities were hereafter to be invested by them, they would not have passed them so carelessly. As it was, there was but little to attract their notice. Highgate was beautiful enough up in the silvery north; but Wellwalk and the eastern end of the Heath, and the "Vale of Health," were not much to look at. As they strolled on, the two younger people listened with delight to a number of old-fashioned stories of her youth, which were told them by Mrs. Lawson, who had all the keen sense of humor which her husband lacked. Sometimes it was difficult enough for them to follow her broad Scotch; but then they were "airted," on to her meaning by the wonderful play of expression across the old woman's face. For herself, she enjoyed these reminiscenses heartily, and she was possessed of the excellent memory which frequently accompanies sharp observation and a happy notion of fun. Her stories of the adventures of her childhood, of the absurdities and superstitions of the neighbors, of the incidents in her own family, were thoroughly dramatic. All the oddities of situation were minutely described, until one could see that she was picturing to herself the whole scene as it actually occurred.

As they descended into the vale, Lilian turned to admire the pretty lake, and grotto-work, and shrubbery down in the hollow. There was no human being about the place on this morning, no trace of the flashy dissipation which at certain seasons invades Hampstead Heath; and in the clear light and the silence, these poor tavern decorations seemed quite pretty and pleasant to look at. They then crossed over and ascended the other side of the little valley.

"Don't you think," said Lilian, looking up to where the line of the road ran along the blue sky, "that when we reach the top, we must find the sea on the other side?"

It was natural enough to think that the strong light and the strong breeze should be coming over to them from a great windy plain of sea; but when they got up to the road, it was a very different prospect which met their eyes. The long stretch of western country lay under the bright spring sunshine, the faint lines of hedge and road fading into a thin blue mist that hovered along the hills, by the horizon. Down in the south the houses of Hendon shone whitely among the thick trees; up in the north lay the scattered cottages of Finchley, with the pale stones of the cemetery glittering in the light; and on the far spaces between and beyond lay clumps of wood, and tiny glints of water, with here and there a farmstead rich in yellow stacks and red tiles. All around them, too, were the dark-green patches of furze of the Heath itself, scattered among the rough sandpits: over there stood a cluster of firtrees, of a still blacker green; and everywhere were the tall, leafless elms rising into the blue sky, with the sunlight shining on their green trunks and black branches. All this spring landscape, cold and clear and bright, was full of anticipation and promise—full of the tingling of coming life: but as yet there was scarcely a bud or a leaf visible. Some of the fields were green and shining (with the glossy rooks watching you warily as you passed), and here and there you saw a tree that was just tipped with buds; but the mild south wind blew as yet over ragged ploughed fields and miry fallow, and the sunlight shone on branches that were hard and black.

"The first wild flowers I have seen this year!" cried Lilian, making a sudden rush downward into a sandpit, and halting by the side of a large patch of furze, which was covered with half-opened yellow buds. She tried to pick a piece, but the jagged spears of the gorse were too strong for her slight fingers; and so she turned away, with a petulant gesture of disappointment. Of course Philip was down at her side in a moment, engaged in damaging his hands severely and unnecessarily in trying to secure the largest piece of bloom. That trophy having been duly presented, they were about to climb up again to where Mrs. Lawson stood, when Lilian turned and confronted him.

"Do you know when furze is out of bloom?" she asked, merrily, with a bright laugh on her face.

"No," said Philip.

"Why, 'when kissing's out of fashion.' Don't you know the old proverb?"

He looked at her with a tantalized admiration and chagrin as she stood and waited for his answer, with some surprise on her face that he said nothing. Why was it that she *would* talk to him in that fearlessly frank way, as if he were merely Mrs. Lawson, or some other old woman? She ought to have been frightened to speak about kissing to him; she was not in the least. And if kissing did not occur to her, it could not well escape occurring to him; for as she stood before him, with the breezy sunlight shining in her blue eyes—shining on her parted lips and pearly teeth, on her bright happy face, and on the wonder of her brown hair—he would have been less than man had not some vague, wild, audacious notion flashed across his brain.

"Come," she said, "must I help you up the bank?"

She climbed up a few feet of the steep side of the place and stretched out her hand.

"Can you pull me up?" he said, catching hold at her fingers.

"Yes; hold tight!"

With which she gave a hearty tug. On level ground he would probably have been pulled forward on his face; but on this incline the result was very different. Instead of moving him, she only overbalanced herself—slipped with one foot—made a despairing effort to steady herself by his hand, gave a slight cry, and knew she was falling. What immediately followed is not very clear; but she presently became aware that he was holding her, and that, but for him, she would have gone ignominiously into the furze-bush. The next second she had released herself, and was standing before him in shame and confusion, with a prodigious blush over her face.

"I was very stupid," she said, looking to the ground; "let us go up some other way."

"Now let me try to pull you up," he said. "You will see I have firmer footing."

"No," she said, almost coldly; "we can walk along until the bank is less steep."

This method of escape took them in the direction of Spaniard's Tap; and when they rejoined Mrs. Lawson they continued in the same direction—passing that semi-rural public-house and following the Highgate road. Lilian was very quiet—not to say reserved. She had a vague impression of having been guiltily thoughtless and indiscreet in her conduct; for, after all, what right had she to treat Mr. Drem as if he were a mere boy, as fond of careless amusement as herself? And so she sidled in by Mrs. Lawson, and paid the tenderest court and homage to that old lady, and was even demonstratively affectionate. The shrewd old Scotchwoman perceived the alteration in the girl's manner, but was rather puzzled to divine the cause. Standing on the edge of the road, she had seen the whole adventure of the sand-pit, and heard every word the two young people had uttered. What was there in either to alter their relations with each other?

That these were altered seemed sufficiently clear. Lilian never by any chance addressed a remark to Mr. Philip, but kept on the other side of Mrs. Lawson, and was assiduously attentive to her aged friend. Mr. Philip was being clearly shut out in the cold, despite all his good-humored efforts to engage both of his companions in conversation. Mrs. Lawson, who could not understand what it all meant, found herself being paid great attention to by both the young people, and yet they never spoke a word to each other. When Philip "talked at" Lilian to Mrs. Lawson, by speaking of something in which the young girl was known to be interested, Lilian said nothing at all, or else spoke to Mrs. Lawson about something quite different. What *did* it all mean?

Nor was Mrs. Lawson, shrewd and observant as she was, less puzzled on their homeward walk; nor was she any nearer a solution at the end of the afternoon. Under a variety of pretexts Philip managed to stay the whole day up at Hampstead; and during the entire time, Mrs. Lawson, who was curious and watchful, saw him continually making efforts to become friendly and confidential as of yore with Lilian. These efforts were met by nothing in the shape of a rude repulse, but were dexterously avoided in a way which showed that Lilian had more of the woman in her than had been suspected. And while the fair young Devonshire girl seemed to draw back from Philip's friendly and good-natured advances, she showed herself unusually affectionate towards all the others. She brought Jims his slippers, and ministered to his small comforts. She showed the like anxiety about the trifling wants of her mother. Towards Mrs. Lawson she behaved with all the duteous regard and respect of a daughter; and, when Alec came home, she set to work to spoil the boy with kindness. Philip alone was shut out from her gracious condescension ; and when he left the house and made his way down to Park Lane, if he was not so much puzzled as Mrs. Lawson, he was a great deal more vexed and disappointed.

Meanwhile Mrs. Lawson's curiosity had not gone down with the setting sun. She watched the girl very attentively during the remainder of the evening; and, when the former retired, she accompanied her and went with her into her room. She had some pretense or other as an excuse ; and as she was apparently about to leave, she said,—

"By the by Lilian, what was the matter between you and Mr. Philip, that ye would na' speak a word to him a' the afternoon?"

"Didn't I, Mrs. Lawson?" said the girl, looking to the ground.

"Come, Lilian," said the old woman, going forward to her in her kindly way and putting her hand on her shoulder, " if ye have quarrelled wi' Mr. Philip, ye should na' be hard on him ; for he does na' know how to be kind enough to you and your mother."

"Oh, it isn't that," said the girl eagerly. "We haven't quarrelled at all—not at all—only——"

And with that the beautiful eyes were upturned to the old woman's face, with a look of piteous trouble in them; as if for the first time in her life, the veil of concealment were drawn over their wonted frankness, and as if she knew not how to bear this barrier between herself and those near her.

"I will tell you all about it, Mrs. Lawson," she said suddenly, and glancing to the door, as if she feared some one might overhear. "I have been so thoughtless until to-day ; and it was only to-day that it occurred to me I had no right to go on talking and playing with Mr. Drem just as if he were one of us—being impudent to him, and careless, and expecting him to be friends with me. I never thought of it until to-day; for you know he has been coming here so often, and has made himself like one of the family almost, and we have all been talking to him as if he were—as if he were—you know what I mean, don't you ? He himself does not reflect—he is too happy and careless—and I don't know how it is, Mrs. Lawson, that it has all at once seemed not quite right to me ; and indeed I wish—I wish—oh, Mrs. Lawson, I wish he would never come here again !"

With that the young girl burst into tears, and flung herself on her old friend's bosom, and hid her burning face there.

"My puir lassie," said Mrs. Lawson, who was startled beyond expression by a suspicion she dared not name, "why should ye blame yoursel' for our fault, if it is a fault? And maybe it was a greater fault o' thochtlessness than ony o' us dreamed o' to hae him comin' here; but that onything should come o' it never crossed our minds. Dinna be feart, my lassie; Mr. Philip is ower sensible to mistake the friendliness he meets wi' here."

The girl raised her head, and there was a strange excited look in her eyes, that were still full of tears.

"You do not think he would notice any difference in my manner?" she said eagerly, almost wildly. "I would not for worlds he should fancy I had been thinking over it—or any' of them—or any of them, Mrs. Lawson! I only wish to be away from him. I was frightened, that was all! and I am not crying because I care about it, but because—because I am frightened—and—and very miserable. You see it is only a trifle, Mrs. Lawson; and so you won't tell mamma, will you? for it would only trouble her about what is—what is only a trifle, you know."

The tears were running down her cheeks, and she held up her hands in a pitiful pleading way, that was full of a child-like entreaty.

"But you have told me naething I could tell her, my lassie," said the old Scotchwoman, gathering her to her, and putting her fond motherly arms round the slight sobbing figure. "I'm no sure that I ken mysel' why ye dinna want to hae Mr. Philip come back here; but it's an easy thing to bid him bide awa'. Sae gude-nicht, my bairn, and dinna ye fash yoursel' about naething."

"Indeed," said Mrs. Lawson to herself as she went downstairs. "I'm thinkin' we hae a' been indiscreet in this matter; and it's the youngest o' us—a mere lassie—who has found it out first. I hope it is no ower late, and that Mr. Philip will bide awa' when we tell him. I'm no so sure that he will; for the Lord kens what an obstinacious devil he is!"

CHAPTER VII.

No sooner had Mr. Philip returned home from his visit to Hampstead than he was summoned into his father's presence. Richard Drem had just finished dinner and was sitting alone at the head of the spacious table, which was covered with fruit, flowers, and wine. The great merchant never allowed his wife to insult his dignity by descending to any homeliness of fare or abandonment of ceremony, merely because they had no guests. Even when, on this occasion, there was no one to dinner but husband and wife, Mr. Drem put on his dress-coat, his stiff white tie, and white waist-coat; he expected his wife to appear in her most resplendant evening costume; the dinner was formally announced in the drawing-room; he solemnly conducted his wife downstairs; and they sat at each end of the large table—far enough away from each other to give Mr. Drem every opportunity of swearing at the servants.

"I ask no one to my house who is better than myself," he used to say with an oath; "and if the master of the house shouldn't have as good a dinner as anybody who comes and gets it for nothing, who should? Damme, don't I pay for it?"

When they thus dined alone—Philip had no great love for these family dinners, as may be supposed, and had a trick of dining in St. James's street—Richard Drem was no such simpleton as to drink his second-class wines himself, and keep the best for his friends. His practice was quite the reverse.

"Half of 'em don't know the value of my good wines when I give 'em them," he would grumble, "and the other half drink them and curl up their nose at me for being such a fool as to waste my money on a pack of ungrateful toadies and sneaks. Oh, don't I know! don't I know! If Richard Drem hadn't a farthing to-morrow morning, where would all his friends be? They're just like other beasts; and they'll fawn round you, and lick your hand, and wag their tail only as long as you feed 'em!"

The gentleman who had formed this comfortable estimate of his friends and acquaintances now sat and waited the appearance of his son. Philip had gone up to his own room. There was a letter lying on the table for him; he opened it and read:

"MY DEAR PHILIP—Captain Dering wishes to buy the black cob you were riding last week, and will give you seventy guineas. You will let him have it, won't you, to please me?
"Ever yours,
"MARY THORMANBY.'

"Captain Dering be hanged!" said Philip, throwing the letter into the grate.

It was Captain Dering he said; but it is to be feared it was Mary Thormanby he meant.

Then he went downstairs to the dining-room, and saw at a glance that his father had been drinking plentifully of the special brown sherry which he generally kept for himself.

"Where have you been, sir?" said Richard Drem, in his most insolent tone.

"Out," replied the younger man, coolly taking up a position on the hearth-rug, turning his back on the fire, and calmly surveying the table before him.

"How dare you answer me with such impertinence, sir!" cried the father, with his red face more aflame than ever. "I know your goings on. I know where you have been. I know where you have been spending day after day, forgetting your friends, neglecting your duties, spending your money—spending my money, *my* money, I should say—and earning for yourself the character of an—hiccough!—abandoned *roue?*"

The last sentence caused a slight sparkle in the eyes of the tall self-possessed young man who stood there: that was all.

"You don't know what you're saying," he remarked, compassionately filling for himself a glass of claret.

"Why, sir, I will teach you that I *do* know. I will teach you to go and spend my money in bribing lawyers to look after the affairs of that woman and her child. Ah, you see I do know; I do know how you have been wasting your time of late."

Philip drank the claret, put down the glass, and walked towards the door.

"If you have nothing else to say to me, sir," he observed, in his most respectful tone, "I may as well go."

"Philip!" cried the father, piteously.

"Well, sir."

"You won't go and leave your poor old father? If I am angry isn't it all for your own good? I only want to see you married, Philip, to a suitable woman. I would give you half my money in a lump to see you well married."

"But I don't see that my looking after Mr. Seaford's affairs —a duty which you, and not I, should have undertaken—has to do with my marriage."

"I thought you had broken off with that girl Thormanby— I was told so," whined Richard Drem: "and then instead of your going to see the Kingscotes—as you would do if you had any sense, and knew the importance of being intimate with people who are of good society; and if you knew what an excellent wife Violet would make—you cast aside all your friends and spend the whole of your time with this woman and her daughter. They are blinding you, Philip, blinding you! *I* know what they mean: *I* know they are trying to inveigle you into marrying her—"

"Into marrying Lilian Seaford?" cried the young man.

"Oh, I have been told—I have been told; and less likely things have happened."

"You must be dreaming," said Philip, and he again turned towards the door.

"Stay sir!" shouted Richard Drem, with the choleric blood rushing back to his face. "I will have you know that I am master in this house, and that I will exact obedience from every one under its roof. You need not pretend to be indifferent; I know your fine gentleman airs; and I will let you understand that it is I who have to decide whether you shall continue this intimacy or not. Do you know who you are, sir! Do you know that you are a pauper? Do you know that to-morrow morning I could close my doors against you, and turn you out into the streets to make your living.

The young man shut the door, and walked back to his father's side, and stood over him.

"Will you do me the favor," he said, quite calmly, "of remembering what I am going to say to you? Perhaps you had better put it down on paper, that you may be quite sure not to forget to-morrow morning. It is this: you have twice made use of these phrases to me, and threatened to turn me out to earn my own living. *The next time you do it, I will take you at your word.*"

The young man turned and left the room. The color forsook Richard Drem's face, and he made a sort of gesture as though he would recall his son. It was too late, however; and so he sank back in his chair, apparently suddenly sobered.

Philip went upstairs to the morning-room in which Mrs. Drem was sitting, all alone, doing some fancy needlework.

"Are you quite by yourself?" he said, as he sauntered in.

"Yes."

"You ought to get a companion. My father's conversation does not improve as time wears on."

"Has he been saying anything to you, Philip?"

"Nothing particular or unusual; only a few of the ordinary domestic amenities. By the way, how came Mary Thormanby to write to me on your note-paper?"

"She called here this afternoon—she and Captain Dering."

"Oh, they came together?"

"Yes; I fancy they met by accident outside. What will you do about selling Bavardeur?"

"I never transact business with women," said Mr. Philip, quietly. "Is Captain Dering afraid of me, that he cannot come near me without catching hold of Miss Thormanby's apron-strings?"

"It was all a joke, Philip," said Mrs. Drem, anxiously. "They were making fun and talking about the cob, and she said she would intercede with you for him. She expects you to go out riding with her to-morrow forenoon; and you will meet Captain Dering at lunch, and the matter can be settled then."

"The pleasure of meeting Captain Dering would be too great," replied Philip. "One cannot stand a dose of his music-hall liveliness more than once a month."

"I fear you are not in a good temper, my dear," said Mrs. Drem, mildly.

"I hope I am not in a bad one," he said, laughing, "for I am come to ask a favor of you."

"And that is——?"

"You remember my speaking to you of Mrs. Seaford and her daughter?"

"Yes."

"I want you to come and make their acquaintance."

"My dear!" exclaimed Mrs. Drem, with a start. "Consider what your father would say! I know there is some one who tells him everything that goes on up there: he knows all the particulars of your visits—everything."

"I suppose that is my kindly Cousin Arthur, who has been getting it out of poor little Alec. But no matter. There is nothing to conceal."

"Oh, but I dare not, Philip."

"But you will, I know you will. I want you, for one thing, to give Mrs. Seaford's daughter a dress."

"I will give her the dress willingly," said poor Mrs. Drem, with eagerness; "but as for seeing her, Philip——"

"Will Bluebeard eat your head off?"

"You must not talk of your father like that."

"I am very sorry: my notions of filial respect have been oddly thwarted. However, I want you to give her a dress that will suit a young girl who has got the most graceful figure you could imagine—something flowing I mean, and simple, without puffs and gathers and flounces and what not."

"I never knew you take such interest in women's costume

before, Philip," replied Mrs. Drem, with a smile. "But I know exactly what you want. Miss Seaford must have the 'Princess shape.'"

"The what?"

"The 'Princess shape,' you know, with the dress apparently in one piece from neck to foot; tight-fitting above, with a long and graceful skirt below. Haven't you noticed Miss Thormanby's lavender dress, with the black bands?"

"No, I don't think so," said Philip, dubiously.

"And yet she fancies it is a special favorite of yours. I don't believe you men ever see what we women wear unless we call your attention to it. However, since she is young, with a pretty figure, and must wear mourning, what do you say to a black rep?"

"I beg your pardon?"

"A black rep."

"It sounds wicked, but I don't know what it is."

"A black rep with crape bands, would be very pretty."

"And so you will see her, and send her the dress as a present?" he said, coaxingly, in the tone he had used to get his first double-barreled gun.

"Oh, Philip, you are asking too much this time," said Mrs. Drem, in a meekly complaining voice.

"Then you'll think over it; and meanwhile I shall go down to the club and have some supper."

"You don't mean to say, Philip," she exclaimed, turning and staring at him, "that you have had no dinner?"

"Well I don't know that I am to be pitied for not having dined at home. The charming family intercourse that prevails at our table is just a little trying at times, you know. But that I think it a shame to leave you all alone, I should never dine here by any chance whatever."

"Don't shay that, Philip," hiccoughed a voice at the door of the room. "You are breaking the heart of your poor old father—your poor old father."

"Good-night," said Philip to his stepmother. "I dare say I shall not see you when I return."

He passed his father without saying a word, and went downstairs and out of the house. Jumping into a Hansom, he was soon driven to his club, where (after some brief snatch of supper), he found "Blue Peter" raging fast and furious. With what success or ill-success he endeavored to rob his neighbors of their lives (which, for the time being, had oddly enough become valuable), does not concern this present history. Perhaps a temperament like his is not the best suited for billiards.

It was towards one o'clock when he got home again. As he turned up the gas and roused the fire in his bedroom, he perceived that Mrs. Drem had left a note for him on the mantelpiece. It merely said:

"DEAR PHILIP.—I will get the dress for Miss Seaford, if you like, and send a card and my compliments, leaving you to make what sort of explanations you can. But I should prefer for everybody's sake, not to visit Mrs. Seaford and her daughter personally."

"She is a kindly little woman," said Philip to himself, "and I fancy she has had rather hard lines of it in this world. I see the dress project must fall through. Perhaps by the time I have acquired sufficient intimacy to warrant my giving Lilian the dress myself, she may be partly or wholly out of mourning."

But if there was to be any chance in Lilian Seaford's costume, it was not to be in the way of lessening the depth of her mourning; for quite suddenly—so sudden that those concerned were too stunned to look back and inquire for the cause—Lilian's mother took ill and died. She died of an illness that is not yet included in medical systems, and has never been subjected to diagnosis. Yet thousands die of it, and die despite the clear reasoning which shows that, as the disease is neither organic, nor functional, it can attack nothing, and consequently can have no effect. The illness of which Mrs. Seaford died was grief; and it killed her quite as thoroughly as if the doctors had recognized it and given it a Latin name. So the small household at Hampstead was again the scene of trouble and desolation; and the young girl, left alone, began to wonder whether it would not be better if she were to go too.

CHAPTER VIII.

THERE was once a fl-a which went hopping about and at length lit upon a child's toy—a small sheep, with long woollen hair. The fl-a thought he was a most fortunate fellow, and said to himself,—

now I shall have a hearty meal! Let us descend to

went along the white wool until he reached the body
eep, which was of wood. On making the discovery his
uncontrollable. He puffed and blew; he rolled his
1 would have twisted his moustache, if he had had

at! *you* call yourself an animal, do you? I am
to be in the company of such an impostor; why,
n't a drop of blood in the whole of your miserable

Major Delaney stood at the window of the drawing-
his club, and absently tapped his finger-nail on the
ile he stared blankly out into St. James's Street. Cir-
:es (and cards) had not been very propitious of late
Major, and he was so far in the position of the fl-a,
'ould have liked at that moment to be told where he
g to get his dinner—for a dinner with strangers, ac-
:es, or friends generally, somehow or other, added to
r's finances. In short, he observed an excellent rule
ily walk and conversation; for while others lived to
dined to live.
st sight you would have fancied the Major's face was
mass of bushy gray hair; so gray and so bushy were
:ers, his large moustache, and his eyebrows. His
on, too, was not red and soldier-like, but seamed and
h a slight determination of color to the nose. He was
small man, but he had a martial appearance, and his
largely seasoned with military oaths when he was out
' society. Indeed, his conversation had frequently a
ous tinge, and in moments of excitement was dis-
d by a profusion of *I*'s.
most men who have little else to boast of, Major
had a habit of letting you know every few minutes that
gentleman. The word "gentleman" was seldom out
)uth, and when it did disappear, it was to make way for
"cad." To divide the world into gentlemen and cads
Major's mission, he himself being the standard by
measured all persons and things which were to be
:d gentlemanly. "By Gad, sir, do they think soup like
r a gentleman!" he would say; and he even exercised
:ude with his favorite adjective that he would venture
n: "You won't find, sir, a more gentlemanly-looking
e in the Park!" He was so severe upon cads, that

you were reminded of the proverbial zeal of the apostate; and so ostentatious about his character of gentleman, that you could scarcely help thinking that the assumption had for him the charm of novelty.

The Major was thus pensively drumming on the window-pane, when he was recalled from his reverie by the voice of Mr. Philip, who asked leave to introduce a friend of his, Lord Cecil Sidmouth. The Major had seen the red-haired young gentleman often, but had never been introduced to him; he was now delighted to make his acquaintance.

"Mr. Drem and you have been bullying the Chancellor of the Exchequer, haven't you, by Gad?" exclaimed the Major, with a laugh.

Lord Cecil—whose hair seemed redder and drier than ever—fixed his eyeglass, looking indifferently at the Major from head to foot, and said:

"We formed part of the deputation; yes."

"Workmen's dwellings, or something of that sort. Suppose we shall see your speech in to-morrow's papers. Tell you what, you young men are going the pace, by Gad—raising up the lower classes, you know, ad giving them ideas about—about—"

"Ventilation, for example," suggested Philip.

"And then," continued the Major, good-humoredly, "it was too bad of you to have ladies at that meeting of your Analytical Society, and talk to them about Malthus—"

"But who ought to be more interested in the question?" observed Lord Cecil, quite gravely, and scowling through his eyeglass. "And, indeed, they might have given us a few valuable hints on the subject, if they hadn't been afraid of the newspapers."

The Major, not knowing whether these graceless young scamps might not be making fun of him, broke off the conversation by abruptly asking them both to dine with him. Lord Cecil had a dozen excuses; Philip had none; for was not Mary Thormanby certain to be of the party? On the other hand, it was to be considered that the two friends, having won their point with the Government in the forenoon, had resolved to dine together in celebration of their victory. At length Lord Cecil's scruples were got over; and, having executed a game or two of Pyramids, in which the Major was content to play badly, they all, dressed as they were, drove up to ask Mrs. Delaney for some dinner.

Mr. Philip was now going to see the woman whom he loved;

and the mission ought to have been a joyful one. It was quite the reverse. His experiences at this time were of a kind which are probably not unfamiliar to many people who have not had the knowledge of life or the courage to break asunder certain bonds. Absence from this woman was more or less painful to him; the thought of being always absent was inexpressibly so. For it represented the voluntary leaving behind of all the beautiful dreams he had once dreamed about her; and even although he had discovered that she was not quite the creature whom his idealizing fancy had created, there still hung over and around her this atmosphere of tender romance. Many and many a time he reasoned himself into determining never to give her up. It was only boys, he said to himself, who imagined that a woman ought to be perfect. Women were not perfect; and perhaps this one, if her imperfections in certain directions were sufficiently obvious, was altogether as good a woman as he might ever meet. Besides, what right had a man to insist that his wife should be perfect, knowing as he did his own failings? If he could have taken the matter down to the Analytical Society for discussion—and if the philosopher of the society would have agreed to accept without proof such promises as that Mary Thormanby was a woman, and that marriage-laws existed in England—they would doubtless have resolved that, all things being considered, Philip Drem ought to marry Major Delaney's niece.

But after having reasoned himself into this decision, and after having experienced all the pangs of absence, he was far from joyful in going to see her. He knew his visit would be full of dissatisfaction, and would end in dissatisfaction. Instead of spending a pleasant evening together, he knew she would be playing some more or less palpable character either to charm or to annoy him; and their conversation would consist of various covert epigrams and retorts (wholly lost on the Major and his wife); and that he would leave the house wishing there was not a woman in the world. Her presence had on him the effect which strong drinks have on some men; they cannot resist the craving, but they dislike the drink as they actually drink it, and they are ashamed of themselves for yielding to the temptation.

It was a peculiar state of affairs for two lovers to be in.

On this particular evening Mary Thormanby was in unusually good spirits, which she betrayed only in the eloquent look of her grey eyes and in the keen quick sarcasm of her tongue. The courteous and cutting by-play, however, which was carried

on between her and Philip, was rather a puzzle to
uncle, and was no less bewildering to the youn
sometimes scowled at her over the table, and w(
this smooth-speaking, cold-looking woman could h;
his friend.

"I can understand your calling Violet Kingsc
woman, if you like," he used to say to Philip. "
I call a smart sort of a girl in talking; but th
common-sense in what she says. Plenty of fun, if
but sensible hearty sort of fun, and none of your sl
ways in it—none of your smooth faces and your add
And what I like about Violet, too, is the uncomn
notion she has of what's going on round about her.
be put upon by anybody; and she's as good a judg(
as any woman I know. I hate a woman who's alwaɣ
to be an angel, and above her dinner; hate wor
who is a sort of half Minerva and half china-doll,
herself too precious clever to talk like other peopl(

It was clear to Philip that Lord Cecil did not mu
Thormanby; and on the evening in question the
the Analytical was inclined to put down the pale-fa
ing woman opposite him, who talked so brilliantlɣ
her white teeth. But the Analytical Society *en*
have been no match for the dexterous wit and inger
Thormanby; and as the Dr. Johnson process of cru
is not permitted in modern society, Lord Cecil wa:
Miss Thormanby only with an occasional scowl, a:
his brief and laconic remarks upon the charmed
Mrs. Delaney.

Meanwhile Philip engaged his splendid sweet
handed, and was alternately charmed by the swift
sympathy she displayed, and chagrined by her p(
pretense. Was she too clever to be sincere, as]
One thing was certain; that not the least reliance co|
on anything she said about her own preferences
To please you, or to torment you, she could expre:
a disliking for anything in a second; and could s.
she had this like or dislike. She really had a dra
imagining herself for a moment in any position :
expressed to you her experiences in that character.
it was, that Philip had long ago convinced himsel
that, for the time being, she believed what she sai
too clever to be sincere, he maintained.

Strange, too, how the least trifle could change ins

her mental attitude. The accidental mention, for example, of Captain Dering's name at once put her into a position of defensive sarcasm—just as a cat that has eaten a canary will pretend to have done nothing, will rub itself against your leg, and be very friendly, until it sees you lay hold of a whip or a Saloon-pistol, and then it suddenly changes its manner and prepares to fly at you. It was Mrs. Delaney who brought up the unlucky subject, by mentioning to Lord Cecil how much she was surprised that Dr. Dering, Captain Dering's brother, when his child was unwell, instead of attending him himself, called in another doctor.

"Nothing more natural," said Philip, curtly. "He might try his skill on other people's children, but he wasn't such a fool as to do that with his own. The one strong point about the Derings is, the knowledge they have of their own stupidity."

"What a comfort it is the poor people have one redeeming virtue!" said Miss Thormanby, with a charming smile, which was as cold as steel.

"By the way, did you let Captain Dering have the cob?"
[*Barometer tending to stormy.*]
"Well, no," said Philip, "I thought you had constituted yourself the agent for the sale, and I waited to see what you would bid."

"You did not thank me for putting you in the way of a good thing," she said, in a tone which was very nearly an insult.

"Didn't I?" he said, carelessly; "I am very sorry. People who meddle with horses invariably forget their manners."

While this petty sparring was going on, Mrs. Delaney sat ill at ease. She could not understand why her niece was so forgetful of her future as to keep constantly provoking her rich lover; and many a sparing admonition she gave her to be a little more mindful. Woman of the world as she was, however, Mary Thormanby was certainly not mercenary—indeed she had too much spirit to be mercenary. No one understood better than herself the advantages of money—for she had been early taught the disadvantages of the want of it; but when she would be prudent and coax this favored lover of hers, the malicious joy of this intellectual strife was too much for her. Her brain took command of her instinct; and made her fight with her best chance of future position. This was heartrending to the ambitious Mrs. Delaney, who knew more intimately than most women what straits genteel poverty entailed, and how hard it was to "make an appearance." Nor was Mrs. Delaney very successful in impressing Lord Cecil with a notion of the magnificence of the Delaneys, former and present; for he, on being told by the aunt that Miss Thormanby, among other qualifications, sang like a nightingale, inwardly remarked,—

"No wonder; for she and the whole family have apparently lived all their life *up a tree.*"

If this is to be regarded as an epigram on the part of Lord Cecil, let us score it down to him at once; he never did it again.

"Now," said the Major when dinner was over, and the ladies had gone to the drawing-room, we are heavy drinkers, are we? The days of the three-bottle men are over——"

"But the results of the three-bottle practice are not," said Lord Cecil, severely. "I suppose we are all suffering now from the over-drinking of the last generation."

"Sure, I don't know," said the Major, cheerfully. "I think we suffer enough from our own over-drinking. But, as I was saying, we are not heavy drinkers; and what do you say to joining the ladies at once, and having a quiet rubber? Three-penny points, Mr. Drem, eh?"

With which he facetiously winked at Mr. Philip.

"That will just suit me," said Lord Cecil, gravely. "I never play over three-penny points."

"Of course not," said the Major, humorously.

"Oh, I'm not joking," said Lord Cecil (like the newspaper-gentleman, who suddenly says, "To be serious," as if some effort were required); "haven't you heard the story, Major Delaney? It was abroad at several of the clubs yesterday; I thought it was everywhere by this time. Haven't you heard of the legacy left me by Lord Carlsmere?"

"I have not," said the Major.

"Nor I," said Philip.

"By all means let me make myself a hero for a few seconds; perhaps I shall never have a chance again," observed his lordship, screwing in his eyeglass. "Some months ago Lord Carlsmere, who was my godfather, was staying with us. He got hold of a book of mine, and ran against a memorandum I had written in pencil on the margin. I cannot recollect the words: but they were something to the effect that, 'if the human mind had ever got beyond the region of its own experiences it was in the mediæval conception of the cruelty of God'——"

"Good gracious," cried the Major, "that is blasphemy."

"I beg your pardon, it is nothing of the kind," returned Lord Cecil, impertinently staring at the Major. "But most ignorant men would, I presume, fancy that my schoolboy effort at being profound had something to do with religion. So thought Lord Carlsmere. He challenged me about the authorship; I acknowledged it. He went home—*and altered his will.*"

The president of the Analytical Society threw out his hands in the fashion of a French *ingenue*—as much as to say, "There went my £30,000."

"He died, as you know, a few days ago," continued Lord Cecil, "and in his will he leaves me property to the amount of £30,000, on condition that I become a member of the Church of England."

"And are you not?" observed the Major, aghast, and instinctively sitting back on his chair. He could make his living by cards; but he was no heretic.

"Well, I suppose I shall be some day," continued the red-headed young man, "if I marry and have a lot of children to bring up. I suppose, in any case, one drifts into the Church of England as offering you as good a solution as any other of a perpetual mystery. But in the mean time, you see, Major Delaney, I am *not* in the Church of England."

"And you mean to throw away £30,000?" exclaimed the Major, who could scarcely credit his ears.

"That is my intention," remarked Lord Cecil, balancing a walnut on his forefinger.

"Of course you will, Cecil," said Mr. Philip, "but it is remarkably unfortunate, is it not? For you won't do anybody but yourself any good by the martyrdom."

As for the Major, he was almost in tears. He begged, and prayed, and reasoned with a vehemence which showed the remarkable force of his good-nature; for what interest had he in his lordship getting the money? And it seemed monstrous to him that a young man, who calmly looked forward to joining the Church of England some day, should decline to anticipate that adhesion by a few years merely through an insane scruple of conscience. Nor was it less exasperating that Mr. Philip, instead of joining in his protest, looked upon the matter as inevitable, and really stared with some surprise at his, the Major's, warm interference.

"You ought to help me," said the Major, "to prevent your friend making such an absurd sacrifice."

"The sacrifice is absurd and unusual, is it not?" said Philip with a laugh, which puzzled the Major much. "Had it been the other way—had he sacrificed his conscience—there would have been nothing unusual or absurd in it, I dare say."

"Suppose we cease discussing the matter," said Lord Cecil.

"I only mentioned it to you, Major Delaney, in case you should want me to play high——"

"By Gad, sir, I am not a professional gambler," remarked the Major with a shrug, "Mr. Drem and I have an odd game occasionally—that is all. The stakes are of no consequence—none."

But he was deeply chagrined and disappointed all the same. Had he thrown away the bait of a dinner all for nothing? What right had this young man to go about with the title of a lord—what right had he to scowl at people, and be ostentatious about his philosophy and his beggarly politics, if he hadn't a farthing in his pocket? Te fl-a had come to the body of the animal and there was not a drop of blood to be got. No wonder the Major was disgusted; and that he muttered to his wife, in a corner of the drawing-room,—

"Don't you ask that Sidmouth here again. The young upstart—he hasn't a farthing; and as for his manners—all the courtesy he has got is in his title."

They sat down at the card-table, however; Miss Thormanby and Philip being partners, as usual. As for Lord Cecil, he was glad to get out on the balcony to smoke a cigar, and watch the passing of the people in the lane beneath, or the motion of the stars overhead. If his gaze were directed upward, you may be sure his thoughts were more scientific than sentimental, and were probably connected with his pet theory of evolution.

The story of his lordship's determination about the legacy was of course brought forward by the Major, who renewed his lamentations, in which he was joined by Mrs. Delaney.

"Sure he won't be thanked by any one for what he's done; and take me word for't he'll be vexed enough when he gets owlder."

Mrs. Delaney spoke with a much more decided Irish accent than her husband did; and, indeed, women seem to retain peculiarities of pronunciation much longer than men. This is strange; for, as Jims used to say to his wife, when she said something particularly Scotch, women ought to speak better than men, having so much more practice.

Mary Thormanby, on the other hand, with her gray eyes waxing almost enthusiastic, said that Lord Cecil had nobly resolved, and that a man capable of doing this was capable of anything.

"If we in the Church," she remarked, with something like a blush of feeling on her face, "had the tender conscience, and the resolution, and the bravery, of many people we find out of it, the Church would be different from what it is."

Philip admired this hearty sympathy, of course, and was glad to see this honest praise in her eyes; but then he knew that, half an hour thereafter, she could have added to the Major's wonder and regret, some contemptuous expressions of indifference about the whole matter. While he played his hand carelessly, trumping his partner's best card, and forgetting to return her lead, he was all the time imagining a little conversation between her and Captain Dering (for example) about this very subject of the legacy. He could see, instead of the enthusiastic color and the frank admiration, the smile of derision and pity with which she would dismiss the poor boy's folly. And here came in the problem: suppose she were married to some one who would carefully cultivate the better side of her nature, and give encouragement to those finer sympathies which sprung up, flower-like, among the careless weeds of her mind, might she not be made a very different woman? And he felt that all the vision of such a possibility he could imagine might at any time be dissipated by one of her cold and scornful smiles.

This was the result, as it had often been before. The brief satisfaction he got from her generous advocacy of Lord Cecil's resolve was speedily destroyed by her expression of sentiments directly contrary in tone—and obviously meant to annoy him. Why should she inevitably subside into this childish trick of provocation—as if she gloried in showing him that she could demean herself in his sight, and yet dare him to go away from her? Why was it impossible for them to speak ten minutes together without finding themselves descending from plain speech into the bandying of meaningless sarcasm? How was it that he could enjoy conversation with any woman except with this one—that she alone was unapproachable?

He rose from the card-table (in spite of his carelessness he had actually won something), more dissatisfied than ever—longing, indeed, to get out of the house and into the fresh air. The false atmosphere of the place stifled him. No sooner did he enter her society than the frank and honest attitude of his intentions was suddenly altered; and he had to assume this tiresome position of useless antagonism. The small word-warfare, the underhand sarcasm, the petty trifling—all this was somewhat wearisome. It was an inexpressible relief to get outside—to get a breath of wholesome air, and a look at the great silent space overhead.

But before they left, courtesy demanded that some show of hospitality should be extended to Lord Cecil, who had been amusing himself pretty well with his cigar outside. There was some more helpless conversation about nothing in particular; some feeble suggestion about wine and biscuits; and then a determined desire on the part of the young men to get away.

But just before they left, Lord Cecil and Philip were standing in the middle of the floor, and had been led into talking of some suspicious movement on the part of the Home Secretary.

"There's more there than meets the eye," remarked Lord Cecil, staring absently before him.

"There isn't much," observed Mr. Philip, following the direction of his friend's glance.

Lord Cecil started and blushed; for he found himself staring at Mrs. Delaney's somewhat *decolletee* figure.

CHAPTER IX.

THERE are many guesses at the mysterious and puzzling circumstances of life which we do not reveal even to those who are most intimate with us; and it may have appeared to both Jims and his wife without either mentioning it to the other, that this girl, who had been, by a series of occurrences, thrown upon their hands, was meant to replace the daughter whom they had lost so many years before. Jims had been, like most Scotchmen, brought up to abhor the word "chance." To him and his wife a special purpose was everywhere evident in events which to other people would have appeared mere ordinary and trivial accidents. When Lilian Seaford naturally fell into the position of a daughter to them—when they almost inadvertently began to assume towards her the character of parents—it gradually became clear to them that Providence had so ordered it. Henceforth there was something sacred and inviolable in these relations; and the old couple at Hampstead found their life grown fuller and sweeter because of this filling up of the blank in their domestic circle.

No one could help becoming fond of the girl, under any circumstances; but there was much in the solitariness of her position and in the characteristics of her own nature (which were daily becoming more and more marked and beautiful) to give her a close and permanent hold upon the hearts of these two old people. And with this gaining affection there became gradually intertwined the possibilities of more tragic circumstances; for love is essentially conservative, and the more tender it waxes on the one side, the fiercer it grows on the other. Jims felt that this poor stray was now under shelter of his roof; that he had pledged himself to accord to her paternal protection; and the grim man, brooding by his fireside over the terrible lesson of former years, would picture to himself how he would now deal with any wolf who should try to invade his small fold. A tender friend, but a dangerous enemy.

During the piteous time after her mother's death, Lilian was too stunned and miserable to take much thought of her own affairs, and she spoke no more to Mrs. Lawson about her wish that Philip should not come to the house. Nor was the old Scotchwoman sorry to let that episode pass into forgetfulness; for she had but dimly comprehended the girl's meaning, and had been greatly at a loss to know how to convey the hint to Philip. Such a return for his many kindnesses would, she properly thought, have been the height of ingratitude; and so she was glad to let the matter slip by, trusting that it had been only suggested by a girlish whim.

As for him, knowing nothing of these things, he took it for granted that his interference and assistance were now needed more than ever, and his visits to Hampstead were more frequent than ever they had been. That unusually considerate lawyer, who would not charge anything for petty services, was again called into requisition, and such arrangements were made about Lilian's present position and prospects as ought to have given her comfort and security. But, in her desolation, she cared only for the kind solace and sympathy she received from the Lawsons, and was content to let other matters shift for themselves. They noticed that her trance-like fits were somewhat more frequent now, and somewhat sadder.

By and by, as the prostration of grief wore off, and she came more into immediate contact with the people around her, Philip began to notice the peculiar manner in which the relations between himself and her had apparently become altered. This discovery only dawned upon him gradually; but it occasioned him the most powerful surprise, and was followed by other discoveries scarcely less unpleasant. In the olden days—and the few months which had elapsed since the arrival of Mrs. Seaford and her daughter seemed a strangely long period—he used to pet this child, and play with her various moods, watching her all the while, as I have said, with the interest one might feel in watching the movements of a new piece of mechanism. All the shifting emotions that were exhibited so clearly in the large, innocent deep-blue eyes represented to him only the workings of a beautiful mental nature, which was a constant curiosity and delight. He seemed to see a new universe, full of wonder and joy, mirrored in these eyes; and he had almost begun to believe in the existence of this fair young world that was full of honor, and honesty, and the joy of health. From Park Lane to Hampstead was for him a leap across a dozen continents—from the cold gloom and artifical manners of our northern land to some happy hemisphere, with the sunlight shining on green islands and blue seas, and the wonder of fresh and simple ways.

Now all this was changed; the old frank communion was gone from between them—nay, she actually seemed to avoid him. At first, he would scarcely believe it; then he was speaking to her directly, and remonstrating with her; finally, with a little more caution, he resolved to ask Mrs. Lawson in what manner he had offended Lilian.

"Mrs. Lawson," said he, "you must find out for me why Lilian seems to get out of the way when I come up to see you, instead of being my constant companion, as she used to be. What have I done? Or do you think she so much associates me with these troubles she has passed through that she would rather not see me?"

"Well," said Mrs. Lawson hesitatingly, and with some wild, woman-like grasping at this proffered excuse, "perhaps—perhaps——"

"Because," continued Philip, in his careless way, and not noticing her hesitation, "if she has any painful feeling like that, you must tell me at once. My staying away from your hospitable and comfortable home *would* be rather a sacrifice, you know; but I should do that gladly if she wished."

Here, then, was the very offer which had been desired: why did she not accept it on the spot? Mrs. Lawson had a sensitive conscience; and it suddenly struck her that, if Mr. Philip must be asked to stay away, he must not go on a false impression.

"You see," he continued, in the same careless fashion, "your husband and I can have our talking elsewhere; or perhaps the world won't be much worse off if we don't have it at all. It is only of late that I have convinced myself Lilian seeks to avoid me; and I know our old confidences and amusements are quite gone. Now it is of great consequence to her that the house should be made pleasant and comfortable to her, while it is of no consequence whatever to me if I spend my evenings elsewhere. You perceive?"

"Yes—but—Mr. Philip," stammered Mrs. Lawson, upon whom his thoughtfulness and kindly feeling had precisely the opposite effect of wishing that he should remain. Nevertheless, her duty towards Lilian was clear.

"Don't say anything about it to her," he observed. "And don't make any remark about my not coming to see you so very often. But I shall by degrees drop off visiting you: perhaps in course of time all these old recollections will have ceased."

"Mr. Philip," said Mrs. Lawson suddenly, "sit down till I tell ye the whole truth about the matter. It's better you should ken, especially as ye're so kind and thochtfu' as to care more about other folk than yoursel'. I say it's better I should tell ye plump and plain, and then ye'll see how ye should na stop comin' by degrees, but stop althegither."

"I must have committed some considerable crime," he said quietly, "to have merited this abrupt banishment. However, tell me."

After all, the honest way was the best way. She said no more than she knew; but that again was not sufficient to compromise Lilian. She told him merely what had occurred on the evening after they had gone for their walk on Hampstead Heath, and left him to draw his own inferences.

He was very grave and thoughtful, saying nothing for several minutes.

"I am very glad you have been so frank with me, Mrs. Lawson," he said at length, rising from his chair. "I only wish you had given me some hint before, and not subjected the poor girl to all this persecution."

"I thought it a' blown over," said Mrs. Lawson, not very certain what to say, and wondering how he should take her disclosures.

He did not afford her much enlightenment. He seemed merely to have grown a trifle more reserved, and he was already dwelling carefully on the matter. Then he said:

"I promised to stay and take tea with you, did I not? I will stay; but after this evening I don't think you will see me for some time, Mrs. Lawson."

The tears started to the old Scotchwoman's eyes. She took

his hand in hers, and thanked him with greater warmth of expression than was customary with her.

At this moment there appeared at the door of the room Lilian herself, who apparently not knowing there was anybody within, was about to enter in search of something. The moment she perceived them she started, glanced with a wild and frightened expression from the one to the other, as if she was divining what they had been talking about.

"Didn't you know I had come?" said Philip, with marked carelessness, and taking heed not to observe the strange expression of her face.

She glanced at Mrs Lawson, and there was more tell-tale confusion in the old Scotchwoman's look than in the cold indifference which Philip had instantly assumed. The girl was still only partially reassured; but she came into the room and shook hands with him, and then turned to seek what she had come for. In shaking hands with her, he could not help looking for a brief second in her eyes; and there was something inexpressibly touching in the frightened, conscious, apprehensive veil that was now drawn over the frankness and joy that had once shone there. It was still a bird-like look; but the audacious cheerfulness and laughter of the clear blue deeps had given place to a troubled fear.

At the frugal meal which shortly followed Philip found himself seated opposite the fair young girl, who was dressed wholly in black. She was very silent and absent; the blue eyes deepening frequently into the mystic trances which he used to observe with peculiar curiosity. She listened as though she heard nothing; and it was only when, by accident, their eyes met, that she seemed to be conscious of his presence, or rendered uncomfortable by it.

Fortunately there was no general conversation to make her reserve apparent. Jims had the talk all to himself, and was discoursing scornfully upon the recondite theological subjects which had puzzled the schoolmen, but were as clear as noonday to the eye of faith. Into these regions Philip never followed him; nor did Jims want any stimulus in the way of pretended argument or opposition. On such matters his dogmatism would have crushed the suggestions of any disputant; and it was Jims' pleasure, on these occasions, to expound the law and the scriptures as if he had just come down from Sinai to confront an idolatrous and backsliding generation. At such times Philip submitted meekly to be considered a typical son of Belial. Jims' fierce arguments were thundered at his head; and he never even protested against his being credited with an amount of heresy and infidelity, of bad logic and general stupidity, sufficient to have ruined a state.

"Why, sir," Jims would say to him, "it is reasonable to think that God would have allowed sin to come into the world, if only for the purpose of allowing us to practice the virtues of charity and forgiveness."

"Probably so," Philip would perhaps answer; "but isn't it a pity so few of us take advantage of the opportunity?"

During this present discussion—or monologue, rather—Philip was unusually inattentive. In spite of himself his eyes would wander towards the girl who sat opposite him there, with the downcast face, the timid look, and absent voice. It is a dangerous thing to give a man the notion that a woman is in love with him : the confidence it inspires paves the way to catastrophes. And there is nothing more certain than this; that a young man is perpetually trying to unlock the puzzle of his future life; and that there is scarcely an unmarried woman whom he meets whom he does not regard as the possible key. It is the instinct proper to this period of existence. But whereas a man sees many woman, and cannot tell how many obstacles there may lie in the way of his marrying this one or that one, the case is very different when he knows, or fancies he knows, that a particular woman loves him. Here, at least, is one solution; and straightway his imagination begins to paint pictures of the coming time; and, artist-like, he puts in this figure to see how it will look.

Jims had gone from original sin to the devil, whose reality as an actual tempter of men he was vigorously expounding. Alec had come home from the City, and now sat on the hearth-rug, looking up with fixed, wistful eyes upon his grandfather, and listening to the strange sermon that was going on. Lilian appeared to listen also; but her thoughts were far away. And farther and farther away did Philip get also; until the whole party seemed in a dream, each regarding his or her own separate world, and living apart. Attentive observers have sometimes remarked this expression on the faces of a whole congregation, and have even hinted that there is nothing more provocative of profound day-dreaming and reverie than a good drowsy sermon.

These five people now, who are apparently at Hampstead, are really very far distant from it.

Lilian is sitting on Paignton Sands, her hands folded on her knees, her eyes looking out on the blue waters of Tor Bay, where millions and millions of white stars glitter on the innumerable ripples, in constant motion under the still sky and the warm sunlight. Over there, on the left, the wooded hills and gleaming villas of Torquay rise above the white water, with the Thatcher and Ore Stone jutting out into the bluer region beyond; away over there, on the right, Berry Head runs out into the clear sea; and the hamlet of Brixham lies amid pale smokes, with the slates of its houses shining through the mist. Then far beyond, and all in front of her, the faint dark line of the horizon meeting the yellow sky, with here and there the speck of a ship that seems to hang between air and water. Beside her, the ruddy sand, the drowsy silence of the mid-day sun, and the crisp white ripples that splash on the beach below.

Philip is at a ball, and Lilian is his wife. Their names are announced; she enters on his arm; and he knows that in all the great room there is no one half so lovely as she is. She is dressed in white, and there is a white rose in her hair, and white pearls round her neck. His friends are there; she has won the hearts of all of them; even the women have taken to petting her. As for his father—— And here the lights of the ball-room grow dimmer, and the scene changes.

Mrs. Lawson is again a girl among the cattle of a small moorland farm in the south of Lanarkshire. She sees Jims as a smart young weaver coming down the road from between the fir-plantations, and he is waving his cap to her.

Alec is standing on London bridge among the dingy idlers who lean on the parapet and look down the great gap in the City, with its steamers, barges, quays, cranes, and what not. Behind him is the roar of carriages; before him the thoroughfare which leads away out to the green islands of the Spanish Main.

By what mental process Jims' valiant encounter with the devil should have been transformed into these aerial pictures we need not stay to determine. They were abruptly scattered by Philip's rising and saying he must be off, as he had to dine with some people that evening.

"And I am going to bid you good-bye for a little time," he said, with excellent indifference of tone.

" Indeed!" said Jims.

"I think of going to Torquay for a month or two."

Lilian almost started. Why Torquay? She had just been there; and it almost seemed as if he knew it.

But the reason for this sudden decision was simple enough.

Among the many places he had been dreaming about, the seaside villages in the south of Devonshire were prominent, for they had many associations with the young girl who sat opposite him; and when, on the spur of the moment, he chose some watering-place as his probable destination, Torquay naturally occurred to him. Yet it seemed strange enough to her.

"What do you mean to do there?" inquired Jims, who was quite ignorant of any reason why Philip should wish to have this excuse for not coming to his house.

"I shall go down with a profound determination to study. I shall read for a day or two; then ask myself what is the use or value to anybody of my doing so: then I shall make a pretense of improving my health—walk, ride, and bathe every day to excess; and then I shall relapse into billiards and idleness. I know the whole programme perfectly, as there is hardly a watering-place in England I have not visited with the like results."

"And you have nothing to do in life but that?" said Jims, with a sigh.

"It is the profession I have been brought up to," said Philip. "However I will not make matters worse than they are. I mean really this time to improve my political education; so that if ever I should get a seat, I shall be able to give the history of every administration since the beginning of the century. I will study all sides of all questions; and in my first speech in Parliament I shall electrify the House as completely as did the Irish member who, the very first time he caught the Speaker's eye, spoke for ten minutes, and managed to propose in that time triennial Parliaments subdivision of the land, the abolition of all established churches, the granting of a sum to construct docks for his native village, the abolition of the game laws, and the repeal of the union. If they had let him go on for another ten minutes, he would have talked the Queen off her throne, and cut the throats of the aristocracy."

"When do you leave?"

"In a day or two, probably. I will send you my address; and if anything occurs about those artisans' dwellings, you know you can tell me."

"Good-bye," he said to them all; last of all to Lilian.

She held his hand just for a moment; and said timidly looking up:

"You have been very kind to me; I must thank you, since you are going away."

He stood on the threshold irresolute, holding her hand, and forgetting that the others were looking at him. Some wild impulses were crossing his brain—that he would boldly give up his intention of deserting the house, declare there and then, before them all, that he would set to work to win this beautiful young creature for his wife, and so settle once for all the uncertainties that lay before him.

The opportunity passed in an instant; she withdrew her hand; and he was constrained to go. And when he went outside, he looked back at the house, and wondered whether again he should ever enter the tender and quiet sanctuary, where he had seen so much of what was beautiful and noble in life.

CHAPTER X.

He had to dine with the Kingscotes that evening, and when he reached Park Lane he found that his father and Mrs. Drem had already left. Accordingly, by the time he had dressed and driven to Sir James's house, he was apparently very late. In the same predicament, however, was a certain Lord Derrosay —an infirm old man, who tottered about on his thin frail legs, and was very deaf; and as Sir James had expectations from this little withered earl, there was no thought of serving dinner until he arrived. Philip, therefore, was just in time; and was making profuse apologies to Miss Violet when Lord Derrosay arrived.

"You must have been very hurried, my dear," remarked Mrs. Drem, with her pretty weak voice.

"Hurried! Yes, hurried!" said Mr. Drem, in his snappish voice; "I dare say he was up looking after that woman at Hampstead, and nursing her baby for her!"

"You forget, sir," replied Philip, calmly, "that Mrs. Seaford is dead."

"Good thing, too," said the merchant.

"My dear!" remonstrated Mrs. Drem.

"Don't my dear me," he said, testily; "I hate your hypocrisy. You want to make people believe we're a loving couple. Very—very!" he added with a sardonic smile.

"Well, it isn't my fault, I am sure," said Mrs. Drem, who was nearly crying.

Philip turned away, as was his wont, from these domestic squabbles; and found that he had to take Violet down to dinner. He found likewise, that on her other side sat the deaf earl, who never under any provocation uttered a syllable during the serious business of dinner; so that Philip could talk to the young lady without any danger of being overheard or interrupted. He began to do so in a fashion which considerably startled his partner.

"Do you know, Violet," he said "that my papa wishes me to marry you, and that I fancy your papa would rather like you to marry me?"

She looked up with her big dark eyes full of astonishment; and then her practical common sense told her that it was impossible any sane man could begin a proposal at dinner.

"Don't look alarmed," said Philip; "I am not going to ask you to fulfil their wishes just at present."

"You are very kind, I am sure," she said; "I hope I shall be grateful and obedient when you do."

"I know you wouldn't marry me," he observed.

"Do not be too sure," she said; "I might be driven to it."

"I think myself you might do worse," he retorted, "and probably will. But that is not to the purpose. I am going to tell you a secret."

"Do," she said; "I like people to go on talking pleasant and interesting things at dinner, and not asking you to answer them."

"We don't mean to marry, do we?"

"We two together?" she asked.

He nodded.

"Well you may; but I don't."

"Very good. Now I am going to tell you all about it, just as if you were my sister."

"But please don't ask me questions. Make it a long story and no questions."

"You little gourmande! Why don't you satisfy your hunger at lunch, and make a dinner what it ought to be—the oramental meal of the day?"

"That is another question and I am busy."

"Greedy, you mean. However, to begin with—I arrived at the resolution when I was in the hansom coming here——"

"Was there a collision?"

"You must not be smart, Violet; for it does not suit the smooth regularity and gracefulness of your face. Besides, what I am going to tell you is serious. When I was in the hansom, as I said, I resolved that I would never marry Mary Thormanby."

"Oh, Philip!" said the young lady, laying down her fish-knife, and dropping at once her provoking air, "I am so heartily glad of that! I am so very, very glad. And I am so pleased that you should have told me in that way—for we have always been very confidential, haven't we? But are you quite sure?"

There was a glimpse of humorous doubt on the smooth, round, pretty face.

"Quite," said Philip. "I have often thought of it; but I never resolved to do it. The fact is, you know, the prospect of having to spend one's life in the continual worry which marks every visit of mine to the house is a trifle too much. There is no frankness between us—no companionship whatever; and when an hour near her makes me as savage as a bear, don't you think the spending all one's life in that state is enough to make one pause?"

"You know," said Miss Kingscote, slowly, and with an odd expression of wisdom on the demure face, "it is a very dangerous thing to say anything against your friend's sweetheart; because he is very likely, after all, to marry her; and then he is certain to tell her——"

"And then you won't have many invitations to dinner from *that* lady. Really, Violet, your prudence is beyond praise. Who taught you all these bits of worldly wisdom?"

"Myself," said Violet, frankly. "I have had to look after a whole household ever since I came home from Bonn; and papa isn't of much help. However, Philip, I am very glad about this; for although I have scarcely ever spoken to her, I have heard a good deal about her, and seen a good deal of her —and I don't like her."

There was just a touch of unnecessary emphasis about these last words.

"Unfortunately I do," said Philip, ruefully. "I think she is a most fascinating woman, and might be a charming companion, if she liked; but she is no more to be depended on than a cat; you can never calculate on her moods, and while you are stroking her, she turns and scratches you. I tell you, Violet, I have had enough of it; it is becoming a little too wearisome. If we were to marry, the house would be insufferable."

"Pray, Philip, don't get so excited," said Violet, who liked to have her dinner in peace. "That is my *menu* you have twisted up."

"It was to hide the bad French in it," said he contemptuously. "You who look after the whole household, might correct the confectioner's phrases. Look at that! *Queues de bœufs en karri; croquettes de homarde.*"

"I suppose there is an *r* too many in *croquettes*," said Violet, with impudent gravity.

At this point the deaf earl lifted his head from his plate, and suddenly bethought himself that he ought to address a remark to his fair neighbor. It was about the weather; and no blazing July day could have made Violet more hot and uncomfortable than the necessity of having to bawl out a reply to him, with the startled eyes of the whole company fixed upon her. When she returned with gratitude and joy to resume her conversation with Mr. Philip, she was a good deal more timid and a good deal less malicious.

"But you know, Philip," she said with some little hesitation, "one seldom gives up one's sweetheart without having the prospect of another one—somebody to fall back upon, as it were."

"Is that your experience, Miss Violet?" he asked gravely.

"If there is anybody else," she hinted, playing with her knife and fork, and speaking in a hesitating way, "you ought to tell me the whole story."

"And suppose I do tell you, Miss Curiosity? Suppose I tell you of a maiden who lived in a kingdom down by the sea, and who looked at the sea so long that her eyes became of a wonderful blue; and the sun made her hair brown: and the winds dyed her cheeks with a clear rose color; and God gave her a perfect soul. Then she left the sea, and the sea sands, and the sea winds, and she came up to London, and lived there apparently; but at all hours of the day her soul fled out of her, and went back to the sea. So I think it was that when the soul was out of her, you know, and she could not see very well, she met here in London a poor idle good-for-nothing, and her eyes played her a trick, and she fancied there was something fine about him, and grew to care far too much for him. And what could he do in return?"

This time her face was more than serious; it was anxious.

"Oh Philip," she said, "do you intend doing that? for I know what you mean—the girl you told me of; and you are not in love with her; and you will marry out of generosity and kindness, and the wish to make her happy. Do you really mean to do all that?"

"I do," he said calmly.

"But you don't know what you propose doing," she said, impetuously, "It is madness to think of it for both your sakes. What sort of married life are you likely to have with a woman you don't love?"

"I should be content to have no other enjoyment than the pleasure I always and invariably experience whenever I am sitting in the same room with her. To look at her is a pleasure; to listen to her is a pleasure; to be near her at any time is a pleasure."

"And you say you are not in love with her?"

"I am not. I never quarrel with her."

"That woman has perverted all your notions," said Violet angrily. "She has irritated you into being so grateful for anything like the pleasure of companionship and gentle society, that you are ready to think there is nothing else wanting in married life. Some men, I know, could pass their life well enough with a woman who could be a sort of a pleasant companion at meals, look after the house, and say nothing if left alone in the evenings ; you never could. You would break the insipid calm of the weather with a thunderstorm. Whatever you do, Philip, don't marry a woman with whom you are not very deeply in love."

So earnest was this little girl, that you would have fancied she spoke with all the authority of an experienced woman. Strangely enough, however, he paid less attention to these words now than he did long afterwards, when he recalled them with a bitter smile, and when it would have been the keenest cruelty to Violet herself to repeat them.

At present she said all she could say on that side of the question ; and now she formed her battery on another position.

"You know what your father will probably do ?" she said.

"The worst he can do is to cut me off with the metaphoric shilling."

"Is that not bad enough ?"

"Yes, certainly bad enough, to one brought up as I have been ; but there are worse things possible in this world, for me as for other men. I don't think I've anything heroic about me, my guide as to conduct being chiefly my own satisfaction. But there are times when my present ignominious position begins to be unbearable ; and I would gladly have something practical to work for—not because I have any grand ambition or notion of duty, but merely out of a selfish wish to feel comfortable within myself. I begin to wish that I was a stone-mason, or a bricklayer, or a cab-driver, and that I could add to my dinner the enjoyment of knowing I had worked for it."

"Is there no other sphere of exertion for one in your position ?" she said, with a touch of her father's manner in her.

"You mean getting into Parliament, I suppose, and preparing additional arguments to back up your leader, to whom your vote is of more importance than your speech. Of the two, I think I could drive a cab to more purpose."

"Miss Seaford would not marry a cab-driver," observed Violet, promptly.

Indeed, she had an admirable faculty of cutting the legs from these tall and weak-kneed propositions.

"You see, my dear young friend," continued Philip, helping her to some grapes, "if all this should come about as you suggest, and if my papa should be inclined to play the tragedy-father, my chances of getting into Parliament would be remarkably small. How otherwise, then, should I be able to do any grand deeds for the benefit of my fellow-men? By writing for the newspapers? Everybody fancies he can write for the newspapers, till he tries. By itinerant lecturing on the rights of man? I should insult my rustic audience in about three minutes. Whereas the life of a cabman is a jolly and healthful life—full of motion, incident, excitement, taking you into the open air during all weathers, hardening your frame, and showing you every aspect of human affairs——"

" And touting along the gutters in Oxford Street on a wet Sunday," observed Violet, scornfully.

" But then you have the delight of catching a prize; for a cabman, like any other angler, fishes best after a shower."

" You are very well off as you are," said Violet. " My advice to you is, not to be too independent. However, I am very glad you are really going to break off with Miss Thormanby."

" But you forbid my marrying Lilian Seaford."

" You ought not to think of it."

" Will *you* marry me?"

" No,"

" Then I am left out in the cold."

" Must you marry somebody?"

" Yes."

" It is a pity you haven't a grandmother——"

" Violet, you are becoming, as Lord Cecil told you, more and more impertinent every day; whereas, with growing years you ought to be acquiring dignity of bearing and extreme courtesy and reserve of manner. Your political notions—Heaven help your pretty small head!—demand that it should be so."

" Very well, Philip, I won't do it again; for I see we are going into the drawing-room presently. Will you come in soon? I have given up the whole of the dinner to talk over your affairs; you must give up the rest of the evening to mine."

" Twenty evenings!" said he.

And with that she and the other ladies left the table.

When Philip went into the drawing-room, however, he found his place occupied by Lord Cecil Sidmouth.

That young gentleman had been asked to dinner; but had given a qualified acceptance on the ground that he was to take the chair at some working-men's meeting, and was uncertain when he might be free. Accordingly, although too late to dine, he had dressed and driven down to Sir James's house, taking up his position in the drawing-room until the ladies should appear. When Philip went into the room, Lord Cecil was in so amiable a mood (although he scowled all the time) that you would have fancied he had dined several times over.

He had been pretty well badgered by diverse malcontents, however, at the meeting. It was broadly hinted that he was in collusion with the Government, and was being paid to betray the interests of the working-classes. Another gentleman would insist that Lord Sidmouth, as he called him, had forsworn his opinions in order to get into Parliament, where he would instantly veer round again; while a third challenged him to say that he believed in the books of Moses. Lord Cecil was not a brilliant young man; but he had a capital notion of being armed at all points on any subject he ventured to speak of; he was not easily perturbed; he had plenty of pluck and patience, and so he at length came off with flying colors. His various adventures he was relating with much gusto to Miss Violet, who listened with a pleasure and admiration only tempered by the thought that, alas! her companion had thrown away his gifts and graces on the wrong side.

CHAPTER XI.

MR. PHILIP did not go to Torquay. He lay awake half the night after going home from Sir James's dinner-party, and next morning he was out early, wandering alone round the deserted walks about the Serpentine and through Kensington-gardens. He had need to consider his resolves just then. He was debating the most momentous issue of his life; and he knew thoroughly and well the terrible importance of it. He had need to consider; and he walked up and down—noticing nothing in his way—with his mind contemplating the two paths which now lay before him, and wondering which he should take. There was no great hurry about the decision; but once made, he knew it was irrevocable.

The more he thought of the happy life he might spend in the society of this young girl, who had already laid at his feet the treasure of her pure and tender affection, the more beautiful and peaceful seemed the prospect. He recalled the pleasant evenings he had spent up in the Hampstead cottage—the joyous rambles they had had together—the singular halo of interest which her association with any place could throw over it. How was it that these south Devonshire villages of which she spoke, and all the wonders of the picturesque coast, seemed to him invested with a peculiar and tender romance? How came it that he had never thought of making any pilgrimage to the perhaps equally beautiful places in Ireland where Mary Thormanby had been brought up? To him Devonshire had become pre-eminently lovely, for her sake. When he saw in the shipping intelligence of a newspaper some mention of one of the small southern seaports, he regarded it with a singular interest, as if it had a message for him.

But with the cool judgment of a man who had seen much of men and circumstances, he proceeded to look at the other side of the shield. Many things combined to make it probable that, if he determined to marry Lilian Seaford, he would have to earn his own bread with his own labor. His father's irascible temper was not to be lightly provoked; and Richard Drem had not only frowned upon Philip's intimacy with Tom Seaford's widow and daughter, but had also cherished schemes about his son in another direction. The mere suggestion of this marriage would make the great merchant furious; and if Richard Drem were driven by sudden passion into quarrelling with his son, the break, he knew, would be perpetual.

Nor was it merely the giving up of certain luxuries which Philip had now to contemplate; but the separation from nine-tenths of his friends. Even if they, out of generosity, would care to keep up acquaintance with a man who had removed himself into a quite different sphere, the calls upon his time and his own temper were pretty certain to forbid his accepting the kindness. In this way Mr. Philip calmly pondered over the very worst that could befall him. He knew as well as any man the advantages of his position, and the various amusements and gratifications he would have to give up along with the income derived from his father. But all at once he said to himself,—

"If life is only valuable to me on account of these luxuries —if I cannot earn for myself a satisfactory way of living—I may venture to consider myself and my position a blunder and failure, and go and put a rope round my neck, like the Heir of Lynne. If things are in this rotten condition, it is better they should be tested. I will make the experiment of living my life my own way; and if the worst comes to the worst, is there not plenty of open land in the Far West where a man and his wife may manage to live?"

Instinctively, in thus contemplating the breaking down of his old surroundings, he turned to the country in which humanity has tried its boldest experiments—in which these are still being tried, with such results as even the next century, or the next again, may not fully reap. Here, in this old land, what remained to him? Indigent gentility, which has not been trained to any of the formal professions, takes refuge as a rule in some endeavor to write. But in the hands of the great majority of human beings, a steel pen is but a poor and small weapon with which to meet and fight the attacks of the elements, the demands of the various appetites, and the eager competitive rapacity of one's fellows. The only alternative which naturally occurred to Philip was to exercise his skill as a whip; but the living is not a very sumptuous one which a man gains by working in partnership with a horse.

In the meantime, after plenty of deliberation, he had resolved to brave all these chances which he had calmly considered. There was no impulsive heroism, or empty braggadocio, about his intention; but the cool purpose of a man who had sufficient reason to control his own hasty and impetuous nature. All this having been talked over with himself, he returned home, had some breakfast, then got into a cab, and drove to Hampstead.

Never before had he felt so much of what was active and resolute tingling in him as at this moment. The world lay all before him, and he had resolved to take it in his own way. The sense of insecurity which accompanies a dependent position was wholly gone from him. There now lay before him some definite object and aim, and his heart leaped up and rejoiced as he nerved himself to meet whatever might come in his way.

First of all, there was the securing of this companion whom he proposed to take with him through life. There was remarkably little of the doubtful and hesitating lover about him, as he drove up to Hampstead on this cool bright morning; there was more of the audacity of young Lochinvar, who came determined to carry off his mistress, thinking neither of "by your leave or with your leave;" and Mr. Philip expected to have nothing more to do than to walk into Jims' cottage and carry off his bride.

He had not arrived at the house, however, when he caught a glimpse of Lilian walking off alone towards the Heath. He instantly dismissed the cab, passed the house without looking in, and by dint of a little smart walking speedily overtook her.

Lilian, with startled and frightened eyes, shrank back from him.

"I thought you were at Torquay," she said.

"I intended going, for your sake; I didn't for my own. Won't you let me walk a little way with you? I have something to say to you."

"I only came out for a few minutes," she said, despairingly, looking round for some means of escape, "and I—I must go back now."

"You must do nothing of the kind, Lilian," he said, in the old kindly, paternal way he was once accustomed to address her. "How is it you have got afraid of me all at once? Don't you remember the walks we have had together—and how very good friends we were? I am going to put a stop to all this nonsense; I am going to make friends with you, whether you will or no. Come along."

Looking up into his face, there was a sort of half-wistful smile came into the blue eyes, as if she were recalling the fashion in which she used to give way to the spoiled boy. So she meekly submitted and walked along by his side—but very slowly, as if she wished to remain at no great distance from her home.

"Now," said he, cheerfully, "look me in the face, and say you are not going to treat me any more as if I were a complete stranger to you."

"Very well, I will not," she promised; but she did not look up.

"You acknowledge you have been doing so?"

"I am sorry if you have thought me ungrateful," she said, in a low voice; "for you have been very kind to me. I hope you won't think anything of it——"

"Not if you promise to be better behaved in the future. And do you know, Lilian, why I wanted to talk to you by ourselves for a few minutes! I want to persuade you to be my wife."

"Your wife!" she said faintly and standing still, as if all the life had suddenly left her.

"Yes. I won't ask you to say anything, dear Lilian—you needn't even look up. You have only to give me your hand."

And he held out his open palm, from which he had a moment or two before withdrawn the glove.

"I cannot, I cannot," she said, in a frightened way; and then suddenly she looked up into his face with that bird-like, quick, innocent scrutiny, which seemed the almost sole weapon of defence that Nature had given this timid and beautiful creature. She seemed to read all he was thinking in that one rapid glance; and for a brief second there appeared on her own face the expression of a great and wistful tenderness, as though she were satisfied with all she had seen in the eyes of the man whom she loved. But there was an infinite sadness in her voice as she merely repeated the words:

"Your wife!"

"Why do you speak like that?" said he, gently, and yet with some reproach. "Don't you care for me sufficiently to think that you could be happy with me?"

And the truth came as simply from her lips as from those of a child.

"I do care for you, Philip—very much; and I should like to have been your wife. But that I shall never be."

Her eyes, that had been wistful and thoughtful, now grew full of tears, and she turned away, as if she would go home alone. But Mr. Philip laid hold of her, and said,—

"I tell you, Lilian, you shall be my wife. What is to prevent our marrying? You have told me enough to let me know that I need fear nothing from *you;* and if you and I make up our minds to marry, I should like to know who is to come between us?"

And he laughed with a joyous, confident laugh, that sent the demons of doubt and fear, with all other gorgons and chimeras dire, howling into the bottomless pit. If a man were not brave under these circumstances—when a young and loving heart confesses its fondness for him; when the whole of life lies before him as bright and cheerful as the young spring morning that is shining all round—when is he likely to be?

The infection of his trust and audacity caught her for an instant, and she looked up with a glad light in her eyes; but presently she drew back from him again, and said, with dispair in her gesture and tone,—

"No, no, no, Philip! You must not think of it. All your people—your father—your friends——"

"Why, you little goose," said he, so glad was he to find that her objections were merely those of detail, "that is my business, not yours. If I enjoy your society more than theirs —if I think that the whole of them taken in a lot and sold wouldn't be worth one of your slippers—how can you alter matters?"

The frank and easy assurance of his manners staggered her for a moment, and she said in a hesitating way,—

"But, Philip, it is so unwise of you! I think you only propose it out of kindness, and that you are not thinking of yourself at all——"

"Indeed I am," said he, in a matter of fact, patronizing tone in which he used to set her right about her French idioms; "you don't perceive that it is out of pure abject selfishness that I mean to marry you, whether you consent or not. So that you really may give up any notion of arguing with me. It is of no use. I mean to marry you, and I will; and if you are obstinate or refractory I will have you carried off in a carriage, your mouth bandaged, and you shipped on board a vessel for South America, just as they used to do in stories, you know. The fact is, Lilian, you are not fit to act or think for yourself; you must leave the affair in my hands, and I will arrange it to your advantage."

"You mean——" she said slyly.

"I mean that it is to your advantage to marry me—at least we will assume that in the meanwhile, and I therefore advise you to contemplate the ordeal with a pleasant face. I should explain, to, that you have every chance of marrying a man absolutely in poverty——"

"Ah, if you were!" she said suddenly; and he saw written in her face what her woman's heart said she would be to him under these different circumstances. That little show of feeling touched him deeply, but he was afraid to speak to her yet as tenderly and seriously as he inwardly felt about it.

"Why," said he, "I believe you would like to see me without a farthing."

"I would," said she simply.

"Then you have every chance of having your wishes gratified."

"And that, Philip," said the girl seriously, "is why I say again that you must not speak any more of this. It was very kind of you—it has given us both, perhaps, a little pleasure even to dream of it for a minute or two; but you must go away now, and not come up to see us any more. That will be better for you and for all of us. Why should you want me to point out that to you? why should I know it, who have not half your knowledge? Yet I do not know it, Philip—I feel sure of it. If you knew how hard it is for me to speak these words, you would not ask me to say any more; and, indeed, I cannot—I cannot. Don't make me any more miserable than I am, but say good-bye now once for all."

The tears were running down her face. She unclasped a

little locket from her neck, and gave it him. He took it, but he took her hand in his at the same time, and he said, seriously enough now.

"I will keep this locket, Lilian, for your sake; but I shall not leave you, and, please God, I never will!"

With that there suddenly appeared on the scene James Lawson, who came hurriedly up, with wonder in his face, and anger and reproach. So excited, indeed, was the old man with what he conceived to be the treachery of Philip and the deceit of Lilian, that he could scarce speak, and there glowed in his eyes, from under the shaggy eyebrows, a fire that boded danger.

"I—I want some explanation o' this," said he, almost gasping for breath.

"And you shall have it," said Mr. Philip with all his old audacity; and, leading Lillian forward by the hand, "Allow me to present to you Miss Lill in a new character—as my future wife."

CHAPTER XII.

AND so these two entered hand in hand upon the beautiful idyllic period of early love, just as the spring was ripening into summer warmth and there was a scent of hawthorn in the air. What a sweet and tender time it was! and the two children wandered carelessly among the flowers, and had little thought of the future. Life was so young and new to them both; for she had won him over to her world, that he had often seen from a distance, and admired and hungered after. Why, he was in it now! He used to think that her eyes looked out on a universe that was far more lovely than any he couldsee; and lo! it had been revealed to him also; and they two entered it, and found it very fair.

Yet, strange enough, at this time when they were really but as children, enjoying themselves in a world that is anew created for every human soul, and which never loses one atom of its wonder and delight, they were unconsciously showing to other people a maturity and self-reliance they had never exhibited before. There fell a certain calm and self-control over Mr. Philip's waywardness, while the more than frank fashion he had of deciding for himself and looking things in the face grew more and more marked. She, too, seemed to have been endowed with an access of keen-sighted womanly sympathy that gradually overcame her girlish timidity, and brought her into more immediate relations with those around her. Philip had been accustomed to pet her in a grave and paternal way; now he sought to make her his most intimate friend, and to receive from her as well as give. He was not madly in love with her, as you know, when he resolved that he would secure this tender life companion—or, at least, he fancied he was not deeply in love, judging by his bitter experiences elsewhere. Insensibly, however, her great affection and sweetness drew his heart towards her, so that he could scarce believe that this exceeding joy and good fortune had befallen him—so that he grew more and more to seek her society and fellowship, as giving a completeness to his own life which was a new sensation to him, and as shedding around him all manner of tender and gracious influences.

You must not suppose, however, that this happy time was merely a blank monotony of contentment and peace. Far from it. After all, they were lovers; and Lilian was too much of a woman to think of throwing away her favors with a careless hand. There was nothing, indeed, tricky or theatrical in her manners, it would have been impossible for her to have played pert comedy-business, and to have preserved the clear shining truth that lay in the dark blue eyes. You could not identify these calm and honest eyes with any self-conscious mimicry; and the face was far too sensitive to be able to provoke for the purpose of trying the effect of provocation. But she was at times very provoking, for all that. She would be coy and distant. When she was coaxed she would become more obdurate than ever. Then Philip, growing peevish for mere amusement, would say vexing things to her; and finally there would be a grand rupture, and reconciliation, and she would condescend to forgive him with the sweet serenity of a young queen.

Philip rejoiced to see her in these moods. He wished she would be more wicked—not with the cynical indifference of Mary Thormanby, but with the sharp matter of fact pleasantry of Violet Kingscote. For what he most feared with this young girl, whose various fancies were matter of such deep study and interest to him, was the suddenly tender attitude she would sometimes assume to him. In the middle of some scene, with both of them playing at cross-purposes for mere fun's sake, she would suddenly break down and say:

"Oh, Philip, I must not vex you! I must make all the

time you can spend with me now very pleasant to you, that you may afterwards look back and think kindly of me, and think I was very good to you."

"What do you mean?" he asked, the first time she said something like this, when he saw her eyes grow sad and thoughtful.

"Because I think, Philip, we shall never be married; and I wish—oh my darling! I wish to be kind to you during the little time we are together."

Sometimes she would burst into tears; sometimes she would only show her wretchedness in the despair of her face, and sit silent and thoughtful by herself at the window,

How to combat these gloomy forebodings? It was a difficult task. Yet he strove with it successfully at times; and it was his constant care to assume with her, in talking however remotely of their future, an easy audacious courage, which was only partly feigned. Indeed, his own temperament was naturally buoyant, and there was much in his determined bearing to teach a girl hope and confidence. He was glad, too, to see her engage in these little sham quarrels; for it gave him the opportunity, in "making up," to be very humble and penitent. In this insidious way he tried to teach her how great a value he put upon her, and how great was the favor she bestowed on him. Joy filled his heart when he saw how this simple device succeeded—how the girl was pleased to think that she was of worth in the eyes of her lover, and that she had the power to make him grateful.

"There are some women," he used to say to himself, "whom you dared not tell of their good gifts, or they would become unbearable. They would take your good opinion as a warranty for their expecting so much more degrading homage from you, and would air their merits as a peacock does his tail, fancying all the sparrows around are turning green with envy. But this tender creature is glad to know that you think well of her, merely because it gives her the power to make her gifts more gracious."

It was no morbid weakness of constitution that made Lilian Seaford regard thus doubtfully the possibility of their ever being married. The sweet color of her face, the light in her eyes, and the natural cheerfulness of spirits she showed whenever the subject was forgotten, were sufficient evidence that the lithesome young Devonshire girl had none of the sickly humors begotten of artificial life—the physical and mental products of heated rooms, late and unwholesome suppers, unnatural hours, and what not. Mr. Philip had only to wean her attention away from this one topic, and she was as bright and cheerful as a spring morning. She went about the house singing; she ran up and down the stairs like a whirlwind, occasionally producing catastrophes and alarming Mrs. Lawson; she would sometimes laugh till the tears came into her eyes over the small impudences of a tiny terrier which Philip had given her—a diminutive sharp-nosed brute, that had a habit of standing with his hind legs on a chair, placing its fore paws very boldly and directly on the edge of the breakfast-table, and barking abruptly when not attended to. "Pop," as they called him, was their common property; and Mr. Philip was vastly pleased to lie back in his easy-chair, with his hands profoundly buried in his pockets, and watch her amuse herself by teasing and fondling her small, quick, abrupt playmate.

There was another method, too, which he discovered of breaking in upon these despondent moods—by making her, ever so slightly jealous. A woman rarely pays a man to whom she is not married the compliment of being jealous; if she feels aggrieved or angry because of his attentions to another woman, her vanity prompts her to conceal her mortification. But in the case of this young girl there was neither mortification, nor spite, nor any other angry feeling in her heart when he spoke of Mary Thormanby; but there was an anxious trouble in her eyes, and just a touch of wounded pride and reserve in her tone. You could read the whole story so clearly in those eyes! There was no malice there, nor resentment—only the expression of a vague hurt or pain.

"You must not make any more of these melancholy forecasts," he said to her one day, as they were walking along the bank of the Thames up beyond Kew-bridge.

They often ran down thither for a short forenoon ramble, the North-London line being convenient. Sometimes Jims accompanied them, and made savage attacks on the tameness of English scenery; but generally they went alone, and had long, and solitary, and happy conversations about the life-journey which they proposed to take together. In after days, Philip dared not go near that bit of the river; but every feature of its scenery was impressed on his mind, and he could bring it all before him with scarcely any effort. And somehow it always wore the same aspect—was always seen under the same conditions of atmosphere. A somewhat cold spring day, with breezy clouds overhead, and a great glare of light coming down the steel-gray surface of the Thames; here and there the wind catching the stream and darkening it with ripples; then the quiet towing-path, with perhaps a solitary figure, in the distance; on either side of the river broad meadows or spacious parks round white houses that had rooks about them; and everywhere the tall twisted elms bursting into cold green, and the cold spring flowers about the damp hedges and banks. But then toward evening the gray day and the windy steel-gray river would undergo a striking change; and away out in the west there would break forth a sudden gleam of gold, with the dark lines of trees underneath growing warm and blue. No trace of the crimson glories of an autumn evening, nor yet of the frosty-red of a wintry sunset; but only, beyond the gray, windy, English sky, the great burning of yellow light, as if it were the reflection of some golden summer shining upon another world far down in the western seas.

On this forenoon the air was unusually warm, and the early summer foliage basked in the heat. There was more sunlight, too, than in the landscape which he afterwards came to regard as typical of all these wanderings; and the river was blue, because of the blue overhead; while here and there a white swan floated on the still surface, under the silent glare of the sky. As they walked on—he had got her into the habit, when thus removed from the haunts of men, of taking his arm, as if she were already his small wife, depending upon him, and ready to look up at any moment for comfort and courage and assistance—she had been telling him that it was necessary she should go down to Devonshire for a few days, to arrange some small matters there. Jims was to accompany her.

"Mayn't I go too?" said Philip.

"Why should you go?" she said shyly, wishing to hear .rom him again the oft-repeated assurance that his greatest pleasure was only to be near her.

"You broke off my visit to Torquay, you know you did," said he, "and you owe me some reparation."

"I hope you did not remain in London on my account?" she said with feigned alarm.

"On whose account, then, was it likely I should stay?"

"Everybody said at that time Miss ——"

But she could not even in jest pronounce the name. This thoughtless approach to it, indeed, seemed to have robbed her face of its sunlight of innocent happiness, and she became a trifle grave. Seeing which Mr. Philip must needs ward off the enemy by returning to the subject of the Devonshire excursion.

"You have not yet given me permission to go with you?" he said.

"I need not," she answered meekly. "You always take it."

"And why? You know you are so ungracious and unkind that as you never give me a proper and courteous invitation, I must invite myself."

"No, no, Philip; not this time!" she said hastily. "I do ask you, now, to come to Devonshire with us. I ask you to come, Philip—if it will please you. You must not say I was ever unkind to you——"

"Now, now!" he remonstrated—for he saw immediately what the sudden tenderness and anxiety of her face meant—"we are not to have any more melancholy prophecies. I cannot allow it, Devonshire or no Devonshire. I accept your invitation; and we shall make the merriest party. I know all the neighborhood of Tor Bay about as well as you do; and we may be able to spy out a house which might suit two young people who are as yet uncertain where circumstances may lead them to live."

"And we will look at it, and think about it a little, in a kind of dream, you know?" she said, looking up to his face with glad eyes. "there can be no harm in that."

"There can be no harm in anything done by so wise a small person as you are," he said lightly. "And when must we go?"

"Whenever you like, Philip."

"Whenever *I* like? What have I to do with it? It is your project—you invite me. I expect you to entertain me all the way, by pointing out the prettiest scenery, and by telling me all the old historical legends."

"But it is whenever *you* like, Philip. And you must not be angry with me if I tell you that I had already thought of it, and that I wish you to come, because I want to have this little trip made very pleasant to us all. It will be so new to us, and removed from everything that may happen afterwards. We shall always be able to look back on it as a thing quite by itself; and we shall think kindly of each other in remembering it. No; you must let me speak this time. I think you and I have only been dreaming, Philip. It was very pleasant, but sometimes a little sad; for when I look forward, Philip, I seem to see you married to some one quite different from me. And I am not angry with her; only you will tell her, when she is your wife, that I loved you very well, and that my love for you was not selfish, because I asked you to go away from me when I thought it was better for you to go."

He was far more impressed by these brief and touching sentences of hers than he cared to show; and many and many a time he thought of them thereafter, when he was sick and sore at heart. But he wanted now to show her that her vague anticipations had no effect whatever upon him; and so he put his hand gently over her mouth, and said,—

"Do you understand what wickedness you are talking? Do you really believe that I should be doing a good thing to my own life in not marrying you? The fact is, you timid little mouse, you are afraid of my father. Why, when I look forward as you are in the habit of doing, I see my father making a pet of you, and showing you off to all his City friends as the wonder of the world. And suppose—as you and I have already considered—that my father, with the admirable suavity of manner which is peculiar to him, should hint that I might as well earn my own living, is there any great hardship in that? Have we not youth and health on our side? And as for courage, I have enough for both of us, surely, or I ought to have, for you have not the confidence of a full-grown robin."

"You do not know me, then," she said simply. "I should have plenty of courage and patience, if the worst were actually to befall us. I should have more courage than you then, I think. But now it is only because I see more clearly than you what you ought to do."

"You mean me, then, to go and marry Mary Thormanby. Was that the happy prospect you were constructing for me?" he asked, making a bold flank attack.

"I did not mean *her*," said Lilian, with just a touch of asperity.

"It is not many months ago," continued Philip, who saw how this movement of his had told, "that I should have thanked you for even imagining that such happiness might be in store for me."

"Perhaps you were wrong in changing your opinion," she said, with a little toss of the head.

"Ah, who knows?" said Philip, with provoking gravity "Don't you think that men are very much the sport of circumstances in their choosing of a wife?"

"They are the sport of their own blindness," said Lilian, "in not being able to judge of a woman's real character."

"By Jove, how fond I was of that woman!" said he, looking absently across the blue river to the green meadows beyond.

For a second or two she was silent, and too proud to speak; but at length she said in a low voice,—

"You ought not to say that to me, Philip."

"But why?" he asked. "You keep continually advising me to go away from you; and how can I help thinking of the woman you say I ought to marry?"

"Not her, Philip. Why, a woman like that! You could not live with her, Philip!"

"You never came underneath the spell of her face, Lilian."

"I should see no spell in it. I could not look with pleasure at a face that was deceiving you; that could smile at any stranger just as it smiled to you; that could wound you with a sweet air, and conceal its malice under a show of innocence. That sort of face may be very engaging to men; but women see what it is and don't like it."

The pretty vehemence of her speech was charming.

"I wonder you can even mention her with so much tolerance," she continued. "If I were a man, and had been subjected to her caprices and made her sport, I should hate her. And indeed, Philip, I think that if you had loved her very much at any time you would hate her now."

"Why, you delicious little fury, I didn't fancy you could hate anybody! Suppose Mary Thormanby were to come before us just now, what would you do?"

"I would tell you and her to go on walking together; and I should walk back to the station myself," said Lilian proudly.

"You would do nothing of the kind. You would go up to her, and you would say; 'Aren't you ashamed of yourself to have treated my Philip so? And aren't you sorry you went just a little too far? And now go away, and don't come near us two any more during your miserable life.' That's what you would say, Lilian, and you would standbe fore her, brave and valiant, ready to defend me from her wrath."

"And what would she say to me?" said Lilian, forgetting her jealousy in her triumph. "She would say: 'Why, you are too contemptible a little thing to do anybody any harm; and I shan't meddle with you. It wasn't you who took him away from me, but his own bad temper.'"

"What is that you say about my bad temper?"

"I don't say it, my dear," replied Lilian meekly; "she does."

Long conversations like those were frequent during this

happy time; and they generally ended in securing at least a quiet acquiescence from Lilian. If she did not wholly give up her dim impression that she should never marry her lover, she was, at all events, reasoned into silence. This attitude left him greater opportunity for turning his attention to the more serious aspect of affairs, and the future now began to press nearly upon them. They could not long remain in this merely tentative state, satisfied to ramble about in the young summer days and enjoy themselves. Their very rambling precipitated matters; for people began to know that Mr. Philip spent all his time with a certain brown-haired young lady, who had a pretty figure and was neatly dressed. He had been met, too, when out upon those suburban excursions, by several of his acquaintances. Lord Cecil Sidmouth among others. Lord Cecil's parents had a house at Richmond; and it was no matter of surprise that he should run against Mr. Philip, when the latter was in the neighborhood. A brief nod was the only recognition between the two friends as they passed; but a couple of days later, when Mr. Philip was lunching at his club, Lord Cecil came and took a chair at the table.

"My dear boy," said he, "let me congratulate you. What an uncommonly pretty little girl that is you have picked up!"

"Oh, do you think so?" said Mr. Philip, furious as a mad bear.

"One of the handsomest women I ever saw in my life, by Jove!" said the red-headed young gentleman, forgetting that he is President of the Analytical, and looking quite fierce in his enthusiasm. "Where on earth did you lay hold of her?"

Something in the expression of Mr. Philip's face startles him.

"What do you mean?" says Lord Cecil, glancing through his eyeglass at the table. "You have broken the head off that wineglass!"

"Confound you!" says Mr. Philip, with his dark face getting a trifle darker; "I should like to break off your head! Do you know you're talking about the girl whom I am engaged to marry?"

"You don't mean to say so!" exclaims Lord Cecil the eyeglass dropping from his uplifted eyebrows. "I owe you a thousand apologies. Upon my life, I'm very sorry! How was one to know, you know?"

Indeed, the misapprehension was one which Mr. Philip was likely to encounter in many quarters. The men and women whom he was in the habit of meeting knew each other so well that his appearance in the company of this spic-and-span new acquaintance was remarked. They knew that she was not one of Mrs. Drem's friends; they had never met her at the house. The men envied him his good fortune, and the women thought he might have exercised a little more discretion, and not gone about so openly.

You may fancy how so proud and passionate a spirit as his chafed under these scarcely-expressed innuendoes. Several times he was on the point of precipitating a catastrophe, and challenging his father either to accept Lilian as his future daughter-in-law, and so bring her about the house, or to cut the connection which bound father and son, and let the latter go his own way and earn his own living. Yet the time was not come for this resolution; for Mr. Philip, having acquired a good deal of prudence of late, wished to make sure of some means of independent livelihood before idly running the risk.

Meanwhile he still enjoyed the profuse means which his father had placed at his disposal; and he employed them to surround Lilian with every little gratification and luxury she could wish. He had to exert no small ingenuity, also, in getting her to accept these things. Many a kindly little deception he practised, with the aid o Jims and his wife, in order to accomplish his wishes in this way; and Mrs. Lawson especially took the greatest delight in devising reasons and excuses for Lilian getting this or that new article of dress, which was supposed to be bought with her own money. The girl would have started back with dismay from the notion that, besides all the various presents he forced her to accept, her lover was paying for three-fourths of everything which Mrs. Lawson bought for her; yet such was actually the fact. Lilian's notions of the cost of feminine finery were somewhat nebulous; and she was far from being aware how much money and how many white lies Mrs. Lawson expended, in sending her out dressed neatly in the costume which was fashionable at the time. For Mrs. Lawson, not having many opportunities herself of observing the *modes* of the season, could only say that all the articles of the girl's dress must be black, and leave the rest in the milliner's hands.

Then Mr. Philip was suddenly smitten with the idea of presenting Mrs. Lawson with a piano. The old jangling thing which Mrs. Seaford, shortly after her arrival at Hampstead, had bought for Lilian's use, was rather a painful instrument; and the young girl used to say she wished she could practice with cotton in her ears. Philip ordered at prety little piano from one of the best makers, and presented it to Mrs. Lawson as a useful piece of furniture. How was she to get it into the house, if Mrs. Seaford's piano remained in the small parlor? It was then suggested that it would be absurd to have two pianos in the house, and if Lilian would consent to let them get rid of hers, she might play on that which had been given to Mrs. Lawson. It was a pretty trick, and quite successful.

Is there any occupation in life to be compared to that of spending day after day in planning little surprises and kindnesses for the woman you love? Is there any happier time than that in which two young lovers, laying their foolish heads together, begin to build their nest, as it were in anticipation, and surround themselves with small articles which may be useful or pleasant in the happy days that are coming? There is no more charming occupation, nor is there any such pleasant time—when the touch of white finger-tips is a mystery and a delight and the heart is full of the promise and the sweetness of the *wunder-schonen Monat Mai.*

CHAPTER XIII.

"I MUST go down to Thurston, to-day," said Mrs. Drem, to her husband at breakfast.

"What do you want to do, gadding about there?" growled he from over his newspaper.

"I must go down to look after the place and the servants," replied Mrs. Drem in a tone of mild remonstrance.

"What do you pay Mrs. Roberts for, if she can't look after the house? Well, and if you go, what then? I suppose you will be late for dinner, as usual."

"I wanted the brougham, my dear," said Mrs. Drem timidly.

"And you want me to go in a cab, I presume?—and catch some infectious disease?—and leave you a widow, with all my money? I dare say you'd like it—yes, I have no doubt you would like it. But I am not such a fool, madam."

"I never meant anything of the kind," said Mrs. Drem piteously.

"It is all your own fault. You *will* keep the barouche down at Thurston—you *will* go about planning visits and excursions, and never say a word about them, so that one might be prepared—and then you want my brougham to take you to the station—Victoria-station, I daresay?"

"Yes," replied Mrs. Drem, who was being prettily served-out for her well-meant renunciation and economy in refusing to have a carriage kept for her own use.

"Then if you want to go to Thurston, you may come to Mincing Lane with me, and go on to London Bridge by yourself," remarked Mr. Drem, decisively.

That was the upshot of it: and Mrs. Drem, mute and miserable, drove down to the city with her husband. He was not in an amiable mood. He had eaten too much breakfast, and was suffering from heartburn. The dock-warehouses were stuffed with unsalable tea; and yet he had seen in the morning papers the announcement of the arrival of two ships laden with consignments from his China agents. Then he had a lawsuit hanging over his head on account of 500 bales of cotton, which the Liverpool lawyers declared were not half the value of the samples. Altogether Mr. Drem was not in a humor to be approached lightly, and Mrs. Drem was heartily glad when she had deposited her companion in Mincing Lane, and found herself driving over London Bridge alone.

When Mr. Drem had glanced over the business letters which his head clerk had left open upon his desk, he whistled downstairs for his nephew. Mr. Arthur came up into the room as clean-shaven, as neat, and pale, and suave as usual; and stood as if expecting commands.

"Well, go on!" said Mr. Drem; "why do you stand there as if you expected to catch flies with your mouth?"

"You mean about Mr. Philip?" said Arthur, gently. "I am sorry to say, sir, that I have no very good news to communicate. I am afraid your suspicions have been too correct. I doubt, indeed——"

And here Mr. Arthur hesitated.

"You doubt, you fear, you are sorry!" exclaimed his uncle, getting into a passion. "What the devil do I care whether you are sorry or not? Tell me what you know."

"You put me in a painful position, sir," pleaded Arthur. "I do not like to become a spy on my cousin: and yet I think a young man of his opportunities and advantages ought to be ashamed of the manner in which he is returning your kindness, sir. The fact is," continued Arthur, hurriedly, seeing something unpleasant in Mr. Drem's eye, "he goes about with her everywhere. He has been with her to Kew several times."

"Alone?" inquired Mr. Drem quickly.

"Yes; then he has given her lots of presents—a piano amongst the rest."

"Does she accept those presents from him?" asked Mr. Drem, again with an eager look.

"I suppose so," said Arthur.

"Arthur, you have done me a great service. I shall not forget it," observed Mr. Drem, suddenly changing his manners, and repressing his satisfaction. "I see I must have wronged my son in supposing he was so mad as to think of marrying this girl. I am sorry she should be receiving presents from him; but then young men will be young men. I am glad there is nothing more serious in it."

"I am afraid there is," observed Mr. Arthur calmly, hastening to rob Mr. Drem of his pleasant surmises. "I believe the young lady has received an engaged-ring from him."

Mr. Drem was too much dismayed to break out into a passion.

"Who told you that, Arthur?" said he. "How do you know that? It must be all a mistake."

"From what I have been able to learn from Alexander, sir, it is no mistake. I could not ask him pointblank; but I got him to confess to many things which are very significant; and——"

"And you mean to say that my son actually intended to marry this girl—that he is going to bring this nameless baggage into my house as his wife? No, by God! he never will—he never will!"

Mr. Drem rose—as if the very thought of it would choke him—and began walking up and down the room.

"If I had another son I shouldn't care," he said almost pathetically. "Arthur, what can we do to prevent him? He must not marry her. I will give a thousand pounds if you go and marry her."

"Well sir," said Arthur with a forced smile, "I don't think it would be very easy for me to go and marry her off-hand like that. And besides, she would then come into the family all the same——"

"The family—the family?" said Richard Drem furiously. "Who the devil are you sir, to talk of the family? You may marry a trull or a Hottentot if you like; but as for my son—to go and bring this nameless hussy into my house—Go downstairs sir, if you can suggest nothing to save us from this shame and disgrace, at least you can get out of the way and hold your tongue."

This abrupt dismissal—a somewhat cruel reward for his secret service—did not put Arthur out as it might have done. He was accustomed to his uncle's gusty temper, and knew how to calculate the cool value of his heated words. He saw, therefore, plainly enough, that never since the great merchant had accomplished the measure of his commercial fame, had he so set his heart on any one object as upon the marrying of his son into a good family; and he perceived that Richard Drem would make little scruple about what he would give in order to prevent Philip's marrying Lilian Seaford. In his own experience Mr. Arthur had known similar cases; for there is nothing more common than this dilemma of a son wanting to marry in one direction and his father wanting him to marry in another. But the peculiarity of the present case arose from Richard Drem's passionate nature, which would leave him to adopt any means in order to accomplish his will. Hence the possibility of a complication which might, Arthur reflected, become of special value to himself; and there was no more likely person than this watchful, calm, mild young man to take advantage of any such chance.

When he went downstairs, he gave a little start of surprise to find Mr. Philip confronting him. But Philip did not observe his cousin's confused look. He nodded, "said good morning," and passed on to Mr. Ewart.

"Mr. Ewart," said he, "I want you to give me a check for £100."

Mr. Ewart opened his eyes somewhat, and said with an odd smile on his face,—

"With pleasure, sir: but I think you have already had paid in to your account something like——"

"Oh, yes, I know," said Philip; "but I must have the money. I had no idea my account was overdrawn."

Mr Ewart took out the check-book from his desk, filled in one of the green leaves, and then called Alec Lawson to take it up to Mr. Drem for his signature.

"How is business, Mr. Ewart?"

"Very dull indeed, sir. Cotton falling every day, and, what is quite as bad, we can find no means to prevent those rascally Chinese from damaging the shipments. They bore holes in the bales and pour water in through a metal tube; and then they cover up the hole so that you can't see it. Consequently the cotton is slowly rotting all the voyage home."

"Please, Mr. Philip," said Alec, "Mr. Drem wishes to see you upstairs."

Philip looked round, and put out his hand for the check.

"Mr. Drem has it," said Alec; and accordingly Philip went up to his father's room.

"Here, Philip, here is the check," observed Mr. Drem in his mildest voice, when his son entered the room.

"Thank you," said Philip, folding up the check and putting it in his waistcoat-pocket.

"There are worse things in the world than a father," remarked Mr. Drem humorously, but still keeping his eyes fixed on the desk before him.

"Indeed I think so," said Philip, suspecting nothing, "especially a rich father. I hope I shall be able to be as obliging to *my* son, if I ever have one."

"And as lenient, Philip—as lenient," said his father. "I think I make every allowance for the calls a young man must have on his money. I wouldn't pinch you in anything reasonable—not in anything reasonable; and, on the other hand, I expect you to remember that I do this. The—the—fact is Philip, I wanted to say a word to you in confidence. We have not been to each other as father and son would be: and perhaps you may have been led to form independent views for yourself—and to think, you know, as some young men might think, that it would be a fine thing to earn one's own living, instead of accepting it from any one. I admire the notion—I say that I admire the notion, Philip, you know—as showing independence and all that; but you may believe me when I tell you that it is not at all a pleasant thing in reality—that having to earn one's own living. I know what it is; you do not."

"I can assure you, sir," said Philip carelessly, "that I have no great ambition just at present to try. When one can get a hundred pounds by driving down to Mincing Lane in a hansom—"

"And you may drive in your own carriage, if you like!" said Richard Drem eagerly. (He would not have made the same offer to his wife.) "I am glad to hear you speak so sensibly on the subject, Philip. Your theories at the Analytical Society are all very well in their way; but they won't keep the pot boiling. Then when you go among other men, it is always more comfortable to know you have money in your pocket—"

"Yes," said Mr. Philip, absently and irrelevantly; for he was beginning to get impatient, and was thinking of a silver collar he was about to buy for "Pop."

"And, you see, all my money will be yours. When I am gone, Philip, you will be a rich man—a very rich man; and you can abolish the firm, if you like, and no one need know that ever any one of the family was in commerce. You will be a gentleman, Philip, just as much as if you could say that one of William the Conquerer's soldiers was your ancestor. I think you ought to be grateful to me for giving you all this."

Mr. Philip did not reply; he was wondering whether Lilian would prefer blue or pink along with "Pop's" silver collor.

"I have heard, Philip," continued Mr. Drem, diving desperately into the delicate subject, "that you go about a great deal with this Miss Seaford"—(Mr. Philip was all attention in a moment)—"now you cannot—after all I have told you—you cannot mean to marry her!"

"I should have told you frankly, long ago, sir," said Philip respectfully, "if you had given me an opportunity. I do mean to marry her."

"Philip," said the old man with a sort of gasping at the throat, "don't be ill-advised—don't provoke me. You have been thoughtless—you have been irritated, I don't doubt, by many things I said—but—but don't do anything rashly. You cannot really mean to marry her. Philip—if you have no regard for yourself and your position in society—won't you for once consider me? Won't you have pity on me?"

The earnestness of this appeal took him by surprise. He had never seen his father so affected.

"Won't you have pity on your father, Philip? I never asked anything from you before. I ask you now— not to marry this girl."

"What can I do, sir?" said Philip, really touched by this pathetic demand. "If we had been better friends—if there had been greater confidence between us—this could never have occurred. Now it is too late."

"No, no, not too late!" said Richard Drem, eagerly. "It is not too late if you are not married. Make her your mistress, Philip—make her your mistress; and you shall have plenty of money——"

The young man rose suddenly from the chair on which he had sat down, with his dark face become ghastly pale. All the effect which his father had produced by his passionate and humble appeal had been destroyed by this unlucky stroke; and Mr. Philip stood there, his anger and indignation shamed into silence by the very fact that it was his own father who had made the infamous proposal. When he spoke, his voice was cold, bitter, and contemptuous.

"I have to thank you, sir, for your prudence in letting others, instead of yourself, educate me. The morals they have taught me are very probably absurd and romantic; still I prefer them to yours. I confess that, until you mentioned it, that way of escape out of the difficulty never occurred to me, and yet it is quite a natural and reasonable one, I dare say. For, as the girl has neither father nor brother, one might ruin her without danger: and besides, as she is a distant relative of yours, she owes you a certain duty——"

"What do you mean?" says Richard Drem.

"I mean," says Mr. Philip, with all the passionate and haughty blood of his mother rushing into his face—"I mean that if any other man than yourself had dared to propose what you have proposed about the woman I mean to marry, I would have felled him to the ground."

"Don't be hasty—don't make bad worse," says Mr. Drem, just a trifle frightened all the same. "You know the hold I have over you. If I have not the authority of a parent, I have at least, the power to reduce your obstinacy in another way. I don't want to speak of that; I don't want to speak of it, I say; better to be quiet and reasonable in time."

"This is beginning to be tiresome," said Mr. Philip. "What do these threats mean? Do they mean that, if I persist in my intention of marrying Lilian Seaford, you wish me to leave your house, and make my way in the world by myself? Do they mean that?"

"Well, then, they do!" thundered out Richard Drem in a sudden access of rage, and bringing his fist down with a bang upon the desk before him.

"Let us understand each other quite clearly," says Mr. Philip as calmly as before; "because we may not have another opportunity of explanation. I do not wish to marry this girl merely out of self-will, or to defy you. I intend to marry her, because I have never seen any woman who could approach her in all the qualities likely to make a married life happy. I say that I don't wish to marry her merely to defy you; for there is no reason in the world why you should not accept her as my wife. There is no woman who visits your house who has a more irreproachable character and disposition; there are few better educated; there is not one half so pleasant in manner. Why do you conceive this violent hatred of her? Only you wish me to marry into some family that is rich, well-connected, has never been tainted by association with commerce. Why should you be ashamed of commerce, or wish that I should conceal my obligations to it. I see nothing to be ashamed of it—there is nothing; and if I were to marry an earl's daughter to-morrow, I should not desire to hide, nor should I be able to hide, the knowledge that my father was a merchant. Yet, merely to satisfy this monstrous prejudice, you are willing to sacrifice your own self respect, my honor, and the happiness of a young girl who is one of the few blood-relations you have. If these are the notions begotten of commerce, then I despise commerce. If my share of your money is to be obtained on terms like these, I think I had better earn my own bread."

"And, by God, you shall!" exclaimed his father, whose anger had been gradually accumulating. "You shall find out what it is to drop your fine-gentleman airs, and consort with wretches who have not a loaf of bread for their breakfast. It is a pretty return for my bringing you up like a gentleman, and spending a fortune on your education and your pleasures and your idleness, that you set up to lecture me as if you were a schoolmaster. You will see whether other people will bear with your fine manners, and your tragedy-airs, and your college logic. Why, sir," continued the irascible old man, his passion quite getting the better of his reason, "go and marry your pauper, and bring up your children in a garret; and when you are starving—you and your brats together—come and beg from me, and I would not give you the bone I would throw to a dog!"

There was something terrible and repulsive in the spectacle of this old man, gloating with a demoniac triumph over his son's possible starvation. The devil that possessed him—to use the old scriptural metaphor, which has given rise to so many curious legends—seemed to be working in the muscles of his face and gleaming in the malice of his eyes. It was not a pretty picture for a son to look at, and accordingly Philip said quietly,—

"You will remember that this rupture was not of my making. I showed you that there was no reason why there should be any disturbance of our ordinary relations, although those were none of the pleasantest. However, after the proposal you have made to me this morning, and after the various rhetorical threats you have uttered, I have resolved to take you at your word. I once warned you that I would do so; and now it is done. There is no need why we should invite any of our neighbors to enjoy the scandal; so you may tell them, if they inquire, that I have taken chambers in Gray's Inn or the Temple, for the purpose of being able to devote myself entirely to study. I throw out the hint to you for your own benefit; it is a matter of profound indifference to me whether or not they know the true cause of my leaving."

"Go—go!" said Richard Drem; "and the curse of the disobedient will follow and fall on you!"

"You needn't do any more of that sort of thing," observed Mr. Philip, haughtily. "If obedience to your wishes means that I am to ruin a girl whom you should have been the first to protect, perhaps Providence won't be so very hard upon me for refusing. And let me say this to you, as I may not have a chance again; I consider our relations as father and son dissolved by mutual consent. Henceforth, if we should ever come in contact, we shall be to each other as two ordinary men are. I say this in case you might be so unwise as to try to interfere further in this matter. As Miss Seaford, from her friendless and isolated position, requires some one to look after her interests and protect her, I have undertaken the duties of the post; and you know enough of me, sir, to guess that I shall make it uncommonly awkward for any man who endeavors to harm her in any way."

You would scarcely have detected any great significance in the measured and reserved tone of the young man; and yet Richard Drem did not care to look into his son's face just then. Mr. Philip took the check from his pocket, tore it in two, and flung the pieces on the desk before him. Then he turned and left the room.

Did he hear his name called as he shut the door? He might have done so; for Richard Drem, catching sight of the retreating figure of his son, was troubled by a great and sudden emotion, which produced a singular change in the expression of his face.

"Philip!" he said, piteously. But the door was shut, and his outstretched hand fell back again on the open desk.

CHAPTER XIV

Mr. Philip went downstairs and walked up to where Mr. Ewart sat.

"By the way," said he, "Mr. Ewart, how is Mr. Lawson pleasing you?"

All the young gentlemen in Mr. Drem's office were called "Mr.;" so that Alec came in for his share of the honor.

"Oh, very well," said the head-clerk, cautiously. "In fact, I may say he's getting on very well indeed."

"You mean to raise his salary, don't you?"

"Yes; he will have £100 instead of £80 a year after this quarter."

"Then I want you to make it £120."

Mr. Ewart smiled.

"You see, sir, we have a regular system of increase in salaries——"

"Oh, yes!" said Philip, carelessly, "I know. But that is only for these young fellows down there, who don't need to care what they get. It only means a little extra pocket-money for them. With Mr. Lawson the case is different."

"Very well, I will give him an extra twenty pounds," said Mr. Ewart.

"Thank you. Good morning."

Nodding, as he passed, to Alec, Mr. Philip walked out of the office and into Mincing Lane. He certainly had not the air of a man who has just been deprived of a fortune, and finds himself confronted by the problem of how to get to-morrow's dinner. He had never felt a more austere sense of satisfaction in his life; and his heart was as light as his empty pockets. Now there was something to live for—something definite to be done; and a thousand vague avenues of action suggested themselves to the busy brain of the young man as he went out into the narrow, dingy, gray thoroughfare. Mincing Lane was certainly not the most enlivening picture for a man just turned beggar. The atmosphere of the place was thick and stifling, laden with the odors of coffee and damp cellarage; and the depressing dinginess of the gaunt buildings was in keeping with the solemn laziness of the groups of men who stood opposite the salerooms chatting listlessly. Here was no active, cheerful, energetic activity—like that of a ship-building yard or an engine-room—but the placid biding its time of capital. You would have fancied that these men who stood there knew that, whatever the dulness of the period, the money they had at their bankers' would pull them through; and that it was only necessary to let this secret agency go on working for them. The only brisk business going on in the Lane was that of the hawkers of small commodities—a new ring-puzzle, elastic bands, Punch-and-Judy calls, or what not; and these eager gentlemen had to move on with their wares whenever a certain police-constable came out of one of the entries. Here and there a cluster of carts and drays, with powerful horses and burly drivers, stood by the pavement, or rattled slowly down the street; while a small genteel clerk would dart across the thoroughfare, just shaving the nose of one of the great animals with his pert hat, or an orange-woman would bargain with a meditative errand-boy about what she should give him for his luncheon-penny.

Mr. Philip's first thought had been to go straight and tell Lilian of what had occurred; but then he said to himself, "No; she will not see it as I do. She will be in despair; she will be for throwing up our engagement; and will accuse herself of everything that has happened. It will be time to tell her when we return from Devonshire."

Was it superstition, or mere thoughtful kindness, which made him respect her pathetic wish that they should make this excursion in every way beautiful and happy, so that in after-life they might look back with wistful eyes upon it? They were to leave London behind them and all its cares—they were to go down together into the gracious land sweet with the fullness of the young summer—and they were to enjoy without measure the happy dreams they had dared to dream. That was her thought: and there was a sad suggestion in it which formed a dark background, and perhaps made this picture shine all the more brighter. As for Philip, he did not see why their happiness together should be limited to this brief time: nor did he share in the tender and melancholy forebodings of the young girl. But all the same he resolved to comply with her wish. He would do his best to make this holiday quite happy to her, let the future have in store what it might. He determined, therefore, to say nothing to her in the mean time of his final break between his father and himself. He would not distress her with unnecessary cares. He would keep the secret himself, and let her see her native country again with glad and shining eyes.

Mincing Lane is not a long thoroughfare, but Philip had time to go over a good many possible schemes of future activity before getting up to Fenchurch Street. Unfortunately no one of these was immediately feasible. Many of them were contingent upon other circumstances which were as yet doubtful; others were vaguely contemplated as a last resource; others again depended on the possession of leisure earned by other work. The paramount thing for him was to get some employment at once, so that his after-career, however humble, should not be hampered by debt.

There was a good many other people in London in similar circumstances on that morning; and doubtless some of them were looking vaguely forward to marriage as the first reward of their success. In such a plight, patience is the most difficult of all the virtues. To Philip, for example, there would have been something inexpressibly grateful in getting actual work to do there and then, however small the remuneration might be—in knowing that he was not wasting time. But a man cannot fight against nothing; and the most invincible courage will droop down and wither when it finds no special obstacle to overcome. Why was it not possible for him to re-enact the old legend of the rescue of Andromeda? He could see the shining maiden on the rocks—over the blue water; and he would fain have taken his sword in his teeth and swam over to her, to slit the throat of the ignoble beast that threatened her. It would have been comforting to him if poverty were some such personal monster to be attacked in fair fight and striven with. But even the soldier of these days, who charges, bayonet in hand, a battery of field-pieces, and finds himself at length confronted by an artilleryman who means to knock out his brains, knows that, even if he slays his enemy, he will only have secured his own capacity of living. Fortune is no nearer him; that is a question of years, and the slow increase of pence. Civilization has destroyed the chances of a moneyless man's becoming rich at a *coup*, unless he joins a band of brigands or robs a jeweller's shop, and both these pursuits are attended with risk. He must wait, and pinch, and gather shillings together; while Andromeda upon the rock pines and tires, and even grows hungry; and then, alas! other suitors sail to her in argosies which are stuffed with pretty dresses, and fruits and spices, and bracelets for the white wonder of her arms.

Philip hailed a cab, and bade the driver drive to Park Lane.

He had only been in the vehicle a couple of seconds, however, when he remembered that he had no business to waste his means in cab-fares. So he stopped the cab, and got out.

"I shall go on a 'bus," he said to the cabby. "Here is a sixpence for you."

The man took the sixpence, and looked at it, contemptuously for a minute.

"I'll lend you this 'ere coin, sir," he said, holding it out.

"Thank you," said Philip, taking the sixpence, putting it in his pocket, and quietly walking on.

The cabman followed him for a minute or two, expecting remorse to shame the gentleman into taking the cab, or giving him a shilling. When he saw, however, that Mr. Philip paid no attention, but was apparently well pleased to have got the sixpence, he abruptly wheeled round his horse and drove off in a boiling rage.

Meanwhile Philip had again changed his intention, having looked with an uneasy qualm at the top of certain omnibuses, at the people thereon, and at the rate of speed of the vehicles. He walked all the way out to the Park Lane, and was just in time to find Miss Violet Kingscote and Mrs. Drem sitting down to lunch together. Mrs. Drem, going down to Surrey, had met Miss Kingscote coming from there; and the young lady had no difficulty in persuading her friend to postpone visiting her country-house, and turn and go shopping with her—indeed, Mrs. Drem never could refuse anybody anything. And now that they had spent all the morning in making purchases—Miss Violet also having the cares of a household on her small shoulders—they were sitting down to a well-earned meal.

"Nothing could be more fortunate," said Mr. Philip, scanning his luncheon-table in a business-like way.

Indeed it was not too liberally furnished; for you rarely find women very particular about a repast which is served only for themselves. Mrs. Drem, in a pretty little flurry, asked Philip to ring, that something might be got up for him; but he said:

"It was my meeting with you two people together, I meant. I suppose you have been shopping. Very well; suppose we have a little more of it. You know the timepiece in my study—that the Countess von Schwachenheim gave me years ago? Ladies, it is a wonderful specimen of art. The gilt cupids are worth a sovereign apiece, and the blue-and-pink china-flowers are fit for the mantelpiece of a queen. Now I want to sell it."

"My dear," said Mrs Drem quietly, "you must have had luncheon before you came here."

"I am quite serious," he said, "I am going off for a holiday; and I want money."

"MY DEAR!" exclaimed Mrs. Drem, "this is an extraordinary subject. If you want money, you know your papa will——"

"I perceive I must tell you both frankly how the case stands. It will save time, too; and I shall be pressed for time in making arrangements for going into Devonshire. The fact is, then, that everything had come about just as we anticipated the other evening, Violet. My father and I had a conversation this morning which was quite explicit and final. We arrived at a perfect understanding. I told him I meant to marry Miss Seaford. He said I might if I liked; but that I should have to earn my own living. He made a few remarks about his wishing to see us all starving, that he might throw the bone we wanted to a dog; but I dare say that was only his notion of a joke. I accepted the alternative; and——"

"And you are going away from us?" said Mrs. Drem, with a pale face.

"Well, yes," said Mr. Philip. "A man of my uncertain income could not afford to live in Park Lane."

"Do you mean that you are going to leave the house?" said Violet, who was scarcely less dismayed.

"Why, of course. I have set about earning some money directly; and I cannot afford to idle about here, even were my father inclined to pay the cost of my board and lodging, which he distinctly is not. That is the short and the long of the matter; and now you will understand why I again offer to sell you the timepiece, which is my own property."

"Philip you must not talk in that way!" said his stepmother in great distress. "It isn't settled. Your father cannot mean this—to part with his only son. He cannot mean it; he must have spoken in a passion; and you did wrong to accept his words literally, knowing how often he speaks that way."

"After all," remarked Mr. Philip, "you must remember that I have a little to say in this matter, and that the decision does not rest with him alone. I have no doubt it will be better in the end for me to go out into the world, find my level, and earn my own living, than to remain in a kennel all my life with a chain round my neck. My father has been reproaching me rather too frequently with the fact of my being a pauper, which may not have been altogether my fault. At all events, I am determined to have a try for myself in the general struggle of the world; and I know the prize that lies before me if I succeed, If I have too much self-confidence, it will be taken out of me; but in the meantime I have no fear. And so, with many apologies for having talked to you so much about myself, shall we drop the subject and continue the auction? As I was saying, the timepiece is a most valuable ornament for a drawing-room. It has as much gold and color in it——"

"But, Philip, this is terrible!" said Violet with anxious eyes. "I feared it would come; and although one cannot help sympathizing with you, and with the motive which has made you do this, I wish—I do wish it had not happened. Now don't you think you were too haughty with your father? Don't you think that if I were to go and speak to him more gently, he would recall what he said?"

"No," said Philip distinctly. "It is no light matter of a quarrel and hasty words, but a definite resolve on both sides. And I don't regret it; I am not anxious to alter matters."

"But you ought to be for the sake of your friends," said Miss Violet courageously. "I know very well what you will do, Philip. When you go out from amongst us you will be prouder than ever; and you will resent any advances your old acquaintances may make, as if these were patronage. You will isolate yourself—separate yourself from all your old friends, and make no new ones. You will withdraw from your club——"

"Certainly," said Philip. "A man who has no income may be a gentleman and a member of a club; but a man who has a small income cannot be either."

"And you will keep away from all our set: you will change your life altogether—just as much as if you had become another man."

"And it is time I should do so, if life is to be worth having," said Mr. Philip, with an abruptness which closed the kindly protests of both the women.

Mrs. Drem sighed: perhaps thinking that the house would be none the pleasanter to her when Mr. Philip has left it. Violet was already sketching the future of her friend as a poor man, and wondering whether she would be able to give him small and secret subsidies out of her own not over-full purse. And both of them thought with a strange curiosity about the young girl who was the innocent cause of this domestic catastrophe ; and wondered whether Philip would find compensation in her society for all he was throwing away.

"You know, my dear," said Mrs. Drem, when Philip had gone upstairs to fetch the timepiece, "there is more in my husband's objection to the girl than the mere fact of her being poor. After all, that need not matter so much to us. But Mr. Drem has had a dislike to the family for years back—some old quarrel, probably; but I don't know, I am very sorry; I wish I could interfere."

"And why don't you?" said Miss Violet. "You ought to step in to prevent such a great misfortune as this would be to all of you."

"Oh, my dear, I dare not!" said Mrs. Drem, anxiously.

"If I were in your position I would dare anything," said Violet, "to secure the happiness of your two nearest relatives."

"But you don't know them as I know them," said Mrs. Drem in despair : "the one ill-tempered and hasty, not to be reasoned with ; the other, proud and unforgiving. I am sure I hope Philip will be happy. I am sure he need never want money so long as I have any to give him."

"But don't you see that he will refuse to take money from you—which would be the same as taking it from his father?" said Violet quickly. "And, instead of letting things drift into that state, I would leave nothing undone, if I were you to avert such a catastrophe. It is your duty."

"But what can I do?" said Mrs. Drem, upon whom the word "duty" acted as a faint stimulus. "What can I do? Neither will listen to me. After Philip is married, I might bring the girl to see Mr. Drem suddenly; and as they say she is so pretty and engaging, you know, she might win him over."

Mrs. Drem grasped this possibility with eagerness, because it afforded her a respite, and postponed the necessity for her interference. Violet, on the other hand, was inclined to be angry, her own generous, active, and courageous nature refusing to make allowances for this feebler spirit. The discussion, however, was brought to a close by Philip's entrance with the timepiece, which he placed at the farther end of the table.

"Now," said he, as he sat down, "you can admire the excellencies of that work of art while you go on with your luncheon. And first, may I ask you, as this is the last time I shall have the pleasure of eating here, to get some sherry of a rather better quality? I don't know why it is that women, when they are by themselves, always manage to light upon the worst wine in the house."

"What is good enough for us is good enough for you, Mr. Philip," said Violet.

"But I deny that it is good enough for you, Miss Violet," said he, ringing the bell. "Indeed, I should like to know what is."

"That is a very pretty speech," she said; "but I am afraid you will make it the excuse for adding five per cent to the price of the timepiece."

"Why do people who know nothing about business always talk of five per cent.—never of four per cent. or six per cent.? That appears to me to be the weak point of the story about the stock-broker who went into a shop to have his hair dressed. 'How much shall I take off, sir?' said the man. 'Oh, five per cent.' said the stock-broker."

"I think you made the story yourself, Philip," remarked Mrs. Drem, with a placid smile.

"Indeed, I should have thought he would have made a better," added Miss Violet, with a touch of scorn.

You would not have thought that these three were eating their farewell feast together; and indeed, Mrs. Drem did what she could to forget it. Mr. Philip was chiefly engaged in demonstrating his right to get a commercial value for this present; and was inveighing against the theory that, because you have some article given you, you must preserve it sacredly, however useless or absurd or ugly it may be, merely because it is a gift.

"If the Countess really meant a kindness to me," he said—"and I doubt it, for she only wanted to pay a roundabout compliment to my father—she will be glad to know that I have at last found the timepiece to be of some value. So with my horse, which poor Tommy Travers gave me a few days before he died. If he could rise from his grave, he would forgive me for selling Cæsar—seeing the circumstances I am in."

However, he did not victimize either of the women. Violet offered him thirty guineas for the timepiece; but he refused the offer, and subsequently got twenty-five pounds for it from a dealer in Bond Street. Meanwhile, he had to see about the packing up of a few things which he wished to take with him to his lodgings; and so he rose from the table, begging his stepmother and her visitor to excuse him on that ground.

"You don't really mean to go?" said Mrs Drem, who had begun to fancy the whole thing was a jest or a dream.

He went, nevertheless; and soon had a few articles heaped together in his room. Then he came downstairs again.

"Will you tell Simpson to put these things together?" he said to Mrs. Drem; "I shall send for them as soon as I have found some rooms for myself."

"And are you really going?" said Mrs. Drem, beginning to cry slightly, "Take this with you, Philip."

She slipped her purse into his hand. He did not know what was inside, but he returned it to her, and said, with a smile,—

"When I am starving, I shall come to you for that proverbial bone. Don't agitate yourself—there is nothing alarming or tragic in my going away. If I can get everything put in order, I shall leave London to-morrow forenoon; but it will only be for a few weeks' pleasuring in Devonshire. I shall see you often in London; and, if I happen to be carrying a hod, I shall forgive your not bowing to me as you drive past. There—take your purse; it is very kind of you, but I shan't need it."

"And I suppose I must say good-bye, too," said Miss Violet: "for who knows when we shall ever see each other again?"

She looked up into his face with her pretty dark eyes as she took his hand, and said almost affectionately:

"Will you promise not to forget your old friends, Philip, whatever may happen to you? Will you promise to remember that they are still your friends, under all circumstances?"

"I promise never to have any doubts about *your* friendship, Violet," said he.

And so he left the house. Mrs. Drem sobbed a good deal; and thought of what a pretty temper her husband would be in that afternoon when he came home.

"I should like, Mrs. Drem, to see Lord Cecil about all this affair," said Miss Violet timidly. "I cannot very well write to him. Would you mind arranging so that I could see him some evening soon at your house?"

Mr. Philip went that afternoon and took a small bedroom and sitting-room in the district of Paddington—rent, twelve shillings a week. Next morning he sold both the timepiece and his horse; and got nearly a hundred pounds. With part of this sum he closed his bank-account, which had been slightly overdrawn; and then he found himself in possession of something like sixty-five pounds.

Most people have experienced, after a run of ill-luck at cards or billiards, the vulgar desire "to go a good one for the last," and crown their dissipation with a sort of climax. Something of this nature prompted Mr. Philip to devote the whole, or nearly the whole of this money towards making the proposed Devonshire trip a pleasant one. Perhaps it was to be his last glimpse of idleness and pleasure for many a day. If so, he would make it notable—within the limits of sixty pounds.

When, having all his arrangements completed, he went up to Hampstead, and demanded when they should be ready to start, no one noticed the least difference in his manner or appearance. He was still the careless, indolent, spoiled boy, who had an easy negligence about his dress, a habit of ordering things his own way, and a matter of fact, business-like way of looking after the comfort of every one round about him. He would have Mrs. Lawson, too, to start upon this pleasure excursion (for which some trifling matters of business offered a convenient excuse), but she flatly refused. Her ostensible reason was that she had to look after Alec's necessities and the house; but her real reason was that she did not care to go about in her old-fashioned dresses, with these two young people. As for Jims, it was quite another thing. Put an old man with white hair into the rustiest of black coats, give him a white shirt and a satin neckcloth, and, if he have plenty of self-assertion in his face (and Jims wanted nothing in that way), he is as likely as not to be taken for some eccentric old nobleman with an annual rent-roll represented by five ciphers.

It was towards evening when our three travelers drew near to the sea; and there was a warm light over the sky. The midday express had whirled them down through Bath, and Wells, and Taunton; and now they were catching glimpses of the Exe river, as it widened out into the great blue plain of Exmouth haven, with here and there the yellow sail of a smack scarcely moving across the still surface. Lilian, sitting snugly in the corner of the carriage, could not withdraw her eyes from the window. As they drew nearer the coast she became strangely excited. The south wind, as it came over the land, had the salt fragrance of the sea in it; and she knew that, but a little way from them, the clear green water was splashing on the beach. Then, all at once, the line brought them close to the shore: and lo! the level sunset was shining along the red coast, and on the great stretch of windy sea, and on the glowing sails of the ships. Close underneath the waves were beating crisply and whitely on the shingle; in front of them the masses of red sandstone, steeped in shadow, ran out with fantastic arches and bald headlands into the sea; and away behind them lay the long coast line in the yellow mist of the sunset, so that you could see the ruddy cliffs of Devon melt into the white chalk of Dorset, and that again disappear in the haze of the eastern horizon. How strangely clear the air was! and the cold water looked so fresh and bright that it seemed to make the blood tingle in one's cheeks.

"And there is Dawlish!" cried Lillian, with something like a sob of delight, as she suddenly clasped her hands.

And she would have her two companions see this or that; and she would have them declare if there was anything in the world half so lovely as Devon. She laughed—she was near crying; and then she seemed to withdraw into the corner of the carriage, as she timidly glanced at two ladies who, from the other end of the carriage, were good-naturedly smiling at her excitement.

Then they got down to Torquay; and the sunset was there, too, shining on the fair watering-place, that looked down from her rocky and wooded hills upon the smooth and spacious bay and the distant sea. Lillian was satisfied with no amount of admiration. Was not the place more lovely than anything they had dreamed about? Was there not a look of Prague about the steep rocks of Waldon Hill, crowned with its scattered white villas that were half hid among deep foliage?

"And you must see the place in moonlight," she said, "when the night is clear and quiet, and you can see the red glimmering of the windows up on the hills there, from among the trees."

Here let us leave them for a little while, by the side of the sea. Another and a greater sea lay before them—the strange sea of life; and these two young souls, looking over the far and mystical plain, stood hand in hand on the beach, and talked of embarking in their frail boat together.

CHAPTER XV.

THERE was a young literary gentleman who lived in Sloane Street, and whose acquaintance Arthur Drem had been privileged to make. Philip's cousin, like a good many commercial men, was rather fond, in after-office hours, of the company of such professors of art, literature, and the drama as were disposed to smoke a cigar with him. They were not the most distinguished persons in their various walks whom Mr. Drem thus met; but, to a far greater extent then their more celebrated brethren, they had about them that aroma of Bohemianism which, in the imagination of the pale circumspect young man, gave a sort of unholy zest to their society. After having spent the day among his decorous *confreres* in Mincing Lane, Arthur loved to stroll down to the chambers of his friend, Mr. Samuel Hickes, and there hover, with a sort of pleased curiosity, on the verge of the realms of fancy and art.

Hickes lived by writing plays—chiefly dramas of a dark-complexioned hue—for a theatre on the southern side of the Thames. He was a quiet, inoffensive, dull young man, with fair hair, rather watery blue eyes, and no sort of will or conviction whatever. He was, perhaps, as ignorant a man as you could find in London; and he had no opinions on any public or other subject, unless it were the flavor of bitter ale. He had as little strength of purpose in any direction; and he would obey, in an unconscious fashion, any wish or whim that happened to strike his companion for the moment. He lived a harmless kind of life; smoking a pipe after breakfast, and planning out a further development of his plot; writing a scene or two before dinner; then walking about in the afternoon; and, finally, turning into a pot-house billiard-room in the neighborhood to finish up the evening.

Yet this rather stupid vacuous person had an astonishing faculty of being able to captivate the imagination of the people who frequented the transpontine theatre. The proprietor of the Rotunda, a worthy sort of man in his way, had been goaded by contemptuous critics into engaging, from time to time, various well-known playwrights to construct a better class of drama for him. These invariably failed. The plays were very clever, but the theatre was empty. No sooner, however, was a new piece of Hickes's put upon the stage, than pit, circle and gallery were equally crammed. How was this? Here was a man who had neither literary culture nor anything like knowledge of human nature. Even the literature of his own profession was closed to him; he knew nothing of the elder English dramatists; he was as unacquainted with the ingenious complications of the modern French stage as with the first pinciples of German art-criticism. He had not travelled, nor mixed much with men; he had gone through no great emotional crises himself; and yet, by a mere trick of manipulation, and by the use of broad coarse color, he could enchain the attention of the rude and ragged multitude of the Rotunda, and confer upon these dull brains the light of an intellectual gratification. He confessed himself that his means were wholly mechanical.

"There," he would say to Arthur Drem, as they sat smoking, "you have the obstacle to the union of the lovers in an angry uncle, with the heroine rich, and the hero poor. In my next piece, I have only to make the hero rich, the heroine poor, and the obstacle an aunt, and you have another drama. I have eight standard characters. The square of eight is sixty-four; when I have written out these sixty-four combinations, I suppose I must begin and translate from the French—after I have learned French."

He would talk in this way to one or two of his familiar acquaintances; but he adopted another tone towards the world at large, and especially towards theatrical managers. *Then* he became a profound analyst of the human emotions; he knew how to touch the public heart, and had seen a whole audience weeping over one of his pieces, with even the critics elevated into the *tears etat*. He generally finished off lightly with this excellent joke, which he had probably borrowed from some burlesque.

Now Mr. Arthur took great interest in the successive combinations of these eight typical characters, or dramatic puppets, which his friend Hickes produced; and occasionally assisted, with his criticisms and suggestions, such literary efforts. When he thought of a good plot or a striking situation he would jot it down for Hicks's consideration; and he became familiar, too, with the requirements of the stage. The consequence was, that he sometimes got into a habit of regarding himself and the people around him as the possible actors in possible dramas —of a Rotunda type, and occasionally amused himself with speculating as to their probable action. How would the grave and discreet Mr. Ewart, for example, conduct himself, if suddenly plunged into a rollicking bigamy case? Mr. Arthur did not understand that his perception of things were being insensibly distorted by the influence of the Rotunda drama.

When, therefore, this complication between Philip and his father occurred, Arthur looked on the affair from a dramatic point of view, and wondered whether he could not play a part in it to his own advantage. It was precisely in such circumstances that the poor young men of the Rotunda stage became rich: and all Mr. Arthur's hopes of fortune were centred upon his uncle. Unfortunately, however, Mr. Drem had none of the grand characteristics of the Rotunda type of patron about him. He was neither to be flattered into doing a romantically-generous thing, nor cajoled into doing a foolishly-weak thing. He was remarkably wideawake. Arthur would not have bet upon his being able to get a five-pound note out of his uncle. Indeed, it was not to be concealed that the nephew looked upon his relative as somewhat of a sneak, because he happened not to be a simpleton.

Nevertheless the position of affairs began to look more suspicious as Mr. Drem's ill-temper drove him into direct antagonism with his son: and Arthur was fairly startled when his uncle declared, in a gust of passion, that he would give a thousand pounds to any one who would marry Lilian Seaford. Here, surely, was a sufficiently dramatic turn that circumstances had taken: for if Mr. Drem would give money to have such a service done him, he would not stop at one thousand as the reward. Arthur Drem, however, despite his Rotunda proclivities was too cool-headed not to know that his uncle only spoke in the violence of his temper, and that if he, Arthur, were to succeed in marrying Lilian Seaford, and then go to his uncle to receive the reward, the latter would either burst out laughing in his face or kick him downstairs.

Long before any one in the office suspected what had taken place, Arthur learned of the distinct and apparently final rupture which had occurred between father and son; here was another aspect which the case had assumed, also diamatic, and full of possibilities. Mr. Arthur's imagination got possession of the reins of his reason.   His cousin Philip once away, who should be Mr. Drem's heir but himself, Arthur? Was it not for his interest that this breach should never be healed?

But no one knew better than Arthur his uncle's invincible and gratuitous spite. He knew that Richard Drem, were he to fancy that any one was waiting and hungering for his money, would take a malicious joy in disappointing him, and would grin in his grave (the possibility being granted) over his relative's rage. Arthur was not sure of becoming his uncle's heir.

On the other hand, he could see that there was nothing in the world which the rich merchant so much desired as a reconciliation with his son, and the abandonment, on the part of the latter, of his marriage. If he could secure both, would not his uncle be glad to reward him by leaving him the whole of the great business of Drem & Co.? And as his small and Avaricious mind—which was singularly like his uncle's in many respects—leapt forward to this practical and happy climax, he sighed to think that the course of events leading up to it could not be compressed into Rotunda time, in which a man's life and career were represented in two hours.

Full of these speculations, he hastened down in the evening to Hickes's rooms in Sloane Street. In such circumstances, who should be better able to advise him? Hickes was quite familiar with these awkward complications; he was a professor of the art of arranging them. And there must have been a certain amount of art in Samuel Hickes's manipulation; for while not believing himself in his stage-theories of life, he had almost persuaded the clear-headed Arthur Drem into believing them.

Mr. Hickes was in the billiard-room over the way, and his landlady sent her little girl for him. Meanwhile Arthur Drem sat down in an easy-chair, and rapidly ran over the possibilities of his position. In these few minutes he conceived the bold project of not only turning them into a drama, but of getting this maker of dramas to play a part in it. To make the master of puppets himself a puppet was a notable scheme, and Arthur began to consider himself a man of genius.

"At all events, I shall be a rich man," he said, rising and pacing up and down the room. "If only I can pull all this through, I shall be my own master, and bid farewell to Mincing Lane. Men have grown rich upon worse schemes; for after all, am I not working for the good both of my uncle and of his son?"

The dramatist, when he arrived, was found to be rather sulky and out of spirits; for he had lost at pool, and some flat ale had given him a headache. However, he brightened up a little over a cup of tea, and proposed that Arthur should accompany him to the Rotunda, it being the benefit-night of the manager, in compliment to whom he had taken a box and paid for it.

"I'd just as soon be here," said Arthur, who was comfortably ensconced in an easy-chair.

"Perhaps it would be more jolly to stay indoors," said Hickes; and he began to look about for his slippers.

"Yet it is a pity you should have your box for nothing. Suppose we walk over and stay for a short time."

"Very well that will be better," and Hickes, who was at all times only too glad to have the trouble of decision take from him. "The manager will be pleased, you know."

So the two walked down Sloane Street, and through Pimlico, and over Vauxhall Bridge, and in course of time found themselves in front of the Rotunda. It was a large gaunt white building, standing at the corner of two thoroughfares, in a not very respectable locality. The front of it, gayly illuminated with gas, was decorated with gigantic pictures of the moving incidents to be beheld within : the rescue of a maiden from a rushing cataract—the stabbing of a nobleman by a person with a mask and dark lantern—the breaking of a bridge over a ravine, and the appearance of a human body, head downward, in the air.

" Nearly all these are my puppets in different situations," remarked Hickes, with a lethargic smile, to his companion. " But the people never see that they are always the same, however much the situation and their costume may differ."

" You like to depreciate your own work," returned Arthur, with a laugh, " like other artists. But you wouldn't care to have your criticisms taken *au serieux*, would you ? "

And, indeed, he would not : he was far more vain of his literary performances than he affected to be. There was in him, also, as may hereafter appear, a vague sort of wish to do right, and be thought well of—a sort of sediment of self-respect, which was sometimes being curiously stirred up in a feeble way. Even his indecision of purpose arose from a kind of wish to please the people around him ; he could not take the trouble to have a will of his own and be disagreeable.

They went up into the theatre, and into the box which had been reserved for them. A frightful din was going on between the acts. The large building, reeking with the smell of escaped gas, oranges, and gin, was crowded with a dense multitude of dusky figures, chiefly those of boys and girls ; and these were shouting to each other, and laughing, and handing from mouth to mouth some dingy green bottle filled with a colorless liquor. Twenty per cent. of the thieves of South London were in the crowded gallery ; while in the tawdry and dirty boxes were tawdry and not very clean-faced girls, with flaunting finery on their heads and coarse paint on their cheeks. In the " dress-circle" were a good many shop-boys and young men out with their sweethearts, while in the pit were a few workingmen and their wives. The majority of Mr. Hickes's audience were not a cultivated or intellectual race ; but then they were human beings. They had all got beyond the tail period ; it is probable there was not one present who could have swung by his feet from a tree.

Mr Arthur and his friend were in time to see the last act of the favorite Rotunda piece ; and a very exciting act it was. The diverse threads of the story had all to be brought together and tied in a knot, so that the dramatist might cut it at one bold and final stroke. All sorts of villainous persons had to be brought to an untimely death, in order that the virtuous people might find the stage cleared for them.

Hard and sharp came the avenging raps of Destiny, until one could almost have begun to sympathize with evil, on account of the harsh treatment it was receiving. For there is much selfishness, not recognized as selfishness, among good people, who arrogate to themselves various privileges simply because they are good. The most humane man in the world does not think himself less humane when, sitting at his dinner, he piously hopes that the rabbit he is eating met with a violent end, instead of having merely succumbed to the ailments peculiar to rabbit life.

The next piece was a still more stirring drama, which Mr. Hickes had written at an early period of his career. Few of his subsequent efforts were more popular than his "Black Chieftain of Lochgoil, or the Vengeance of Binnoire," and, indeed, there was a good deal of rough vigor about the construction of the drama and the interest of the story. Hickes complained, naturally enough that the appointments of the theatre—the weak kneed clansmen, the ranting hero, and the chieftain's daughter, whose accent had a twang of Camberwell Green about it—would have burlesqued a better piece; and even the much believing audience were inclined to be satirical about the kilt and tinfoil shield of the Black Chieftain himself. Mr. Arthur, however, paid little attention to the drama. He was aware that the chieftain's daughter kept tossing about her h's as a juggler does his glass balls, and that her father had an indescribably hoarse whisper. But his thoughts were with another drama, and he was wondering what part he should have to play himself. He had not yet an opportunity of mentioning the matter to Mr. Hickes.

At length (after having gone behind the scenes and drunk some sour half and half in a celebrated tragedian's dressing room), they returned to Hickes' lodgings; and having dispatched some brief sort of supper, they settled down to their smoke and their talk. Mr. Arthur proceeded to tell his friend as much of what had occurred, with reference to his uncle and cousin, as Hickes did not already know, and then he said:

"I came naturally to you to ask for advice. It seems to me that here is just one of those things out of which one might make something; and you ought to know how. You have studied all these domestic complications, and you know what men are likely to do in them."

But Mr. Hickes had no such belief in the creations of his fancy as Mr. Drem had.

"I know what men on the stage would do," said he with a vague smile. "I would not advise you to attempt any theatrical *coup* in private life."

"But why?" said Arthur. "It does not look improbable on the stage; why should it be in real life? And, after all, a deal of nonsense is talked about improbability, merely because some people fancy certain things unlikely to occur to them. A man in a quiet way of living—who does not mix with various men, and who has, perhaps, not very much money, and not very much passion—finds strong passions, and daring acts, and hazardous resolutions in a drama or in a book, and then cries out, 'Oh, improbable!' Take your own case. It seems improbable to you that Mr. Drem would give you an annuity of £200 a year for marrying this girl I have been speaking about. That is only because you are not rich enough to understand that £200 a year may be a trifle to a man like him, determined to have his own way. In higher spheres of life than yours or mine, there are greater opportunities for romance, and I think they become greater the higher you go. Men who have been accustomed to study their lightest whim—who have had unlimited command of money—whose temper has become headstrong by constant indulgence—are they not likely to do things improbable to either me or you, who are merely mice in a wire wheel, going our small round, and never moving beyond?"

Mr. Arthur delivered himself of this argument with emphasis, for he had been studying it the whole evening.

"By Jove! there is something in that," said Hickes, whose powers of reasoning were very small, and who had a leaning towards agreeing with anybody.

"Fancy what Mr. Ewart would call probable," cried Arthur; "a man who goes on like clock work from year's end to year's end, never varying by five minutes his hour for luncheon. Anything sudden, or passionate, or dramatic would look impossible to him. So with you. Don't imagine a thing improbable because you would not do it yourself."

"I understand you—I understand you," said Hickes. "Perhaps my combination of puppets are more possible than I ever fancied them."

"We may leave them out of the question just now," said Arthur, "with the assurance that you will never make your fortune by them. You may go on working to the end of the chapter, and never earn anything beyond a precarious income. And then, when you are old, what's to become of you?"

"True enough," said Hickes thoughtfully, coinciding at once with every suggestion of his companion. Indeed, his mind was continually being blown about in this way; and he seemed rather to prefer that some one else should accept the task of thinking for him.

"Now, Mr. Hickes, said Mr. Arthur seriously, "I have been considering all this afternoon whether you and I mightn't find something profitable in this business; and I begin to believe we might. One way I will tell you. If you were to marry this Miss Seaford, and so prevent my cousin's marrying her, I believe my uncle would give you a couple of thousand pounds."

"But suppose he didn't—it would be rather awkward, wouldn't it?" he said, with a smile.

Indeed, Mr. Hickes had no belief at all in Mr. Arthur's proposed transference of stage-business to real life.

"Or get her into a position that you could go and say to my uncle, 'Give me £2,000, and I will marry her.' I am certain he would give you the money."

"Perhaps he might. And how to get the girl to marry me —or to promise to marry me?"

"Good heavens! You ask that of me!" exclaimed Arthur. "*You* ought to know—that is why I came to you."

"Oh, I know how it could be done on the stage," replied Hickes, carelessly. "Nothing simpler. You get a dying mother to lay her commands on her——"

"Her mother is dead already," said Arthur.

"Or you ruin her, and make her glad to marry you."

"Why not?" said Arthur.

"Or you threaten to kill her unless she swears an oath that she will marry you. But all that is mere bosh, you know. It couldn't happen in real life. If you tried it on, somebody would punch your head, or the girl would laugh in your face."

"Don't be so sure," said Arthur. "If these things hadn't happened some time, they would not be in dramas; and, having happened some time, they might happen again. I'll tell you what it is, Hickes: if you had the courage to pull yourself together and act a little bit of one of your own dramas—just as you would write it down—you might do a rare good turn for both yourself and me."

"I think you're stage-struck," said Hickes, with a little dull laugh, but showing a little more curiosity and attention all the same.

"I know more of life than you do," retorted Arthur, coolly; "and I know that stagey things are quite practicable, if they are done boldly. It is only your pet canary, that has been brought up in a cage, that disbelieves in the picture of the eagle striking the lamb. You think life is not full of violent changes and accidents merely because you live in Sloane Street, and have the same sort of bread and butter for breakfast every day."

"Well, I give in on that point," said Hickes (was there any point on which he would not have given in?) "Suppose I admit that there are more chances of dramatic business among rich people than among us humdrum middle-class people—what then? Do you propose that I am to turn into one of my own villains, and strike at the lamb, as you practically put it? Upon my soul, it is the richest notion I have heard of for many a day! There is something sublime about it."

And he lay back in his chair and laughed; it was seldom his sense of humor was so touched.

"And if you, who have made so many villains, cannot yourself play the part of a villain, who should?" said Arthur, also laughing.

"But then," said Hickes—making a true remark by chance—"it is the very essence of the stage-villain to show his villainy, and inform everybody how bad he is. In real life he would be kicked out of the house at once."

"My dear fellow," said Arthur, "it is getting near midnight; and I am a commercial man, who must be at business in the morning. Let us stop this joking, and talk over the matter seriously. I don't want you to play the part of villain, or do any harm to any one. On the contrary, by getting this girl to marry you, you would do everybody a vast deal of good. If my cousin marries her, he will be a poor man all his life; she will be wretched in thinking she has made him poor; his father will be a miserable man all his days. On the other hand, you step in; you get yourself a pretty wife and a considerable addition to your income; you will make her a good husband; you will restore Philip to his proper position; and you will gladden his father's heart."

"But what am I to do for you, since I am conferring favors on everybody?"

"Leave that to me," said Arthur. "Now, do you see that all this is to be done by your accomplishing one thing—your marriage with an inexperienced young girl ? If you cannot do that, what is the value of all your dramas ? "

"I never said they had any—in *that* direction," replied Hickes. "Really, Drem, you seem quite serious about it."

"I *am* serious."

"But it is absurd."

"Why?"

"Why! why, how should I make her consent to marry me, when she is already engaged to another man?"

"Did you never hear of engagements being broken off? I tell you that, with one bold stroke out of your dramatic experience, you ought to settle the thing at once."

"I could not even become acquainted with her—how is it possible?"

"I say again that you should not ask me. You ought to be familiar with every detail. A man in your position should be capable of acting in any emergency."

"Nonsense! You *will* confuse this stage-stuff with real life."

"I tell you, nine-tenths of people do not know the difference, and, if you boldly brought the stage-stuff to bear upon them, would accept it in perfect good faith. You ask how to become acquainted with her? There are a dozen ways. She teaches in a Sunday-school; why not go and become a teacher yourself, and touch her sympathy that way, and make the acquaintance of the whole family?"

"I become a Sunday-school teacher! I should not be able to tell the first from the fifth commandment, nor the ninth from the tenth."

"That is because you did not observe a regular series in breaking them," observed Arthur, gracefully.

"And if she were to consent to marry me because I became a Sunday-school teacher, she must be supplied with a good many possible husbands already."

"Of course; I only meant that to be the first step," said Arthur, testily. "If I am to describe everything you have to do, I might as well do it."

"What is the use of keeping a dog and barking yourself, you would say? Well, why not marry her yourself?"

For it was plain that Mr. Hicks still remained in the outer regions of scepticism. The pendulum of his mind swung towards faith in the representations of his friend, but inevitably swung back again into infidelity. He had a terribly definite consciousness of the mechanical nature of that stage-business by which he made his living. Far more intimately than Arthur, he knew how artificial it was in construction. Had Mr. Hickes been acquainted with some faint rudiments of philosophy, he might have argued that all the emotional and other complications of the Rotunda drama were nevertheless only combinations of what must have been actual human experience at some time or other; but he knew only the remarkably matter of fact method in which he, as a handicraftsman, whipped up the old materials into new forms. It was not the case of a shoemaker disbelieving in leather; but that of a shoemaker refusing to believe that a skin of leather could be mistaken for a living ox.

Samuel Hickes, however, was a weak man, easily persuaded. Despite his own puzzled doubts as to the feasibility of the project mentioned by Arthur Drem, he had nearly been won over to trying it by his adviser and friend. Even Arthur Drem was interested in watching the curious spectacle of the vacillation of this man's belief. At one minute he would start back from the proposal with scorn and derision, laughing at himself for having entertained it for an instant. To attempt to carry out a tragedy-plot in real life—it was too absurd! And then, again, yielding to the influence of Mr. Arthur's persuasion, he would incline the other way, and would admit that, after all, this melodramatic climax might be reached by a succession of possible and natural steps.

"There you have hit upon a great truth!" exclaimed Arthur, who, following the example of more celebrated and wiser men, was fain to term a great truth that which accorded with his own beliefs. "People call certain situations in plays or books melodramatic and impossible because they do not see the small stages by which these points are reached. The drama, or the story, omits all the dull or tentative passages in a man's life, and gives you the sharp and striking incidents; and then the critic cries out that these things are too sharp and striking. Would he like to spend three weeks in a Japanese theatre to see the events of a drama brought about naturally and without crises?"

Mr. Arthur was pleased to find himself talking so fluently, and began to think the society of literary persons improving. As for Hickes, his intellect was too wavering and "woolly" to follow out any piece of clear reasoning, or accept its conclusions; but he was impressed by it all the same. The engine of an argument rushed past his bewildered head, and he could not tell whither it had gone; but the force of the wind which it caused made him stagger backward. He was not very sure that Arthur Drem had demonstrated all these things. Perhaps he had; perhaps he could prove himself to be right. All that Samuel Hickes knew was, that a very curious and difficult matter had been set before him; and that he felt half inclined to study it more closely, merely out of curiosity.

CHAPTER XVI.

"THIS is a very pleasant hotel," said Mr. Philip, as he stood at the window one morning before breakfast, and looked out over the spacious bay. "And really the attention of the domestics is surprising. Fancy their having these fresh wild flowers brought in for our breakfast-table every morning!"

With that he caught sight of a grim smile on Jims' face; and then, turning to Lilian, remarked that there was a glow of color in her cheeks, and a light in her eyes, as if she had already been out in the cool breeze and the early sunshine.

"My dear child," he said, "you don't mean to say that you have been out every morning before breakfast to gather these flowers? When *do* you get up?"

"Ye may well ask her!" said Jims. "I think the young witch has been flying about all night on a broomstick; for the earlier I get up, the earlier I find her coming back over the hill up there, wi' her hands fu' o' flowers, and singing like a lintie, wi' nae ane to hear her. And this mornin', I'm sure, there was na a bird awake when she came to my door and bade me come out wi' her. And here was I, a poor auld man, dragged away by this will-o'-the-wisp down the fearsome rocks, and round bits o' shore, and up over the hills, wi' her laughin' and runnin' and caperin' like a mad thing. 'Deed, it's time, miss, ye sat demure and respectable on the sofa there, lookin' as if ye'd ne'er been out o' the house!"

"And I have been supposing these flowers were brought by the servants!" said Philip.

"I thought you might like to have some every morning," said she, timidly, and not looking up.

It was only one of the many little ways in which she strove to please him, in her innocent, tender fashion. She had somehow or other got it into her head that he was her guest. Here, down in Devonshire, she was at home. She knew every lane and bay, every quiet nook and old ruin, and all the secret haunts of the wild flowers; and she took her two companions about with a sort of anxious care that they should be amused and gratified, and was filled with a proud satisfaction when she saw them pleased. The tender little show-woman forgot all about herself. How was her comforts or convenience to be considered, when she had two guests to entertain? And so she was out in the early morning—away over the cliffs and down in the wooded coves by the sea—to gather some sweet-scented and sweet-colored wild flowers for the breakfast-table of her lord.

It may be remembered that Mr. Philip had been permitted to accompany Jims and Lilian on their business-excursion as a sort of *attache*. It was soon very clear, however, that Mr. Philip was taking the management of the whole affair. On arriving at the small town. Jims proposed that Lilian and he should go to some smaller hostelry than that Philip was likely to go to, so that Lilian's friends might see her there. But Mr. Philip said No; they should all go to the same hotel, where they might have a private sitting-room for the reception of visitors. Accordingly, he carried them off to the big building which, a little way outside the town, stands on a platform of rock above the sea, fronting the rippling waters of Tor Bay, the long neck of land on the other side, and then the far horizon, where the sky and water meet.

How could they tire of the perpetual change of picture visable from the large windows, or the warm terraces, or the exposed promontories of rock? Was there any hour in the day in which the land and the sky and the sea preserved the same aspect? On the evening of their arrival, a misty yellow sunlight lay over the bay, and the opposite coast seemed far and dreamlike in the haze. But next morning the land opposite had come strangely and sharply near, so that you could see every house and field and hedge; a brisk breeze from the southwest was bringing up heavy, swift masses of cloud over the sky, and these threw splatches of shadow on the great tumbling breath of green waves that ran, white-crested, in for the shore. The boats rolled in the harbor, with creaking cordage: and the wind that blew through the small town was laden with the smell of seaweed. Towards mid-day the wind moderated, and the sun was faintly hidden by a fleece of gray cloud, the opposite shore receeded, and the long line stretching out to Berry Head lay like a dusky bar of blue in the blinding gray light of the sea and sky. And then again, towards the afternoon, the clouds thickened and grew thunderous; and suddenly—when one had forgotten all about sunset, and expected a gray and listless evening—there appeared a lurid glow of dusky brown in the west; the masses of cloud over Paignton shore became illuminated as if with fire; and their lower edges, with sunlight shining on the other side, came down in a red smoke of rain. Behind these ragged streaks of crimson, again, there were glimpses of the far green and gold of the sunset; and this keener and clearer color, as the thunder-clouds slowly lifted, sent a pallid glow over the waters of the bay and the full tide of the harbor. Finally above the clouds there rose the clear stillness of the twilight, that glimmered on the fronts of the houses high up on the wood hills; and overhead, in the pale green sky, yellow stars began to burn.

They explored all the neighborhood too, and had small picnics down in the secret clefts of the coast, where the sea had eaten out a semicircle in the red sandstone or the gray rock, and washed up a shelf of clear white shingle. They drove down the narrow, leafy lanes, with the tall banks and the wilderness of foliage about. Mr. Philip hired a yacht, furthermore, and they went cruising round the land looking up at the precipitous cliffs, with their great caverns or bold arches jutting into the water, or looking far out on the blue plain of the sea, with the sails of distant ships or a faint string of wild ducks sinking down into the horizon. It was a happy time, and Mr. Philip was glad to perceive that, so busy and anxious was Lilian in making everything pleasant, she had nearly forgotten why she so wished the time to be happy.

One morning he missed his wild flowers and Lilian was a few minutes late for breakfast. She came in almost breathless, her face suffused with color.

"Where have you been?" said he.

"After some daft trick, I warrant," said Jims.

"I have been to Paignton," she said, with a smile of triumph in her eyes.

"To Paington!" exclaimed Philip; "it is three miles off."

"Well," she said with an anxious apology, "I thought it was a pity to take you there, and break up the day for me, when I knew you wanted to go to Watcombe. So I thought I'd start off and see Mrs. Rossiter myself."

"And you have walked there and back before breakfast!" said Jims rather angrily.

"No," she said, with a laugh; "I ran nearly all the way back, for I thought I should be late."

What was Mr. Philip to say when he saw the great unselfishness and affection that were shining in her eyes? He had not the heart to scold her. He was going to do it, but something at the back of his throat prevented him.

In the evenings they had plenty of company; for among the first persons whom Mr. Philip met at the hotel was the M. P. for a Northern Radical borough, whom he knew very well, and who had, without asking leave of his constituents, run down to Torquay for a fortnight with his three daughters. This Mr. Stanberry was himself a sort of "philosophical Radical," with very definite convictions; and nothing pleased him better than to get into a fierce controversy with old James Lawson and with Philip, in the smoking-room, while Lilian was in the drawing-room, submitting timidly to be petted by the three girls.

It was the first time she had ever met three such young persons, who had run the gauntlet of several London seasons, and acquired an excellent coolness of manner. Catch a timid little wren, and put it in a cage with three calm and well-bred canaries, and watch how they will regard its frightened, wild-eyed wonder. The three girls were amused by this young creature, who was so fascinatingly pretty; who dressed, and talked, and walked and sewed as they did, yet who had an indescribable something about her which made her *piquante*, unfamiliar, and captivating. They did not meet her with the cool criticism and with the somewhat distant courtesy they would have assumed to an ordinary stranger. They began to pet her, as they would have simultaneously rushed to kiss a pretty child or tease a kitten. They were consequently very frank with her, and revealed their various dispositions in the most open fashion.

There was Catherine, the eldest, who was rather good-looking, and conscious of it—who was graceful and dignified, yielding to her two sisters with a condescension and a sweetness for which she gave herself ample credit.

Mary, the second, was the fat one, who was rather selfish—especially at meals—and a trifle irritable and ill-tempered. She was the plainest of the three—had flaxen hair and tepid blue eyes, while the others had darker hair, and dark eyelashes over their gray eyes—and was quite frankly jealous and angry when she saw her two sisters monopolizing the attention of gentlemen whom they might meet when out riding or walking.

There was Lucy, the youngest, quick, pretty, sharp in her look and speech, and a notorious and wicked flirt. She had a habit of modestly keeping in the background when her two sisters were present; but that was only her cunning. Ten to one you found her flirting desperately in a corner with some grave gentleman whom she had inveigled thither; or engaged in the same occupation with another gentleman as she lagged behind her sisters' horses, and conversed in a series of pert whispers with her companion on foot. Catherine patronized Lilian in a kindly way; Mary had a sort of sleepy liking for her; but this Lucy put her arm around her neck as she sat in the chair, and talked nonsense into her ear. She was a dangerous young person, this Lucy, as more than one young gentleman can testify.

"What a pretty ring that is!" she said one evening, as she somehow had got Lilian's hand in hers.

"That is my engaged ring," said Lilian with a conscious blush of pride.

"I thought so," said the other, still holding the small white fingers. "Do you know what serious things engagements are? They very often lead to marriage."

Lilian did not quite understand the coolness of this remark; but Miss Lucy went on.

"How odd it is we should never have met at Mr. Drem's house! I have only been once or twice, to be sure; but my sisters have been there frequently."

"I never was in the house," said Lilian. "My father was a half-cousin of Mr. Drem, and they were never very good friends."

"Oh, indeed," said the other, opening her eyes very wide.

She guessed in a moment that there was something very peculiar in this complication, but she had too much delicacy to show her curiosity. There had been a good deal of confidence, however, between the two girls during these few days; and so Lilian said to her, simply:

"I like to look at this ring, and I know I am engaged. But I do not think we shall ever be married."

"Why not? I think you like him very well; and anybody can see how despertely fond he is of you. It is quite pleasant to see the anxious way in which he tries to make everything nice for you. But what amuses one most of all is his chivalrous way of proving you to be the wisest little woman in the world. When we are all chattering together, you never say anything, or express any preference, without his instantly taking it up and showing how right you are, and giving some profound reason for it. The first evening I met you I thought you must be some authoress travelling in a petty disguise—Minerva going about as Venus, you know—until I found out that you were—that you were, indeed, rather stupid, just like the rest of us."

Miss Stanberry had a sufficiently good and accurate opinion of her own cleverness to know that she was paying a compliment in saying so.

"We women are poor creatures," she said, with a sigh. "Whatever originality of character we start with doesn't matter; for destiny compels us to become stupid at last, and fall in love with men. Nature is too much for us."

"And have you fallen in love yet?" said Lilian timidly, yet with an eager curiosity.

"Oh yes; ever so often," replied the other gayly. "Turn over my music-books, and see. If gentlemen had any sense when they go flirting and pretending to make love (and expecting to find that you have never spoken to a man before), they would examine these painful records of by-gone *affaires*. I think music-books are awkward things for us girls; for, you see, every man who comes about one must inscribe his name— in large and sprawling letters generally—over the title-page of the songs and pieces he sends you, just as if he were doing something bold and original. And then some one takes up the book; and there is your music-master's name, with whom you flirted when you were still in short petticoats; and there is this cousin's name, and that cousin's name; and then follow the names of other gentlemen, who have had their brief hour of bliss and departed. Then supposing you were to have a real *bona-fide* lover, and supposing he were to get into a temper, he'd be sure to provoke you by referring to these names, and asking you about them. When I have a real lover, I think I shall burn my music; I cannot have him turning over the pages to prove previous convictions."

"What have you done with my *eau-de-Cologne*, Lucy?" said Mary, sharply, coming into the room. "I told you to get *eau-de-Cologne* for yourself before you came down here."

"You may have my bottle," remarked imperial Catherine with calm sweetness, looking up from her book.

"I don't want yours," retorted Mary, going off hot and sulky to her chamber.

In this beautiful scenery, in this pleasant company, Mr. Philip almost forgot that in a few days' time he might have to become a cabman or clerk, or tide waiter. He even forgot that £60 was not a large sum with which to live for a fortnight *en prince* at a fashionable watering-place. That manner of living was so natural to him, that he found no difficulty whatever in being careless about half sovereigns. It was the knowledge of their value that he had yet to learn: and he staved off the evil day.

In the mean time Lilian and Jims had seen all the people whom they wished to see, and the rest of their stay in the South was to be given up to pure idleness and pleasure. Ten days had passed; there were fewer than ten to come; and all that Lilian could wish for, in the thankfulness of her heart, was that the remainder of the time might be as sweet and beautiful as that which had passed.

"In London," she said to Jims, as they sat together on the rocks over the gleaming sea, "we shall be able to dream of this place. It may be years and years before we see it again."

"You may see it again," said the old man; "I never shall. Or, wha kens, but that in the next world we may have wonderful powers o' vision, and may be able to look frae the blue up there to the blue doon here. And if that were the case, d'ye think ane could get a bonnier place to look at than this blue bay, wi' the green hills round it and the jagged gray rocks out there?"

The jagged gray rocks presented no problems to Jims. They were not half so firmly imbedded as was his faith. The next world, which his imagination had pictured to him was a firmer reality to him than this one; and he would have regarded only as dreams the demonstrations of the geologists that these planetary bodies must in time be dashed into the sun. It was for a poet, not for this practical and determined old weaver, to conjecture as to the possible inhabitants of that splendid orb, when, like our present globe, it may have cooled sufficiently to produce living forms; and to wonder whether Nature has only one system of evolution, or whether, under these new and magnificent conditions, the line of life will reach a climax as superior to man as he is to the first reptile that crawled: Jims would have scornfully asked you to point out anything of that kind in the first chapter of Genesis.

Now there were to be some steeplechases in the neighborhood and as they all decided to go, Mr. Philip must needs drive thither four-in-hand. Mr. Stanberry and his daughters were invited to be of the party; and so it was that Lilian found herself seated next to the driver of the handsome drag as it started from the hotel-door—Jims looking anxiously ahead for sharp corners and obstructions; Mr. Stanberry taking the matter more coolly, for he had constantly seen Mr. Philip driving in the Park.

"You have a valuable freight, Mr. Drem," remarked the youngest Miss Stanberry, as they rolled along.

"Don't you be afraid, Miss Lucy," said he. "I have driven four-in-hand all over the South of Russia,"

"But there it didn't matter how many people you killed," she remarked, "as you were only doing service to your native country."

"At critical moments you mustn't talk to the man at the wheel," said he, as his off-leader showed symptoms of shying at a newspaper which lay open on the road, and which the wind was blowing about.

"The horse didn't like the politics of that paper," said Miss Lucy, when the danger was past.

"It was the leader that was wrong," observed Lilian, very timidly, and only for Philip's ear.

"Lilian, how dare you," said he; and she hung down her head and was overhelmed with a pretty shame.

Nothing of any consequence occurred until they reached the course. A sum of twenty shillings was demanded for the admission of a fourwheeled carriage into the inclosure, and Mr. Philip tossed down the sovereign to the man as if the events of the past fortnight and his present position were alike forgotten. The drag was driven up by the side of the rope, the horses taken out, and the people on the top of the carriages turned to look at their surroundings.

They were on the side of a large circular hollow in the neighborhood of St. Mary's Church, and round the pretty wooded valley they could trace the line of the course, marked by small yellow-flags. A short distance in front of them stood the grand stand—a huge, bare, wooden erection about half filled with people. Down before it, the crowd that moved about and stared at the Punch and Judy shows, or listened to the nigger songs, or watched juggling feats, was denser than elsewhere; and, indeed, one was puzzled to discover how the neighborhood of Torquay could have turned out such an assemblage. The scene, is short, reminded one of a Derby day in miniature; only that the men and women who walked about in their stiff Sunday customes had brown faces, thick-set frames, and stupid look. There was none of the smartness and the gaudy finery that distinguish the holiday of the pale-faced London clerk and his sweetheart. A good deal of beer was being drunk in the refreshment-tents by burly farm servants and stout tradesmen from the neighboring villiages; but you did not see some pallid boy of fifteen, with a flashy tie, sham jewellery, and a big cigar, produce a bottle of champagne for the delectaticn of his mistress—a coarse woman of thirty with green ribbons, and paint on her face.

"You have never told me, Philip," said Lilian, "what you have been doing these last two or three days, when you disappeared in the afternoon and no one could tell where you had gone."

"You must not be curious. Must she, Miss Stanberry?"

"I think she has a right to be," observed the eldest Miss Stanberry, with a graceful smile, as she glanced at Lilian's gloved hand, where the circle of the ring was visible through the glove.

Philip caught the direction of her eyes, and laughed. He had no time for explanation, however, as there devolved upon him the duty of getting up a sweepstake for the first race. It was an open handicap for seventy sovereigns, added to a sweepstake of ten soverigns each; and there were seven horses down on the card.

"That is one for each of us," said Philip. "But I forgot. Perhaps you won't go in, Mr. Lawson?" he added.

Jims gave him distinctly to understand that he would join in no such games of chance, that had a smack of the devil about them. So Philip took two horses; and when they had paid up their half-crowns, and picked their cards out of Philip's hat, and scanned the name of their horses with eager curiosity, the bell rang for the course to be cleared.

There was nothing unusual about the race. Having shown off their horses to the crowd, and allowed the spectators to identify the colors of the riders with the description on the card, the competitors walked their horses up to the brow of the hill opposite the stand, where the starting point was. A man waved a flag; down came the seven horses, with the gay colors of their riders glancing in the sun. A murmur ran through the crowd as the three leading horses simultaneously cleared the first fence; and the curiosity increased as a certain blue and white horseman was seen to steal ahead. But the others were only nursing their animals for the fine run down the slope in front of the stand and the water-jump in the hollow. Then up the hill and round again; the seven horses tailing off with cries of "Rose has it! Rose has it!" as a gleaming point of pink was seen in front of the rest crossing the high broad field. And this rose-colored rider kept the lead all the way round—for they had to go twice over the course—and finally won by a neck, letting Miss Mary win the first prize in the sweepstakes.

But why did Mr. Philip disappear? And why, as the preparations for the next race began to be visible, did the three young ladies begin to glance nervously at Lilian? And why did Mr. Stanberry come and seat himself beside her, and take to conversing with her in an unusually sprightly way? Mr. Philip had gone down by way of the grand stand.

"If he does not come back soon," said Lilian, glancing all over the crowd, "we shall have no sweepstake for the next race."

"Let me get it up," said Mr. Stanberry, "in case he should not be back in time."

"But where is he?" she asked.

"He has probably met some one he knows down at the stand."

So Mr. Stanberry got up the sweepstakes, collected the half-crowns, and doled out the bits of paper, reserving one for Philip, and taking two for himself. The race was down as a "Maiden Steepleshase" of fifty sovereigns for horses that never won before, and, it happened, Lilian got a horse called Rocketer, whose jockey colors were green and gold.

"Do change with me," said Miss Lucy to her. "I have got Black Dart; and my rider's colors are scarlet and black."

"If you like," said Lilian; "it is quite the same to me."

So Lilian came into possession of Black Dart, and naturally began to look out for her own horse with its own colors. When the course was cleared, the various riders cantered up the course in front of the spectators. One of them, however, hung rather in the rear; and Lilian said, "That is my horse—the rider with the black jacket and scarlet hoop. Why doesn't he come nearer?"

Indeed, he seemed rather to avoid being seen; and it was not until he had turned, and was making off for the starting-place, that he rose in his stirrups to give the assemblage a look at the pace of Black Dart. But at the moment of his turning the sunlight caught his face; and Lilian cried out, with a sudden qualm of fear:

"Oh, that is Philip!"

"So you have found out," said Mr. Stanberry, with a good-natured smile. "He did not wish you to know at first. But don't be alarmed; the course is a very easy one, I think; and there was not even a spill in the first race."

She sat mute and still, and with her face fixed, apparently hearing nothing of what was said around her. When the horses were ranged on the brow of the hill, her heart was beating as if it would choke her; and she held Jims' arm with a tight grasp.

"They're off!" cried the crowd; and down the hill came the line of horses, like a charge of cavalry, their various bright colors almost in a line.

"The Dart leads—the Dart leads!" was the long murmur among the crowd, as the rider with the scarlet sash across his black jacket got a few yards to the front. Along the bottom of the hollow lay the first fence; and as the line of horses came down upon it, Black Dart was seen to rise first. Yet, strangely enough, when the horse was high over the fence, and had apparently cleared it, he seemed to expose his side to the people on the drag; and the next moment he had gone down to the ground on his shoulder and head, throwing his rider heavily. In the same instant the next horse came thundering over on the top of them, and there was a cloud of brown dust.

Lilian uttered a cry that seemed to be the breaking of her heart, and covered her face with her hands.

"Good God!" exclaimed Mr Stanberry; "I hope he isn't hurt."

"Help me to get down," cried the girl, with a white face and piteous eyes. "I must go to him."

But Mr. Stanberry seized her arm and pointed. She caught sight of an old man with white hair, fleeing like an arrow through the divided crowd; and at the same moment—for all this had occurred in a couple of seconds—she saw the scarlet-and-black rider pulling the reins back over the horse's head, and putting his foot in the stirrup.

"See—he is in the saddle again!" cried Mr. Stanberry. "There he comes! Bravo, bravo! Well done! And listen to the people now!"

For as Black Dart came along the empty thoroughfare, laying himself down to a long swinging gallop, with his rider sputtering the dust from his mouth, and looking forward to the rest of the horses, there arose a long, hoarse murmur of applause from the crowd. It was taken up by the people in the stand and around it, as Black Dart's splendid stride let him gain slowly on one—two—three of the horses; and it broke into a ringing cheer as the horse was seen to rise to the water-jump and clear it, placing himself within a few lengths of the leader. Until that moment Lilian had sat icily cold and stiff, clasping Lucy Stanberry's hand tightly. When she saw Black Dart get safe over the dreaded jump, she uttered a strange sort of laugh, endeavored to say something, and then trembled slightly, and finally sank backward, white and apparently dead, with her companion's arms around her neck.

"George!" shouted Mr. Stanberry to his servant below, "some water—quick!"

"I don't think there's none, sir; nothing but the wine."

"Give me anything, you fool! Knock the head off one of the champagne-bottles."

The broken bottle was handed up; Lucy Stanberry dipped her handkerchief into it; and presently there was a cold fragrant dampness on the girl's forehead. To the pale cheeks there gradually came a color as faint and tender as the blush in the inside of a white shell: and no sooner had she recovered life than she steadied herself on her companion's arm, and looked anxiously all round the valley.

"Don't be alarmed," said Lucy Stanberry, coaxingly. "He is all right; he won't get such another fall as that. The odds are against it, my dear."

The horses now came into view again as they rounded the opposite hill. They were bearing down again on the same jump that had already nearly produced a catastrophe; and it was no consolation to Lilian to hear the people cheering Black Dart, which was now a good third. She saw with dismay, too, that the fourth horse—a fine chestnut animal, whose silken coat shone in the sun—was running with an empty saddle. He had thrown his rider; and so determined was the brave brute to win, that he came valorously on with the others, with briddle-reins flying in the air. When they had got down to the fence in the hollow, the riderless horse was running second. All got well over the fence, himself among the rest; and as they came up to the corner near the stand the order was: White Star, first; Rocketer, (without his rider), second; Teignmouth Lass, third; Black Dart, a dangerous fourth. Just opposite the stand, however, Rocketer with his flying reins, overtook White Star, and pretty nearly cannoned against her. The latter horse swerved, and ran down the line of the crowd, scattering back the people, and tossing her head in the air, as her rider kept sawing at her mouth to get her into the stream again. When he had accomplished that object, he found himself at the tail of the field, with the race now lying between Teignmouth Lass and Black Dart, Rocketer having been caught.

"Now you may look at them with safety," said Lucy Stanberry, when they were coming round the hill. "There are no more jumps; they have only to run in."

"And that is Philip who is first!" cried Lilian, who was picking up a little interest with her reassurances.

"No," said Miss Stanberry with a smile, "Teignmouth Lass is first; Black Dart is second."

It was a close race. From the brow of the hill the two leading horses came down almost neck and neck; and the excitement of the crowd was intense. Their admiration for the pluck of the rider, who had not despaired of the struggle after getting a remarkably bad fall at the very commencement, doubtless increased their sympathies with the second horse; and there were eager and frantic bets that, after all, Black Dart would win. There now lay between these two competitors and the winning-post but the breadth of a field, and a line might have been drawn across the noses of the horses.

"The Dart wins, the Dart wins!" was the cry everywhere.

But, alas! Philip called upon his horse in vain. The brave animal had been severely tried to make up the leeway lost by his first fall; and now, when half a yard was all that had to be won, Black Dart did his best; but his best wasn't good enough. Teignmouth Lass won the race; and her owner got the fifty sovereigns. But Black Dart, as he was led back to the stables, the reins hanging down on his neck, and the rider taking a little more of the dust from his own mouth and eyes, had all the cheering of the crowd, as was natural.

When Philip, in his ordinary attire, made his way back to the drag, and got on the top, they were all for talking to him at once; but Lilian, from the various emotions that possessed her, could say nothing whatever. She only took his hand in hers, as if to assure herself that he was alive and safe.

"Ah! you don't like to scold him," said Lucy Stanberry. "Let me. I think it was shameful."

"Well, it was a bad one," said Philip. "I had a very odd sensation when I saw the hollow inside of two hoofs just over my face, but they lit on the other side, fortunately."

"I did not mean the fall; I meant the riding in the race, and causing us all to suffer such agony. This young lady, for example, fainted; and we were all in a condition worse than fainting."

"But why did you tell her?" he said, turning upon Miss Lucy with some sharpness.

"We did not tell her. She recognized you from the first—by your moustache, I suppose."

"And arn't you hurt at all, Philip?" said Lilian, looking up.

"Nothing beyond a bruise or two. I have a peculiar impression, though, that I am in a merry-go-round, and that this circular valley is revolving on its own axis. The trees over there have a tendency to float backward and forward; and as for that hill, I believe it is breaking into waves. I propose that we have luncheon, to dismiss these phenomena."

After luncheon they waited to see the ladies' purse run for, and also a selling steeplechase. Thereafter they drove around by Watcombe, and so back again to Torquay.

When, in the afternoon, they came down upon Torquay from over the hills, they fancied they had descended into Italy, so rich and pure were the colors that lay before them; the town itself, with its wooded rocks and white villas, lying in a flood of yellow; with the tossing waters of the bay darkly blue, and broken only by a speck or two of red, where the sunset hit the sails of some herring-smacks off Brixham; and with the far-off line of Berry Head stretching out into a sphere of deepening purple.

This was their last evening in Torquay, and it was a very beautiful and memorable one. After dining at the hotel, they all went out together to stroll about the small town and its neighborhood. The night had come on, and yet there was a peculiar glow where the sun had gone down, and this yellowish-green light shed a strange metallic glare on the lapping waves of the harbor. Overhead there was darkness; but on the water this level, cold brilliancy fell, and twisted the dark hulls of the boats that lay and rolled. In time that light died out, and there arose in the east a new light, which changed the hue of the sky into a dull warm olive. As yet there was visible only a glimmer of radiance from behind the trees on Warberry Hill; but as the silver rim of the moon rose among the firs, the town became gradually whiter, and the orange lights of lamps and windows high up along the rocks began to lose their intensity. The bay grew lighter, too, and Paignton Sands showed a curve of gray along the dark sea. Down in the harbor the boats were dark in shadow, and you could see the yellow and red lights of the quay: but up there on the tall rocks the villas stood in the flood of the moonlight, and the ruddy lamps had grown pale. How fair and still and beautiful the place looked when the moon had fully risen! and over the black harbor rose the silvery heights of the town, with its faintly crimson windows; and overhead lay the calm of the still green sky. As they walked round by the shore the murmur of the waves seemed to say farewell. It was their last evening there. *O lente, lente currite, noctis equi?*

CHAPTER XVII.

"ARE you a gentleman, sir?"
"Are you?"
"Yes, sir."
"Then I am not, sir."

That was the anticipated overture to the interview which Mr. Philip expected to have with Major Delaney—a sort of preliminary breaking of the balls, as it were. But, with his adversary in hand, the Major was too experienced a player to chance any such losing hazard; and matters remained as they were, each refusing to make a decided stroke. Indeed, the Major was somewhat puzzled, as well he might be.

The first intelligence of what had happened between Philip and his father was brought by Miss Thormanby herself. That young lady was surprised to find Philip's visits, which had gradually become fewer, and were evidently mere courtesy-calls, cease altogether, without any explanation on his part. They had not quarrelled—indeed, for some time back, their relations had been rather more civil and agreeable than was at all customary. Mr Philip had certainly avoided anything like a *tete-a-tete;* but he was very amiable and complaisant, even when Captain Dering was present.

What, therefore, had become of him? Mary Thormanby was much too proud to inquire—for some little time; then she thought she might walk up to see how Mrs. Drem was. As it happened, Captain Dering had also been struck by the same notion, and was helping himself to a glass of sherry in Mrs. Drem's drawing-room when Miss Thormanby was announced.

Mrs. Drem was rather in a dilemma; for she had been effectually mystifying Captain Dering about Philip's absence from the house and from town, and she knew well that no mystification of the kind was possible before Mary Thormanby. So, facing the danger with something like boldness, Mrs. Drem begged Captain Dering to excuse them for a few moments, and walked off Miss Thormanby to the conservatory.

There, with all her sweetness and tact, she told the news to her companion—how Mr. Drem and his son had had a misunderstanding, and how Philip had, for a time, left London. Now there was no word mentioned about the cause of this quarrel; but Miss Thormanby divined it instantly. Perhaps she had heard some vague rumors; but at all events, she knew that nothing less serious than the question of Philip's marriage could have produced this catastrophe. And the moment she perceived this, so soon did she assume the proper attitude for a woman under the circumstances.

"I am very sorry," she said, with a good-natured smile; "Philip was always a pleasant companion; and may not be quite lost to us yet, even although he marries."

"Do you know anything about it?" said the innocent little Mrs. Drem, with a faint start.

"Oh dear, no," said Miss Thormanby. "But of course one imagines what is likely to be the cause of such an unfortunate occurrence."

"And you can understand," Mrs. Drem said, in a whisper, "that I had a little delicacy in not mentioning this matter to you."

"But why?" said Miss Thormanby, with the big gray eyes widely open.

"I thought—I fancied Philip's marriage, or any talk of it, might be a surprise to you."

"And so it is," said the young lady, boldly. "A very pleasant surprise, indeed. You know the nonsense people talked regarding him and me, but of course there was nothing in it. We were too intimate—too near friends—to think seriously of marrying. I assure you no word of such a thing passed between us."

"Oh, I am so glad!" cried Mrs. Drem.

"Why?" said Miss Thormanby, with a peculiar smile, and wondering whether the small clever woman before her actually believed all this.

"For your sake, my dear," said Mrs. Drem, with an affectionate look—she would have tried to smile away the appetite of a hungry tiger, had she met him, in the same fashion—"I was afraid Philip had behaved badly."

"Oh, not at all," said Mary Thormanby, formally; and

then she added, so as not to compromise her uncle, "You know it is impossible to say what other people may have expected. My uncle, for example, is hasty in his inference, and may have imagined there was something between us more than mere companionship—flirtation, you know—and so forth. But Philip and I knew better."

Mrs. Drem did not believe a word her friend said; but she almost persuaded her to believe that she believed. Mary Thormanby was astute, however, and was not wholly convinced that Philip's stepmother had not been acting simplicity.

Thus it was that Miss Thormanby got the news to carry to her uncle; and its effect on the burly and hairy warrior was surprising. He stamped up and down the room; he fumed, twisted his moustache, and slapped his thigh as if there were a sword dangling there on the wrong side.

"This is *my* business; *I* will see to this!" he exclaimed.

"What do you mean to do, uncle?" asked Miss Thormanby quietly. "Do you mean to make him marry me?"

"I *will* make him marry you, or he will answer me else. By gad! am I a gentleman, or am I not?"

"Of course you are, uncle," said his niece, dutifully. "But as to your making Mr. Drem marry me, pray consider that I would rather not marry him. I am not more mercenary than other people; but still I don't think Philip, with his education, is likely to have a comfortable establishment to offer one for some time."

"Do you mean to say," observed the Major, solemnly—"do you mean to tell me that Philip Drem is really without a farthing?"

"That is precisely his condition, uncle, as far as I can learn," said his niece.

"By gad! what a deal of time I've wasted on that young man!" said the Major reflectively.

"Sure ye won't ask him to marry her now?" said Mrs. Delaney.

"It is not a question of marriage, madam!" exclaimed the Major, breaking out in a new vein. "It is my honor that is concerned; and I will let that shopkeeper's son know what it is to insult a gentleman. By gad! ma'am, am I in her Majesty's service, or am I not? And if I am, have I not a duty to perform to every man in it?"

"If you let Philip alone, uncle," said his niece, with a laugh, "I don't think the army will be any the worse. Why should you bother about it? Even if you get up a breach of promise case

—and you couldn't—do you think I would allow my name to be dragged into the papers?"

"And there's not a shillin' to be got out av him," said Mrs. Delaney, with a shade of contempt.

"No; but there are bones in him—bones, ma'am; and some of them shall be broken before long. I am not the man to sit down tamely under an insult—from a grocer's apprentice, by gad! We'll see what a sound thrashing will do for him!"

"Then you had better hire somebody to give it to him," said Mary Thormanby, with a touch of pride (for no woman likes to hear a man whom she has honored even by a flirtation made light of in this fashion). "I don't know any man of our acquaintance likely to thrash Philip Drem without wishing heartily, in a very few seconds, that he hadn't begun."

"It isn't you that should stand up for him any way," said Mrs. Delaney.

"And if he *is* a bully," continued the Major, accepting Mary's hint, "can't I shoot him?"

"He might shoot you; and I don't see what good shooting would do either of you. Indeed, uncle, it can't be helped; and I am not sure you pay me much of a compliment in making a fuss about it. Is he the only man in the world likely to marry me?"

"Think of the money I've wasted on him!" said the Major, pathetically.

This was too much for his niece, who could not restrain from breaking into a hearty laugh. The warrior looked at her, scowled, and then grinned also.

"You must have lost so much at threepenny whist, uncle," she said, with mock sympathy.

"Ye young baggage," he said gayly, and assuming a broad brogue, in imitation of his wife, "'tis yourself that knows how to chate a poor man out of his revinge. Give me a kiss, and we'll let the desavin vagabone go his ways."

Philip was consequently dismissed from the consideration of the Delaney household for the time being, and Mary Thormanby began to wish that Captain Dering were not so very stupid.

But farther up Park Lane Mr. Philip's absence was more marked. There an irascible old man sat and complained of being left alone in his declining years by his only son, and revenged himself by heaping reproach on the head of his meek and despairing wife. He blamed her for everything that occurred. It was she who had spoiled Philip as a boy; it was she who had nursed his pride as a man, and taught him to apply ridiculous standards to the people around him. He forbade her to mention the name of Philip to him; but he himself never ceased to harp on the theme, and to visit innumerable petty tyrannies upon her because of her want of sympathy.

Poor Mrs. Drem had, indeed, a hard time of it. She began to think that, after all, she had made a bad bargain, and that life would have been altogether more pleasant to her had she remained an humble teacher of music in a small provincial town. She had plenty of money at her command; but what avail was it to her? She went out less and less now; for her husband, when he came home in the evening, inquired minutely after her day's occupations, and grumbled about her gadding. Had he settled down calmly to the purpose of making her life wretched, he could not have succeeded more effectually.

In the old days Philip afforded her some aid and shelter. His father feared to expose himself before his son, and was never so unreasonable aud capricious in his presence. Philip, too, was some company for her when she dreaded having other company in her house. She never dared ask her own special friends to visit her; and Mr. Drem's temper was getting so much more wayward, that she gave dinner-parties as seldom as she could, even to his friends. Above all, she was afraid of his breaking out into open conflict with Sir James Kingscote; for the society of his light-hearted and charming daughter was one of the few pleasures remaining to the poor woman. And Mr. Drem seemed to have got it into his head that Sir James was somehow connected with Philip's departure, and that Violet had done him an injury in not marrying Philip without being asked.

Mr. Arthur was too prudent to speak to his uncle about his cousin unless the former alluded to the matter. Even then the subject was dangerous. But the observant placid young man saw that Philip's desertion was telling on his father, and that the old man was gradually, in spite of all his scornful boasting coming to wish that the rupture were healed.

Healed, that is to say, in his own fashion. Had he chosen to do so, he could have made everybody, himself included, a good deal happier, by quietly recognizing Philip's right to choose his own wife, and accepting Lilian Seaford as his daughter. But Mr. Arthur saw that as time went on, this solution of the difficulty became more impracticable than ever, so bitter and determined had grown the old man's obstinacy and his anger with her whom he regarded as a chief agent of his trouble. Mr. Arthur thought he might possibly meddle in the affair, but he had not the courage to recommend *that* settlement of it.

CHAPTER XVIII.

THERE is nothing very tragic or even dramatic, in the aspect of Sloane Street. That lengthy thoroughfare is not calculated to familiarize one with the poetic side of life; and it is conceivable that a young man of receptive nature, like Samuel Hickes, by constantly looking out on the monotonous gray pavement, and listening to the melancholy echoes of distant organs, had come to regard existence as a rather tame affair. The effect of Sloane Street on the mind must be to produce at length a disbelief in anything approaching melodrama; and it is even probable that a man born and bred there, were he to become a geologist, would insensibly espouse the Uniformitarian theory of geological phenomena, and scout the Catastrophic. It is well known to students of natural history that many animals—especially certain fishes and birds—seem to borrow their color from that of their habitat. Now the prevailing hue of Sloane Street is gray.

Besides the fact of his living in Sloane Street, there were other reasons why Samuel Hickes should be rather sceptical about the possibility of applying a fragment of melodrama to the affairs of the actual world around him. He had lived, as Arthur Drem pointed out, a colorless and uneventful life, his chief cares being the securing and economical spending of a small income. A man with straitened means has seldom the chance of exercising the heroic passions, unless when he thrashes his wife. A man with plenty of money at his command can afford to indulge the whims of his fancy and affection—he can do mad things, and approach the region of the stage. What is impossible to a man in a narrower and more methodical manner of life (and this impossibility leads him to imagine it improbable in the case of another), is possible to him whose actions are not confined by the limits of so many sovereigns a week. The life of the one is a series of impulses; the life of the other is measured by the slow progress of office hours. And not the least curious feature of this complication was that Arthur Drem, himself educated under these formal conditions, had been led to conceive the possibility of getting beyond them by this very Rotunda drama, in which the author himself disbelieved.

The two oddly-assorted friends had several conversations about the theatrical *coup* which Arthur meditated, and that young man was several times on the point of abandoning the matter in despair over the weak faith of his companion. It was not that he found any difficulty in persuading Hickes that the project was feasible. On the contrary, Hickes admitted readily that his friend's proposal was reasonable, and, at the time, would almost give his assent to it and undertake the singular duty. But on the next occasion that they met, Arthur would be mildly enraged to find that his companion had fallen backward into doubt, and that the old arguments had to be again forthcoming.

At length Hickes said:

"I do believe, Drem, you're wrong. You don't know what stuff those Rotunda plays are, or you'd see that it was impossible to do that sort of thing in real life. It is all very well in the theatre, where you can get everything made to your hand—the hero always comes round the corner at the right moment, and the villain always kills himself at the proper time. However, for a lark, I don't mind doing this: I will go a certain way, just to try."

"You promise that?" said Arthur, who was only too glad to get the engine on the rails.

"A certain way, I say. I will try and get admitted into the Sunday-school. I will try and get introduced to this Miss Seaford——"

"And then?"

"Then I might ask her to marry me, to crown the joke. Of course in the drama she would consent—for I am now acting the hero who is to do everybody a deal of good; but as it is, I wouldn't back my chances with half a sov. And the first steps are not so easy as you think. What do I know about a Sunday-school? You never saw *that* at the Rotunda. And the only clergyman we have there is the Irish priest of the fat, humorous, generous kind—a splendid character to go down."

"Well, you don't need to be afraid of a clergyman; he won't eat you."

So it was that, on a certain warm Sunday evening, Mr. Arthur and his friend walked up to Hampstead. Hickes was rather sulky—partly because he dared not drink anything, and partly because he felt he was being goaded into making an ass of himself. If they had been doing the Rotunda drama in its pure simplicity, he might have felt more confident: but here they were approaching it by unfamiliar paths. Fancy trying to get to a melodramatic climax by way of a Sunday-school.

Sometimes, indeed, he submitted to the soft enchantment of the pictures which Arthur Drem painted for him. He was to touch the heart of this girl by his generosity and piety. He was to point out to her that her duty was clearly to throw over Philip Drem, and restore him to the position in society which he had forfeited for her sake. He was to show her that her path in life were with that of a poorer man, and he was to win this pretty companion for himself. Then there was Mr. Drem, with his check of £2,000 or £3,000, and the grateful Arthur, endowed with a partnership, heaping favors upon him. Hickes dwelt upon this prospect chiefly after his midday dinner, when he drank a good deal of ale, and was smoking a thoughtful and drowsy pipe.

The evening was yet light when the two drew near the schoolroom, the arrangements of which had been unwittingly described to Arthur by Alec Lawson. Mr. Arthur said he would go for a walk over the Heath, and return in an hour.

"You need only wait long enough to see how they go on. Keep up your courage, old boy!"

"I'd rather venture into a fighting-crib in Ratcliffe Highway than into this confounded Sunday-school," said Hickes with an uneasy smile. "I wish I could have a glass of brandy."

"You might as well go in with cloven feet, a tail, and blue fire coming out of your mouth."

"Well, here goes!"

Arthur Drem walked on; and Mr. Hickes went boldly up to the door of the schoolroom and knocked. It was opened by a young girl, of whom he asked if he could see Mr Miall. There came to him a tall, elderly gentleman, with a bald head, a bland expression of face, white whiskers, and gold-rimmed spectacles.

"I hope you will excuse my troubling you, sir," said Mr. Hickes in a hesitating way; "the fact is, I should like, if you have no objection, to see how your classes are carried on."

"By all means," said Mr. Miall at once. "Pray come in."

Hickes followed the clergyman into the place; and the latter said:

"Perhaps you have had some thoughts of joining us? We are always glad to add to our list of teachers."

"I am afraid," said Mr. Hickes with a charming modesty, "that I should betray a greater ignorance than the children in my class."

"We do not profess to be very learned," said Mr. Miall with a smile. "If you think of it, I would suggest your remaining simply as a spectator for an evening or two, to see what our method is. Then, as we have always set lessons, which the teachers as well as the scholars prepare at home—those of them, that is to say, who have no great experience—I think you would find no difficulty in taking the position. Do not let me press you; yet it is a good and necessary work, and the Lord is mindful of His servants."

"I wonder whether Mr. Drew will be pleased?" said Hickes to himself, with a sort of pathetic glance over what he was about to endure.

Yet he did not find this hour pass heavily. He was accommodated with a seat in front of a row of round faces, some of them not particularly clean; and, after the usual religious exercises had been gone through, and the catchising of the various classes commenced; he found it not uninteresting to listen to the odd matter of fact replies which the younger children gave to the questions. The lesson was the story of Eli and the young Samuel; and it was curious to notice how many of the round little heads in front of him had been busy in interpreting the relations between the highpriest and his young assistant by their own experiences. Curious, too, it was to see how tags of other explanations—vacant theological phrases, and so forth—lingered about the small brains, and were brought out to cover the retreat from a dilemma.

"What do you mean?" asked Mr. Miall, who had relieved one of the teachers from his duties to give the benefit of his example to Mr. Hickes, "by, 'Samuel ministered unto the Lord before Eli?'"

"He liked the Lord better than Eli," said one.

"He ran errands for Eli," said another.

Of course an explanation of Samuel's duties in the Tabernacle followed, finishing with the remark that Samuel most likely lay down near the lamp which he had to trim during the night.

"That was very naughty," said a wise young woman of ten, who was vainly nudged to silence by her elder sister.

"Why?" said the teacher.

"He might ha' been burned.

There followed another explanation, and a discourse upon God's calling little children now as well as then.

"Should you be afraid to die?" was the next question.

"I wouldn't, if it wasn't for the doctor," said one small and practical philosopher.

"But the doctor visits you to do you good, does he not?"

"No. He gives you physic."

"But the physic is for your good, is it not?"

"N—no," was the answer, coming rather timidly, as if the philosopher knew he ought to be moral and uphold physic, while certain recollections constrained him to be honest and defy it.

"The physic doesn't do you good?"

"No; for it's bitter to take, and God will make you die whether you take it or not."

Mr. Hickes began to think that, if he got many remarks like this addressed to him, his vocation as a teacher would not be such plain sailing as he had hoped. Nor did he find it very easy to maintain his gravity in listening to certain homely explanations of such phrases as "the ears of every one that heareth it shall tingle," or "And all from Dan even to Beersheba knew that Samuel was established to be a prophet of the Lord." With regard to this last verse, Mr. Miall asked whether Dan was in the north or south of Palestine; whereupon a profound exponent of Scriptural history replied that he was in the Den of Lions.

Mr. Miall now handed over the duties of the class to the official teacher, and, turning to the stranger, observed that he had seen something of the manner in which the teaching was conducted.

"There is not much difficulty, you see, when you know the lesson beforehand."

"But I should be afraid of meeting with a poser in some of these chance replies," said Hickes modestly. "You can't anticipate the odd things they may say."

"No; but you soon get accustomed to them, and treat them as you treat the perpetual 'why' of a very young child. I have a little boy of five who, I can assure you, is a serious trouble to me in that way. It is necessary that he should believe me to be infallible, for I am laying the basis at present of all his moral knowledge, and he must have no doubt that I am absolutely right. But what are you to say to a child who asks you *why* the lining of your coat is blue, *why* the fields are green, *why* the river is blue, or *why* the birds sing? I was telling him the other day that the lark sang up in the sky to cheer his mate, or perhaps to warn her in her nest below; whereupon he instantly said, "But Miss Seaford's lark sings in the brass cage with nothing below." By the way, that reminds me—we have one of our young ladies absent just at present—I believe she has gone down into Devonshire to see some friends—and we have had to apportion her class among the others. Now if you thought of joining us, I should collect this class again."

"But I should be in the way when the young lady returned," said Mr. Hickes.

"Not at all," said Mr. Miall. "We have always plenty of work for willing hands, as it is desirable the classes should be kept small. I find a teacher has not time to get acquainted with his or her class when the lesson has to be hurried over. In any case I could not give you Miss Seaford's class—I think we have no teacher to whom the scholars are more warmly attached; and they would resent being separated from her when she returns. But if you like to take up the class until she comes back from Devonshire, we can then find you some independent sphere of labor."

"Thank you; I am very much obliged," said the young man, whose suavity and modesty and gentleness had evidently made some impression on the kindly clergyman. "Perhaps, however, I had better only look in on next Sunday—I mean Sabbath evening—before actually beginning.

The fact was that Hickes pleaded with his own conscience for this respite, for his stomach turned from the work before him as the stomach of a strong man might turn from gruel. He would go through with the task he had undertaken, but he could not plunge into it all at once. It was with a sensation of unspeakable relief that he shook hands with Mr. Miall, and found himself once more in the open air.

Mr. Arthur soon rejoined him, and Hickes found his friend in the cheerfulest of moods.

"Now," said Arthur, "was there anything easier, once you tried it? A few days ago you'd have said it was impossible to get acquainted with Miss Seaford—now the way lies clear before you."

"Yes; and a pretty way, too," grumbled Hickes. "I'll have to begin and learn the New Testament off by heart."

"You couldn't be better employed," said Arthur, with grim malice; "it will do you a world of good. In the mean time have a cigar, and we will get down to my room, where you can reward yourself for your recent temperance."

When they had at last reached their destination, Hickes was found to be somewhat discontented and sulky. Like most feeble natures, he had a good deal of small cunning, and he was determined that no one should make a cat's-paw of him. What guaranty had he that Mr. Arthur would fulfil the vague promises he had made, in the almost impossible event of his, Hickes's marrying this girl? Might not he find himself saddled with a penniless wife, and the whole Drem family vastly obliged to him, but refusing to acknowledge that they ought to give him a penny?

Other and no less uncomfortable reflections crossed his mind as he walked up to Arthur's lodgings. Hickes was a weak, irresolute sort of man, with no very definite convictions of right and wrong; but, after all, he had a dim sentiment about what was right; and, on the whole, he rather inclined to that. He would prefer doing right, if the right were easy, and if the wrong were not too tempting. He had no conception of any obligation to be honest, to tell the truth, or to respect other people's property; but whereas breaking the law laid one open to the risk of exposure and punishment, doing right was productive of a certain small glow of satisfaction. On the other side, doing what was unfair or dishonest was distinctly unpleasant—it was rather shabby and mean.

Arthur had a notion that they ought to celebrate the success of the first step; and, while his landlady was getting up some supper, he produced a couple of bottles of sparkling Burgundy, one of which he opened.

"Here you are," he said, handing a full glass of seething crimson to his friend. "Here's good luck to our melodrama!"

Hickes could not resist the appeal, for he was very thirsty. He swallowed as much as he could at once without choking, and then he put down the glass with rather a sullen air.

"What's the matter with you, Hickes?" said Arthur, gayly. "Has the singing of hymns been too much for you?"

"I'll tell you what it is, Drem," said the other, "I don't half like this sort of thing. I'm not more thin-skinned than other people but it does seem to me precious mean to go trying to get this girl into trouble. You needn't tell me," he added doggedly; "I say, getting her into trouble. I don't think we can do it; but if we do we ought to be horsewhipped, and that's the long and the short of it. I don't say but what you're right in arguing that in the end it might be better for her not to marry your cousin. Very likely not; and, of course, it would be better, as you say, for him that he should not marry her. But that does not excuse us."

"Why, the singing of the hymns *has* been too much for you!" cried Arthur. "Whoever heard you preach morality in that way before? I declare you are quite impressive; and I foresee a grand career for you at the Sunday-school."

Here the tray with the supper was brought in; and, when the woman had left, Arthur remarked, in a cool and careless way,—

"Of course it is for you to judge; I don't insist upon your doing it. I have already bothered myself too much in convincing you against your will that the whole thing is feasible; and as you would reap more benefit from it than I should, I don't see why I should trouble further. Let us drop it, if you like. As you say, there are difficulties in the way. I undertook to show you that the preliminary difficulties were not so great as you fancied; and I think I have done that successfully—witness the events of this evening. But I can see from your manner that I should have continual trouble in arguing the matter with you, and there is no reason why our friendship should be broken off by some probable quarrel. Let us agree to drop it, from this moment forward. It was not of so much consequence to me, as I have always the chance before me of suceeding to my uncle's business in the case. As for you I dare say you would only be withdrawn from your proper sphere of literary labors by receiving a definite sum of money. Let me give you some of this cold tongue."

Hickes looked up in a hesitating way. He had been advancing these objections chiefly to have Arthur answer them the more strongly and so pacify his conscience. But he did not anticipate that his friend would quietly accept the situation.

"You see," he remarked, "the last time we talked over the matter, it was all theory, and it didn't much matter which way the argument went. But *now* the thing is coming closer, and getting to be practical, and one naturally pauses. I may consider myself as already a Sunday-school teacher. Next Sunday, or the following Sunday, Miss Seaford is coming to this school, I shall meet her. The certanty is that, if I like, I may become acquainted with her. Then there are many ways of getting introduced to the house—by calling on her friends for some subscription, or some such means. Then, as I get better acquainted with her, I may see her home, as I walk that way."

"My dear fellow," said Arthur, "now you are showing your inventive faculty. Didn't I tell you the successive steps would come readily enough when you made up your mind? And take my word for it, the climax we look for, though some distance off, will be reached in the same natural, easy fashion. Look at it as at the top of a mountain—a very striking and imposing thing; but, after all, it is only a matter of half yards."

"Writing these plays is such precarious work," said Hickes, as if he were already putting in a plea with his own conscience. "One never knows what may happen; and if anything did happen, it would be such a comfort and security to have a snug little sum by you."

"And a pretty wife to console you. Depend upon it, Hickes, that the girl will very soon perceive that her marrying my cousin would have been a vast injury to him, and she will be grateful to you for having secured everybody's happiness. She mayn't be very complaisant at first, until she is tamed down a bit."

"Oh, oh!" cried Hickes; "you mean me to marry her by force?"

"Well, not exactly," said Arthur; "but it is possible—one doesn't know."

"You mean really to go in for melodrama? I didn't know when my Rotunda experience was to be called for. Bless you, I know twenty ways of marrying girls by force. There is the grand abduction on the part of the wicked nobleman—carriage-and-pair, with servants in masks; there is the running off with the heiress, a sham priest, and a couple of men with horse-pistols standing by——"

"Don't talk nonsense," said Arthur; "you can choose your own way—you ought to know which is most likely."

"If Miss Seaford and all her friends would only stand for ten minutes on the Rotunda stage, I'd settle the affair directly. *Then* there would be no humbugging about a Sunday-school, and mincing airs, and the 'Land of Canaan.' I do think, Drem, that since the creation of man there has been no rummer thing than this project of yours, of getting a bit of sham drama to run in the same harness with our own affairs."

"There won't be anything sham about the drama," said Arthur, "unless you spoil it. I should like you to tell me how you draw the line between what is possible in a drama and what is possible in life. The line is apparently a broad one in your eyes; I can't see it."

"As I said before, you're stage-struck," retorted Hickes, with a laugh. He was evidently getting over his despondency and conscience-qualms.

"We shall see who is right when you've got a cottage on the banks of the Thames at Mortlake, with a charming wife, and a nice little fortune, with a garden all round the house, and a study in which you can compose dramas for theatres on this side of the water."

"Dramas got out of my new experiences, I suppose," said Hickes, with a hiccough.

"Why not? After your old dramas have taught you what to do in life, you will put your new life back into new dramas."

"Good! good!" cried Hickes, with a woolliness about his speech, for it took but a moderate amount of wine to upset this young man's balance. "That's very good—I take the Rotunda drama, pass it into my own experience, and turn it out again as a more genteel drama for the West End. It's like the circ'lation of the blood—comes in one sort of blood into the lungs, goes out another. Or a machine that takes in c—cats, and produces sausages. Or it's like a magical hat, that takes in raw eggs and turns out a—a pie——"

"By Jove! you're making metaphors sufficient to stick all over a comedy, like a pudding stuck full of raisins. Why don't you get into this brilliant vein when you're writing your plays?"

"Mustn't drink at work," said Hickes solemnly. "I'd be puttin' jokes in, and openin' the people's eyes—I'd be for chaffin' the villain, and makin' the sweet young lady cuss and swear when she burst her gloves. The fact is, I'm not so dull a dog as I look; and if I was to open out on these characters of mine, I'd play old 'Arry with 'em. Law bless you. I'd pay them out for the trouble the've cost me this ma'y a day; and, if I was to get a fortune to-morrow, dash my eyes if I wouldn't sit down and write a burlesque of every blessed man, woman, and child I ever made talk in a drama. And I'd get some clever fellows to take the parts, and b'lesque the actin' too; and I'd have the tragedians, and the old heavies, and the scraggy chambermaids all sittin' in the front row of the orchestra, and I'd watch 'm gnashin' their teeth. Wouldn't I pay 'em out? Tell ye what, Drem —'s a grand notion. I once had an idea of bringin' all the chief people in Shakspeare's plays into a play by themselves; but that's nothin' to this—nothin'! For wouldn't I make it a real scarifier, and have the people told the morality that the upper gallery believes in and practices, and not the clap-trap stuff it applauds? And wouldn't I stick into the play one o' them costermongers, that are satisfied with nothing but superfine sentiment on the stage !—and I'd show him sick wi' gin, and tearin' his wife's hair out, and thrashin' the brats when he gets home. And I'd—I'd—thank you for some so'-water."

These pictures of the revenge of the dramatist on the creations of his brain, and on his patrons, were thus brought to an abrupt conclusion; and shortly afterwards Mr. Arthur put his friend into a cab and told the driver to go to a certain number in Sloane Street.

Mr. Arthur would have been more tranquil in mind had he not begun to see more and more of the vacillation of this young man. That one accustomed to revel in wickedness, and utter the most atrocious sentiments through the bass throat of a capricious tragedian, should be visited with squeamish doubts on a minor question of fairness, was not unnatural; but that he should be determined one minute to carry out this peculiar project, and the next minute to turn away from it altogether, was to Arthur a matter of much anxiety.

CHAPTER XIX.

"Don't you think," said Phillip, as they sat down to breakfast on the morning of their departure, "that it would be very hard to die at Torqnay, and leave behind one the sea, and the clear air, and the sunlight? I shouldn't mind so much dying in a dingy hole in Islington, I think—in a sickly atmosphere, with blinds drawn and bottles on the table. One might almost be glad to get quit of the smell of physic. And going away from here—leaving that blue bay and the green country round about it—seems in itself a sort of little death."

"I am so glad we are getting a beautiful day, though, to leave," said Lilian. "This morning, when I looked out, the sea was green and windy, and over there at Brixham the land was quite hidden behind a mist of rain."

"And when I came down and caught her," said Jims, "she was nearly wud wi' delight, for there was a glimmer o' sun behind the mist."

"And it was so curious to see a light green color beginning to shine through," said Lilian, " the sunlight, you know, breaking on the hills behind the rain; and then the clouds lifted, and you could see the slates of the houses in Brixham glittering across the bay, and the sea changing from green to blue. And now, look! the clouds have all disappeared, and the bay has grown still, and Berry Head has got misty and white out there!

When their luggage had been despatched to the station to be sent on to Totnes by rail—they went down to the harbor, got into a small boat, and were pulled out to the yacht which Mr. Philip had hired. It was to be their last excursion in her —they were to leave her at Dartmouth.

And when the tiny vessel outside the harbor dipped over to the gentle wind that was coming up from the west, Torquay was already receding from them. How fair and stately she looked, seated white and radiant on the summit of her green hills! The morning sunlight shone on the great gray crags, and on the gleaming fronts of the houses, and on the dense foliage around the old abbey; while round at Livermead the masses of red sandstone that finished the curve of the beach fairly burned in the sunshine, over the intense blue of the water. As they got farther out into the bay, a sort of silvery haze seemed to dwell over the place, only broken here and there by the glitter of a window that happened to catch the rays of the sun.

"Oh Philip, we have been so happy here!" said Lilian, with tears coming into her eyes. "Why should we ever go back to London?"

Ah, why? And it seemed to him that behind and encompassing the beautiful and smiling picture that lay before them, there was hidden a darker circle—full of dismay, and trouble, and the weariness of waiting—into which they must soon enter. Why could they not stay here forever? He was almost on the point of confessing to her the tender hypocrisy of which he had been guilty during this brief and happy time; and then he looked at her face and her anxious eyes, and could not.

"You're no fitted to be the wife o' a man that has to battle wi' these times," said Jims, putting his hand affectionately on her shoulder. "Ye mind me o' a white kitten, that likes to play and frisk about a while wi' a reel o' cotton, and then snoozle down afore the fire on a thick rug. What would you think o' a man that could content himself to live a' his life up at the big hotel yonder, and do naething but kick his heels on the grass in the sun, when around him the world is working and storing, and they who have time are up in the great centre o't—in London—fechting in Parliament for them that are otherwise engaged? Them that are working have nae time to think and understand about laws; and yet the laws are crushin' them, and takin' frae them to give to the wealthy idlers in the land what ocht to gang to them that are starvin' for want o' work. The taxation o' the workin'-man should gang to help his poorer brethren, instead o' helpin' to fill the pockets of them that are rich enough already. But folk are beginning to understand the duties o' the capitalists now; and there's many a rare battle to be focht o' mair consequences than Waterloo, or Peterloo either. And wi' a' this coming forward—singing i' the air, as it were—ye would like to have him leeve a' his life down by the shore here, like a limpet on the rocks or a dandelion in the grass!"

"Then there's to be no pleasure in life for anybody!" said Miss Lilian, contemptuously. "For if you happen to have no troubles of your own, you are to go and take up the trouble of other people—who won't thank you. What difference does one man make? If the nation wanted Philip, it would have told him so long ago. He is not of much consequence to it; but—but—he's of some consequence to me."

She glanced timidly at Jims, with an arch look in her eyes and a conscious blush on her face.

"You selfish little heathen!" said Philip. "Do you know what blasphemy against the whole duty of man you are talking? If every single person were to take as an excuse that he individually would not be of much service——"

"I am not going to argue," she said defiantly, changing her position. "You always get the best of me there, because you have been to college; but I know I am right all the same."

"Well, of course," said Philip; since the beginning of time women have been celebrated——"

With that she put her hand over his mouth.

"I have told you before," she said petulantly, "that I will not be called 'women.' You are always putting me in the ranks with all the thousands of women you know; and some day you will be losing sight of me. I don't wish to stand to be compared with everybody you know; I wish to be all by myself. I am not a woman, or a girl, or anybody, or anything, except—just what you see!"

And she threw out her two hands with a laugh, as if she were showing herself off.

"Do you think you could ever be lost in the ranks?" said

Philip, taking hold of a curl of golden-brown hair that was near the white neck. "Wouldn't this be a decoration to single you out? Do you think that Perdita, dressed in her lover's clothes, would have passed muster among Frederick's Pomeranian giants?"

"I don't think Perdita lived in the time of Frederick the Great," said she demurely.

"Perdita lived then, lives now, will live always. When you and I shall have got out of this dream that we call life, Perdita will still be going about with her flowers, and singing her snatches of old ballads."

"I wonder if she ever did live, and if she was happy?" said Lilian "I wonder if Shakspeare ever saw any girl that he thought might be Perdita? Don't you think he must have been desperately in love to have written so tenderly about love?—and don't you think he must have suffered dreadful misery about love to have written so much about that? Other things he could imagine—ambition, or pride, or avarice—without actually experiencing them; but I think he must have been very miserable about some one he loved before he could have written about it."

"Why, what do *you* know of it?" said Philip, with a look of wonder.

"I know only by anticipation," she said wistfully. "I know what I should suffer—if—if——"

She never completed the sentence. It was as if her soul had gone out of her, and was already moving in the years to come. Jims never liked these fits of strange brooding which fell over the girl's eyes, and he invariably interrupted them.

"I'm thinking," said he, "that Perdita had an extra chance of being happy, as there was nae Parliament then to tak' her sweetheart frae her."

"Parliaments are for old men," said Lilian sharply. "I would have no man go into Parliament till he was sixty, and fit for nothing else."

"You are too hard on me," said Jims with a smile.

"Oh, I didn't mean you!" she said anxiously, and at once taking his hand, as if to atone for her indiscretion. "You know I didn't mean you. I ought to have said that no one should go into Parliament who has got any relations, or any friends, or anybody who cares a pin about him."

"But look what such a Parliament would immediately do," said Philip. "They would set to work to destroy all conjugal and domestic ties, and make everybody as miserable as themselves."

"But nobody would pay any attention to what they did," said Lilian scornfully.

"And we should have a very efficient Parliament," said Jims.

So the desultory careless talk flowed on, as they slowly made their way southward with the drowsiness of a hazy sunlight around them, with the blue waves lapping along the side of the boat, and a curl of white at the prow; with a gentle wind just filling the sails, and causing the pennon overhead to flutter. And now they were about to see the last of Torquay and its beautiful neighborhood, for they had nearly reached the point of Berry Head. The spacious blue bay lay behind them; down there, on the left, the Creek of Brixham, with its clustered houses and fleet of smacks; then the white line of Goodrington Sands; then the long brown curve of Paignton beach, on which Lilian had played for many a day when a child; and so round by the sandstone cliffs of Livermead to the massive hills and shining villas of Torquay, with the Thatcher and Ore-stones jutting out from the point.

"Good-by, Tor Hill, and Waldon Hill, and Warbery Hill, and all the houses and trees you have!" said Lilian, standing up and looking with a wistful smile towards the receding shore; "good-by, dear Paignton, with your pretty sands!—good-by, Brixham, with your fixing-boats and your rocks! I wish I could take you all into my arms and kiss you! Good-by! good-by!"

And then, as the great cliffs of Berry Head interposed, and cut off, one by one, the various places on which her eyes lingeringly and fondly dwelt, the smile died away from her lips; and when the last house of Torquay was shut out from her sight she sat down in the boat, and covered her face with her hands, and sobbed bitterly.

The gates of the Old World—the fair world of her childhood and youth—seemed to be forever shut; and there now opened before her another world, full of indeterminate terror and sadness, and the pain of renunciation. What might come she knew not; but she felt that she would have to meet it alone.

"My darling," said Philip, laying his hand tenderly on the downcast head, "we shall see all these places again."

"We shall never see them again, we two together," she said, looking up with a white face.

"If you say anything like that again," said he, "do you know what I shall do? I will have this veritable and actual boat in which you sit turned round, and in an hour or so we shall run into Torquay harbor. Then do you know what will follow, you timid little bird? Mrs. Lawson will be telegraphed for to bring down a special license with her from London; we shall be married in Torquay; and not only shall we see all these places together, but we shall not have them out of our sight ever after; for I shall remain in Torquay, and support my household by becoming—what shall I say?—a billiard-marker? No; I should lose form down here. I shall become a coast-guardsman, and spend the day in leaning over the parapet of the quay and staring at nothing, or I may drive a cab. Do you know there is nothing more probable than that I may have to earn our joint living by driving a cab?"

She looked up with a glance of surprise; and he saw that he had made a mistake. It was not time yet to speak of what was ahead in his affairs. So he adroitly continued the conversation, as if the chance remark had been only a bit of the idle talk in which they had been indulging; and so by and by he won her round into a more cheerful humor.

And now the new line of coast, stretching down into the white haze of the south, opened out before them; and they sailed past the immense cliffs of limestone and rock, which fell sheer into the green water, with here and there a shelf of slate gleaming through the thin veil of mist that the sun had thrown over the land. Spectral and vast loomed these silent cliffs through the heat, their craggy headlands throwing natural bridges out into the water, their steep sides seamed with rugged scars and black lines of caves. Over their smooth summits stretched a faint surface of green, with a few sheep or cattle visible only as specks in the light, while in some sheltered bay the rocks sloped more gently down to the water. There were trees and a cottage or two lying warm and snug in the valley, and a line of white shingle where the dark sea met the shore. From the splendid masses of Sharkham on to Downend Point, these successive promontories and bays were sufficiently familiar to Lilian; and yet she did not care to name them, so strange and unfamiliar they appeared in this dream-like haze. Indeed, at any time, there is something very solemn in the look of the tall and silent rocks that stand unmoved above the great murmuring plain of the waves, and are so still. You cannot but think that an awful quiet has fallen upon them, because they have through so many years held commune with the night and with the stars: and that they have grown mournful because they have looked over the sea towards the gray east, and beheld the mystery of innumerable dawns.

Then, as they drew near the estuary of the Dart, they ran close under the black Mewstone—the solitary jagged mass of rock that stands out in the sea. Far below them stretches the long blue lines of Start Bay, losing itself in a silver mist in the south; and as they turned inward from the sea, they found themselves in the green haven of Dartmouth, with the old-fashioned little town huddled along the side of the steep hill that overlooks it.

Having rowed ashore to Kingswear, on the opposite side of the river, they put up at the Yacht Hotel there; and Jims must needs go out on the balcony to look at the broad stream, the boats, the quaint houses, and the lofty stretches of pasture and fields of wheat that seemed to be tumbling over the chimneys. The midday sun was shining down on the place: but the hills is so vertical that while it remained in shadow, the light only caught here and there on the top of a tree or the slates of a house; and these shone out in yellow from the misty blue behind. A still, sleepy, old-fashioned little place, with picturesque houses and walls built down into the clear green deeps of the Dart, with glimpses of rounded hill and sunny pasture glimmering at the end of precipitous streets, and with a few villas on the outskirts buried in trees, and perched upon the steep rocks that rise from the water.

"This is anither place like Torquay," said Jims. "A man must either have his nóse level wi' his neighbor's doorstep, or else find himsel' lookin' doun his skylight-window. I wonder how they keep the bairns fra flinging stanes down the chimneys."

But Miss Lil, as they sometimes called her, would have no one to say a word against the place; for it appertained to the Dart, and the Dart she had insisted on their seeing before returning to London. She had conducted them all over the neighborhood that she was familiar with; and now, like the proprietor of a merry-go-round, she was going to give them "a good one for the last." When they praised the beauty of the county, she was pleased; but she always said, "You have not seen the Dart yet." And now they were on the very threshold of the mystic and beautiful region; and they were to carry the memory of this day's wanderings with them to London, whither they were bound on the morrow.

"What if it were to begin and rain now?" said Philip, as they sat in the hotel.

"I should make you wait here for days or weeks till it cleared," said Miss Lil, decidedly.

"You talk as if you were the owner of the whole county, you arrogant little woman!" he said; "whereas all that belongs to you is some of the blue of the sea that you have stolen into your eyes by constantly looking out on Tor Bay."

"The Dart is my river," she said proudly. "You talk of those rivers abroad that you have seen. My river is the Dart, and you will see whether it is not prettier than any river you ever saw."

"What shall be my punishment, if I say it is not half so fine as the Danube, for instance?"

"Why, your own blindness," she said, with a toss of her head.

"But you have never seen any foreign river."

"That doesn't matter," she observed sententiously. "I *know* the Dart is the prettiest river in the whole world."

"And I know who is the absurdest little woman that ever looked on the prettiest river in the whole world. I wish I could write poetry, Miss Lil, and I would call you the Wild Rose of the Dart."

"But roses don't grow in rivers, you stupid boy!" she said.

"They grow by the banks of rivers; and isn't that the same?"

"There, again!" she remarked, petulantly. "Whenever I talk common sense——"

"Which isn't often," he interjected.

"You bring logic into it, just to show you have been to college."

"I wish college had taught him simple addition," said Jims, following over a scrap of paper which Philip had handed him. Mr. Philip, on being called upon to say what was the share of the hotel expenses at Torquay which fell to Jims and his young charge, replied vaguely £5. Jims was not satisfied, for he would not entertain the notion that Mr. Philip should pay anything beyond his own expenses; so that Philip was forced to draw up an imaginary bill, which he presented to the old man.

"Three pounds ten and three pounds ten make five pounds!" said he. "I'm thinking ye'll no make your fortune as a clerk."

"Very well," said Philip, getting hold of the paper, crumbling it up, and pitching it into the grate. "You *would* have a statement, and now you're not satisfied. If you want to give me other five pounds, do. Between the two of you, I lead a happy life ; bullying and grumbling from the one, sneers and contempt from the other. Now it is my arithmetic, now it is my logic, that is faulty. When I undertook to come down here, it was to have a pleasant trip, not to go into training for a senior wranglership."

"When you gentlemen have quite done fighting," remarked Miss Lilian with a gracious politeness, "you may follow me to the church out at the point ; " with which she left the room.

The next moment Jims, still looking down from the balcony, cried out,—

"Losh me ! there she is, all by herself, in the ferry.'

"Come along, then," said Philip ; "we shall soon overtake her."

"'Deed no," said Jims ; " I'm for nae mair scrambling among rocks like a partan. I've had plenty o't lately. Gang after her yersel'."

Mr. Philip, rushing downstairs, found that the ordinary ferryboat had left, but that a horseferry with two or three horses and a wagon, was just being pushed off. Without considering, he jumped on to the raft as it was leaving the landing stage, and took his place by the neck of one of the horses. It was an unlucky resolve. The small steamtug which generally drags the ferry across was not in use ; and there were only two men, with long oars, to pull this heavy craft across a broad stream, with a swift current running down. Their plan of operation was to pull the thing up the bank, where there was a slight backcurrent, and then let it float down with the stream to the opposite side ; so that Mr. Philip found himself being slowly taken up the river, while the ordinary ferryboat was quietly plying both ways below. Nor was there much more progress made when the raft got farther over ; and indeed, a more ridiculous spectacle could not well be conceived than he then presented, standing angrily and helplessly, in the middle of the river, with Jims grinning at him from the balcony of the hotel, and with Miss Lil ready to die laughing at him from the opposite side. He shook his hand at her ; in reply, she kissed her fingertips to him in mockery, for there was no one near to see. When at length he gained the opposite shore, and began to scold her for her hard heartedness, she was drying her eyes from the effects of her merriment, and was assuming a more sedate and gentle air, with which to walk into and through the old town.

"If the Dart is your river," said he, "you might find some better means of taking people across."

"Did you never try a horseferry before?"

"No."

"Then you deserve credit for your courage," she said, laughing.

"Like the brave man who first ate an oyster. But wouldn't the oyster have been braver if it had eaten the man?"

With this sort of nonsense being bandied about, he was glad to see that the happy light never once died out of her eyes. She was, in truth, in the brightest of spirits; for she looked forward to charming the hearts of her two companions with the scenery of her pet river as they sailed up in the afternoon. In the meantime the day was warm and fine; and there was overhead a clear intense color, almost as deep as that in her eyes, as she and her companion wandered out to the rugged point on which the old church of St. Pedrock is built, overlooking the narrow channel of the river and the broad ocean. They entered the small graveyard that is perched out on these rocks, and glanced over the brief narratives of deaths by sea and land which were inscribed on the weatherworn tombstones, with pathetic assurances that these poor men and women were only "gone before."

"And here we must bid good-by to the sea," said Lilian, with more cheerfulness in her tone than when she saw Tor Bay fading out of sight. "How blue it is."

They had strolled up from the old church, and the ruined castle to the lonely downs above; and from the summit of the hill they were gazing out on the sea and the far ships. The wind had risen somewhat, and the great blue plain before them, had ruffled streaks of green across it, with here and there the deep purple of a cloud shadow moving briskly over the water.

"Look at it hard," she said to Philip, "and then shut your eyes suddenly, and turn round, and let us go away. And then ever after, when you want to see the sea, you need only shut your eyes and you will see it, just as it is now."

"When I want to see the sea," he said, "I shall look for it in your eyes, not by shutting my own."

And so they turned away and left the sea. When they had gone down to the hillside, and got into the cool shadow of the trees that overhang the road, Lillian stopped and put her hands over her eyes.

"Yes, yes, yes," she cried; "it is all here! Shall I tell you what I see. First, there is the old gray church and the castle, and then the steep rocks going straight down to a little bay, with green water, and rocks, and seaweed, and white sand. Then out there is the sea, blue and green, with a few tiny tips of white; and then, farther out, it gets gray, and there are ships on the line of the sky. Don't you see it too, Philip?"

He took down her hands from her eyes, and held them.

"Look up," said he; and she turned the beautiful, frank eyes towards him.

"Yes," he said, "I can see it all here—every bit. Only the sea that I look at is all blue; there are no clouds near; and it is safe and kind—not treacherous and angry like the one you speak of; and then, besides, it is a sea that I can take up to London, and it will shine there among the smoke, and people will not know where you and I get the sunshine for our house."

"Our house!" she said, almost sadly; and so, to prevent her thinking about this hazardous future, he began to try the effect of various wild-flowers in her hair, and she took one of them and kissed it, and gave it to him. They were so young then, both of them, and overhead the sky was so fair.

By the time they returned, Jims had got luncheon ready, and had provided a suitable and modest repast. Philip grumbled, nevertheless, saying that in honor of the Dart, and of the fair young show-woman who was to be their guide, something more decorative in treatment should have been ordered. You would have thought that this young gentleman had the mines of Golconda in his waistcoat pocket, to hear him speak: whereas the fact was, of the two, Jims was the moneyed man, and Mr. Philip he who ought to have been economical. But Mr. Philip was possessed by the thoroughly masculine notion that one way to please and gratify a woman is to give her ostentatious meals, such as would suit an elderly clubbist; and was not this the last day of Lilian's prilgrimage in Devonshire?

You should have seen the sedate little empress—dressed all in black, with a touch of white muslin round her neck—seated in the stern of the small steamer that was about to go up the Dart. At first she was calm and gracious, suffering herself to be pleased with the cool breeze, and the sunshine, and the moving by the various vessels. But when the tiny steamer had left its moorings—when Dartmouth was slowly left behind, and the wonders of the river began to unroll themselves as they steamed up the green tide—her repose and gentle satisfaction quite left her. She became anxiously delighted, and would give her companions no peace until they had examined every corner and bend of the stream. Now it was,—

"Oh, Philip, isn't it lovely?"

Or again,—

"Look, look, Mr. Lawson! These are the Mount Boone woods; and see how they come down to the river's edge! And that is Dittisham—that cluster of cottages smothered in orchards—and above it is Bramble Torr! Do you see how green the water is with the sea?"

So they sailed up between the overhanging woods, that lay dusky and warm in the sunlight, and had their masses of light foliage mirrored in the smooth stream below. They glided as in a dream past the pleasant banks of this pretty Devonshire river—past the tiny villages, with the gray spire of a church visible over the trees—past steep hillsides with cattle and farm-yards on them—past verdant knolls, surmounted by some big old house. It was all very pretty, doubtless; and perhaps to one who was familiar, as Philip was, with the Scotch lochs and the south German rivers, it was no more than pretty; but they had to vow and swear, both of them, that there was no river like Lilian's river.

At length even the wonders of the Dart came to an end, as the small steamer was finally roped to its moorings outside Totnes towns. And here they found their luggage waiting them at the hotel; and, having wandered about the old place and visited the castle, as in duty bound, they had some tea, and prepared to go out for a pleasant walk in the sunset.

Jims preferred to stay indoors, probably fancying that the two young people would as soon walk by themselves. Philip, however, got an opportunity of telling, in a few minutes' private conversation, of all that had occurred and all that he had concealed. Jims was astonished nearly out of his powers of speech.

"Were ye clean wud, to come down here and spend money, when every shilling was o' consequence to you?"

"Don't you remember Lilian saying something about wishing to have this little trip a time of perfect enjoyment?" replied Philip, as if that were a complete answer.

"Bless me!" said Jims, "if a man is to make a fule o' himself every time a woman asks him!—and I'm sure the lassie would never have allowed it, had she known——"

"That was precisely why I didn't tell her."

"And ye'll catch it when you do!" said Jims, with an angry smile. "'Deed I never heard the like! When you should ha' been saving up every farthing ye had—when you should ha' been looking out for work—to come stravayging down here, and living like a king at that wearifu' hotel in Torquay. I never heard o' sich a daft-like trick in my born days."

"I think I never did anything more sensible all my life," said Philip. "The chances were that she and I should never have an opportunity again—at least, not for a long while—of having such a pleasant time together; and, if I had told her, she would not have allowed it, as you say. What signifies a few pounds?"

"Tell me this," said the old man abruptly. "Do you mean to make your own living, marry a wife o' your own choosing, and be master o' your own coming and going? Or do you only mean to make believe you're doing that—and hang on i' th' expectation o' your father turnin' round?"

"You don't know my father," said Philip, "or you wouldn't speculate on that chance. You might as well hope for Bramble Torr to turn round."

"Then you are positeevely determined to gang your ain gate?"

"Most decidedly," said Philip—"that is to say, I mean to do what that probably would be, if translated into English. I dare say I know what you mean; and I mean to 'gang my ain gate.'"

"I'm no sayin' you're right," said Jims, with grave Scotch caution, "and I'm no sayin' you're wrong. Every man has his ain notion o' what's better for him in this world; and it is no great matter in any case, for it lasts so little a time. But, my certes! if you mean to make your own living, you'll find out that a few pounds is of mair consequence than ye seem to think."

"Probably," said Philip with a fine carelessness. "But the money I spent down here would have been good for nothing in the way of helping me to work. The want of it will be a better spur."

The entrance of Lilian at this time prevented their further talk over the matter. She had on her out-of-door costume, and stood at the door of the room.

"Who is coming?" she said. "It shall be your *valet de place* again."

Philip and she left together. They passed out of the town, and got down to the side of the Dart, by the alders. The great glow of light from the west was shining along the tops of the woods, and farther down the crimson overhead was reflected in the bend of the stream that lay like a line of blood between the green meadows. Most of the birds were silent now; but the blackbird's flute-like note was heard from among the trees down by the river; and occasionally, as they strolled along the narrow path, a thrush would send out a long, clear, wavering thrill from the deeps of the bushes along the bank. They met no one but a young girl, who was coming home with both hands filled with flowers. She bade them "good evening" as she passed, and her voice seemed strange in the silence of the place. For Lilian had spoken scarcely a word since they had left the inn.

"Why are you so very quiet?" he said. "Are you not pleased that our trip has been so pleasant throughout, and has closed so pleasantly?"

"It has been very pleasant, has it not?" she said (her veil was down, and he could not see the expression of her face). "And this is our last evening, and our last walk together."

"For the present, yes," said Philip cheerfully.

She said nothing further for some time, and they had gone down to the bend of the river, where the red color lay, and beyond that there was the dusk of the twilight, from which they instinctively turned.

"Let us go back," she said; and there was something in the tone of her voice, as they turned away from the ruddy stream and the silent trees, that made him regard more attentively the inscrutable veil that was over her face. The hand on his arm had been trembling for some time, and all at once she said, in heart-breaking accents,—

"Oh my love, my love! Shall we never be here again, you and I?"

She turned her face up to him, and he saw now that she had been crying all this time, as they were walking down the river-path. And it seemed to him then that something more was required than the ordinary gentle assurances, to remove the passionate despair into which she was plunged. So he said,—

"Why do you ask that, Lilian? What are you afraid of? Do you know that, before I came down here, I gave up everything in the world for you, so sure I was that we two should go through the world together?"

He then he told her, rapidly and clearly, the position in which he stood towards herself and towards her friends.

He had long dreaded this necessity, and he had pictured to himself what her reception of thèse disclosures would be. She would not consent to this abnegation for her sake; she would implore him to go back to his family; she would be in misery over what had happened, and blame herself for it.

Surely she could not have understood? The veil she had drawn back from her face; and now she looked up to him with a strange, proud, confident look in her eyes.

"Is what you tell me true?" she said. "You have done all this for me?"

"And have I not done right?"

There was an almost wild look—of courage, and joy, and triumph—passing across her face, and she said,—

"I am not afraid now, Philip. It seems to me that you have come so much nearer to me, that I need not be afraid. We will go to London together. It will not make us afraid now, will it? Oh, my dear, my dear, you have made my heart full of love for you!"

Her eyes were wet and wild; yet there was joy shining in them. She turned round to have one last look at the Dart; and then she said to him, in a low voice,—

"A few minutes ago, Philip, I wished that I was lying underneath the stream. You know they say,—

"'Oh river of Dart! Oh river of Dart!
Every year you break a heart!'

and I thought if was mine the river had taken this year, and now I feel so strong and brave, because you have shown yourself so brave; and I am ready—oh, I am ready, my dear, to face twenty Londons, and fight them all for your sake!"

Then he stooped down and kissed her, almost solemnly, and he felt on his forehead the light touch of her lips, as though the wing of a butterfly had touched him. It was the first embrace she had bestowed on him; it was his royal accolade; and there he became her knight, and swore to be faithful to this sweet mistress forever.

CHAPTER XX.

SHORTLY after his arrival in London from Devonshire, Mr. Philip walked from his lodgings in Paddington to a "livery establishment," kept by a certain Mr. Dufton, in Euston Road.

Dufton, in former days, had been coachman to Philip's father; but had, through a quarrel, left Mr. Drem's service and started as a cabproprietor. He had succeeded so well that, in addition to his small and well furnished house that overlooked the stableyard, he had bought a pretty little cottage at Ewell, whither he occasionally sent his wife and children.

At present the family seemed to be at home; for no sooner had Philip been shown into the parlor (the extreme brightness and neatness of which showed that Mrs. Dufton was an excellent housewife), than a small and sturdy young gentleman of about four years of age walked boldly into the room, stood in the middle of the floor, and critically examined the stranger.

"Well, do you know who I am?" asked Philip of the owner of the wide blue eyes that were staring at him.

Having again coolly surveyed him from head to heel the hero of the flaxen hair and the sturdy legs said,—

"Oo is him what belongs to the big dog."

"How do you know I ever had a big dog?" again asked Mr. Philip.

The small gentleman walked to the table, and pointing to a photographic album (which he dutifully refrained from touching), remarked,—

"Him is in here."

Sure enough, on opening the book, Philip found in one of the pages a portrait of himself—a lad of fourteen, with a velvet jacket, shiny boots and a riding whip, standing beside the big dog which had earned for himself the honor of remembrance and recognition from Master Dufton.

"What's your name?" he said to the boy.

"Henry Dufton," he said; adding, somewhat irrelevantly, "The butcher wasn't been to-day."

"Would you like to have a big dog, that could eat up all the bears and the wolves? Wouldn't you be afraid if you saw a bear coming down the street?"

"No," said the young hero valiantly; "me ood like to see a bear; me ood take a gun and bang him!"

"Isn't that a pretty gentleman?" continued Philip, pointing in the album to a portrait of a very High Church clergyman in magnificently colored robes, and with a touch of pink in his cheeks.

"What oo says?"

"I say isn't that a pretty gentleman?"

"Her is a lady," objected Master Henry.

"Did you ever see a lady with a moustache?"

"Her has a gown and 'ticoats on," replied the boy, as if that settled the matter about the sex of the person; and then he added sagely,—

"Her cannot put on her boots and go out, for her is a pitture."

At this moment Mr. Dufton senior entered the room, and was at once greeted by his son's asking him—pointing to Philip meanwhile—"What's him's name?"—a question which he ventured to overlook.

"Law bless me, Mr. Philip," said the small wiry man with the tight trowsers, stiff little collar, and the brown-red face that reminded one of a frosted pippin, "it's a long time since I see you. Times are changed since then, ain't they? You see," he added, looking around the comfortable and cleanly room, "I ain't got much reason to regret the row as 'appened between your father and me, when he throwed the bottle at my 'ed. And I don't bear him no malice, Mr. Philip; and if so be as you want anything in my way, I'll let you 'ave as good a thing as you'll see."

"I do want something in your way, Mr. Dufton," said Philip. "I want you to give me some work."

"Law! you're joking, Mr. Philip!"

"No, I'm not."

"Well-a-day!" said the good-natured Dufton compassionately; "and, as it come to that? Poor old gentleman! It's a bad thing for him at his time of life: and if I can do anything, I will. I don't bear no malice, as I say. And them downfalls will happen to the richest on us——"

"No, you mistake," said Philip. "My father has suffered no change of fortune. He is as rich as ever he was."

"Ah, I see," said Dufton with a sage nod. "A quarrel. Well, if I must tell the truth, Mr. Philip, I'd sooner do you a good turn than him—not that I wouldn't let bygones be bygones if things was come to the worst, and the old gentleman become hard up. But as for my giving you work, Mr. Philip, you must be joking, as I said——"

"I am not at all," said Philip. "I don't propose to start as a cabby all at once; but I want to know that I have that to fall back on, if everything else fails. Do you understand? Now tell me, how much could I earn if I were to persuade you to let me have one of your cabs?"

"You'd have to persuade me first," said Mr. Dufton with a dry laugh. "I don't say as you can't drive, or that you'd be bad to the 'osses—because I know you're all right both ways. But law, sir, I have the character of my cabs to keep up; and think of the chaff you and me would get when you was on the ranks, and didn't know a single place as you was asked to drive to."

"But I could learn that easily," said Philip. "I know a good deal of London; and I could walk about for a few days, and study a map."

"Oh, maps is very fine!" said Mr. Dufton; "but they ain't got brick walls down on 'em. You can go slick through a row o' houses or a brick wall on the map, but your horse wouldn't go. Now suppose you was to come to a brick wall with your cab, what would you do?"

"Turn round, and go back."

"And have your fare cussin' and swearin' at you hawful. Oh, I know plenty of men as thinks it's a jolly easy thing to drive a cab because they know the road from Pall Mall to Charing Cross, or from Waterloo Place to Regent Street. But bless you! if they was to go on a stand, they'd find out they knew no more o' London than the babe unborn. I don't say as I won't give you one o' my cabs, if nothing else is to be done; but I'd rather let you help my clerk, or do some other work—if so be as you're serious about it, Mr. Philip. And it's dry work talkin' like this; and perhaps you won't mind having a glass of sherry wine with me?"

This was only a *ruse* on the part of Mr. Drem's old coachman. He was proud to hear himself called "Mr." by Mr. Drem's son, and he wished to show Mr. Philip all the comfort and luxury that he had fairly earned for himself by his own industry. So he invented this excuse for sending for Mrs. Dufton —a smiling little woman, with rosy cheeks and black hair—who forthwith not only placed wineglasses and cut decanters on the table, but must needs bring in Miss Sissy, a small girl of six, and the baby, to have them shown off. All these three wonders had flaxen hair and blue eyes, like their father; and, indeed, nothing could equal the cab proprietor's pride in exhibiting these and the other ornaments of his snug little household.

"She's the most intelligent child," he said, taking up the baby, and looking at the small lump of soft humanity. "She's only eleven months old, and we can understand what she says perfectly."

To Philip's uninitiated ear all the language the prodigy could utter was "Goo, goo, goo!"— but that goes a long way with admiring parents.

Then there was Miss Sissy, who was not at all so amiable a character as the frank and sturdy young gentleman her brother.

Sissy was conscious of being looked at; was greedy, and knew that the presence of a stranger gave her the whip-hand of her mother. No sooner had she caught sight of Mr. Philip than, standing at some distance, and keeping her eyes on him, she began to say,—

> 'Pity, O Lord, Thy feeble child,
> By sin, alas, too often 'guiled.
> Thou hast 'passion for the weak,
> The boosed reed Thou 'not break.

which was immediately followed by a demand for a "bistit."

"Dear me!" said Mrs. Dufton with a sigh of happiness, "Sissy *will* repeat them hymns—she's choke-full on 'em! Get away, Sissy, and don't annoy the gentleman."

Sissy had gone forward to Mr. Philip's knee, and informed him that she could spell "sugar."

"If you do," said Philip, "I'll give you another biscuit."

"Thus encouraged, Sissy began; and keeping an eye on her mother's face, said tentatively, "B, u, t, t—." Something in her mamma's expression told Sissy she had gone wrong; so she instantly changed the direction of her efforts, and said,—

"M, i, l, k, sugar; and Samson was the wisest man, and Moses was the strongest man, and Sommon" (presumably Solomon) "was the man wis the longest hair. Sissy ood rather have a piece of sugar than another bistit."

Indeed, Sissy sulkily refused the biscuit which Philip offered her, and said to her father,—

"Sissy want a piece of sugar, dada!"

The father, finding no sugar obtainable, and seeing a storm brewing in the distance, proposed that Sissy should go upstairs and play a tune on her papa's concertina. These Chiltern Hundreds of infancy were accepted by Sissy, who, like 'some more elderly people elsewhere, made a pretense of retiring into private life only to make more noise than ever. The remainder of Philip's interview with the cab proprietor had a running accompaniment of melancholy howls and squeaks from the chamber overhead, representing the torture of the concertina; while the more thoughtful and manly Henry sat still and quiet on the hearthrug, watching Philip's face narrowly, and only interrupting the conversation by an occasional appeal to his papa in these words,—

"What him says?"

Perhaps the glass of sherry had thawed Mr. Dufton's cold calculation of Philip's chances; for when Sissy and her mamma had left the room, he admitted that, after all, a knowledge of London streets would not be difficult to learn.

"You can always ask your way, *after the fare is inside.* You get him inside, and make sure of him, and then you can ask the nearest pleeceman."

"And how much do you give your drivers?"

"I don't pay them no salary," said he. "I lets 'em have the cabs for so much, and they make what they can get. Sometimes it ain't much, if they have a bad day or night; and there's some on 'em so slow in catchin' the eye o' people, that they miss hall their chances. And there's others as is always dawdlin' in publics, and leavin' the cab on the stand, and when fares come they take the next cab. That's one on 'em, just come into the yard there for his second 'oss. He's one of the few as have two 'osses a day, and little he does wi' em—except at the stations early in the morning."

"Well," said Mr. Philip suddenly, "let me have that cab for the rest of the day, that I may see how much I can get."

"It ain't mine," said Dufton; "he's hired it."

"Here's a couple of sovereigns you can give him for the loan of the cab."

Dufton looked at Mr. Philip with some suspicion, and with a twinge of anger. Was a man applying for work likely to have sovereigns running loose in his pockets? And was the whole matter a joke?

"If this 'ere is a lark, Mr. Philip," said he, looking at the two sovereigns, "I think you might ha' spoken more plainly."

"It is no lark," said Philip. "Do you wonder I should have money? A man need not be penniless because he wants to work. See—I will leave the two sovereigns with you, to make what arrangements you like; and you will let me have the cab from now until the evening."

"You couldn't go out drivin' a cab in that 'ere coat and hat," said Mr. Dufton with a smile.

"You can lend me both," said Philip, as carelessly as if it were in the olden time of his ordering everybody about.

"They wouldn't half go on you."

"Then the man who was driving the cab can lend me his— he is as tall as I am, I should think."

So Mr. Dufton descended to the stables. It was not the first time he had obeyed the whims of a certain young gentleman.

In less than half an hour Mr. Philip was perched on the

box of the handsom, rigged out in a sun-faded brown coat and a glaze billy-cock hat. When he drove out into Euston Road, he had an uneasy consciousness that he should laugh in the face of any one who might hail him, and rather hoped that nobody would. His speculations on that point were disturbed by the angry admonition of a policeman, who wanted " none o' that ere crawlin' ; " and so cabby had to touch up his horse and move on at a brisker rate.

" Cab, sir ? " he said to an old gentleman who was standing at the corner of Albany Street.

He felt rather ashamed of making this white haired old gentleman the subject of a joke ; but, to his surprise, the clergyman—for such he was—nodded. Mr. Philip drew up by the curbstone. His fare got inside, and cabby opened the little port-hole by which prayers and supplications arise from those condemned to temporary punishment below. Mr. Philip inwardly trusted he should not have to drive to Islington—the part of London of which he knew least.

" Eccleston Square," said the fare.

" Right, sir," said the cabby, delighted to get an "easy one" to begin with.

No accident befell them on the way ; and at the prescribed number the passenger got out.

" What is your fare ? " said the old gentleman mildly.

Here was a problem which neither Mr. Philip nor his employer the cab proprietor had thought of; he knew only the fares for such distances as he had been accustomed to drive himself.

" Leave it to you, sir," he said, touching his cap.

" What is your fare, young man ? " repeated the clergyman severely.

" I don't know, sir. I suppose it is about three miles."

" I cannot remain in conversation with you on the pavement, as you ought to know. It is your business to inform me what I should pay you. If you do not care to do so, I will go inside."

" Then suppose you give me two shillings."

" I do not think the charge exorbitant," remarked the clergyman, tendering the half-crown.

" Then you might give me another sixpence to drink your honor's health," said Philip, touching his cap again.

" I will encourage no such practice," replied the clergyman, going up the steps to the house.

So the somewhat listless Rosinante between the cab shafts was slightly admonished with the whip, and our hero set forth in quest of new adventures.

CHAPTER XXI.

The more Arthur Drem saw of his friend Hickes, the better he understood how to manage him. Like most men of weak nature and confused perceptions Hickes would trot peacefully and evenly along a well known road, but would shy like a frightened horse if he saw anything new or startling in the way. Mr. Arthur had therefore to lead him up gently to such obstacles, show him there was nothing dangerous about them, and so coax him onward to the next stage. Whenever he looked forward to the climax of the journey, and spoke of it, Hickes recoiled from it in mingled dismay and derision; but when Mr. Arthur merely contemplated the immediate and practicable steps with which both were familiar, Hickes was content to do as he was bid.

This was very singular; for these steps were useless, and a cause of a great deal of unnecessary trouble, if the future climax were impossible. Mr. Arthur's object during this time was to keep his friend from looking forward altogether, and put his present action in the light of a harmless prank.

"After all," he said, "you can suffer no injury by becoming intimate with such a pretty girl as I hear she is."

Mr. Arthur's faith in the practicability of his scheme had grown more assured with time. All his previous doubts were gone now. The Rotunda drama had at first only captured his imagination; and he had the most admirable belief in the processes of his own logic. At times, when Hickes would indulge in a little anticipation, even he caught a faint warmth of enthusiasm from the ardor of Arthur's convictions. He was only dissatisfied as to the means. He did not believe in the drama. Yet an extraordinary difference in his manner was produced when he found himself in the second scene of the living comedy or tragedy which Mr. Arthur—at once his pupil and teacher—had so boldly sketched out. He had now become acquainted with Lilian Seaford, and he came down to Arthur's lodgings, radiant and triumphant, to announce the fact.

"What did I tell you?" said Arthur coolly. "Was there ever anything more easy and natural?"

When Hickes began to speak of the girl, and to describe her beauty, his somewhat expressionless eyes and face brightened up with a dull glow of admiration.

"I told you that also," said the imperturbable Arthur.

"But you have no idea how pretty she is," said Hickes; "nor would you have if I were merely to tell you what she is like. You must see her. I have often read what would pass as descriptions of her, you know—very dark blue eyes, a high white forehead, lots of hair of a sort of—sort of—sort of——"

Hickes waved his hand in the air, in default of words.

"I know," said Arthur.

"But all that tells you nothing."

"Not much," said Arthur.

"Then her manner—to the children, especially. She was like a small mother to them; and she laughed once or twice at some absurdities of their answers, and I'm hanged if I didn't wish I was in her class."

"That she might laugh at you?"

"No; you mistake. There was nothing cruel in her laugh —it had the same sort of frankness that she used in speaking to you, quite frank and simple, you know; and apparently not caring to think what you thought she might be thinking of——"

"Hickes, you must have gone straight to the public-house on coming out," said Arthur, reprovingly.

"I didn't—I couldn't. You may laugh as you like, but I declare that, when I left that schoolroom, I wished I was a deal better fellow than I am, and I wished I could go back and tell her so; and when I came to think of you——"

"Well, what did you think of me?"

"That it was a confounded shame——"

"What was a confounded shame?"

"Why—you know, I was nearly throwing up the whole affair on the spot."

"Well, you are the most vacillating and illogical creature I ever met. You think you ought not to marry a girl because you find her pretty and pleasant in her manner. If she had been plain and a dragon, you would have seized the other excuse. But you have not told me how you became acquainted with her."

"Simplest thing in the world. I was to be merely a spectator this evening, as before, and so I went up to the place. I was rather before the hour; and while I was loitering about, in comes a young lady dressed in deep black, with a black veil over her face. Everybody crowds round her, and shakes hands with her, and she is laughing and talking with them all at once. She lifts up her veil—I see a charming face and the prettiest pair of eyes—and then somebody calls her 'Miss Seaford.'"

"Quite dramatic," observed Arthur. "You might put it in a play."

"*You* might; my clients wouldn't stand anything so weak. No; I should have had her come on the stage from the top of a house on fire or carried on in a fainting fit, by me, her lover; or——"

"Well, to continue."

"To continue. I hung about the various classes, while the performance was going on, by way of gaining experience. I sat down near her. She lent me a book and told me where the lesson was."

"Of course you looked very modest and pious, very amiable and good-natured."

"You don't believe in modesty, or piety, or anything else, but I do," retorted Hickes, whose vibratory nature had not yet shaken off the influences of the schoolroom and of Lilian's unconscious kindness. "I tell you frankly that I thought you and I were two confounded scoundrels."

"Perhaps you are right," said Arthur; "but it is no matter; go on."

"I was very near telling her all about it."

"She would have had you arrested as a dangerous lunatic."

"But at the same time I thought I might as well make her acquaintance if I could. One does not often get the chance of speaking to such an amiable and nice-looking girl, I can tell you. And so I put the book, by accident, into my pocket, and forgot to go near her during the rest of the service."

Across the rather vacuous face of the young man, which had been a few seconds before quite penitent and earnest in its expression, there came a brief smile at this stroke of cleverness.

"Then you overtook her on her way home, and gave it to her?" said Arthur.

"No, I did not. I kept behind her on her way home—she went the roundabout way by East Heath Road—until I saw her knock at the door of the house. Then she entered. I went up immediately afterwards, and asked if I could see Miss Seaford for a moment. The maid-servant looked rather surprised, said that Miss Seaford had gone upstairs, and would I walk into the parlor?"

"The fly inviting the spider. Well?"

"Of course I went in. There an old gentleman with white hair, and rather a fierce look about his head, turned on me, and I wished that I was out of the house. I'd have given twenty pounds to be out of the house. Mind you, you may think it very good fun, but it was uncommon awkward to go like this into a bear's den, and not have a word to say for yourself."

"Didn't you say you had called with the Testament, or whatever it was?"

"Certainly I did; but not until I had stood in the middle of the floor, looking like an ass, with my throat choking. You say my experience in inventing awkward situations and getting out of them should prepare me for anything. That's all very well while you're in your own house with a pen in your hand; but when you're in another man's house, with him looking as if he was going to eat you, it's different—precious different. I'd rather have faced an alligator with jaws as long as Southend pier. Everything behind my eyes began to swim round, so that I could neither look in nor out for anything to say or do; and then at last, I stammered and bungled, and hoped that Miss Seaford would accept my excuses for my carelessness in carrying off her Bible from the Sunday-school. Sir, that word was my salvation. The enemy began to thaw. He said something about the school, and at this moment Miss Seaford entered the room, and, though she appeared a little amazed—as may have been natural under the circumstances—she was very gracious, you know, and accepted my apologies, and tried to make the thing rather pleasant. So did the old gentleman; for he asked me to sit down, and then he began to unfold his views on all sorts of religious points connected with establishments and what not. I was in a precious fog."

"I dare say," said Arthur.

"And so would you have been," returned Hickes, rather angrily. "Who was to know what an Episcopalian was? I began to think that Henry VIII. had precious little to do to kick up such a dust; and that his eight wives——"

"Six," said Arthur.

"Well, what's the difference, when you go in for a lot? I

wish they had given him something else to do, as I say. Luckily the old gentleman had most of the talking to himself; and I had only to sit in a sort of mist, and hope he would ask no questions. Then Mrs. Lawson came into the room, and I was more afraid of her than of the other two. She has sharp eyes, that woman, and she looked at me from head to foot, until I began to feel quite weak, and quaking along the back. Talk about an ordeal!—the Spanish Inquisition was nothing to this. All I could do to escape from that woman's eyes was to pretend to be greatly interested in what the old gentleman was saying; and so I had councils, and popes, and Scotch Covenanters, and James II., and Archbishop Wolsey——"

"Cardinal Wolsey, if you please."

"And Charles I., and Carlyle—I mean Cromwell—all dancing quadrilles within my head. And sometimes the quadrille was changed into a regular cracker of a waltz, round and round; and then all of a sudden I'd catch sight of Mrs. Lawson's eyes, and these confounded gyrations inside my head would stop in a second, and I'd be wondering if she saw anything in the shape of my necktie to tell her that I knew you."

"Why all this is splendid material for you," cried Arthur. "You are amassing experiences for future dramas."

"Rubbish! How could I put that into my dramas? Would you have the principal actor open his head on the stage to let people see what was inside?"

"No; they would hiss the blankness of the show. But you ought to try something different from merely rearranging these eight puppets you speak of."

"We will discuss that some other time," said Hickes, fortifying himself with another glass of Arthur's claret, as if the present business he had in hand was sufficient worry to have before him. "I was going to tell you that my listening so meekly to Mr. Lawson had apparently produced a good impression on him. He wanted me to stay and have some supper with them; but as neither Miss Seaford nor Mrs. Lawson seconded the invitation—indeed, I will go the length of saying they looked a trifle surprised—I did not consider it prudent to remain. Old Lawson, however, said I might always come in there and rest when I was up in the neighborhood; and so, thanking them all, I left and came down here."

"In excellent spirits," said Arthur, "over the discovery that your future bride is fairer even than you imagined."

"Ah" said Hickes, moodily, "that's another thing."

"What do you mean?"

I mean," said Hickes, lazily stretching out his legs, and speaking in a determined tone, "that I have had enough of this thing. If it is only a lark, as you say, it has gone far enough. At least, it has gone far enough *for me*—you may carry it on, if you like."

There was an interval of dead silence. Mr. Hickes looked at his boots; Mr. Arthur bent in two the penholder he had in his hand, to prevent himself flying out into a rage. It was not the first time his irresolute companion had suddenly assumed an air of resolution; but on this occasion he seemed more in earnest than he had ever been before. Mr. Arthur treated the matter with much apparent indifference; said it was of more importance to Hickes than himself; hinted that perhaps Hickes was right in considering their scheme impracticable; and finally changed the subject altogether by proposing a game of chess.

The table and pieces were brought and the game commenced. Hickes was at no time a brilliant player; but as he now played, or pretended to play, the keen eyes of his opponent easily perceived that something other than the taking of pawns or the development of an attack on the white king was uppermost in the weak young man's mind. Indeed Mr. Arthur was content to let this growing discontent increase, rather than again open the matter; and, as he expected, Hickes himself suddenly reverted to the subject of their previous talk.

"The first steps, I grant you, were easy enough," he said, "quite easy. I admitted that from the beginning. But now we are at a dead stop."

"You can't castle out of check," remarked Arthur, keeping his whole attention on the board before him.

"I beg your pardon," said Hickes hastily, and sifting his king into the next square.

"That square is commanded by my queen," observed Arthur.

"Bah! of course!" said Hickes impatiently, and then he managed to get out of his chess difficulty.

"You were speaking of that affair with Miss Seaford?" said Arthur carelessly. "Ah, well perhaps it would be a risky matter. It is true that nothing could be more certain than the hold you would have over my uncle, if you succeeded. Every day he is becoming more wretched about Philip's absence. He does not say so, but I know it; and I know that anybody who removed the cause might dictate his own terms.

"Confound it!" said Hickes, "you are always dangling

that before my eyes, as if you meant me to murder the girl. I'd very nearly do that as soon as the other thing you propose."

"Murdering her *would* smack a little too much of the Rotunda, wouldn't it?" said Mr. Arthur with a smile. "In the meantime may I inform you that a knight does not generally jump from a black square to a black, and that it is unusual to have both one's bishops on the same color?"

Hickes regarded with dismay the mess into which he had got his pieces, and gruffly withdrew from the table.

"Let us sink this stupid game, and have a talk."

"I should have given you checkmate in two moves," observed Arthur, as if the game were of greater consequence.

"I say we have come to a dead stop. I have become acquainted with the girl; I should like well enough to marry her—but where is the chance of such an impossible thing? You say she is engaged to marry your cousin. Perhaps she is married to him already. In any case, is it not absurd to think of carrying on this wild speculation any farther? As I say, we have come to a dead stop."

"You mean *you* have," said Arthur. "I have nothing to do with it—beyond giving you my advice as to a possible way of bettering yourself—of securing for yourself a pretty wife and a tolerable slice of fortune. As to the project having come to a dead stop, that is a matter of opinion. I do not see that it has."

"You don't see that it has!" exclaimed Hickes with a burst of anger. "Then, you're either blind or mad, that's all! Why, what on earth would you do, if you were in my case?"

"Rather, what would you do, if the same problem confronted you in a drama?"

"In a drama!" repeated Hickes, with bitter irony. "I would kill your cousin, perhaps. Or I would carry off Miss Seaford by force. Or I would make her swear an oath to marry me——"

'Then why not make her swear an oath to marry you?"

'Because she wouldn't be such a fool," said Hickes, contemptuously.

"Would she appear a fool in the drama?"

"Well, no. Because I could get her into a predicament, and frighten the life out of her, and extract the oath from her."

"Why not do all that up at Hampstead?" said Arthur, looking with cold, careless eyes, upon his companion.

Hicks stared in silence.

"Don't look at me as if *I* were the devil," said Arthur.

"I believe you are," returned the other, jumping from his chair, and beginning to pace up and down the room.

Arthur sat still, apparently quite indifferent to what was going on, and yet keeping an eye on the strange alterations of expression which crossed Hickes's face. At one moment he would be serious in look, with his breath going rapidly, and his finger twitching a button nervously; then the next minute he would throw his hands out and laugh derisively, as if dismissing the phantom project that had arisen before him. When he finally stopped before Arthur, there was an excited flush on his usually dull face; but he still had a sceptical smile on his lips.

"It is a capital notion," he said, "for a drama. But suppose I were to corner that girl, as you suggest—suppose I were to frighten her into swearing she would marry me—do you know what the result would be?"

'Yes," said Arthur; "she would marry you."

'Quite the reverse," said Hickes, with a scornful laugh. "The old gentleman who talks about the Covenanters would come down and punch my head—that would be the result."

"What then? Suppose he did punch your head; that wouldn't matter much, if she married you all the same."

"She wouldn't do anything of the kind."

"She would keep her oath."

"She wouldn't be such an uncommon ass."

"There you mistake. An oath has probably no sanctity for you; but such an oath as you *might* dictate to a girl brought up as she has been, she would keep, though it would involve the sacrifice of her life."

"Perhaps," said Hickes, dubiously. "But that only shifts back the impossibility another step: because, if she would keep such an oath, rather than swear it, she would sacrifice her life."

"You needn't threaten *her* life in order to get her to take the oath," said Arthur. "You would have more chance in threatening to destroy your own if she did not consent. Don't you see?"

"I see a good situation for the Rotunda," said Hickes, sinking helplessly into a chair, "nothing more."

The extreme excitement and agitation which the conjuring up of this vision had produced, suddenly left him, and with the reaction he had become mentally quite limp and flaccid. He asked for another cigar, anxious to get something trifling and immediate to do. When he held up the taper to light it, Arthur noticed that his companion's hands were white, and trembling nervously, even to the shaking of the cigar.

'What is the betting on Bluebeard for the next Derby?" said Arthur; and he was himself startled—not so much by the odd irrelevancy of the remark as by the sound of his voice.

Hickes sat silent for several minutes, and then he roused himself with a violent effort.

"I'll tell you what it is," he said. "I believe I should grow mad if I had that idea you mentioned always before my mind; mad enough, at least, to go on with it and venture everything for it. I once heard it said that a man would grow mad if he kept thinking about what some people say—that the world never had a beginning; and that the mystery would possess him so that he would be certain to commit suicide in the hope of discovering the truth."

"If he did not discover the world's beginning," said Arthur, with a rather ghastly effort to be jocular, "he would at least discover his own end. But I never knew such a despondent fellow as you are—talking about murder, and death, and suicide, when you are looking forward to marrying a charming girl, and enjoying yourself with a lot of money! You should be thinking of your wedding-trip, rather—down to Herne Bay, let us say; or will you cross the water? For myself, I wouldn't advise you. Newly-married people shouldn't start off for Paris just directly they are turned out of the clergyman's hands, because the bride is likely to have all her notions of the heroism of her husband destroyed by watching him become a helpless and ignominious lump as soon as the vessel begins to pitch; and I don't think *she* is likely to be any the prettier if she gets sea-green, and asks faintly to be taken downstairs. Better look at the waves, Hickes, my boy, from the solid earth of Herne Bay. Can she sing, do you know? I picture to myself her and you living in a cottage, window open; you smoking on the sofa, she playing the piano; both of you as happy as two pigeons. And when one of you gets up and goes to a table and opens a desk, I know whom you are going to write to; it is to Arthur Drem, Esq., Mincing Lane, London, E. C.; and you say you will be happy to see him down on the following Friday, with his 'Friday till Monday bag' with him. And you think he won't be jolly glad to go?"

Hickes looked up as if he had neard nothing, with a dazed look in his eyes.

"I think," he said, slowly, "if I were to become fond of that woman, and if she were to look me in the face and tell me that I had destroyed the happiness of her life, I would shoot myself."

"More suicide!" said Arthur, gayly. "You are mistaking your vocation in life, Hickes. Tragedy is not your line. You excel in drama, and you might in comedy—only there is not an audience for genteel comedy at the Rotunda. As to your getting fond of Miss Seaford, no doubt you will. You spoke of her with quite the rapture of a lover when you came in to-night. How could you live in the same house with her without becoming fond of her? And as for her reproaching you—and I honestly admit that she may be a little angry at first—she will see in time that everything has happened for the best, and for the especial good of them she cares most about. Bear that in mind, Hickes. Cheer up, lad! None but the brave deserve the fair!"

Hickes said nothing, and in a few minutes left the house. When he had got outside he paused, and vaguely looked up and down the silent street, with its lines of gas-lamps. The sky was dark overhead, and there was a high wind blowing. Although the night was warm, he trembled slightly; and as he walked away he buttoned his coat around him, as if to assure himself that it was only the wind that made him shiver.

CHAPTER XXII.

WE left Mr. Philip in Eccleston Square. When he turned his horse round, he had no very clear idea as to what he should do next, or as to the most likely place for touting in the neighborhood. He was divided between the wish to make as much money as he could that afternoon, and really see whether he could compete with professional cabmen, and with a vague desire to have the fun of driving through the haunts most familiar to him, and looking at the people he knew. By the by the great ebb and flow of carriages would begin in the Park, and he only regretted that he could not, in his present disguise, join the stream.

As he was turning the corner of Gillingham Street, he observed a man standing at the door of a house with a large picture-frame in his hand. He drove down that way, and was immediately hailed. The small brown-faced, bearded gentleman, having put the picture carefully into the cab, told Mr. Philip to drive to New Bond Street.

Just as he was getting into the vehicle, a small crowd that had gathered on the pavement appeared to be shaken with laughter over something remarkably interesting that was happening in its midst, and both Mr. Philip and the artist stopped to have a look. The crowd consisted of a lot of big, hulking, idle fellows, who had been attracted to the show from Vauxhall Bridge Road. There was much cheering and howling; and presently the circle of dingy ragamuffins moved into the road in front of Mr. Philip's horse. The cause of the excitement was now visible; two very small boys had been provoked into fighting, and the men were goading them into further display of their science. Neither of the children was above eight years of age, and one of them had his face covered with blood; while the method of their fighting was to catch each other by the hair, and tug and struggle until both fell into the road, whereupon the men would pick up the bewildered infants, set them on their legs, and urge them to renew the fight.

"Disgusting brutes!" cried the man with the frame.

Now on the right of Mr. Philip's horse there were three men who were particularly active in the matter; and these three men happening to stand in a row, displayed three grossly fat and bare necks above their greasy coat-collars. The opportunity was too tempting. Across that line of dirty human flesh the thong of a cabman's whip came suddenly down; while an appalling yell, rising simultaneously from the three men, startled the crowd into forgetting the children altogether. A splendid uproar ensued, for the sufferers, smarting with rage and pain, called on their fellows, and made a dash at the cab and the cabman. There was but one way of escape. With a sharp touch to the horse's neck, Mr. Philip sent the animal straight in among them, scattering them on each side, and knocking down at least one. He just managed to get clear of the two small boys, and then he sent the horse forward. A man was hanging on behind, and trying to get up into the box. Him he easily disposed of with a decisive tap from the butt of his whip on the top of his cap. The last that Mr. Philip saw was a stone going through the window of a shop near the corner—a weapon which had doubtless been aimed at himself. Then looking down through the trap-door in the roof of the cab to see if his fare was all right, he caught a glimpse of the little brown man rubbing his hands with delight, and grinning all over his face with ferocious glee.

"My good fellow," said the artist, when they arrived in Bond Street, "your fare is eighteen-pence, I suppose. Here is half a crown for you. The yell from those ruffians was magnificent—magnificent—worth five shillings, in fact, if I could afford to give it to you."

"Thank you, sir," said Philip, touching his hat. "Glad they didn't overtake us, or they'd have been down on that ere picture o'yours."

While he was thus speaking to the artist, and receiving the half-crown, he became aware that two ladies were looking at him. When the picture had been got out, and he was now ready to receive fresh commands, he turned to these two ladies. One of them was Mrs. Drem, the other Miss Kingscote; and both were regarding him with horror and dismay.

"Oh, Philip!" said Mrs. Drem, coming forward to him, with her face quite pale, "what do you mean by this? It is too cruel of you—too cruel! Why did you not tell your father, rather than threaten him in this way?"

"You mistake altogether," said Philip from his box; "it is no threat at all. I am only trying whether I can earn myself a living this way, and what sort of one. I had no idea in the world of meeting you; and, to tell you the truth, I can't stop here talking to you under two shillings an hour."

"I will give you two shillings—twenty pounds—anything —if you will only come down, and come home and change those dreadful clothes you have got on. Do you know that Mary Thormanby and Captain Dering are in the silversmith's shop over there?"

"Getting the wedding-ring, I hope," said Philip.

"If they come out and see you, they will publish your disgrace over the whole world."

"I don't mind if they do, if only they will pay me for the copyright. What disgrace is in it. But, you know, I can't stop talking to you."

For indeed a policeman came along at this moment, and stared at the cabman who was having a conversation with two fine ladies.

"My fare is three shillings, mum, neither more nor less, mum," remarked Mr. Philip.

"Oh, what shall I do?" said the timid little Mrs. Drem to her companion.

Violet Kingscote had been standing somewhat demurely on the pavement, with the suggestion of a laugh in her bright dark eyes, but still hoping that her father's coachman—seated on the box of Sir James's brougham, a few yards farther down the street—might not recognize Mr. Philip.

"If you like," said Violet, "I will send Richards and the carriage home, and Philip can drive us somewhere where you can talk with him."

"Oh, thank you, darling, if you will be so kind!" said Mrs. Drem effusively; and this course was immediately adopted. Richards thought his young mistress was mad; but he received her commands as gravely as though he had been ordered to drive to his own funeral. As Mrs. Drem and Miss Violet got into the cab, and as Mr. Philip again woke up his industrious but rather languid horse, Mary Thormanby came out of the shop opposite.

Philip had but one glance at the figure and face he knew so well. It would be affectation to say that he did not suffer some quick flutter or spasm of the heart in catching sight once more of the pale fascinating face, and the eyes that had at one time held his whole future in them. He used to try to read there what was in store for him, as if they were a book inscribed with the decrees of destiny. And now another man—for there was the patient and heavy Captain just behind her—was reading the same book, and tracing out in its mystic characters a special revelation to himself. You can never get a man to believe that the language he finds in the eyes of the woman he loves is a language common to the whole race of mankind—that it is as simple as a big A B C—and that one man can read it as easily as another.

Fortunately she did not see him. Mrs. Delaney, who was also of the party, called the attention of her niece to some article in the silversmith's shop, and so the gray eyes were turned in another direction. Mr. Philip drove on, not regretfully, yet rather saddened by the recollection of old times which her unexpected appearance had called up.

"Where shall I drive to?" he asked through the small trap-door.

"Anywhere," said Miss Violet.

"I warn you," he said "that you will have to pay handsomely for this conversation. You should consider whether it is likely to be worth the money."

"My dear," said Mrs. Drem, "I don't care if it is fifty pounds. I am only anxious to save you from this disgrace."

He drove up to the west side of Regent's Park, and there paused in a deserted nook.

"You may have the glass down and speak to me through the trap, if you would rather not be seen," observed Mr. Philip.

They decided on getting out, however; and so Mr. Philip got down from his box. Mrs. Drem was very much agitated; but Violet, looking at his costume, could not held laughing.

"You must have employed an artist, Philip," she said, "to paint everything in the proper color. But he has forgotten your hands; they are far too white for a cabman."

"You should be ashamed of yourself, miss," said he gravely, "to go about in your silks and your satins, and laugh at the clothes of people poorer than yourself. A poor but honest man is above such sarcasm, which is unbecoming to a sweet young lady, and she not out of her teens. And I'll drink your good health, miss, if you'll be so kind——"

"Here is something for you, my dear man," she said, picking a sixpence out of her pocket; "but I thought poor and honest people never drank anybody's health."

"But this is distressing!" broke in Mrs. Drem, with a piteous expression of face. "It is no joke, Violet, and you, Philip, should not encourage her. What would all London say, if the story were to be told to-morrow? What would all your friends say, Philip—how could you ever meet them again? Think of the men at your club."

"Indeed it's true, ma'am," he remarked. "I shouldn't be standin' here a-talking to you, when I've a job to get the shilling saved every week for my club. And I hope, ma'am, that I shall be moral, and not drink that ere goose before it's paid for; for what should I do at Christmas without the goose and the bottle of rum, and only a shilling a week, although it's not more than five on us out o' thirty subscribers as ever sees it? My fare is eighteen-pence, ma'am, and sixpence for waitin'."

"Philip, your father——"

"I hope the old gentleman is very well, ma'am."

"Philip?" she began again; and then she broke out into a vexed and angry laugh, and turned away. "I leave him to you, Violet—I give him up."

Whereupon Miss Violet assumed an air of responsibility, and said,—

"Once for all, Philip, you do not mean to become a cabman, do you?"

"Certainly not," said he, "if I can find anything more lucrative to do. But employment is not very plentiful in London, and I am anxious, above all things, not to starve. The life of a cabman does not seem to me unpleasant in weather such as this, but I am willing to give up its freedom and picturesqueness for more solid advantages. In the meantime, my dear Violet, I am making an experiment to see how much one may get this way, and you are disturbing the conditions of the experiment."

"Philip why won't you come home?" said Mrs. Drem, suddenly.

"Why won't I go home!" he repeated in some surprise, as if that alternative had long ago passed from consideration.

"Your father is wretched about this affair—thinks over it from morning till night. I am sure, so anxious is he that you should return, that he would recall anything he may have said to you in haste and anger. I am sure he would. I have no doubt he expected, when you left the house, that you would soon find discomfort and anxiety, and be glad to return. Now that he sees such is not the case his only thought is to get you back on any terms."

"On any terms!" said Philip, opening his eyes.

"Well," said Mrs. Drem, drawing back somewhat, "you must be reasonable, too. You have to consider——" And here she glanced somewhat anxiously at Violet. Why was she unwilling to speak before her of the real reason of Philip's withdrawal from the house?—why, but that the well-meaning little woman had been thinking over a wonderful plan for rectifying all these wrong things, in which Violet was to play a chief part?

Such was the truth. Mrs. Drem found all the people around her at sixes and sevens—the whole condition of affairs disturbed—and she proposed to come in as general mediator and pacificator. It was no selfish wish to secure her own comfort (although that was also involved) which prompted her to undertake the thankless task; it was merely that she saw before her a grand opportunity of doing everybody a service. The timid hypocritical little woman felt almost heroic as she contemplated the prospect, and one of the pet portions of her scheme—that on which she dwelt most lovingly—was to get Philip to marry Violet Kingscote.

There was nothing improbable in all this, Mrs. Drem reasoned with herself. Both Violet and Philip had the sincerest esteem and likening for each other; and nothing could be more opportune and pleasing to both their families than their marriage. She suspected that Violet was a little too well-disposed towards Lord Cecil Sidmouth; but then, thought Mrs. Drem, was the grave pragmatical young man, who had no money, and who was always propounding puzzles about metaphysics and scowling at one, to be compared with her Philip? Philip himself would have to give up this absurd fantasy that had taken possession of him. Mrs. Drem's own experience of life had not taught her much respect for the importance of the affections. She did not believe in grand passions. Young people got cured of these whims, at the bidding of prudence; and she did not believe it possible that this monstrous rupture of domestic relations could be permanent. Of course Philip would come back; of course Violet would throw over the red-headed young man with the eyeglass. There would be universal reconciliation and forgiveness: and, on the wedding-morning, Mrs. Drem pictured to herself Violet Kingscote's tightly brushed dark hair being surmounted by the folds of a veil, and the fastening of these folds would be pearls, and the giver of them Richard Drem's wife.

It was partly the project, that had grown dear to her through much thinking of it, which induced her to make such a constant companion of Miss Kingscote; and during their shopping, and their drives in the Park, and what not, Mrs. Drem was continually endeavoring by little hints and remarks to make light of Philip's secession. She explained to Violet that young men were rather fond of these wild flirtations, but they came to nothing. It was only the opposition to their wishes, she observed, that gave the pastime some zest; and when the temporary excitement was over, the youthful heroes returned from their campaigns, and settled down quietly into domestic quietude.

"You know, my dear," she remarked with a smile, "it is hard to say whether men or women flirt most; but men like to carry on these meaningless love affairs to a greater length. Girls prefer to sit in a room and amuse themselves by playing hide-and-seek behind a fan; but men want to look big and grand, and have their love affairs bold and picturesque. Don't you think so, Violet? Don't you think they are no worse than we are—or as you are, I should say, for my youth had not much of that in it? And so, you see, you must not place too much importance on anything of the kind. It is only in books that the nice young lady, who has never looked at a gentleman, marries a husband who has never thought of flirting with anybody before. You are too sensible to think of such a thing."

Violet was a sensible young person, as Mrs. Drem said, and had in her own way about as much shrewdness and knowledge of the world as her mentor. She not only perceived that Mrs. Drem was preaching at her, but she knew also the whole story of Philip's adventure. Miss Violet did not think it necessary to tell Mrs. Drem that she had so far been Philip's confidante. She had got rather to like this well-meaning and kindly little woman, and even sympathized with her unselfish wishes touching Philip, his father, and herself. Violet did not think it likely she would marry Philip, but she sensibly thought there was no use in robbing Mrs. Drem of the pleasure of anticipation by stating her reasons. And, if the truth must be told Violet Kingscote honestly reflected that, although she did not particularly wish to marry Philip, still such a marriage would have its compensations, and it was therefore no disagreeable subject of talk.

"When Philip marries," she said one day to Mrs. Drem, "what will his wife say about Mary Thormanby?"

"My darling," exclaimed Mrs. Drem with a surprised look, "you don't expect to marry a man who has never before shaken hands with a woman!"

"I was not talking about myself, Mrs. Drem," said Violet, with a gentle laugh; and Mrs. Drem's pale little face flushed.

Up here, therefore, by Regent's Park, Mrs. Drem found herself in a dilemma; for she did not wish to let Violet see the gravity of the situation. She had been treating the rupture between Philip and his father as a very awkward circumstance, but still one that could easily be mended by a little forbearance on both sides. She was unwilling to mention the name of Lillian Seaford.

"I have considered," said Philip, in reply to her hesitating suggestion, "and I am afraid that to talk of my going home is out of the question—you know why. But do not let that distress you. I promise never again to make you uncomfortable by driving up Bond Street while you are in it."

"Promise me," said Mrs. Drem, pleadingly, "that you will at once give up any notion you may have had of—of——"

"Becoming a cabman? I never had such a notion; but I give it up, to please you. I shall assume my ordinary costume this evening. If I were subject to such interruptions as these, how could I make my living by cab-driving?"

"And you will let us know, Philip," said Violet, earnestly, "how we can assist you."

"But I don't want assistance, my dear child; though I am very much obliged to you. Don't you see what trusting to assistance would really mean? Shall I put it into plain English for you?—for, in these days, a beggar does not live on alms—he is supported by voluntary contributions. Now my case is simply this——"

"Philip," said Mrs. Drem angrily, "I will not have you call yourself a beggar."

"I was just going to prove that I wasn't one," he replied, with a laugh; and then he moved towards the cab. "Will you ladies step in? You are only wasting time here—though it is very kind of you, I am sure. Believe me, that I shall not starve. Keep your tender and anxious minds quite at rest on the point."

"Are you still at the same address, Philip?" asked Mrs. Drem.

"Yes," said he; "and I can see in your eyes that you mean to send me a big check. I won't have it."

"My dear boy," she said, almost in tears, "you will starve—I know you will starve! And while we are living with every comfort, you will be toiling and slaving in poverty, with scarcely a crust of bread. I cannot bear the thought of it, Philip. Why should you do this? Why should you encounter such fearful trials—hunger, want, anxiety? There is nothing in the world to repay you for such a terrible life."

"Thank God, there is!" he said; and there was a look in his eyes which she had never seen there in the old languid days. "Don't let us have any heroics in this dull neighborhood," he added, however. "Get into the cab, please. Shall I drive you down to Park Lane?"

"Not for worlds!" cried Mrs. Drem. "Think of the servants, Philip! We will walk—I am sure we can, Violet."

"Yes," said Violet, dubiously.

"And indeed you will do nothing of the kind," said Philip with perfect decision. "I will drop you, if you like, at the foot of Edgeware Road, but I shall not allow you to walk from here to Park Lane."

Somewhat disconsolately, Mrs. Drem got into the cab, and Miss Violet followed. Philip drove them down to Edgeware Road, and there they got out and went away, quite forgetting to pay the cabman. Mr. Philip would have asked for his fair wages but that he was busily engaged in watching the motions of Lord Cecil, who, with his hat considerably on the back of his head, was walking absently along towards the corner of the Lane. Would he meet the two ladies? Mr. Philip hoped not, for he wished to have the pleasure of accosting his friend from the box of a hansom. Unfortunately, however, Miss Kingscote and her companion passed so close to Lord Cecil that he was obliged to see them; and he immediately turned to walk down to Mr. Drem's house with them.

Mr. Philip followed at a distance, but was disappointed at

seeing Lord Cecil, yielding to an apparently urgent invitation, enter the house. So he turned away.

By this time, it must be confessed, he was rather tired of his perch, and had become hungry besides. His effort at calculating what he would be likely to earn as a cabman had been spoiled by this interruption; and the final result of his deliberations was that he let down the glass of the hansom, and drove straight up to the stables. He was, on the whole, very glad to get into his own clothes again; and it was with a rather vague promise about seeing them again that he bade good-by to Mr. and Mrs. Dufton, to the saucy Sissy, and the manly little Henry. Master Henry happened at the moment to be in great depression of spirits, through an accident which had happened to a couple of recently-born kittens.

"Us did not have the two kittens in the yard," he explained, "and they weren't been cleaned this morning and nurse did take them, and her put them in the pail what is in the yard to wash themselves, and the stupid kittens didn't wash themselves, they went and drownded themselves."

As he was leaving, Mr. Dufton insisted on returning to Philip two of the four half-sovereigns which he had got for the loan of the cab; and Philip, bidding farewell to the chubby small boy who was in grief about the kittens, consoled him with one of the half-sovereigns. It was not until he was outside that he suddenly recollected how unwarrantable was this piece of extravagance in his present circumstances. Half-sovereigns were of consequence now.

He partly made up for this folly by dining for a shilling in a dingy restaurant, and went on foot all the way home to Paddington. As he had also to contemplate walking from there up to Hampstead, farther on in the evening, the walking home was a creditable sacrifice. He saved threepence by it, and felt himself entitled to a modest share of self-congratulation. It was true that he had thrown away about thirty shillings that day in an idle and useless fashion; but then he had saved half a crown by eating a bad dinner, and threepence by walking from Euston to Paddington.

Late at night Lord Cecil Sidmouth called up at these lodgings, and found Mr. Philip returned from Hampstead. Lord Cecil was in evening dress, having just come from dining at the house of a Cabinet Minister; but there was no after-dinner gayety about the young gentleman's manner. Indeed he was more than usually important and grave; for, during the previous two hours, he had been propounding his theories of the relations that ought to exist between England and her colonies, and the affairs of the empire still hung heavily over him.

"Philip," he said, with the sternness of a mute at a funeral, "if you have nothing to do at present, and if you will take up a light occupation, why not become secretary to the Analytical? The post is vacant. We will give you £150 a year."

Here Lord Cecil fumbled with his loosely-gloved fingers in his waistcoat pocket, and, scowling more than ever, said,—

"In the meantime I wish you would take that."

Mr. Philip opened the bit of paper which Lord Cecil, rather nervously, had put on the table. It was a check for £100, drawn on a bank in St. James's Street, and signed, 'Cecil Sidmouth.' "

"My dear fellow," said Philip, "don't think me impertinent; but when did you ever have as big a balance at ——'s?"

"Never you mind."

"Let me ask you one question; if I were to present this check to-morrow morning, the moment the bank opened, would it be paid?"

"There is no need for such hurry," rejoined Lord Cecil, rather uncomfortably twisting the cord of his eyeglass. "If you present it during the forenoon, you may be sure it will be all right."

"One question more, Cecil. Who put you up to this? Who gave you the money, in short? Mrs. Drem?"

"No."

"Violet Kingscote?"

"Confound you! what business is it of yours?" cried Lord Cecil angrily, and all the more vexed to see Mr. Philip quietly fold up the slip of paper and push it towards him across the table.

CHAPTER XXIII.

A DULL October day was drawing to a close, and over Highgate and Hampstead there lay the sultry haze of the afternoon sunlight. All the morning—it was Sunday morning—had been gray and dismal; now there was a bronze-colored glow in the west, and the spire of Higngate Church caught a tinge of the warm light. It was a drowsy, silent afternoon, fit for a quiet talk, and nothing else.

"We may have thunder," said Jims.

"Why must you go to that perpetual school?" asked Philip of Lilian. "Suppose you should be caught in a thunderstorm on your way home?"

"Dinna mind him, my girl," said Jims severely. "Do your duty, in spite o' thunderstorms. He has persuaded you to enough o' self-indulgence by takin' ye every Sabbath mornin' to that play-actin' church, to listen to music, and look on pictures pented on the windows."

For Mr. Philip had stepped in to relieve Lilian from going to the somewhat dreary chapel which Jims and his wife frequented. Lilian, he knew, was an unwilling convert. She was familiar with the Church of England service; she liked sweet music; she even preferred stained-glass windows to whitewashed walls. And so Philip, despite Jims' opposition and sarcasm and argument, carried her off each Sunday morning to church, and together they sat in a small pew, and listened vaguely to what was going on, and watched the sun shine through the color in the windows, and dreamed dreams of all that was coming to them in life. If all this was, as Jims insisted, but a pampering of the eyes and ears—but a feeble, sensuous, emotional sort of worship, as contrasted with the vigorous denunciations and the rough argument which he himself preferred—it was not very harmful. It suited the ease and quiet of those still and peaceful autumn days.

Lilian would go to the Sunday-school this evening; and so Philip accompanied her thither.

"What time shall I come for you?" he asked.

"Don't come at all, Philip," she said. "The children are to be addressed by a missionary just come home from China, and it is rather uncertain when we may get away. You need not be alarmed about my safety," she added with a smile. "There are always one or two of the teachers going down that way."

A young man passed them and entered the school. As he did so, he took off his hat and bowed to Lilian.

"I hope that is not one of them," said Philip, laughing. "He is either tipsy or a maniac."

"Oh, no, Philip," she said, "that is Mr. Hickes, who has become so friendly with Mr. Lawson of late. He is a very pleasant and modest young man, and very obliging."

"He has an odd appearance, at least," said Philip. "He stared at you then as if you were a ghost, and his own face was rather ghostlike. Good-by, darling. Tell little Carry Jepps that I shall bring her the pocket-knife for her brother next Sunday."

He waited until she was gone inside, and then he hurried away into the dusk. A slight wind had sprung up, however, and there was a mildly damp freshness in the air which had not been perceptible during the day.

"This does not look like thunder," he said, looking northward, where Highgate was now on a blue mass in the deepening gray. Red lights were beginning to burn in the windows of the houses around him, and here and there overhead there was dimly visible a single star. He returned to Jims Lawson's house, and resolved to wait for Lilian's return.

Meanwhile the young monitress had begun her duties of the schoolroom. By this time Mr. Hickes had been accommodated with a small band of pupils; and it was generally remarked that he showed great industry in being very well-informed about the particular lesson of the evening. He had got into great favor with most of the teachers; and towards Lilian, in especial, he was never tired of showing a wish to do her small kindnesses and services, which were offered so modestly that they could not well be refused. On one or two occasions, also, he had spoken to her while out of doors, and had walked part of the way with her. Indeed, his manner was so kind and respectful at all times, that it disarmed suspicion; and Mr. Hickes had become quite a favorite with Mr. Miall and his young friends.

On this particular evening there was something restless and *distrait* about the new teacher. His face was paler than usual, and his general bearing was far from having its ordinary placidity and calm. He was not well at ease, his eyes were rather bloodshot, and he was evidently laboring under some excitement which disturbed the customary quiet of his demeanor.

"I fear you are not well," said Mr. Miall to him, kindly putting his hand on his shoulder. "Shall I relieve you from your duties?"

"Not at all! not at all!" said Hickes quickly. "I never was better in my life."

Mr. Miall left him, thinking that the new teacher had probably received some intelligence that day which had unnerved him, although he did not like to reveal the cause of his perturbation. The scholars, however, with the observant eyes of children, wondered not a little at the abrupt sentences, the absent look, and the general disquiet which their teacher evinced,

Occasionally he seemed to forget altogether that his class was there, and subsided into an odd sort of reverie. At other times he asked ridiculous questions, and made remarks which were quite foreign to the lesson in hand. There was, too, a certain unusual look in his face and eyes which did not escape the children's notice.

When the ordinary lessons were over, the teachers came together in a little crowd, and then sat down on one of the benches to hear the address of the Chinese missionary. At such times Hickes had been in the habit of getting near to Miss Seaford, as being the one of his companions whom he knew best; but now he seemed to keep away from her as much as possible. He glanced at her once or twice; but hastily withdrew his eyes, and kept them fixed on the floor. When the missionary had finished his brief address, Hickes rose with a violent start, as if he had just been awakened.

In leaving the schoolroom, Lilian was one of the last, and Hickes was standing at the door when she got outside. He moved away to let her pass, and did not even bid her good night, as was his custom. She was rather surprised at this want of courtesy, and hoped she had not offended him in any way. She did not speak, however, but put down her veil over her face and set off homeward, going round by East Heath Road, as was her wont.

The night was quite still now and clear. The slight wind had carried away the mist, and then died down itself, leaving the stars overhead to throb in a cloudless, transparent, and dark sky. There was no rustling in the trees, so still and silent was the night; and the only sign of life or motion abroad was the tremor of the innumerable white stars in the great dark vault. But when Lilian had got round to the Heath, she was surprised to see, once or twice, the flash of a pale blue shaft of lightning up in the direction of Highgate—a sudden, vivid, pallid line of light, that flickered for an instant and then disappeared, followed by no distant rumble of thunder. There was something strange and weird about these blue shafts, that played silently about the horizon in the deep stillness.

She was looking northward at these frequent glimmerings of the lightning, and rather hastening her walk, when she was accosted from behind. The suddenness with which her name was pronounced startled her, and she inadvertently paused and turned. It was only Mr. Hickes, who begged her pardon for interrupting her, and hoped she would allow him to see her home. There was something in his voice which struck upon her ear with a peculiar ring; and she could only hasten to say that there was no need, that she was near the house, and that——

Here Hickes came closer to her, and she now fancied there was some truth in what Philip had said. She was not actually alarmed, and yet she would rather have been two or three hundred yards nearer James Lawson's door.

"Do let me go with you," he pleaded, in that forced voice which jarred on her ear. "The night is so dark: you ought to have gone the other way. And, indeed, Miss Seaford, I want to speak with you for a few minutes, if you will be good enough to let me."

"To speak with me!" she said, in great surprise, and endeavoring to hasten her steps a little. She heard the sound of people walking further down the road, and hoped she might be able to overtake them.

"Yes, Miss Seaford," said Hickes; "you have been very kind to me since I have had the pleasure of knowing you—very kind; and now I ask you to add to your kindness by letting me walk home with you, and speak with you on the way. It is a trifle—a trifle, is it not?"

She fancied that he tried to smile; but the unnatural and husky tones of his voice showed that he was laboring under some powerful emotion or excitement which he was trying to repress. She gradually became more alarmed; and she was on the point of breaking away from him, and desiring him not to follow her, when he suddenly confronted her in the road, and seized her hand. She now saw that his face was quite white and wild, and the hand that he closed over her fingers trembled violently. She tried to draw away her hand—she was powerless; and indeed at this moment a sense of danger, and a terrible consciousness of her own loneliness and weakness, came upon her so suddenly as to wholly unnerve her. She was stunned, frightened, confronted by a man who had the appearance of a madman; and she felt herself helpless.

"Listen to me, Miss Seaford," he said, or rather gasped. "Don't be alarmed; don't tremble so. I'd sooner kill myself than harm you—you know that. There is no danger—none at all. How do you think I could harm you when you know I worship the ground you walk on? Listen! I would give you my life if it would please you. I think I have gone mad with love for you; and I will kill myself if you don't become my wife. Life to me without you is not worth having."

"Oh, let me go! let me go!" she cried, terrified by his

wild manner. "Some other time you may tell me—I wish to go home—I wish to go home by myself."

"You must forgive me, he said, with a desperate effort at self-control, "if I say you must hear me out now. I cannot have you go away thinking I have been violent with you, and without knowing what has made me speak like this. God knows I may be mad, but it is through love for you; and you know whether I have ever been anything than respectful to you since ever I knew you. You *must* hear me."

"Another time," she murmured.

"No—now!" he replied; and here again a strong shiver of excitement passed over him, and he struggled for utterance. The man was not acting. He had dwelt upon this interview until his part in it had assumed a morbid reality in his mind. He had almost got to believe that he was madly in love with the girl, through the fierce desire that had been stirred in him to be successful and win her for his wife. At first he had shrunk from the project with aversion and distrust; but, once in the act of carrying it out, he seemed to have lost self-consciousness, and to have become the victim of a mania. There were conflicting passions raging in his mind, about the reality of which no doubt was possible. Fear as to the terrible consequences which might ensue from this wild scheme if he failed in it—the lust for the money which was now almost within his grasp, and even a stubborn kind of pride that made him dread the ridicule of defeat—all these worked upon his feeble and impressionable nature until they produced in him a kind of delirium. For the time being he was really a monomaniac. He forgot all the set speeches he had prepared; and adjured this girl to have pity on his life, as if he really were mad for love of her. Frigtened beyond the power of recovery, she listened to his ravings, and could not help believing them. Was there not plenty of testimony to the reality of his excitement in the haggard face and eyes and the shivering frame?

Escape from him was impossible; he held her arm with the grasp of a maniac, while he poured forth his protestations and entreaties. The footsteps in the distance became more indistinct; and she was too much terrified to listen for others. All around them was the ghastly stillness of the night and the stars, while ever and again a pale line of blue light would flicker silently along the northern sky, and then disappear in the void. If Philip would but come?

"You *must* listen—for what I have to say concerns the life of one of us. I cannot live without you; I will not live without you. If my case were not so desperate, I would tell you how kind I could be to you—I would win you over into taking pity on me—I would show you how you will do the greatest kindness to Mr. Drem by letting him go back to his friends. Don't you know that you have ruined his life if you marry him?—don't you know that you will be my murderer? I swear before God I will not live to see you his wife!"

"Oh, you terrify me!" she cried, piteously. "You cannot mean what you say. I have done you no harm—pray let me go!"

"You only care for your own safety!" he said, bitterly. "You have no thought what this night may do to me. Miss Seaford, I beg you to believe that I have come to a grave decision. I am not speaking to you out of any hasty impulse. I have tried to go away from you—never to see you again—long before I became incapable of controlling myself; but now that is impossible. There is but one alternative. As I tell you, you are ruining the man whom you wish to marry; you have estranged him from all his friends; you have thrust him into poverty. I tell you that you will not have been married to him a year when he will bitterly regret that he ever saw you; I tell you he will look on you as the cause of his worst misfortunes, and hate you and curse you!"

"Ah don't say that!" she cried. "You do not know what you say! If I have caused you pain—or if I must cause you pain—I am deeply sorry; but I cannot help it. I never sought to harm you. Mr. Hickes, won't you let me go? I cannot do what you ask; you will think better of it—you will forget."

"Forget!"

He came so close to her that she was forced to look up into his face, and she saw that it was ghastly pale, and that perspiration stood on it. His breath came quick and hard; his teeth were set; he was in appearance like one possessed. And yet when he spoke, it was with a cold, implacable resolution in the tones of his voice that startled her even more than his vehemence.

"Forget!" he said calmly, and he still held her hand tight. "Do you know where forgetfulness is to be found? In the grave! You have chosen for me. I will bid you good-by now. You may go."

He released her and stepped back. The next moment she saw before his breast the glitter of steel. With a faint cry she sprang forward and caught his arm.

"Oh, this is dreadful!" she cried in an agony of terror. "What can you mean?"

"I told you there was forgetfulness in the grave," he said in a low, clear voice, "and I mean to find it. As sure as there is a God above us, unless you swear, on the ground where you stand, to marry me, you will have for your companion a murdered man—murdered by you. I do not ask you to choose. You have chosen."

"No, no!" she cried. "Only wait till to-morrow—give me time—I cannot see you kill yourself—only till to-morrow. Have mercy upon me. I cannot, cannot do it!"

She sank at his feet, shuddering and holding up her hands. All things seemed to whirl round her, and there was only a murmur in her ears. And yet the murmur seemed to say, "Not to-morrow, but now—this minute. You are not prepared!" And then she vaguely knew, in her agony, that he was holding up her right hand, and that she was repeating the words of an oath, every one of which seemed to be written in fire and blood on the utter blackness of the night; then a sinking backward, and a sweet, dull uuconsciousness of pain.

He was kneeling down over the prostrate figure of the girl, endeavoring to bring back the life to her by chafing her hands. Large drops of perspiration stood on his forehead, and his brain throbbed as if it were surcharged with blood. At last, being terrified, he called to her; and she roused herself, and awoke with a cry of terror on meeting his face near her.

"You are not hurt?" he said.

"Oh, have pity on me, and go away!" she cried; and she looked round with a shudder. "I wish to be alone—I wish to go back by myself."

"But you know you have sworn—"

"I know, I know!" she cried wildly. "Oh my God, what have I done?"

"It will be all for the best," he said soothingly. "You will forgive me when you come to see what made me do it. I knew you would not marry me otherwise—and I could not live without you. I hoped—I knew—you would have compassion on me. Oh, Miss Seaford, I feel that I am a wretch and a coward to have treated you so; but I couldn't help it—I couldn't help it. And I will make it up to you—I will!"

She did not seem to hear him. She stood dazed and bewildered, with a pale white face and tearless eyes, as if she had not yet realized to herself the horror of what had occurred. Was it true, then, that these few minutes had destroyed her life, and that the cold stars overhead were as they had been when she left the schoolroom door? But a few minutes had passed, and what was this that had happened? There was a pain across her forehead, and a mistiness about her thoughts. She only knew that Philip awaited her at home, and that she dared not go to meet him.

She turned away, trembled, and was forced to take Hickes's proffered arm to prevent her sinking to the ground. Then, suddenly, she broke from him with a sharp cry, as if her heart had at length found utterance.

"Oh, Philip! Philip! was I not right in saying we should never be married? And how can I tell you, my darling —how can I tell you, and look into your face, and say goodby!"

She burst into tears, and went away by herself, weeping. Hickes dared not speak to her then. He watched her figure go down the road, and he followed her at some little distance, with a terrible weight at his heart. The excitement was all gone now; he had wiped the perspiration from his forehead, and his eyes did not throb and burn as they had done. The subsidence of the mania that had taken possession of him left him full of vague apprehensions, with a low dull sense of remorse, and a strange susceptibility to physical cold. He shivered now, not with excitement, but with the chilliness of the air. The stars above him glittered as if in a frost, and the silent flashes of the lightning were steel-cold and bright. His very teeth began to chatter, and then he recollected that he had a flask of brandy in his pocket. He took it out, and drank every drop of the burning liquor, and yet it did not give him the desired warmth—the night seemed so cold.

And meanwhile the young girl had paused at the railings in front of James Lawson's small garden, as if she could not enter. She looked up at the small windows—there was a ruddy glow in them.. Presently the door was opened, and the figure of a man came out towards the garden gate. Hickes saw the man approach the girl; she turned her face up towards his; a few words were spoken hurriedly, and then Lilian Seaford went into the house by herself, leaving the other standing by the gate.

Hickes turned and passed up the East Heath Road again. He went round through Hampstead, and then, having gone into a public house and drank some, more brandy, he proceeded to make his way towards Sloane Street.

CHAPTER XXIV.

"Why does not Lilian come home?" said Philip that evening, as he sat and turned over a few photographs that he had given her during their happy sojourn in the South. They were precious talismans, those tiny pictures of the places they had visited; for, now that there was but small chance of their being able to leave the din and smoke of London for the sweet air and the pure color of Devonshire, Lilian would often sit with one of these views in her hand, and dream herself back into the beautiful solitudes of her youth. There was the wooded picturesqueness of Anstey's Cove—the white shingle below, the bold rocks falling sheer into the green water; and in the distance the far glimmering of the Dorsetshire coast. There was Babbicombe Bay, with its cliffs of red sandstone; and the Livermead rocks; and the white beach of Goodrington; and the fishing fleet of Brixham. But, above all others, she had a view of Torquay, which was inseparately associated in her mind with one beautiful evening which she well remembered. She would sit and gaze at this poor little photograph until it was transfigured—until the bit of pasteboard faded wholly away, the horizon widened, and she saw in a dream the colors of that rare evening—a glow of pure pale pink over the clouds in the west—the tall heights of Waldon Hill growing transparently blue underneath this clear flame; low down in the south, the white crescent of the moon in the cold green of the twilight; and over the bay and far into the east, a pale metallic light fading out on the mystic sea.

"I must go and meet her," said Philip, at length.

"I'm thinking," said Jims, going to the window "that I saw something like lightning."

"I hope not," said Philip anxiously, following him to the window.

They had not remained there above a second, when one of the pale steel-blue shafts glimmered across the northern sky. There was no thunder—only a harmless flash of light, which was presently repeated.

"That is very often the precurser of a serious storm," said Philip. "Mrs. Lawson, please give me a cloak or two, and I will go up to the schoolroom. That China fellow ought to have more sense than to keep a lot of children and young folks so late."

"Indeed, Mr. Philip, you're quite right," said Mrs. Lawson indignantly: "and I am sure I dinna like the look o' him, missionary or no missionary. A big, heavy cheekit, greasy, fat, thick neckit, idle sumph—"

"Peace, woman!" said Jims, severely. "Ye should have mair respect for men that imperil their life in spreading the Gospel: and what has his neck or his cheeks to do wi' his doctrine?"

"A good deal," said Philip, looking about for an umbrella. "A man with a neck like that would imagine that heaven is peopled with Rubens's women instead of angels. But pray give me those cloaks at once, Mrs. Lawson; we will settle that missionary's hash when we return."

Mrs. Lawson was very proud to hear Mr. Philip pick up her Scotch phrases.

"We will take him down to the Analytical," continued Mr. Philip, folding up a big shawl, "and have him dissected. We have a man who is just on the point of discovering how the brain acts in thinking. We will open the missionary's skull—the formation will be nice and loose; we shall have the same chance that a botanist has of watching movements in the large cells of very flabby vegetables. The missionary will be of great service to us, I daresay; so we shall not abuse him further. If Lilian comes down the other road, tell her that I shall return in a few minutes."

He put the shawls over his arm and went out, shutting the door behind him. The night was dark; but the starlight was sufficient to show him the figure of a woman, who was apparently standing outside the garden, in the road, regarding the house. He advanced a few steps, and by this time the dark figure had opened the gate and came down the path.

"Lilian," he said, "what is the matter with you?"

She had run forward to him, and taken his hand in both of hers, while she looked back up the road with terror on her white face. She could not speak: but he knew that she was trembling violently, and that her appearance was strange and wild.

"Lilian," he said, "what do you mean?"

She only clung closer to him, and grasped his hand tight; and then she turned her face up to his, and said, with a terrible calm in her voice:

"Philip do you know that it has all come true at last? I knew we should never be married. I knew it when I asked you to come with me to Devonshire, that we might have a pleasant dream there—something that we could remember with kindness, if we were never to see each other any more. And now, Philip, it has come true; and you and I are never to be married, and we are to forget all we have been thinking about, and we are to go away from each other forever. You do not seem to hear—you do not seem to understand me, Philip. Don't your hear what I say; that you are to go away—that I am speaking to you now—oh, my love, my love! for the last time?"

What could it all mean—her wild manner, the tears streaming down her cheeks?

"Lilian, are you mad?" he cried: and he caught her to him, and smoothed back the hair from her forehead, and looked into the beautiful eyes that were full of fear and despair and pain. All at once she shrank from him, almost in terror, and released herself.

"I shall go mad, if you do not go away," she said; "I cannot bear to see you, Philip! See—I will kiss you this once, and then you will go away."

"My darling," he cried, "what has happened to you? Come into the house and tell me."

"I must tell you here," she said, in an excited way; "not before all of them. Oh, Philip, don't be angry with me; I am far more wretched than you can be. I have sworn a terrible oath not to marry you; to marry———"

She could not pronounce the name: she only glanced with a shudder up the dark road.

"I have sworn it, Philip, and there is no going back—no going back! Oh, my darling, how well I have loved you!—and now you must go away, Philip, for it will break my heart to see you. Do not come into the house. Your face is white, my dear; but you are not angry with me? you never were angry with me? Look, I will give you this one kiss, and it will tell you that my heart will always be full of love for you—always, always; but you must not see me again. God bless you, Philip—you have been very, very good to me!"

She had fled into the house, and he was standing, bewildered, under the stars, that seemed to be throbbing blood red. A gulf had suddenly opened before him in front of his feet, and, as he shrank back with horror, he knew that his eyes were growing dim, and that he must fall. A strong instinct of self preservation took hold of him; he would rouse himself from this dreadful sleep, and prove to himself that the danger was only a dream. It already seemed to him that the apparition of Lilian —the wild words she had uttered—the frantic grief visible in her face—must all have been phantasmal; and yet it was true that he had come out to meet her—it was true that the door of the house stood open before him.

He entered the house, and went into the parlor which he had recently left. James Lawson sat there, alone.

"Where is she?" cried Philip. "Haven't you seen her?— didn't she come in just now?—has she not returned at all?"

"Do you mean Lilian?" said the old man looking up from his book with some surprise.

"Yes! Hasn't she come in?"

"You look as if you'd seen a ghost. I'm thinking I heard her come in; for the gudewife went upstairs wi' somebody. But what has happened?" said Jims, turning to his wife, who now entered the room, with a most unusual excitement in her manner.

"Oh, this is dreadful!" she cried; and then she looked at Philip almost with alarm.

"Go on," said he; "tell us all you know about it."

"That young man Hickes——"

"Hickes!" ejaculated Philip, with all the vague wrath in his heart suddenly directed towards one object.

"Has done what he should be hanged for. It seems he was determined to marry our Lilian, and he met her to-night, up the road there, and frightened her into swearing that she would be his wife."

"Hickes will answer to me for all this," said Philip, with his face set hard and pale. "But as for the oath, Mrs. Lawson—as for the oath—surely you had enough sense to tell her that it was nothing—pure nonsense! What value is it? Why, you must go and tell her not to disturb herself about it; an oath got under such intimidation is worth nothing. If a man threatens to blow your brains out if you don't swear not to reveal that he has broken into your house, there is nothing binding in the oath."

"But he did not threaten to kill her," said Mrs. Lawson, wringing her hands in her perplexity and dismay. "He only threatened to kill himself—he says he is so deeply in love wi her. Its' a terrible misfortune, Mr. Philip, terrible!"

"But you don't mean to say that you consider she must keep her oath?" he said, not so much in anger as in dismay.

"You don't mean to say that you will allow her to marry him?"

"I canna think o't! I canna believe it yet!" cried Mrs. Lawson in despair. "And yet, what is she to do? She must answer for her oath at the judgment seat. It is no the first time I have heard o' sic a thing. I mind o' a lass that was in service in Kirkintilloch being frichtened into marryin' an auld man o' fifty, because he was aye swearin' he would murder either himsel' or her. And there's mair nor ane lass I've kenned that was half coaxed and half frichtened into marryin' young men they didna much care for, through some such threat. Oh, it's a dreadfu' thing, that love-making, when it gets into a man's head and mak's a madman o' him. The newspapers are fu' o' cases o' murdering and wounding, and if Lilian hadna sworn as she was bid, who kens but that there would have been a man's corpse lying up the road there?"

"Better a good deal that the corpse should be there," said Philip fiercely, "than that her life should be ruined. And, indeed, if there is no other way out of it——"

He did not give expression to the thought that rose within him then, and caused his dark face to grow darker; but if ever there was murder in his heart, it was at that moment; and it seemed to him in his passion and despair, that the blackness of the crime grew lighter as he thought of the suffering girl upstairs, and that her sorrow lent a sort of consecration to it.

"Mr. Philip," said Jims, gravely and sadly, "this may be a severe trial to you, and to all of us; but we are bound to guard against the grief and disappointment provoking us into sin or sinful imaginings. Do not give way to your anger, however just ye may think it: it may be that this is a merciful dispensation——"

"I will have none of such merciful dispensations!" exclaimed the younger man, with a vehemence that startled them. "I tell you that you have no right to let evil and wrong take its course, and then say it is a merciful dispensation. If this is a work of Providence, it is time we were taking our affairs into our own hands. I will not believe it. I will not believe that either she or I should submit to such a monstrous thing, though she had sworn a thousand oaths on her mother's grave; and I tell you that, sooner than see her sacrificed to this man—sooner than let such a horrible crime be enacted in the very face of Heaven—by God, I will kill him with my own hand! If this is your religion and your law of right and wrong, I have done with both. I tell you, you should pitch your petty code of justice into the fire, and get up some other tables of the moral law, and put at the head of them that the first act of virtue in a man is to kill, as he would kill a reptile, a ruffian who would debase and ruin the life of an innocent woman."

"Philip," said James Lawson, with an anxious sadness in his eyes, "there is worse might befall you than what has already happened. God grant that may not come also!"

"Go upstairs and tell Lilian that she is not to fret—that she will not be the victim of such a monstrous theory," said Philip to Mrs. Lawson.

"Indeed I will go up and comfort her as well as I can," she said. "It is comfort and consolation, not revenge which she needs."

"I will bring her consolation before twenty-four hours have passed," said Philip, with his teeth set. "Tell me where Hickes lives."

"I will not," said Mrs. Lawson, firmly; and then she suddenly caught the young man's arm, and cried, with tears springing into her eyes, "Oh, Mr. Philip, it is not at such a time that you and we should fall out. Do not be vexed with us if we dinna see these things as you see them. Think o' the puir lassie upstairs."

"I do think of her," said Philip; "and it is for her sake that I deny your right to impose your notions of right and wrong upon her. I say it is shameful you should think for a moment that such an oath—whatever its terms—should be regarded. It is monstrous, incredible that you should think so."

"Mr. Philip," said Mrs. Lawson, "we have advised her in nothing—it is of her own will that she swore she would marry him; it is she who must answer at the last day for the keeping of her oath; and it is for herself to say whether she will dare to break it."

"It is not for her to say," said Philip; "it is for you—you who are older than she is—who ought to advise her in her distress, and help her. Instead of that, you leave her to herself, and to her own frightened notions of what she ought to do; you let your superstitions come in to blunt your own sense of what is right, and leave her to her fate. This is what you call your conscience, I suppose?"

"Mr. Philip," said James Lawson, "I can make great allowance for you in your present position; but there are some things I will allow no man to say in my house. It has been your boast that you were drawn towards this girl by the great purity and nobleness of her nature—by her strong sense of honor and truth and honesty—by that very delicacy of conscience you are bitter against. I ask you whether you would rather see such a woman be true to herself and her sworn word, than debase herself and purchase her present happiness by laying in store for herself unending remorse. It is hard, hard to bear; but it is better she should bear it than forswear herself, and live with a crime on the whiteness o' her nature. If I were a young man, I should be proud to know that I had been the friend o' a woman capable of keeping her solemn oath at the expense of her present happiness. I would not, whatever it might cost myself, ask to see this noble woman debase herself to live a life of ease and comfort."

"Why, these are the morbid dreams of a priest, not the sentiments of a man," said Philip, with angry disdain.

"When a year or two have passed," said the old man, "you will think differently. You will know that there is nothing rarer, nothing more beautiful in life, than to see a tender-hearted woman content to suffer hardships rather than fall away from her own ideal of honor. It is so rare a thing, Philip! The present trial will be bad enough for both of you, God knows. And yet people have borne worse, and have grown stronger and wiser and better for it. The young do not see the purification that sorrow brings, until they have passed through it and look back; and then they know the joy of having remained faithful in trial. You may think I am heartless in speaking in this fashion, yet I have come through as hard trials as fall to the lot o' most men; and now I can scarcely regret them."

"And think," added Mrs. Lawson, "o' this other young man, who was near killing himself this very night. Doubtless it was a cruel thing to do—to compel our poor Lilian to marry him; and yet he was desperate. He was so gentle and quiet every time he was here, that something must have driven him near mad. She says if she were to break her oath, he would make away wi' himsel', and you and she would ha' a stain o' blood on your married life."

"I see you have both decided against me," he said, bitterly, "and you are the keepers of her conscience. My only chance is with herself. I must see her. Mrs. Lawson, will you kindly say to her that I wish to speak with her for a few minutes?"

"She will not come down," said Mrs. Lawson. "She heard you coming in and bade me tell her when you had left."

"I must see her!" said Philip.

Mrs. Lawson knowing what would be the result of her mission, went upstairs and opened the door of Lilian's room. The girl was seated on a chair in front of the bed, her head buried in the pillow. When she lifted her head, Mrs. Lawson could see by the dim candle-light that there were tears on her face, and that she held in her clasped hands a small prayer-book that Philip had given her.

"He wants to see you," said Mrs. Lawson, gently.

"My poor boy!" said Lilian, with a wistful, sad look in her eyes. "He must not see mê—how could either of us bear it? I shall be able to bear it better than he, for I have all along been prepared for the sorrow of parting with him. He never would believe me—he was always so full of hope and confidence."

She went forward to her kindly old friend, and said, with her head bent down and in a low voice,—

"Is he very much grieved?"

"He is more angry than grieved, my poor girl," said Mrs. Lawson; "for he does not believe it possible yet. Oh, I hope nothing more dreadfu' than we dare think o' will come o' this!"

"What do mean, Mrs. Lawson?" said the girl, but in a tone which said that nothing worse could happen now.

"He is so angry at the way you have been treated—so determined that you will not marry the other—that I know he has it in his heart to murder him."

"Oh, no, no!" cried the girl, covering her face with her hands; "there has been enough of wickedness and wrong done already. Tell my poor Philip that he must not mind about me; he must go away abroad for a time—away from London altogether, and forget all we had been thinking about. He will soon forget, will he not, Mrs. Lawson? He is young and strong; all the world is before him; he will go abroad, and see people and places; and when he comes back to London"—here there was a sad, uncertain smile on the girl's face as she looked up—"he will not remember the poor Miss Lil, who was such a trouble to him long ago. You know he will go to his friends now; he will get plenty of money, and then he will go away, and come back with no sorrow on his face at all. And if ever he remembers me, it will be perhaps when he finds himself down near Tor Bay, where—where we were so very happy!"

She could add no more. She turned away, and threw herself on her bed, and sobbed bitterly there. Mrs. Lawson went over to her side, and gently drew away one of her hands.

"My darling," she said, "you must come downstairs, in

stead or sitting here and crying by yourself. Will you come downstairs now?"

"Not while he is there," she said. "Tell him, Mrs. Lawson, to be kind to me even now, at the last moment, and not ask me to see him. I could not say good-by again. See—give him this, and tell him all that I told you about his going abroad."

She turned to her writing-desk, which stood on the small table beside the candle. She opened the little ivory-boarded prayer-book; on the fly-leaf were these words: "*From Philip, to the little girl who is always wasting her books with pressed flowers.*" Her eyes were blinded with tears, and her hand trembled, so that it was with a pitiable effort that she wrote underneath: "*And who gives it him back, with her whole heart's love, and bids him good-by, and knows he will be brave and hopeful for her sake.*"

"There," she said to Mrs. Lawson, "give him that, and bid him good-by for me. There are some flowers in the leaves; perhaps—perhaps he will remember having gathered them for me one evening by the side of the Dart."

This was the last message he received from her. He looked at the little volume he knew so well, and he saw here and there a withered scrap of some wild-flower that he had picked up and given her. All his anger seemed to have gone from him. He held the book tightly in his hand, said good night to Mr. and Mrs. Lawson, in an absent way, and went out into the cold night.

By and by they got Lilian downstairs. She was much calmer, the sadness in her eyes having grown far more intense and still. She told James Lawson, in her simple way, all that had ever occurred between Hickes and herself at the Sunday-school. It was very trifling and unimportant, as we know. The only occasions on which Hicks had really had an opportunity of speaking to her in a friendly way were those chance visits he had paid to James Lawson himself; and then he had been so singularly gentle and unassuming that no one could have dreamed of this sudden outburst.

"But it will be so much better for Philip," said Lilian, gazing wistfully into the fire. "He will go back to his own people; he will no longer have to trouble himself about money; he will forget all about me."

"There are some things a man cannot forget," said the old man. "He will never forget you so long as he lives; and your brief friendship with him will have a pure influence over his life so long as he has memory. He will never forget you,

Lilian; and, whatever happens to you, you will have to show yourself a courageous and a noble-minded woman, that you may be worthy of his best thoughts of you."

"And if he does remember me," she said," I hope it will not be in connection with this terrible evening. He must think of me as he knew me in Devonshire. Do you remember, Mr. Lawson, that I said he and I should never again see Tor Bay together? And you were so angry with him for spending that money in going with us. Was it not better now that he went? To him, perhaps, it will not matter so much. Men have so much to do, so much to think about, that these pleasant memories are not of so great importance to them. But I should feel myself far more wretched now if I could not look back to that happy time. It was all a dream—I knew it was a dream—and yet it was so very beautiful! Do you remember the bright mornings, and the sound of the blue water outside, and how far away the ships seemed to be? Do you remember the days we left Torquay and sailed round the coast, and went up the Dart? That was the end of the dream, you know. I think it wanted only one thing—that, just at the end, I could have lain down and died, and freed Philip from all the care he has had about me."

Then she said presently, in the same low voice:

"Perhaps he will marry Miss Thormanby. He must not think it will please me that he should marry no one."

"My poor girl!" said Mrs. Lawson, with tears coming into her eyes, "you are always thinking about every one but yourself; it is you who ought to be pitied. You need not think of Mr. Philip marrying any one—for many a long day, at least. I have never seen a man so fond of a woman as he has been of you."

"And he will not wish that he had never seen me," she said; "for we have been very happy together. He cannot regret having known me, I think, when he remembers that time in Devonshire. Perhaps, when next he goes there, he will be married, and he will tell his wife about me—that I was very fond of him; but that was a long time ago, and she need not be angry with me. I don't think she would be angry if she knew me, and knew my story, and knew that I bore her no ill-will."

And so the sad and gentle creature talked on, half forgetting her sorrow in thinking of him and his future. But when they were about to retire, she said to Mrs. Lawson:

"Would you mind sleeping in my room to-night, Mrs. Lawson? I—I am afraid——"

"Of what?" said Mrs. Lawson.

"Only," said the girl, pressing her hand over her heart, "that I have a great pain and weight here. Don't they say that people sometimes die so suddenly of heart-disease that they cannot even say a work to their friends!"

"My darling!" cried the old woman "you must not talk like that."

She slept in her room, nevertheless. The girl was somewhat restless and feverish all night; but towards morning she sank into a soft steep. The old woman looking by the pale light at the beautiful face that lay on the pillow, with the soft golden-brown hair lying in small curls and coils down on the white neck, saw a smile occasionally cross the girl's lips, and heard her murmur in her sleep. And when she caught a word or two, she knew that it was about the sea that the girl was dreaming; and once she caught the name of Philip, and then some mention of the River Dart.

CHAPTER XXV.

"ALL the brandy in London won't make me drunk to-night," said Hickes gloomily, as he sat in Arthur Drem's lodgings.

"Why should you wish to be drunk?" said Arthur. "You have been successful—you have come home triumphant—you ought to be as gay as possible."

"Yes," said Hickes with a sneer, "we have been victorious, haven't we, over a girl! I like to see two men sitting down to congratulate themselves over having frightened a girl! Hang me," he added, with a sudden burst of anger, "if I don't think we two ought to be drowned like rats! I will back out of this; I won't go any farther. However I managed it I don't know, for I can scarcely remember what I did. I was as mad as any man ever was; and I'll swear the girl was not half so much frightened as I was. Confound it, Drem, why don't you make that fire burn?"

He shivered as he spoke, and rubbed his hands together.

"I begin to see what I have done," he continued in quite

another tone; "I did not know at the time. I think I was bewitched by her pretty face, or else frightened into madness; for I know I spoke as if I meant to kill myself for love of her, and she believes it! By George! if she would only marry me, I'd make up to her for all this—I would indeed."

"And why not?" said Arthur.

"Why not? Do you think she is such a fool as to keep her oath? Do you think they would let her?"

"My dear friend," said Arthur calmly, "you are committing your old mistake of judging what other people would do by what you would do yourself. Of course, *you* wouldn't keep such an oath, or any oath that was distasteful to you. You have no more idea of the way in which such people as they regard an oath than you have of the dramatic incidents that befall people of violent temper and great wealth, who give the rein to their whims. You judge of human nature by the experiences of one man—who is rather poor, who leads a tame and monotonous life, who has no great passion, and no great belief about the sanctity of an oath. I tell you the girl will marry you. Of course, it musn't be done in an abrupt way—so as to make the ceremony look like the buying up of her pledge—like a sacrifice, you know. No; you must go up and see her; win over her friends to liking you; pretend it was only the suggestion of an impulse that led you to exact this promise; and, in short, make the fulfillment of her oath as pleasant to her as possible. If you were to go up as the villain of a play, and demand her hand in lieu of her oath, she would probably kill herself first. But she believes you are desperately in love with her, she believes that you have a gentle and kindly nature (I don't think she is far wrong you know); and so, as I tell you, she will marry you."

"If she does, I will make it up to her," said Hickes eagerly; "I will, indeed. You couldn't help being fond of such a charming face, could you? I have never seen any woman who could come near her in appearance; and then her voice—you wish she would always go on speaking, so soft and pleasant it is. I'll tell you what, Drem, I'm knocked this side and that every time I think about what I should do. It does seem a beastly shame to make her marry me, and I make up my mind to cut it altogether; and then, again, when you think of herself, if seems as hard to give her up. And then this money! I declare I wouldn't have gone to Hampstead this evening—I would never have spoken to her again—but for the Rotunda people losing that play which they were to have copied. They won't pay a farthing for it; and now they're going to run one of Dolent's plays, and that may carry them on to the pantomine, which is good till February. Do you really think your uncle will give me the money?"

"Of course he will," said Arthur, "and be precious glad, too."

"Mind you, Drem, I'm not as bad as I seem. I declare to you I would marry the girl without any money, if I had the chance and if she was willing. But then, without the temptation of this money, I should feel bound to set her free."

"You are a victim of compulsory vacilliation," said Arthur, laughing. "And as you seem to have no will of your own, you had better be guided by me."

"If your uncle were to refuse to have anything to do with the affair, I wonder what I should do," said Hickes, absently. "I should be inclined to marry her, and inclined as well to set her free, because, after all, it's such hard lines for the girl."

"You are only getting into a fog," said Arthur, impatiently. "by guessing at the right and wrong of the thing. The facts of the case are simple enough. Here are you, very fond of a remarkably handsome girl; you get her to swear to marry you, and she does so. There is nothing wonderful in it; it occurs constantly. Only, as it happens that the marriage is, at the same time, very convenient to another man, there is no resaon why he should not make you a present—a wedding-present, as it were."

"And that *is* the sensible way of looking at it," said Hickes boldly, and sitting up in the chair. "And I might explain to any one what I have done; and how could they blame me?"

This conversation with Arthur Drem gave Hickes far more courage than any brandy could have done. He went home to his own place in Sloane Street, thinking there were much worse men in the world than he; that, indeed, he had done nothing that he had not a right to do.

"Isn't universal competition the first law of existence?" he said to himself. "Isn't everybody trying to better himself at the expense of other people? Generosity and forbearance, and all that sort of thing, is only possible to people who have plenty of money and can afford it. If I had plenty of money I would be generous. If I could afford to deal fairly, I would deal fairly. Make me an emperor, and I'd astonish the world with my goodness—I'd encourage the arts, and give money to beggars, and go about visiting the needy, and be a general favorite. But at present I'm in the ranks of those that are fighting for their bread. I have as good a right to mine as anybody else; and if anybody else suffers, well, I'm sorry, but it isn't my fault. It is *not* my fault; and if everything were known, perhaps I'm quite as good as my neighbors."

With this comfortable theory he got to sleep: and next day he went into the City to learn the results of Arthur Drem's meditation with Philip's father. While Hickes waited in an obscure coffee-house, in a thoroughfare leading out of Cornhill, Arthur was deliberating as to the chances of his finding Richard Drem in an approachable mood.

At last he ventured upstairs. Mr. Drem was fast asleep when he tapped at the door and entered; he started up with a look of anger which did not bode well for Arthur's chances.

"I wished to speak to you, sir," said Arthur gently, while he shut the door behind him, "about a matter not entirely relating to business."

"You want money, do you!" said Richard Drem. "Got into debt, I suppose. The best thing for young men who have got into debt is to let them get out of it for themselves."

"It was not about myself, it was about Philip I wished to speak to you."

"Very well," said the uncle, sharply. "Go on—go on. What have you to say? Do you want money for him?"

"No," said Arthur.

"I thought not," said Richard Drem, with an open sneer. "There is this one good thing about you, Arthur—you don't waste your time in thinking about other people."

"He intends marrying that young—that young person," said Arthur, too well used to taunts to mind them: "and I am sure, sir you will be as glad as I am to meet with any means of preventing such a calamity. I am deeply sorry for my unhappy cousin, sir, since he has been so unfortunate as to earn your displeasure. I should like to see him restored to his family."

"Yes, yes, yes!" said Mr. Drem, hastily; "we know your generous intentions and sentiments. Let us pass that over. What is the means you propose to take in order to get Philip back? Do you mean to marry the girl yourself?"

It was a difficult thing for Arthur to withstand the insolently mocking tone in which his uncle spoke; but he had an admirable command over his temper.

"You may well disbelieve the possibility of such a thing, sir; and yet I know a man who may, if he chooses, marry Miss Seaford. He is not in wealthy circumstances——"

"And you want me to say how much I will give him if he will marry her?"

"Well, sir, some recognition——"

"How much do you propose to get for yourself?"

"You mistake my motives altogether, sir, if you regard them as mercenary in such a matter as this. I wish to save Philip from committing a blunder which will ruin his life. I wish to do you a service also; and here, as I say, is the chance of making his marriage with Miss Seaford impossible. After that, of course, Philip will return to your house, Who can doubt it! He has plenty of common sense, he knows the advantages of a comfortable home and an easy income. That I don't ask anything for myself should show you that what I say is true, and that I am not trying to impose on you."

"Will you kindly tell me whether you are drunk, or whether you really believe what you say?" observed the merchant, contemptuously.

"I do believe it—I can prove it," said Arthur, warmly.

"And what was the sum which the gentleman who is to marry Miss Seaford proposed to have?"

"You yourself, sir, some time ago, said you would give two thousand pounds."

"Two thousand devils! Do you think I have nothing else to do with two thousand pounds than to hand it over to some swindling friend of yours, who will bolt with it to Australia, and drink himself to death with it?"

Arthur looked rather crestfallen. His uncle, indeed, made suspicion a matter of personal vanity. He was proud of saying that no one could take him in; and he would rather have thrust a banknote in the fire than give a halfpenny to a beggar who might perhaps be an impostor. Richard Drem was clearly not in a conciliatory mood; and, on the other hand, could he expect Hickes to marry on the vague chance of wakening some gratitude in the breast of this cantankerous old man? But Richard Drem was growing impatient of his presence, and at last Arthur blurted out,

"You don't believe me, sir. But will you give this man £2000 when the marriage has taken place?"

"Yes, yes; I will," said Richard Drem, pretending to be merely anxious for the whole subject to be removed, but in reality more struck than he chose to show by this dim hope of having his son back again in his own home.

"Thank you, sir," said Arthur. "You will see that there was more in the proposal than you appear to imagine. I should not have ventured to speak about it, but that my anxiety about my cousin——"

"Very well, very well; go away now, and don't tell me any more lies," said Richard Drem, hurriedly. "And you may tell Mr. Ewart to bring me up those 'salted' invoices of which he complains. I must teach these people with whom they are dealing."

For that the great Richard Drem, who could at once establish lines of commerce stretching over a hemisphere, and detect the sham old soldier who asked him for a penny at the corner of the street, was to be imposed on by a trumpery China firm, that were glutting the market in order to get fancy sums on the consignments, was not to be thought of for a moment. What would Napoleon have said to one of his puppet kings had the latter attempted, in his own little sphere, to mimic the great emperor, and turn his master's weapons against the master himself?

Arthur Drem put on his hat, and walked up to the coffee-house in which Hickes was amusing himself with some brandy and water and a newspaper. When it was explained to him that Mr. Drem would give him the money only after the marriage, he looked rather blank.

"What guaranty have I?" he asked. "Suppose he were to change his mind, what should I do?"

"You can't expect him to give you the money beforehand," said Arthur; "for he knows nothing about you, and you don't want any guaranty from a man like him. Do you think he has got the habits and tricks of the manager of the Rotunda? I tell you his word is as good as if you had the £2000 in your hands. You must remember with whom you are dealing;" and Arthur rather drew himself up, to let Hickes know that a merchant was a gentleman, and to be trusted.

"What did he say to you?" asked Hickes.

"You mean as to my share in the results? That, I can tell you, is likely to be merely a deal of abuse for meddling in a matter for the good of other people."

"Two thousand pounds is twenty hundred, isn't it? Twenty hundred!"

And here Hickes drew mental pictures of the various things he might do with this potent sum. There was very little consideration for Lilian Seaford likely to occur now. The money had come almost within his reach; he had but to put out his hand and pluck the golden grapes.

"How soon after the marriage will he pay it?"

"Oh, directly. Such a sum is a mere trifle to him, you know."

"And you think she will marry me?"

"Of course; unless you frighten her by letting her see the real reason why you wanted to marry her; and then she would probably drown herself rather than become your wife. Everything lies clear before you. You can do all that we planned ever so long ago without harming or paining any one. It is now as it was then; the climax seemed an abrupt and impossible thing; but the steps towards it, as I told you they would, have been easy and gradual. And so with those to come."

"Ah, yes," said Hickes: "I'm not out of it yet. I can scarcely believe——"

"You never could believe anything, unless it was at the point of your nose. But I mean to have something to eat. Shall we have luncheon here?"

"No. I have been watching the struggles of the man over there with his food until I am nearly sick. A steak that looked like the back of a mahogany chair that had been blistered at the fire; vegetables that looked as if you'd worn them in your buttonhole for a week; beer that should have been in a doctor's bottle, with a glass-stopper and a label."

So they went elsewhere to have some brief lunch; and the time that Arthur could spare from the office he devoted to counselling Hickes as to how he should conduct himself towards the Lawsons and his future bride.

CHAPTER XXVI.

VERY strange indeed was the first interview which the accepted lover had with his betrothed wife and her friends. Jims sat fierce and still, compelling himself to be calm, and yet looking as if he might at any moment rise and throw the intruder out of the window. Mrs. Lawson, no less angry (for both husband and wife, though looking on a solemn oath as irrevocably binding, were none the more disposed to forgive the means by which it had been obtained), bustled about the room in her excitement, making bitter speeches, and stopping every moment by the side of Hickes's chair, as if she meant to box his ears. Lilian herself sat mute and pale in a corner, anxious that there should be no outbreak of wrath, and rather inclined to pity the timorous young man, who so vainly endeavored to deprecate their hostility.

At the very moment of his entrance he had offered to them a carefully studied apology for what he had done, with such extreme nervousness of manner and hesitation of speech that they never dreamed of doubting his sincerity. And then, to each of them separately, as occasion served, he made an appeal for forgiveness. He had been maddened to do it; he regretted it now: but, since it could not be helped, he would atone for it in the future: he would convince them afterwards that Lilian's happiness had not suffered by this violent shock.

"Jims," said Mrs. Lawson, that same evening, when they were alone, "if that young man is to marry our Lilian, it would be wise o'us to put the best face on the matter, and no anger him. We are powerless in his hands: and he might be angered into dealing harshly wi' her afterwards."

"There's some sense in that—there's sense in that," said Jims. "And he seems a well-disposed lad, gentle in his manners, and anxious to please folk. I'm thinking we ought to make Lilian believe the best o' him, so that she may bear what is to come wi' greater composure. There can be nae doubt o' his being very fond o' her——"

"Or he would never hae done such a mad thing," said Mrs. Lawson.

"And yet," said Jims, "I fear he is unstable: and as for his ignorance, it is quite extraordinar'. On nae single subject does he seem to hae the least information. Can ye believe that such a man come to his time o' life doesna ken the qualifications o' a voter in his ain country, and actually had never inquired whether he hae a vote or no?"

"Folk are no a' wud about votin' and votes," said Mrs. Lawson, with a touch of contempt. She suffered so much from Jims's political harangues, that she almost looked on this ignorant young man as a sort of ally.

"And his asking whether the Lord Chancellor was going to tak' something off sugar in his next budget!"

"I'm sure I wish he would," said Mrs. Lawson, who would have accepted the reduction gladly, whoever made it.

Accordingly, Hickes found himself received in a much more courteous fashion on his next visit. Indeed, the two old people were quite kind to him. As for Lilian, she still seemed to regard him with fear, and was very silent while he remained in the house. He was content to accept this neutral attitude, in default of any more gracious welcome. He never tried to force her to speak more directly to him. He was to her quite as respectful and distant in his manner, until his unassuming ways, and his anxiety to learn anything he was told, most favorably impressed the Lawsons, and they were almost disposed to forgive him for what he had done. His visits increased in number. He made them all little presents, the prettiest of which he offered to Lilian; and how could she refuse them? Sometimes she looked at these trifles with absent and wistful eyes; and Hickes, watching her, fancied she was asking herself what these might have been to her had they been the gift of another.

In those days, the young man became aware that he was beginning to regard her with a tenderness which was almost painful. For the more he thought of her, the farther away from him did she seem. Sometimes the calm resignation of her face was like to drive him to despair; and when she tried to be kind to him—when she smiled as she shook hands with him—there was a look in her face and in her eyes which troubled him more than he cared to confess.

"I am getting to love this woman, whose love is so far away from me," he said to himself, one night as he walked home; "and if that should happen, what will happen to me?"

One evening he brought her some photographs.

"You often speak of Devonshire," said he; "but you don't seem to have any photographs of the places you know."

"I had some once," she said. She did not tell him that these were now part of the sacred possessions which had been associated with her bygone love, and were hidden away in a secret place, never more to be shown to mortal eyes.

"I thought I might bring you these," he said; and he gave them to her.

She was sitting in the twilight, with her back to the window, and he could not well see her face. She took the photographs and began to look over them: at one of them she stopped. Why was she so silent? he asked himself. Why did she hold the picture before her, down on her knee, as though she scarcely saw it? She did not turn over the others; she merely sat in the shadow, and regarded this tame little copy of one of the Devonshire coast-scenes, a glimpse of Tor Bay and Berry Head being included in it. And then she rose, and gently put the photographs on the table and went out of the room. As she passed him silently, with her head rather bowed down, he fancied her face was wet with tears.

A fierce pang shot through his heart. He went to the table, lifted the photographic-album, and turning over one or two leaves, arrived at a portrait of Philip Drem, which was placed opposite one of Lilian. The former he took out of the book, tore it savagely into several pieces, and flung the fragments into the fire.

"She will never forget him?" he said, between his clenched teeth.

"Why, where is Lilian?" said Mrs. Lawson, coming into the room.

"Gone to see if Philip Drem isn't coming up the road, I suppose," said Hickes, angrily.

"Deed, ye should be the last to say anything about that," said Mrs. Lawson, indignantly. "Three times has he been here trying to get speech o' her; and she has considered it her duty no to see him. Mr. Drem is a gentleman." continued the old woman, nettled into something like scorn, "and wouldna force himself, where he is no welcome, and so he didna see her: but he has written to her again and again, begging her to see him for a few minutes."

"I won't have him write to her! He has no business to write to her," said Hickes. "I don't wish to interfere, but I will not have him write to her!"

"Ma certes!" exclaimed Mrs. Lawson vehemently. "Ye force me to say, Mr. Hickes, that ye seem to forget what ye hae done to both Philip and her. Interfered! If ye wish to have a whole bone in your body, dinna you interfere with Mr. Philip! That he has never sought a meeting with you on his own account quite astonishes me; and maybe it's because he is waiting to hear from her. But if ye are so far misguided as to provoke him to settle accounts wi' ye, tak' my word for't, my man, ye'll no ask for twa lickings o' *that* spurtle!"

"I'm very sorry, Mrs. Lawson," said Hickes; "I didn't intend to speak like that. And to tell you the truth, I scarcely know what I say, when I find things going against me like this. I don't believe she cares for me one bit."

"Indeed," said Mrs. Lawson, whose moods did not veer round so rapidly, "I canna wonder at it. I am quite astonished to see her so kind to you as she is."

"Mrs. Lawson," cried Hickes suddenly, "I sometimes think I am a devil, instead of a man. I am not worthy of her. I will go away; I will release her from her promise."

"Can ye tell me," asked Mrs. Lawson calmly, "how ye propose to get her to break a solemn oath harmlessly?"

"Ah, don't you see," cried Hickes with great eagerness, "don't you see that I couldn't do it? I couldn't do it, if I wished. I have not the power to do it, Mrs. Lawson, have I? And I am not so much to blame, after all; for I *would* release her from her oath if I could. It was not to me she swore. *I* can't release her; *I* can't help it."

Mrs. Lawson turned away with a gesture of impatience. She was unable to conceal her contempt for this petty, weak, vacillating nature, that was so anxious to throw the blame of its own actions on outward circumstances.

Shortly afterwards Hickes left the house, a prey to much restless anxiety and trouble; there were new emotions in his breast which terrified him. He knew not where all this might end. Hitherto he had been proof against whatever might happen, simply because he was equally indifferent to all the various issues which he considered possible. He had not contemplated this one, however; and now his indifference was wholly gone. He had played with events in a careless fashion, fancying that he could at any moment withdraw; and now they were catching him up, as the wind does a withered leaf, and whirling him onward, whither he knew not.

"What am I to do? What am I to do?" he exclaimed, as he and Arthur Drem sat in consultation that evening. "I tell you I am becoming mad about this woman. I cannot bear to see her leave the room, unless I know she is coming back presently; and when I heard of Philip Drem writing to her, I felt I could have murdered him, or drowned myself, or done something desperate. I will not degrade her; I will not have her sold for this money. I will go away rather, and leave her——"

"To my cousin Philip," said Arthur, quietly. "That will be the result of your romantic nonsense."

"D——n him!" said Hickes savagely. "I would murder them both rather than that!"

"My dear fellow," said Arthur, "let us say you are in love with this woman. The chance of marrying her is at your disposal. Instead of that, you prefer to hand her over to somebody else. Very good; you are generous, I must confess."

"If I had only known, I should never have made her swear that oath—I'd have made her acquaintance, and have asked her fairly and honorably to marry me."

"And she would have laughed at your impudence," said his adviser coolly.

"Was there ever anybody in such a position as I am in?" said Hickes, in despair.

"Yes; you are badly off," said Arthur Drem, with a sneer. "You are going to marry the woman you are in love with, and you are going to get a couple of thousand pounds for doing it. Certainly you are badly off! Perhaps you would like somebody to give you five or six thousand a year, to complete the list of your miseries?"

"It's all very well for you to laugh; but I'm not ashamed to say that I've a good deal more tenderness of feeling than you have; and the more I think of this girl, the more I am determined——"

"You never had a particle of determination in your life."

"You may find out very soon that I have. And if I must marry this girl to get the money and keep myself from starving, I tell you I will not force her to live with me and keep herself wretched. Rather than that, I will get some means of sending her home to the Lawsons' house, and spend years in gaining her free and full consent to live with me. I won't have her remain in my house on compulsion, and have myself tortured day after day by her meekness and her suffering. What is coming of all this, I don't know. Sometimes I get afraid; I feel myself helplessly drifting into such a position as I dare not consider; and I am tempted to go off direct to America, and never set foot in England again. But I cannot leave her—I could not leave her; and so, I suppose we must wait to see what may happen. One thing I am resolved upon, Drem. You may laugh as you like; but until she comes of her own free will to my house, I will not ask her."

"Why ask her? She will go with you, of course, after the marriage is over."

"And I will get some means of sending her straight back to the Lawsons."

"So as to have the pleasure of courting her a second time? Do you know, my dear Hickes, that you have grown quite a romantic person of late? When we first talked of this matter —when you scouted the possibility of its all happening—did you ever contemplate uttering such an absurd speech as that? You are in love with a woman—you marry her——"

"I am in love with a woman!" said Hickes, vehemently. "Heaven help me, that is true enough! And I tell you I will not be more of a brute and a coward than I can help; and if I marry her to get this money, I will leave her to freedom until I can persuade her to have some liking for me. This will I do; and I declare to you, Drem, that sometimes, when I look at her, and see the way in which she tries to be kind to me, and tries not to let me see that she is forcing herself to do it—I declare that I feel I could go out and put a bullet through my head, and relieve her from her misery forever."

"She has turned your brain," said Arthur with some pity.

CHAPTER XXVII.

OVER the north of London there lies, on this November morning, a thick white mist, and the sun that is visible through it is a distant globe of faint rose-pink. Now and again the folds of the white smoke waver hither and thither, and the luminous circle becomes pale and silvery, while occasionally the fog deepens into a turgid yellow, and the sun is of a dusky copper color. As yet there are few people abroad; the shutters of the shops are just being taken down, and the first omnibus has not yet started for the city. Alec Lawson gets stealthily out of the house—unknown to any of its occupants—and makes his way down to Paddington and to Philip's rooms.

The secretary of the Analytical Society is at breakfast—the table being plentifully littered about with newspapers and opened letters. He is surprised to see Alec at this early hour—indeed, a trifle dismayed. And the lad bears ill-tidings in his face; for he has of late carried news to Philip of all that was going on at Hampstead, and comes now to report the climax.

"Oh, Mr. Philip, she is to be married this morning!" he blurts out.

"This morning!" says Philip, turning suddenly pale.

"I did not know till last night. None of them expected it; but it seems Mr. Hickes has had it all arranged, and came up yesterday, and now the marriage is to be this forenoon."

"What does she say?" asked Philip, quite calmly.

"Nothing at all," said Alec. "She is no longer sad and vexed, as she used to be. Instead of that, she seems to be very reserved and determined. I wonder what she means to do."

"She does not complain?"

No; she does not even like to hear grandmother say anything against Mr. Hickes. She says that is of no use now. I think she tries to appear more cheerful and contented than she really is before me; for she knows I see you often, and I fancy she would not wish you to know that she was unhappy."

"You are going into the city now?"

"Yes."

"Thank you very much for coming to tell me. I may go up to see the marriage."

With that Alec left, wondering not a little that Mr. Philip should be so grave and so composed.

Somewhat later on, Philip went by rail to Finchley Road, and walked over to Hampstead, and to the church were he understood the ceremony was to take place. There were several idlers—chiefly women—hanging about, apparently waiting to have a glimpse of the bride.

"There is to be a marriage here this morning, is there not?" he asked of one of them.

"Two, sir," she replied.

By and by the clerk appeared, and Philip, having spoken a few words with him, begged permission to be allowed to go into the church. This was granted; and he entered the silent, damp-smelling building, with its rows of gloomy pews, and dim windows, and melancholy altar-railings. He went into one of the pews and sat down in a corner, where he could not be seen by any one passing up the centre of the church.

So this was the end of all his dreams! There was a prayer-book lying before him; mechanically he opened it, and found himself reading carelessly these words, which had been written on the fly-leaf by some penitent sinner:

"Peccavi peccatum grande, et mihi conscius multorum delictorum; nec sic despero, quoniam ubi flagitia abundaverunt, gratia superabundavit. Qui de aeccatorum suorum venia desperat negat Deum propitium esse. Deo magnam injuriam facit, qui de ejus misericordi diffidit."

"'He does an injury to God who doubts His compassion,'" he repeated. "What compassion have I to be thankful for?"

How slowly the minutes passed! And now, upon one side of the church, a frail glimmer of ruddy sunshine fell, sending a few dusky shafts of light through the panes. It was cold, too, in this damp pew; and there was a frosty odor in the air. This was not the picture of Lilian's marriage that he and she had drawn in the olden times, when they had looked forward to walking down the dim aisle together—out into the warm air and the sunshine, with the song of birds around, and the blowing of the summer wind. How long ago it now seemed since they had talked together! His memory wandered backward until it came to a beautiful period, at once beautiful and sad. He was still looking at the Latin inscription; but in place of it he saw the blue waters of Tor Bay, and the white sunlight on the sails of a small yacht, lying at anchor outside the harbor, and Lilian with an open book on her knee, and a sunshade over her head. Had that time ever been? He might go down now and see the white shingle, and the rocky cliffs, and the far horizon-line; and he would not be able to believe that he and she had ever been there. And yet there were odd phrases of hers belonging to his period which still seemed to sound in his ears; and he could see before him the piteous figure of the girl, as she bade farewell to the bay, and sat down and covered her face with her hands. Then the sail round the coast—the warm day on the Dart—and the tender evening they spent together down by the river, under the sunset, thinking of the great future that lay before them. Was all that a dream? or was this a dream—these ghastly pews, and the voices of one or two people without who waited to see the arrival of a pale bride?

There is a sound of carriage-wheels outside the church door. Presently three men enter and pass along the aisle; one of them, who has a large flower in his coat, he recognizes as Hickes. He trembles as he sees this man; for during these recent days he has had strange thoughts about him: and now that he is actually there, would it not settle this agony and misery once and forever if he were to spring upon him and choke the life out of the coward body? The small prayer-book gets twisted and torn; but Philip does not stir.

And then—in all the pale beauty of her innocence, and with a calm, heroic light on her face—Lilian Seaford walked up between those dismal pews, Mrs. Lawson and Jims accompanying her. How lovely she was then, as the red sunlight tinged the white figure in passing, and fell warmly on the soft yielding golden-brown hair that he knew so well! Yet she seemed to have changed greatly since he last saw her. Whence had come that new light to her face—the calm courage that dwelt in her eyes—and the firmness that was visible about her mouth? Never before had he seen anything like this. There was in her bearing a dignity and self-possession which gave her beauty maturity and perfect repose. The face was paler, too; and there were traces in her eyes of a sadness which no semblance of courage could quite conceal. Yet he saw that she made no effort to appear cheerful. She was grave, calm and firm; there was no tremor of the hand or hesitation in her manner. So she passed on with this simple majesty of bearing; and he could not see how they began the service; for in thinking of his poor girl and of her probable fate his eyes were blinded with tears.

He bent his head down over the book, and heard only the confused muttering of a voice at the farther end of the church. He felt as though his life was slowly ebbing away from him, and that he should never stir from his present position. Those words that were being uttered were the dirge over a bygone life, and he had no wish to arise and face a new one. After this terrible, slow, acute torture were once finished, might it not be possible to sink into sleep, perpetual and dark?

And all at once there came to him a recollection of the time she had kissed him on the banks of the Dart, and looked up into his face with her pure and truthful eyes; and he started up as from a dream, and nearly uttered a cry of despair. For there was his love being separated from him for ever: she was kneeling in her white dress, with a ray of dusky sunlight falling on the beautiful head, and her hand was in the hand of another. She was leaving him now, and placing between them a barrier eternal, insurmountable.

"Oh, my darling, whom I loved so well!" he groaned, in his bitter, unavailing grief.

He could not remain longer there. The place seemed to stifle him. He rose and went outside into the cold air and the wintry sunlight, that now gleamed down on the strange faces around the church gates.

"They are waiting to see the happy bride," he thought.

He would wait, too. But he dared not meet her eyes; so he went some little distance off, and remained there. He heard the talk of the people standing about—some of them seemed to know Lilian, through the Sunday-school, and were discussing the merits of the bridegroom in rather a contemptuous way.

"She did not seem over-happy, did she?" said one.

"Them Sunday-schools are a rare place for courting, I hear," said a second.

"She might 'ave done better than him," said a third.

"You wouldn't find a prettier girl about here, I'll take my oath."

There was a slight bustle and murmur among the crowd when the bride came out. For one moment she seemed to glance round the faces, as if expecting to meet there with one she knew. The people observed with surprise that she was not on her husband's arm as she came out, and that, indeed, he hurried forward in a somewhat awkward way from behind old James Lawson. There were two carriages there—the second being the one in which Lilian and the Lawsons had arrived. The first, of course, was reserved for the newly-wedded bride and bridegroom; and Hickes now hastened up, to offer his arm and conduct her to the carriage.

"No," she said, in a low, clear voice; "I go back with Mr. and Mrs. Lawson. You made me promise to marry you—I have kept my promise."

How cold and calm she was as she turned away from him, with her face pale and her lips white and firm!

"Lilian," he said.

Jims had come before him and taken her hand. She stepped into the second carriage, Mrs. Lawson remaining valiantly to the last, as if she would dare any one to lay a finger on her girl.

"Lilian," he said again, "you mistake altogether. If you had only come with me, I'd have shown you I wished to set you free. I did, indeed. I was going to send you home; I wanted to prove to you that I am not so bad as you think. Won't you believe me—won't you believe me, Lilian? I will let you go; I don't wish to prevent your going; but you will believe what I tell you?"

She sat quite pitiless and cold in the carriage, apparently hearing nothing. The small crowd now began to suspect that something was wrong, and drew nearer to the wheels of the carriage.

"Driver," said Jims, in a loud and firm voice, "drive back to the house."

"Stay for one moment," cried Hickes, in great excitement, for the crowd was surrounding him, and had begun to testify a lively curiosity. "I only wish to assure you, Lilian, that you need have feared no persecution from me. I had determined to win your full consent to be my wife."

"Drive on," said Jims.

The carriage began to move, and the crowd drew back. Philip, who had been left alone, saw only part of what had occurred. He was concerned chiefly in trying to get one last look at Lilian—perhaps the last for many, many years. As the carriage turned in the middle of the road, he caught a glimpse of the beautiful pale face that was inside; and in the same instant he knew that the girl's eyes were fixed upon him with a look of piteous pain which he never forgot.

"God help her!" he groaned. "My little girl seems to beg for forgiveness from me!"

He saw the carriage drive off; and he turned to go away, not caring whither. He was so occupied with his own bitter thoughts that he scarcely knew that a hand was laid on his arm.

"Look here," said a voice beside him; "it is you who have made her do this—it is you who have done it! You think I am afraid of you. I am not. I will let you know that you can't always be master and lord of everything you see!"

The voice was husky and wild with excitement; and Philip, turning, saw himself confronted by Hickes. A powerful effort of self-control enabled him to resist the first impulse he felt to knock the man down. He merely shook off his hand, and said,—

"You had better go away."

"I will not go away!" cried Hickes, who was apparently quite mad with jealousy, or rage, or mortification, or all three combined. "I suppose you laid a pretty plan to make me the laughing stock of my friends; and you think I am afraid of you, and you can do what you like."

"I tell you to go away," said Philip, again passing on, but with a darker light growing in his eyes.

"I will not go away; I mean to settle with you *here—now!*——"

"Then, by heavens, if you will have it, take it!"

He turned rapidly round, and the next instant Hickes lay stretched on his back on the pavement. His two companions now rushed forward, and were for closing upon Philip; but the crowd came round them, crying, "Fair play!"

"What do you want?" said Philip, whose blood was now thoroughly up, to Hickes's friends. "Do you want to provoke a street brawl? I think the best thing you can do is to pick up that fool who is lying there and bring him to his senses, and preserve a whole skin on your own bodies."

There was something in his manner even more persuasive than his advice; and Hickes's companions thought better of it, and did as they were bid. Philip walked away from the group and from the crowd, with no great compunction for he had done. Indeed, it very speedily escaped his memory; his heart was full of other and sadder things.

It was as in a dream that he wandered on, until he had reached the parts of the river between Kew and Richmond, with which he and Lilian were once familiar. He had come hitherto without set purpose, scarcely knowing, indeed, the direction of his steps. The various successive things that he saw did not distract his attention; he was aware of their presence under this chill and wintry sunlight; but it seemed to him that, outside the immediate circle of these familiar objects, there was another and greater world that was full of pain and darkness. What he did all that day he was never able to remember. Towards nightfall he returned to town, and overhead there hung the crowded silence of the stars.

He glanced up at them as he walked along; but he did not know that another face, pale and sad, was also looking up to them, and wondering if they knew of her grief—if they could tell her how her love fared, and bear to him one last despairing message from her, now that they were separated forever. Was he angry with her? That did not matter now; and yet she hoped that he had gentle thoughts of her.

"Oh, my lost love!" she said to herself, " I must not think of you any more, but you will think of me and of the old times and of the Dart. How sad you looked this morning! but there was love in your eyes and kindness for me. And did you think I was hard hearted because I sat there so silent, and did not cry to you for help? Would you have come to me, my poor boy, whom I used to pet so? And you must forgive me for all I have done, for the sake of our old, foolish, wretched fondness; and when you marry you will tell me. and I will send your new love some flowers for her hair, to show her that I am glad you are happy."

So she talked to herself and cried bitterly, now that the cold, red, fearful day was over, and she sat in the dark room alone. The world had grown so cruel to he rof late, and now she had reached the close. There was an end of the happiness of her life; and she wondered whether she could not fly for sympathy and safety to the sheltering bosom of her mother. Alas! when she gazed, with eyes blinded with tears, at the great throbbing vault of stars, they only deepened her misery. Those melancholy stars! that have been sought by the weary and the wretched since ever the mournful Pleiades looked down on a breaking human heart. Are they sad to us because we know that they are the only link between us and the forgotten nations that have lived out their little life and passed away long before history had a voice—between us and all the races of men that have looked up to them, and wondered, and died? We know only that since ever human sorrow forced men to puzzle over the mystery of life the pale stars have been there; the young husband, turning from the bedside of his dead wife has stretched up his hands to them, and piteously entreated for one glimpse of the fair young soul that has gone from his side, and wondered in which of the great worlds of light she is walking with shining feet; the young mother, in the dead of night, has listened to hear her child call to her from out of the wonderful star plain, and has grown sick of the cold silence; and the lover, from over his loved one's grave, has questioned the vague mystery of the heavens, and wept because he saw no sign. So sad they are!—for we know that all this sorrow has passed before the cold unpitying eyes; and we know that the same stars will shine down on our small world when every trace of human life shall have been brushed from off its surface—when an ocean may lie over the graves of Abelard and Heloise, and all the manifold voices of by-gone centuries be mute. Is it possible we ask ourselves, that this must be—that a future comes in which there is no sound and no light—that the human race will be as the dead man who lies beneath the Atlantic, and cannot hear any more the bells of town or village ringing even in dreams? This is the question we ask of the stars; and they will not answer.

CHAPTER XXVIII.

CRISP and clear was the weather that now shone over Surrey and over Thurston Place, where Mr. Drem lay very ill. It was Christmas time; and not for years had we such appropriate Christmas weather. The windows of Thurston Place had their blinds down, and the sunlight could only struggle in parallel lines through the crimson curtains as it entered the dusky, thick carpeted rooms; but outside there was the sparkling whiteness of snow, and overhead the clear blue of a bright sky. Snow on the lawn, which was marked by the interlacing footmarks of partridges that had been running about during the early morning—snow on the heavy laurels and evergreens surrounding the house—snow on the black branches of the lime-tree walk skirting the garden—and snow on the thick squat oaks in the park that sloped down into the valley. Thurston Place was a big white house built on the face of the hill, with a semicircle of fir wood behind it to shelter it from the northeast winds. It looked towards the south; and on a clear and sunny day like this you could see far over the glittering white plain, marked by black lines of hedge and coppice, towards the blue line of the chalk hills that lay down near the sea.

Richard Drem had suffered a severe shock of apoplexy and the three doctors who attended him began to fear at one time that he might not, by Heaven's mercy, be spared to lengthen their bills. However, he so far recovered as to become the terror of them and of his wife, until, in the end, they would not enter his room except on urgent need. They prescribed to Mrs. Drem; they studied what she told them of the case; they ordered her, instead of admonishing him; and so constituted the timid little woman a sort of go between. The office was neither pleasant nor easy; yet she undertook it so willingly— she worked with such solicitude to prevent her husband killing himself with brown sherry—that you would almost have imagined that this amiable creature after all she had suffered, was actually anxious that her husband should live.

Richard Drem lay and alternately broke into fits of passionate defiance of the doctor's directions, and into pitiable anticipation of his doom. Then it would. In his abject terror he would call for his wife, given up Bill to him and beg for some assurance that he was likely to die, and then he would stormily demand whether he was not master in his own house, and went on having some more wine.

"I'll play you a pretty trick, my lady," he said with a malicious look, " when I get better. We shall see then who has the keys of the wine cellar."

" It's only for your good, Richard," she said.

"Don't Richard me!" he cried, at imminent risk of having another apoplectic stroke. " My first wife used no such vulgar familiarity. But she was a lady born and bred."

" You might let your first wife rest in her grave," said Mrs. Drem, with just a touch of bitterness. " I dare say she was glad enough to get there."

" She was a lady," said Mr. Drem hotly. " She had the manners of a lady—she had a civil tongue in her head——"

" It is a pity the rest of the house did not learn something from her," said Mrs. Drem very quietly, but with a tendency to compression of the lips.

" Yes," he said, " show your spite, because she was not a nobody like you. She had the best blood in Spain in her veins —the best blood in Spain. If *she* had been by my deathbed— it may be my deathbed, for all you think, do you hear?—she would have treated me with some affection. But no matter. If I must die, I will go to her—do you hear? I will go to her——"

"She's welcome to you," said Mrs. Drem, with a curl of her lip.

"And when you come, where will *you* be? You'll rather be out in the cold, won't you?" he said with a malicious laugh.

"Perhaps that is where you'd like to be, then," she said sharply.

But the next moment she was sorry she had been goaded into hinting anything about such a subject; for her husband sank into one of his fits of despondency and terror, and began to whine about his penitence and what he would do if he were spared.

"It isn't my fault that Philip will stay away like this," he said, "when there is no need for it, now the girl is married——"

"Who told you the girl was married?" said Mrs. Drem suddenly.

"None of your business," said he. "I will give him anything he wants, if he will only come back to the house. I will give him £3,000 a year. Counselhake Sir James give him Violet for a wife—and where a better wife could he get?"

"But you know," said Mrs. Drem, "that you will only make matters worse if you try to force such a marriage. Young people nowadays are not bought and sold——"

"As they once were, do you mean to say?" he put in with a sneer. "Well, I didn't pay much for *you*?"

"How did your first wife bear those insults?" said Mrs. Drem calmly. "Had she something of Philip's nature in her?"

"She had the nature of a lady not of a nobody!" said Richard Drem. "And I tell you, madam, when I see her in heaven——"

"You make very certain of going there," said Mrs. Drem, knowing well how to puncture the wind-bag of his boasting.

Here Mr. Drem had another fit of apprehension and penitence. Indeed, his swaying between these moods of self assertion and abject cowardice resembled much a similar alternation between prayer and brandy on the part of a great person of these realms who was once about to bombard a sea-port. He now took Mrs. Drem into his confidence, and said he could not rest for thinking what his son Philip might be doing.

"If I am going to die," he remarked, with some pathos in his voice, "if I am going to die, it is the place of my son to come and smooth his father's pillow. Go and tell him that—tell him to come at once, if he would see me alive."

Mrs. Drem knew very well that there was now not the least fear of her husband's dying, if he would only avoid brown sherry, But it seemed to her that here was a favorable opportunity for inducing Philip to return to the house. It was a project she had been puzzling over for a long time ; and, if the truth must be told, there had been a time in which she speculated as to all she should do for Philip, in the event of his father dying and disinheriting him by will. It was a proof of the amicable relations existing between husband and wife, that she had not the faintest notion as to what was the purport of Mr. Drem's will—as to whether he had fulfilled his threat of cutting out Philip altogether from the document. Should such be the case, she speculated at such moments, what delight it would give to her to hand over to him all that should have belonged to him! She had plenty of poor relations. She was young enough to marry again; and the greater her fortune, the greater choice of suitors she would have. On the other hand, this Philip was the son of that woman whose manners and birth and beauty had been used to irritate her for years. Yet Mrs. Drem would have given up half her fortune to Philip with the greatest joy in the world, and would have given him with it her little finger, if he had asked her to cut it off.

Here, then, was a chance of promoting that reconciliation between father and son which she had for long set her heart upon. She dared not of herself have suggested such a scheme. If she had managed to inveigle Philip to the house on the pretence that his father was seriously ill, Richard Drem, out of pure contrariety, would have been sure to have spurned the offer of reconciliation, and sworn that he never was better in his life. But now he was in the humor. She knew that if Philip were to come now, his father would make believe that he was on the verge of the next world, in order to move his sympathy and remorse.

"And to-morrow is Christmas-day," said Mrs. Drem. "How pleasant it would be if Philip were to come down and meet Sir James and Violet, who promised, as I could not go to them, to come here!"

"And have their orgies in a dying man's house," grumbled Richard Drem. "Say it was out of kindness to you, when you know they only want to guzzle at my expense. You think of nothing but eating and drinking the whole lot of you. Give me another glass of sherry."

"I daren't," remonstrated Mrs. Drem.

"You shall, though."

"Really, Richard, you must not have any more wine just now."

"I will rise and throw you out of the window if I have not some more wine instantly!" he cried; and with that his face became suffused with blood, and he sank back on his pillow, breathing heavily.

Mrs. Drem ran forward.

"You are killing me," he continued in a weak voice, "killing me to get my money. Never mind; I am going to a better world. Send for Philip—send for my son. Go yourself and bring him; nobody can tell lies like you."

"I should be afraid to leave you," she said, with some hesitation.

"Afraid to leave the devil!" he retorted. "I daresay you'll be precious glad to get out for a holiday. Go away at once, I tell you, and bring him back. Promise him anything. Take a blank check with you, and I will sign it. No, I won't; I'm not such a fool. You can tell him he'll have one when he comes down—a blank check, without a signature."

Richard Drem chuckled to himself over this excellent joke.

"Do you know where to find him?" he continued. "Go to the rooms that that Society meets in, and you'll get him there. You'll find him, I dare say, trying, with the rest of them, to get capital punishment abolished. Why, Mrs. Drem, why? Because they're all interested in having no more hanging to look forward to!—it's their own necks makes them anxious!"

He chuckled again; and Mrs. Drem took advantage of his good humor to slip out of the room, sending Mrs. Roberts, the housekeeper, to officiate as nurse. Mrs. Roberts was a tall, thin woman, with a sharp tongue, and Richard Drem was rather afraid of her. It would have been better for the whole of them if Mrs. Roberts had always command of the sick room, instead of the pliant, timid little wife.

Fearful that his humor might change, Mrs. Drem hurried on the preparations for her departure. In a very short time the carriage was at the door, and, before any counter-command had reached her, she had started for the small rural station. There were no express trains from this little place; but it was still early in the forenoon, and she hoped she would be in London soon enough to catch Philip.

It was the first time she had been out of the house for weeks; and there was something fresh and invigorating in the keen air, and the sunlight, and the change from the dull monotony of the sick room. The carriage did not go rapidly along the narrow lanes, in which the snow lay thick; but there was plenty of motion and variety abroad—in the blowing of the frosty wind, the glittering of the sun on the white arms of the trees, and the startled scream and rapid flight of the blackbirds, as they dipped down from the holly trees to fly along for some farther hiding-place in the tall hedge rows. Mrs. Drem felt quite elated and happy. She was going on an errand of charity, which should do good to everybody concerned.

"And who knows," she said to herself, "but that he may marry Violet, after all?"

She was continually asking herself that question. It haunted her like some vague refrain, following every fresh speculation about the future. He might marry Violet, after all.

At this moment, Mr. Philip was putting a few things into his small portmanteau, preparatory to going down to Wimbledon to spend Christmas with an old gentleman, who was a member of the Analytical Society. This Mr. St. John was a rich old bachelor, who had but few friends, and who was glad to have an occasional visit from the Society's secretary. He was an amiable, benevolent, cheerful old man, with long white hair, very bright blue eyes, and the most astonishing ignorance of the world around him. He was a skilled entomologist, and was familiar with beetles, domestic and foreign; but he had a number of theories about his fellow creatures which showed that he had yet a good deal to learn from the Analytical Society. It was he who proposed, when the Contagious Diseases Acts were first spoken of, that all persons who might be apprehended on suspicion, should be allowed to go free on giving their word of honor that the provisions of these measures did not apply to them.

Philip was just about to start for Wimbledon when Mrs. Drem, having already been to the rooms of the Analytical Society, and found them closed, drove up to his lodgings. She had not seen him for some time; and now he seemed to her to have grown somewhat paler and there was a sort of a listless indifference in his voice and manner.

"You must come down with me to Thurston," she said. "Your father has sent for you."

"He is very kind," said Philip, carelessly. "I am engaged to go to Wimbledon."

"But your father is very ill," said Mrs. Drem.

"Seriously ill?"

"Yes," said Mrs. Drem, with just a twinge of compunction.

"Then, why have you left the house at such a time?" he asked.

The question would have confused a less dexterous woman.

"Oh," said Mrs. Drem, at once, "you know that in such an illness mental rest is the very first thing to be considered. Nothing would please your father but that, at any risk, I should at once start for London and bring you down. And nothing could have given me greater pleasure, Philip. You will come—won't you? What is the use of your remaining apart from us when the cause of the estrangement is all over?"

"Yes; it is all over—isn't it?" he said, absently. Then he added, abruptly, "Do you know that Miss Seaford is married?"

"Yes," said Mrs. Drem, timidly, "I heard so. I am very sorry, for your sake, Philip, and yet it may be better in the end. Only to think of your living in a place like this!"

She cast her eyes round the small room, with its litter of books, pipes, photographs, and what not.

"Your father is not absolutely in danger," she said, "but he is very, very anxious to have you back in the house. And really, when you reflect, Philip, what is the use of living in this way? You have suffered a great disappointment; but you are young, and there is plenty of amusement for you. Your father offers you £3000 a year."

"I have been living on three pounds a week, and did not find it starvation either."

"Oh, Philip," said Mrs. Drem, "why wouldn't you let me send you money? Three pounds a week! You *must* have starved; for I know you never could look after money."

"On the contrary," said Philip, "there are six sovereigns of savings on the mantelpiece there. And there might have been eight, only somebody has taken two since last night."

"And you have made no inquiry after the thief?"

"No," he said, indifferently. "I suppose it was the old woman who lights the fire in the morning. If so, she is welcome to them. She has rather a hard life of it, I think."

"Nothing will change you, Philip," said Mrs. Drem. "You must come away from here. A month in the country will do you good; and then, if your father is well enough, we shall be returning to town. Consider, Philip, what a pretty mail-phaeton you might have for the Park on the income your father proposes to give you. And I'm sure, my dear, if it is not sufficient——"

"Don't alarm yourself," he said with a smile. "I never knew before that I was of so much importance. I had begun to fancy that my commercial value was three pounds a week; and lo, I find myself quoted at nearly ten pounds a day! If my father did propose to buy me over, he has offered a very handsome price."

"My dear!" said Mrs. Drem, in a tone of mild expostulation, "why do you always talk like that of your poor father? If—you knew the affectionate way in which he has been speaking of you of late; if you knew how anxious he is to have you return to the house——"

"*Connu,*" said Philip. "How does he treat you?'

"Oh, very well indeed," said Mrs. Drem, without a faltering look or a blush on her clear pale face. "Of course, he is a little irritable at times, like all invalids; but we must bear with him, you know. And you will have plenty of amusement," she added, hastily getting away from the subject, "When the snow clears, you will have abundant shooting, for your father hasn't allowed anybody to shoot this autumn, and there are plenty of birds all about, though they will be rather wild, you know. And Sir James and Violet are down at Margery House just now, and they will dine with us to-morrow; and if there is nothing else for you to do, you and Violet can play *les Graces* in the drawing-room. Violet and I had a little game the other day," she continued with a smile, "and Violet did a good deal of damage with her hoop. She ran one of her sticks, too, into the Chinese drawings, you know."

"Then my father is not so *very* ill," said Philip quietly.

"Not in danger—far from it," said Mrs. Drem, with demure composure; while she added, in her gentle way. "There is a train at five minutes past four, Philip."

"Ah, well," said he, "I suppose we must resign ourselves to accepting that three thousand. What if I were to give Cecil Sidmouth a thousand of it every year?"

"My dear,' said Mrs. Drem, sagely, "one always has some project like that in looking forward to getting a lot of money; but when one gets it, one always finds enough to do with it for one's self. When you return to London, you will find there is not much real difference between that and your former income."

"You forget I have been living on three pounds a week, and have acquired economical habits."

In the end, she persuaded him to go down into Surrey with her. What reason was there for his refusal? The old possibilities were now over, and he surrendered himself, with something of a sigh, to his old way of living. Life had been robbed of the great purpose which he had dreamed of; now there was nothing but the old routine of somewhat monotonous pleasures. Doubtless, when once he had entered on his new career, it would be rather less dull than it now looked. He had been so long apart from the occupations of fashionable life that they appeared to him rather tiresome; but he knew that, once again in the old sphere, he would rewaken his old interest in his old hobbies. And hobbies— which are of the mildest form of insanity—are very necessary to a man whose sole occupation in life is his own amusement. They distract the attention from regarding the vanity of life, and by occupying his mind, prevent a man so dwelling upon death as to anticipate it.

"I must telegraph to old St. John," he said. "He won't mind my secession, as he has a lot of men going down to him to-morrow—some of these bachelors and relationless fellows who have no family dinners, and get distributed at Christmas among their domestic acquaintances. And may I consider myself the owner of three thousand pounds a year? And may I walk into the Park without offence to my neighbors? And may I ask you to drive with me to Regent Street and have some luncheon?"

"All these things you may do," said Mrs. Drem, with a smile. "And if you want any money now, you will not refuse to take some of mine?"

She held out her purse.

"I have six sovereigns," he said. "Surely that will carry us safely through Blanchard's and down to Thurston. I haven't tasted wine, nor been in a hansom, nor smoked a cigar for weeks. I haven't been in the Park for six months. I have been as socially dead as Sacville Brett. By the way, did you hear what he did in revenge for their having turned him out of the Park? You know, he was so tipsy that he fell backward out of the phaeton, and nearly got under the wheels of the princess's carriage."

"I heard," said Mrs. Drem, solemnly, "that the woman who was driving was as bad as himself."

"It seems he took it into his head that it was a general conspiracy of the Park to disgrace him by shunting him into Piccadilly; and so he went down next day in a dingy shooting-jacket and wide awake, and smoked a clay pipe in the faces of all the people he knew as he walked up and down. The last I heard of him was, that he had gone deeply into the prophecies of Daniel, and his friends were rather anxious about him. *Delirium tremens*, I should think, was the matter."

So they went and had some luncheon in Regent Street, and afterwards drove through the wet and dirty streets to the station, where they caught the appointed train. It was nearly six o'clock, and was quite dark, when they reached Thurston Place, and there were yellow lines of light falling from the windows on the snow of the lawn. Philip and his mother at once went up to Richard Drem's room, and entered.

"I cannot speak to you just now," said the invalid in a weak and querulous voice. "I am too ill; I am very ill; and you go away and leave when I may be dying."

"You said I might go," said Mrs. Drem.

"Never mind—never mind; I shall shortly be out of your power to torture me. Is Philip there? Very well. Go away; don't bother me. Go downstairs, and eat and drink; and if I must die, let me die in peace."

"You may as well say that I am welcome in the house," said Philip.

"Don't you see I am too ill to be bothered? There's plenty of meat and drink for you downstairs. What more do you want? You will have a nice time of it, both of you, when I am gone."

"Come away" said Philip to his stepmother, as he opened the door and waited for her to precede him. "We have had enough of the private theatricals."

"Oh, Philip, you must not mind what he says," she cried, in great alarm lest this reception should have frustrated her kindly intentions. "He does not know what he says; he is really very glad to see you."

"So it would appear," said Philip. "However, it does not matter. Are the Kingscotes coming over to-night?"

"No—to-morrow night. Would you care to ride over there and dine with them rather than dine here?"

"And leave you alone? That would be a poor return for all your kindness of to-day."

"I shouldn't mind, really, Philip," she said. "I am quite used to dining alone. I am sure they would be so glad to see you at Margery House."

"I shall walk over in the morning. What rooms am I to have?"

"You cannot have what used to be your study until tomorrow. Would you mind smoking in the conservatory this evening? I will come in and keep you company if you like—you know I rather like tobacco."

He knew, on the contrary, that she hated it; but this was only the renewal of her old system of sacrificing herself to please the people round about her. This little woman was always telling lies and making pretences, which were as often unnecessary as not; but she was as full of kindliness as of hypocrisy, and, indeed, was a miracle of considerate and thoughtful goodness. She was a very tender-hearted and well-meaning woman, although there was no particle of sincerity in her facile nature. You could trust her actions, but not her words; and, indeed, the whole of her white lies and little misrepresentations were caused by her anxiety to gratify and make things pleasant for her neighbors. She would not have told a deliberate lie to have saved herself from any pain, physical or mental, but she would have told twenty to heighten Philip's enjoyment of a glass of sherry, or to have put Violet into a good humor for a few minutes. In short, in her motherly way, she treated those around her pretty much as if they were children, and told them only what it was good for them to know.

Mrs. Drem was pleased to observe that Philip never spoke of Lillian Seaford; and although he was at times strangely silent and moody, and again restless and discontented, he did not appear to her to dwell much on his disappointment. He would in time, she made no doubt, forget all about the Devonshire girl, and perhaps might marry Violet, as was her constant wish. She recollected, however, that there were some photographic views of Torquay and its neigborhood in a book which lay in the drawing-room, and she contrived that evening to hide away this book before he saw it.

CHAPTER XXIX.

"What am I to do? what am I to do, Mrs. Lawson?" said Hickes, as he walked up and down the parlor of the small house at Hampstead in a condition of extreme nervous agitation. "Why will she not see me? Is it fair? How can I persuade her that I am in earnest unless I see her?"

"She doesna doubt your being in earnest," said the old Scotchwoman, with some surprise and expostulation in her voice. "Doubtless she kens ower weel that you were in earnest when you went so far as to make her marry ye."

"She is driving me mad, Mrs. Lawson," he exclaimed in accents of complaint. "She ought to listen to me. What is the use of her being so determined as that? Doesn't she know that I can't live if I have to go on thinking that I have done wrong to her, and she never gives me a chance of repairing it! I tell you, she is driving me mad, Mrs. Lawson, and none of you will help me to persuade her to speak to me. It is a conspiracy among you, and I never did any harm to any of you, except her—except her. I tell you, if I could make her happy by killing myself, I'd do it—this minute."

He threw himself into a chair, and Mrs. Lawson was astonished to see tears running down his face. There could be no doubt about his being in earnest.

"You aye fly to killing somebody to set matters straight," said the old woman with some scorn. "There has been enough o' that. She kept ye frae killing yourself by marrying ye and destroying the happiness o' her life."

"Don't say that—don't say that, Mrs. Lawson," cried Hickes. "She may be happy if she likes. If she only knew how fond I have become of her—how I worship her—she would have pity on me, I know. And if I can't persuade her that I am sincere, there may be other means. You think I haven't the courage to kill myself if I thought it would please her?"

"Toots, toots, man!" said Mrs. Lawson, "the lassie is no a wild animal wanting to be the death o' decent human beings."

"I tell you what I'll do," said Hickes, eagerly. "I'll give her the chance of suing for a divorce—will that prove to her that I am thinking only of how to please her and not myself? I'll go away and do anything that may be taken for evidence against me—and then she could be quite free, don't you see, Mrs. Lawson? And if they want to prove cruelty, too, we could get up some story among us."

"And ye would have her name made a byword, and make her the talk o' London?"

"What else can I do?"

"Ye should ha' thought o' that earlier," said a severer voice, and Jims entered the rooms; "ye should ha' thought o' that earlier. It is over late to bring back the past."

"It is not—it is not," said Hickes. "I can set her free. I can make her just as she was before I ever saw her. I can kill myself."

"Ye might do worse," said Jims grimly, for he did not quite believe the gusty declarations of this unstable young man.

"I know what you mean," cried Hickes. "You want me to shoot myself, and leave her to marry Philip Drem. Do you? I won't do anything of the kind. I am her husband—I will insist on my rights. I will see her this instant; I will go upstairs and see her, and tell her to her face what I have to say. If a man cannot speak to his own wife——"

With that he rose, and was making for the door. Jims stepped in between him and the passage, and said firmly:

"Young man, this is my house, and the girl upstairs is under my protection. If you step out of this room, it is with me, not with her, ye must settle; and although I never laid hands on a stranger who was under shelter of my roof——"

The sentence was left unfinished, but Hickes thought it prudent to relinquish his intention. He threw himself back into the chair, and said gloomily:

"It isn't you I am afraid of. I am not afraid of any man, only I don't want to quarrel. Quarrelling won't do any good. You know I could insist on seeing her if I liked; I could bring the law to bear on both her and you. But what would that do? It would only make her hate me worse than ever."

In his vexation, he kept pulling and twisting at a new watch-guard which he wore until it snapped in two. Apparently, he paid no attention to the circumstance.

"And you know that," he continued, "and you ought to help me to make friends with her, instead of coming between us. Suppose things are bad enough, here is no use in making them worse; and it is very hard that she will not give me a chance of telling her how wretched I am without her—yes, wretched. And why shouldn't she be as comfortable in my house as in yours? I have plenty of money. I have near nineteen hundred pounds; and I will give it to her to spend on any house she may take a fancy to. I'll go anywhere she likes—out of London, if she prefers the country, and I will work for her like a slave. What dislike has she taken to me? What does she say against me? And what was the meaning of her cheatery and hypocrisy in being very complaisant before the marriage, and pretending she was quite well satisfied, and now breaking off, as if I was her greater enemy?"

"If there was any cheatery or hypocrisy," said Mrs. Lawson, warmly, "it was none of hers. Do you think she liked the marriage because she was barely civil to ye? Do you think she was happy when onybody wi' een could see that wretchedness was clouding her face from morning till night, in spite of the way she tried to be cheerful? And, my certes, if ye canna understand why she is no in love wi' ye, after a' the ill ye have wrought, ye are a bigger gomeril than I took ye for."

"But all that is past and gone," said Hickes. "There's no use in bearing old grudges. Why not make the best of what is left to us?"

At this moment he heard steps on the gravel path outside. He started up.

"She is going out to escape me," he cried. "But I will see her before she goes."

He ran to the window, however, and saw that Lilian Seaford was coming to the house, instead of going away from it. Unknown to the rest of the household, she had gone out for a short walk, and was now returning, unconscious that Hickes was within. As he looked at the slight and graceful figure dressed all in black—at the beautiful calm face which seemed to have lost all its girlish mobility and cheerfulness, and to wear a look of resigned and uncomplaining suffering—his anger and haste died wholly away. What a pure and sweet face it was! although it was somewhat paler than it used to be, and there were hard lines about the mouth. Perhaps it was this paleness which made the dark blue eyes look darker and larger than they had been before. It was a beautiful face, but it was not a merry one; all the light-heartedness had gone from it—all hope and expectation had vanished. With that resigned and steadfast air, she seemed a woman to whom no more delight, no more interest, no more surprise was possible.

Hickes sank down in a chair with a groan and buried his face in his hands. The next moment the door was opened, and the pale face looked into the room. For an instant her eyes lighted upon Hickes—who did not raise his down-bent head—and there was no sudden shrinking in them, nor any sudden look of fear on the face. She merely retired, shutting the door behind her; and when Hickes looked up, he saw only Mr. and Mrs. Lawson.

"You see, she has no pity," he said, bitterly, "none at all. She only cares for her own misery, and thinks that nobody else suffers. Why wouldn't she speak to me? Doesn't she know that I worship the ground she walks on, and that the sight of her face, grown sad like that, makes me think of strange things? You think I am raving—perhaps I am—I don't quite understand it all—God knows that I am very miserable!"

"I am very sorry for you," said Mrs. Lawson, for there were tears again running down the young man's face, " but what can we do? So long as she is with us, no one shall be allowed to force her to go out of the house against her will, and if ye were to force her, ye would be a' the mair miserable afterwards. Dinna think we are fighting against ye. We leave her to her ain choice. Perhaps it might be better for everybody if she could be moved to take a liking for ye; but while she does na do that, there is na help."

"Does she know that I have plenty of money?"

'I will tell her."

"Perhaps she doesn't think I could keep a house," he said, eagerly. "Perhaps she thinks I'd be unsteady and plunge her into difficulties. But I declare to you, Mrs. Lawson, I'd work my fingers to the bone for her sake—I would indeed; and if she would only give me a chance of showing her how I'd work for her—how attentive I'd be to her—how much I think of her —I am sure she would not be so hard-hearted."

Very soon afterwards he left, and yet he wandered about the place, as though loath to go away. He walked up the East Heath Road, to the fatal spot where so much wretchedness had been wrought. He stood there and tried to recall the madness of that wild night, and asked himself what devil had been in his blood and brain at that time to provoke him into working so cruel a wrong!

"But I did not love her then," he said to himself—"I did not love her then; and now, when everything in the world seems wretched and miserable without her, I find myself no nearer winning her love than I did when I made her swear to marry me. What is to be the end—what is to be the end?"

He wandered about there, and returned down the road, and passed James Lawson's house. He fancied he saw, at a window above, the shadow of a face—the face whose mute suffering so rose up in judgment against him and punished him sorely.

"Well, she has her revenge," he said to himself as he walked on, on this cold, gray day, into the town. "How many months is it since I fancied this accursed money was all I wanted to make myself happy?—and now when I could fill my pockets with sovereigns—when I could scatter them about to the children in the streets—I can't buy myself a minute's peace. I wish I could always live drunk, for then I begin to believe that she must in time relent; but the waking up next morning is like hell."

"I'll go and see the Martens," he said, suddenly. "I am not a baby, to be always puling and crying about nothing. If I have the money, I'll have the money's worth. I'll get hold of the Martens and have a flourish."

He called a cab and drove into Kentish-town. He made his way to a decent-looking house in one of the larger thoroughfares, and asked whether Mr. Marten or Miss Marten was upstairs. All the Martens—the two brothers and sister—were at home; and he was accordingly shown into their parlor on the first floor.

It was a large apartment, furnished in a curious fashion; for it was the practising-room of Signor Martini, the celebrated Italian juggler, and all around were balls, bottles, swords, and the other *materiel* of the signor's art. The professor himself, as Hickes entered, was in the act of catching on the point of a cane a bottle thrown him by his sister; while the brother, in accents more Irish than Italian, criticised the performance.

Signor Martini was a tall, stout, dark-faced man, with jet-black and very oily hair. A pair of earrings he wore gave him a somewhat foreign look. His brother—who was known as Senor Tomazo, the Spanish champion equestrian—was a much slighter and younger man, fairer in face, and with no superfluous flesh on his supple and well-knit figure. The girl—who was of yet another nationality, being celebrated as Mademoiselle Cecile, of the lofty wire—was the youngest of the three, and was a comely damsel, with rather a pretty face, coal-black eyes, hair of luxuriant length, and a frame which was evidently rendered hard and sinewy by her gymnastic efforts. For while, at a certain great circus Tomazo flew round the sanded arena on his famous Spanish mule, and while the signor balanced balls on the edge of a sword or kept the atmosphere full of twinkling plates, it was the province of mademoiselle to walk backward and forward on a slack wire, to lie down on it and make her bed in mid-air, to kneel on it in an aspect of picturesque devotion, and to execute a series of tricks that kept the audience from breathing, and made them sigh with relief when the performance was all over. Mademoiselle, with her pretty young face and her shining costume of blue and gold, looked really very charming when she lay all her length on this bent wire, and swung herself as if in a cradle, while the balancing-pole was kept beneath her neck, as if by way of a pillow; and she was consequently a great favorite at the circus. The three lived very happily together, except when Tomazo abused his power of drinking during the day, and made the other two envious.

"Look here," said Hickes, "cut this, and come and dine with me. I'll give you the best dinner I can get in London."

"No use," said Mademoiselle Cecile—who was familiarly known as Kate—with pert frankness. "Neither Bob nor I can touch wine, as you know, until the performance is over. Would you have him miss every ball? and would you have my head swim on the wire, and me come down a cracker? Call it supper, and we are with you. What do you say, Bob—Jack?"

"That's right," said Bob, the signor." "Shall we call it supper—the wedding supper? What's come over your wife, man?"

"D—n it," said Hickes gloomily. "Let her alone—I don't want *you* to talk about her."

"And yet we were to have met her on her marriage-day." said Kate. "I can't help thinking it would have been such a lark, us all pretending we were drunk, and you beginning to bully her, and she thinking it was all in earnest, and running home. What did you mean by it, Sam?"

"I am very glad now she didn't come," said Hickes. "I only wanted then to get rid of her for good; and if I had done it that way, I should never have had the chance of speaking to her again."

"Then you *do* want to make it up with her?" said Kate, with lively interest. "And it is she who has got rid of you?"

"I didn't come here to talk about her," said Hickes angrily.

"Why don't you let him alone, Kate?" said Signor Bob. "You women are always a precious sight too curious. And if you really mean this supper——"

"I can't wait for supper," said Hickes fiercely. "I want something to do *now*—I want something to drink. Here, you Jack, you and I can go and get some dinner; and at night I'll give you all a supper, if you like."

"All right," said Jack the equestrian, jumping up with alacrity, while his brother and sister eyed him with some chagrin.

"You were to have helped us to try that candle trick," said Kate sulkily.

"Never mind," said her brother; "I dare say Monsieur Bertrande will come up to console you."

"Is that Bertrande a Frenchman?" asked Hickes, when they had got outside, glad to get talking of anything.

"A Frenchman!" cried Signor Jack contemptuously. "No more a Frenchman than you are. He was born in London—*there is the identical gutter*," he added, with a sneer, as he pointed to the side of the pavement. "And I won't have him come after my sister. I'd rather you married her—only you can't."

"Confound you!" said Hickes with impatient irritation. "The whole of you seem to talk about nothing but my marriage! Can't you let it alone?"

"No offence—no offence," said Jack, who was rather a dull and sleepy young man, not willing to quarrel with any one.

They got into a cab, and went down to the neighborhood of Leicester Square, where they dined at a French dining-place. There they smoked and idled until it was time for Jack to go to the circus, whither Hickes accompanied him, and was accommodated with a private box. There he sat all alone, listening rather drowsily to the dull jokes of the clowns, and gazing wearily at the old and well-known comic business, at the performance of "highly-trained steeds," supple acrobats, and a stout lady who walked over a tightrope with a child on her back. At last he fell sound asleep in a corner of the box.

He was awakened by being tapped on the shoulder, and, starting up, found himself confronted by Arthur Drem, who was in evening-dress, and in the gayest of moods.

"Saw you from a box opposite, old fellow," said Arthur. "You shouldn't sleep like that—it isn't complimentary to the poor devils. I have two or three friends here; will you join us?"

"No, I won't."

"In another fit of the dumps? Has your pretty one been treating you badly?"

"Look here!" said Hickes, with a sudden spasm of rage, "it would take precious little to make me throw you head over heels down there. I'll do it some day. I warn you to keep out of my road!"

"Hoity-toity!" cried Arthur—but he receded a step all the same—"what's the matter now? Is this the way you rejoice over your good fortune? You are the luckiest of men, and this is the way you thank me for helping you. But there, I forgive you. I see how it is. It is the old story. Man was made to mourn, and women to be the cause of his mourning. A fellow is never satisfied unless he is breaking his heart about somebody, instead of enjoying himself like a reasonable being. But you might at least be civil."

"I don't want any more of your chaff."

"Come, come," said Arthur, "you've waked up on the wrong-side—that is all. Let's go to the bar and have a drink; and you can come back and tell me how you have been getting on of late since you fell heir to your fortune."

Hickes at last consented to be appeased—indeed, he was rarely of the same mind for five minutes. When they returned from the bar to the box, he unbosomed himself to his old confidant, and told him, in piteous accents, of all that had happened, and of his own wretched plight.

"I don't believe," he said, "that there's as miserable a man as me in all London—not in all London. I don't blame you, Drem—it's all my own doing. And, now it's done, what way am I to go? Day after day passes, and I am getting madder about her than ever; and when I see her, and see how wretched she is—God help her!—I feel as if hanging was too good for me."

"That's only modesty on your part," said Arthur soothingly. "You must do something active instead of lounging about and moping. You should enjoy the money you've got. Why don't you run away with somebody, and give yourself something to think of? I hear you are carrying on a gay flirtation with Mademoiselle Cécile."

"You hear a lie, then!" said Hickes, suddenly altering his mood into one of savage attack. "Do you remember the stories you told me of all the good that was to be done by that infamous scheme we got up? Wasn't everybody to be made happy? Wasn't Philip Drem to go back to his father's house? Wasn't I to have a pretty wife and a lot of money? Weren't you to have your uncle's business?"

"My dear fellow, if you were less irritated by your sleep, you would see that all these things have occurred. My cousin Philip went down to Thurston on the day before Christmas, and is there now. Not only is he good friends with his father, but I think he is likely to marry a certain young lady down there."

"Do you think he will?" said Hickes, with great and vivid interest.

"I think he will. But what is it to you?"

"Oh, nothing," said Hickes, falling into a brown study. Were Philip Drem to marry, might not Lilian be induced to turn from thinking of him?

"As I say, you have done all the good I said. Philip is reconciled with his father; you have a pretty wife and a lot of money; as for my chances of my uncle's business, I am quite satisfied. Now, what more would you like?"

At this moment, Mademoiselle Cécile came out and tripped with a pretty grace into the middle of the arena, where she bowed and kissed her hand to the spectators. Then she climbed up a ladder, got on to the "lofty and invisible wire," had her balancing pole handed to her, and began her performances. She was dressed in a tunic of blue satin, glittering with silver lace and spangles; she had knickerbrockers of the same material and hue; and on the top of her mass of jet-black curls, that hung down her back, she wore a white rose that Hickes had sent her. But she had no opportunity—as an actress might have had—of sending him a brief swift glance of thanks during the performance; for while she put herself into pretty positions, representing various well-known statues, and while she walked backward and forward on the yielding wire with all the muscles of her body in a state of extreme tension, poor Kate's eyes never left that thin line of iron which rose in front of her towards the opposite pole. Had her head grown dizzy—had she lost sight of the wire for an instant—there would have been a shriek from the great concourse of spectators, and a huddled heap of blue satin and senseless humanity would have had to be carried out of the ring by the attendants, with the two clowns hovering in the rear, and quite forgetting to make any joke.

"You may as well break off with your friends in the box," said Hickes to Arthur, "and come and have supper with us. I'll introduce you to Kate Marten. If I'm not to be jolly one way, I'll be the other. I'd be as straight as any other fellow if I had the chance; but everything is against me—and so I mean to take what fun I can get—and you'll see how I'll make this money spin."

Hickes, spite of his money, had returned to his old notion that the world was using him ill, and that it was not his fault if he fell into evil ways. That night he conducted himself like a madman—until even Kate Marten said she would rise and go home by herself if he persisted in throwing away his money in preposterous extravagances. Arthur paid such particular attention to Mademoiselle Cécile, that he let Hickes go on as he liked; and the latter in turn shouted and laughed, made the waiters drink champagne out of tumblers, and then fell to crying over his wretchedness and ill-luck. He seemed to be making desperate efforts to become intoxicated, and to fail. He could not reach the goal of frantic excitement or of happy stupor. The more he drank, the more restless he became, and the wine only provoked him into magnifying his misery.

"My boy," said Arthur to him as he got him into a cab, "you may make your money spin if you like. Easily got, easily spent. But you are killing yourself."

"It isn't my fault," said Hickes, who began to cry again. "she won't listen to me ; she cares for nobody but him."

"So much the worse ; but why should you kill yourself because a woman won't speak to you?"

"You say that, of course !" said Hickes. "There's no woman born would put you out. You don't care for anybody but yourself. You have no more blood than a fish. And you don't need anybody to care for you ; for all the world is with you—you have lots of friends—you are respectable—you look forward to having plenty of money——"

"All this is nonsense. You must come to your senses, and consider what you mean to do."

"I have considered," said Hickes wildly ; "I have considered. I know what I shall do before long, if this continues, and if she will not speak to me."

CHAPTER XXX.

Mrs. Drem was overjoyed with the turn things were taking in these spring months down at Thurston Place. Her husband gradually got better, and as he became well he evinced an extraordinary desire to be friends with his son. He was almost respectful at times, and showed such efforts to control his temper and be considerate, that Philip was really touched by his forbearance, and did everything in his power to respond to these signs of altered times.

"We need not have separate stables," said his father to him, as they were talking of going up to town. "When you buy your horses, I will keep them for you, and you will lend me them should any accident happen to mine. I think I shall make one serve for the brougham, and we must send the barouche up before we go."

"Oh, not for me, Richard," said Mrs. Drem. "I am sure, when Philip gets his phaeton——"

"He will drive you in it !" said Mr. Drem, with a sneer. "I suppose you'd like to be driven up and down the Park in a mail-phaeton? But young men have their own friends; and that sort of thing is not suited to your time of life, ma'am."

Mr. Drem had not included his wife in the list of those to whom he wished to be more civil than formerly, and, indeed, seemed inclined to visit upon her the ill-nature he no longer extended to Philip. Nevertheless, Philip and his stepmother had been all along too firm allies to suffer this peaceably, and the young man interposed on behalf of his more timid companion with a vigor which his father was forced to respect. And on this occasion he declared that the very first person he should drive in the Park would be his stepmother, and that she would be heartily welcome to the seat whenever she chose to occupy it.

Violet and Sir James were much at Thurston during the spring of this year, and the intimacy between the two families became more and more familiar, if that were possible. Philip and Violet were, of course, thrown continually together, and Mrs. Drem looked on the pair of them like a smiling little providence in petticoats, and secretly speculated on what was to result from this constant companionship. Again and again she was on the point of talking to Philip about the chance that lay before him, and as often a certain feeling, which she could not well define, told her that it would be imprudent. At last her anxiety to have this great hope of her heart fulfilled overcame her caution, and she said to him one morning, with a little inward tremor:

"What an excellent wife Violet will make—so bright and cheerful, so clever, and engaging, and sensible!"

"He will be a fortunate fellow who marries her," said Philip rather carelessly, and scarcely looking up from his book.

His stepmother was rather disappointed by the indifference of his tone, but she half suspected him of dissimulation.

"Come now, Philip," she said, laying her hand on his shoulder, "confess that you enjoy very much this constant rambling about with Violet, and that you are not so blind as you pretend to be about the natural consequences. If it doesn't matter to you, think of her. Why does she come here so often —why is she so glad to walk with you, or ride with you?"

"Well," he said, looking up from his book with a laugh, "you have a pretty way of paying a compliment. Do you think every woman must be as much in love with me as you are?"

A slight blush passed over Mrs. Drem's pale face, and the pretty stepmother said :

"Of course it is natural that I should expect women to fall in love with you, because I know so much of you."

"Thank you very much. I begin to have a very good opinion of myself, when I find myself able to withstand all this nice flattery."

"But as for Violet," continued Mrs. Drem, "you must remember, Philip, that you ought not to trifle with her, if you are not in earnest. She is a particular friend of ours. When you return to London, you may go on as you please with other girls; but with Violet—I would not have her feelings hurt for the world."

"What does all this mean?" he said, with a look of profound surprise. "Are you serious? You cannot be. Violet and I have not altered in the least our old relations. Hurting her feelings! Yes, if you forgot to help her at lunch, or made fun of her ferns. She is too sensible; the most perfect confidence exists between us."

"But there are some things which a girl dare not tell," said Mrs. Drem insidiously.

"But Violet tells me everything, from the wine she would rather have at dinner to the plans she has laid for spending £5,000 a year, should she ever get it—which is not likely. And I know the name of the man she would like to marry."

"She cannot have told you that," said Mrs. Drem, somewhat aghast. "You don't mean her old schoolgirl liking for Lord Cecil?"

"I am not going to tell tales," said Philip, "but you may rest content about Violet's feelings; she is a remarkably sharp young woman."

"You are most unjust to her!" exclaimed Mrs. Drem.

"I am nothing of the kind," said Philip. "Is a girl any the worse for knowing what to eat and drink—for knowing the value of money—for having a pretty correct notion of the people around her? Violet is the most charming girl who comes to your house—out and away the most charming; and if I were condemned to marry, I should ask for no greater happiness than to have her for my executioner. There!" he added impatiently, as he flung down his book and walked to the door; "why will you always talk about marriage?"

He strode out of the house, and she watched him descend into the valley and disappear down one of the lanes.

"I know what that means," she said with a sigh; "the old

story coming up again; and he will walk about the country all day by himself, and come home at night looking so tired, and wretched, and miserable. Will he never forget it?"

Philip had just disappeared, when she saw two figures on horseback riding along the bottom of the valley; and these she soon discovered to be Sir James Kingscote and his daughter. A few minutes thereafter the horses were at the door, and presently Violet was in the room.

"What is the matter?" said Mrs. Drem, alarmed by the unwonted trouble that was visible in the young girl's face.

"Oh, Mrs. Drem," she said, "such a dreadful thing has happened? That railway, you know—the company has smashed up, and papa is ruined—absolutely ruined! Where is Mr. Drem? He wishes to see him at once."

Sir James was in the hall, and he had already sent a servant to ask whether Mr. Drem could be seen. The man forthwith conducted him to the room in which Mr. Drem was to be found, and Mrs. Drem returned to Violet.

"Everything was going on so pleasantly," said the girl, "that I had begun to fancy it was all right. You know papa would not tell me anything about it, and it was only through Philip that I heard. And as Philip has said nothing for some time, I thought it was getting quite straight again."

"My dear," said Mrs. Drem, "don't excite yourself; the failure of a single company is nothing. Your papa may lose some money——"

"He will lose everything, Mrs. Drem," said Violet. "All his money—and it wasn't much—was sunk in that company years ago, when it looked so promising; and Margery House was heavily mortgaged to get the funds."

"You mustn't mind, Violet," said Mrs. Drem. "People don't die because a company breaks. You won't have to leave Margery House, depend on it. You may have to endure a good deal of pinching until you pull through, you know, but you will pull through. Why, my husband will be sure to give Sir James whatever he wants."

"Oh no!" said Violet. "Woman might help each other in that way, but men never do. If Mr. Drem helps papa, it will be in the way of business; and what are we to offer him for the money?"

"*We!* So you have made yourself a partner? Well then, you must sell us yourself."

"What use would I be to you?"

"I would give £50,00 for you if I had it," said Mrs. Drem, kissing the girl in an affectionate way.

"I wish I was worth that to anybody," said Violet, with a sigh.

"You would be worth far more than that to Philip, if you would only be his wife," said Mrs. Drem, blushing somewhat.

"I thought you meant that," said Violet, rather absently, "and I am afraid both Mr. Drem and papa will propose it,"

"My darling!" cried Mrs. Drem, taking both her hands, "I should bless the day that made you my daughter. And what are you crying for, my dear?"

For the tears had sprung to the girl's eyes, as she stood there silently contemplating what the future might have in store for her; and this exhibition of grief was so new on the part of the light-hearted Violet that Mrs. Drem, at first surprised was profoundly touched, and fell to kissing and soothing the girl as if she had been her own daughter.

Sir James entered the room in the middle of this pretty business.

"What!" he said; "has she taken this company-matter so much to heart?"

He was looking quite cheerful; and Violet started up with a curious searching glance directed towards her father's face.

"Girls don't understand these things, do they?" said Sir James' "But they know enough to vex themselves and get a good cry."

"Were you not vexed as we rode over, papa?" said Violet.

"How long ago is that?" said Sir James, gayly. "Aye; the fact is, you timid people must know that my friend Mr. Drem has proved himself a true friend and that together we mean to get over this troubled time."

"Didn't I tell you so?" said Mrs. Drem reprovingly to Violet.

Violet looked with a doubtful expression from the one to the other, and said nothing. But no sooner was the visit over, nor had they ridden a hundred yards from the house, than Violet abruptly asked:

"Papa, what arrangement did you make with Mr. Drem?"

"Now how could I explain such matters to you?" said Sir James.

"I want to know," said Violet. "He is to give you money, I suppose—what does he expect you to do in return?"

"My dear child," said Sir James, in the blithest of humors. "What if I were to tell you that, in order to give security to

Mr. Drem, I have effected a mortgage on the most valuable piece of my property—that is to say, yourself? How now? how now? Bridling up? Well, you girls are always like that —angry if we translate your wishes into plain terms."

There was no anger visible, however, on Violet's face but there was a hard look in the dark eyes, and a certain coldness in her voice, as she said, stiffly——,

"How much did you sell me for, papa?"

"Violet!" said Sir James, with some asperity.

"These are plain terms; you see I don't dislike them."

"Are you serious, or are you only pretending a little mock-modesty? I should have thought nothing could be more agreeable to you than to learn that your marriage with Philip was a subject of pleasure to all of us; that it most opportunely comes in to save us from ruin: that it renders easy transactions otherwise impossible."

"I know," said Violet, in the same tone. "But he has not asked me to marry him."

"But he will."

"I think nothing is farther from his thought, and I am sure nothing has been farther from mine."

There was a little sigh of resignation accompanying this statement which made Sir James turn in his saddle and regard her with some surprise. But presently he had recovered his equanimity.

"I never knew one of you different. Wayward, intractable, pretending to be hurt when you're pleased, angry with those who are doing their best for you. Never mind, my girl, I don't want you to say you wish to marry Philip Drem. It isn't time yet, if he has not asked you. But everybody takes it for granted. Here are you and he continually together."

"That is our doing, not his," said Violet. "We go there ten times for once he comes to us. And he and I have been playmates ever since we were children."

"The more reason you should carry on the game until you get into your second childhood," said Sir James. "Why, everybody knows he is going to marry you."

"Everybody knew he was going to marry Mary Thormanby. I am sure it is not his fault. People won't let him alone. They are always fancying he is going to marry somebody."

"I suppose I represent the 'people' you talk of? But I don't understand you Violet. Do you mean to say you dislike Philip Drem?"

"How could I, papa? He is one of my best friends."

"Friends! friends! That is what all girls say. Have you anything to say against his marrying you?"

"Papa, he has not asked me," said she in despair. "Please don't talk any more about it—you don't understand."

"I understand very well, and I won't talk any more about it. Only you must listen to this like a good girl. Don't go away with any notion in your head that I have sold, or bought, or made any money transaction about you whatever. I would sooner see Margery House sold inch by inch than that you should suffer any such wrong. Now don't begin to cry, Violet, you know I can't bear crying. This monetary transation has nothing to do with your wishes. You are quite free. Only as both Mr. Drem and myself took it for granted that Philip and you will marry each other some day, that conviction made it easy for Mr. Drem to advance me a certain sum to meet these present difficulties. That is the whole transaction. You are not bound by it. Marry Philip Drem or not, as you please, only don't go and cast him off through contrariety, merely because you think we want to bind you to it. Oh, I know you little plagues very well. But I have confidence in your good sense, Violet. You must not do anything wilful, for my sake. Consider what our home has been to us. You would not like to leave it, I know. And although I daresay, if the worst came to the worst, I could go into some sort of business, and earn enough for both of us——"

"Oh, don't speak of it!" cried Violet; "don't speak of it, papa! I will do all you want; I will do anything you like; only you must not leave Margery House."

Three or four days elapsed before Violet saw Thurston Place again. London was beginning to fill, and the mental eyes of innumerable families, hid away in the corners of counties were turned to the great centre, and saw the gathering crowd begin to enjoy the rush and run and glitter of the season. Mr. Drem was just about to return, although Mincing Lane, and not the Row, was the object of his thoughts. Sir James, too, although he could better have afforded to remain in the country, deemed it prudent to arrive with the stream, for his daughter's sake.

The Kingscotes were to spend the second last day at Thurston Place, and accordingly Sir James and Violet went over in the forenoon, and idled about until luncheon time. During that practical, sensible, and satisfactory meal, Violet told Philip she wished to speak a few words with him by and by. Accordingly, when they rose from the table, he and she passed outside to the lawn, then chatted a bit, then drew off a space farther, then finally went off for a ramble, fancying themselves unperceived. Of course everybody saw them, and was not grieved when they disappeared, alone, round by the lime-tree walk. It was a beautiful day, full of sunlight and the odor of opening buds.

"Are you going to town to-morrow," said Violet.

"Yes," said Philip, a little surprised by the oddness of her tone.

"I have something very particular to say to you, Philip, You know that my father is in great money difficulties?"

"I heard something of it."

"And that he asked Mr. Drem to assist him?"

"So I understand."

"Do you know anything more?"

"No; that is, I believe my father has relieved Sir James from all present anxiety, and I am very glad. Look here, Violet—you and I are such old friends that I am going to say something rather odd to you. I have a lot of money, and nothing particular to do with it. Now, you won't be offended—"

"But you don't seem to know," she exclaimed in great excitement—" you don't seem to know why Mr. Drem gave papa that money. Oh, Philip, they want me to marry you?"

And she burst into tears.

"That is no discovery, is it?" said Philip, with a smile.

"But don't you see, Philip, papa cannot have this money unless I marry you. Oh, tell me what I am to do!"

"Poor little thing!" he said compassionately, "they want to marry it against its will, do they? Why, Violet, where is the common sense you used to be so proud of? I don't think your great desire not to marry me is any great compliment; but still, my poor Violet, do you think I am an ogre to eat you up in spite of yourself? They cannot make us marry. I won't marry you—unless you ask me prettily. Didn't you ever hear of the young lady who was asked by a young gentleman if she would marry him, and answered, 'Yes, please?' There, dry your eyes like a good girl, and resume your ordinary amount of self-possession, which I may say, is considerable. I won't marry you until you come some day and very nicely, 'Please, Philip, will you be good enough to become my husband?' And then I'll consider it."

Miss Violet bridled up a bit at this.

"You'd better not wait for that time," she said, "or you

will be rather tired of waiting. But you have not told me what I am to do, Philip. We are both of one mind, but here is this business of money. Your father won't give papa the money unless he thinks we are going to marry,"

"Now you are talking like yourself, Violet. We will let him think it, and your papa also. The money Sir James wants is, I daresay, not so vast a sum—*and he must have it directly.* Let us act the part of affianced lovers until he gets the money. There can be no harm in the deception—for the money he will get is in one sense mine."

The girl reddened violently, and he said, "I beg your pardon Violet; I didn't mean to remind you of that, but it would occur to you in any case. We are going up to town. You must exercise your skill so as to lead people in general to believe we are only friends as before (that you may not be compromised), but at home we may conduct ourselves like engaged people. Do you know how?"

"Oh, yes," said Violet; "at least I know how a gentleman conducts himself when he is engaged. He seems to be always pulling on his gloves nervously, as if he wanted to go out, and always simpering anxiously at the young lady, and bothering her with what he thinks funny speeches—and disarranging her music—and getting angry if she goes down with anybody else to dinner—and stands in a corner and scowls when she is dancing with anybody else—and is particularly civil to her brother, and to her sister's governess, untill he finds out that she dislikes the governess, and then he turns round and hates that meek lady furiously—and he is always hanging about in the afternoon when one wants to go to the library—and he thinks it fine to neglect his duties, and makes a boast of it, for her sake —and generally to make himself rather ridiculous and desperately in the way."

"That is how gentlemen who are engaged conduct themselves?"

"Such as I have seen."

"And how do girls who are engaged conduct themselves?"

"I don't know," said Violet, demurely.

"And how do young persons who are engaged conduct themselves, when they find themselves together? For we must begin and try."

"Oh," she said quietly, "if it is that you mean, I will give you a kiss—for your kindness."

And so she granted him in a very matter-of-fact way that

tiny reward; but it was not the first, nor yet the hundredth time, that a similiarly meek and cousinly embrace had marked the even and gentle current of this friendship.

CHAPTER XXXI.

In one of the saddest of his songs Heine bids his sweetheart lay her hand on his heart and listen to the knocking in the small chamber within. There is a cunning and wicked carpenter living there, he tells her, and the carpenter is working and hammering at a coffin. The carpenter hammers and knocks by day and by night; and soon the coffin will be ready and sleep near. Is it true, then, that Love, that makes the heart beat faster, is the colleague of Death? Lilian Seaford began to dream dreams and see visions during the long evenings up at Hampstead; and in these *traumbilder*—gazing on which she was withdrawn from the world around her, and wholly unconscious of it—she seemed to see Love and Death together; the one angry and passionate and wretched, the other calm and serious and sweet. And it appeared to her that Love, whom she feared, had taken her by the hand, and led her a little way, and confided her to Death, whose pale and earnest face was full of kindness to her.

"Ye maun go to Torquay," said Jims abruptly, looking at her.

"To Torquay!" she said, with a blush of color mantling into the wan cheeks, and a wistful light appearing in the dark-blue eyes.

"Yes, indeed!" said Mrs. Lawson, with no less decision. "Ye want something to put new life into your blood. You've been sitting and moping here until your hands are thin and blue-white like paper, and your eyes are sunken and dark, and your cheeks are no as fresh and rosy as they used to be. Torquay—that's your doctor."

"I should like to go down to Torquay—for a day or two," said Lilian; "but the fares are so expensive."

"Expense or no expense," said Mrs. Lawson, "ye are going to Torquay; no for one day, nor two, nor three—but until we've got the pink into your face again."

The end of it was, that the whole family migrated to Devonshire; Alec getting his month's holidays then instead of in the summer, and going with them. They went down in a second-class carriage; but in view of the spring sunlight, and the mellow air, and the young fresh colors of the woods and hedges, they did not mind that. And when the first salt breath of the sea blew through the carriage, it was like the touch of a magic wand, waking a whole crowd of recollections, some pleasant and sweet, some tender and sad. As for Lilian, sitting in the corner and looking out vaguely on the scenes that rushed past, you would have thought she had no memory. Did she recall nothing of that former journey down here with Philip, that she sat so cold and reserved, with a wan look in her eyes? Jims reminded himself of that journey—and of the eager delight of the young girl, who was alternately laughing and crying with the joy of seeing again the old familiar places. Could this be the same creature, who had grown so impassive—whose lips were white, and thin and hard? When they caught the first glimpse of the sea near the mouth of the Teign, her eyes dilated somewhat, and seemed to drink in the rich blue color of the great sweep of sunlit water; but otherwise she betrayed no special interest. She mentioned to Alec, briefly and curtly, the names of the places as they went along, and that was all their conversation.

Nor did she betray any emotion when, in the calm yellow evening, they came in sight of Tor Bay, with the long sweep of coast lying under a ruddy haze, and the green hills and white houses of Torquay shining in the sun. They were fortunate enough to get some lodgings without any trouble—in Higher Terrace the rooms were, looking out over the harbor towards the bay. They all went out for a walk afterwards, except Lilian. She remained in the house alone, in spite of their united entreaties. She said she was a little tired—did not feel disposed to walk—would rather remain by herself.

"My lassie," said Mrs. Lawson anxiously, "ye maun be out o' doors from morning till night until we see your color back. We have na brought ye down to Torquay that ye should sit in a room."

"You are very kind, Mrs. Lawson," was all she said. "I will go out as much as you like by and by, but not to-night."

The Lawsons did not remain out long; but when they returned Lilian had retired to her own room.

"I guessed as much," said Mrs. Lawson; "for when we went out, I saw she had in her hand that little prayer-book that Mr. Philip gave her."

Then, when Alec had gone off, also, and the old people were left by themselves, Mrs. Lawson said, in a complaining way.

"Nothing seems able to break this dreadful stillness that's ower her. I would rather she were ever so wild wi' grief rather than this settled look on her face, that makes ye think she only wants to get into her grave and have done. Who would ha' thocht that a' this would come o't? It would have been far better for her to have done as Hicks wanted—let him come about the house until she got accustomed to regard him as her friend, and then as her husband. Whatever he may be, he aye seemed anxious to please her and be kind to her."

"We maun leave her to the decision o' her ain heart," said Jims. "I'm no inclined to think that Hickes is a stable young man: but she might have made him better and given him a house and household affairs to look after and steady him. But that's neither here nor there. Let her be his wife, or nobody's wife, I carena—if only she gets well."

"Jims," said Mrs. Lawson, "I'm fair terrified when I look at her white face, that is like stone. I hope something'll break that hardness that seems killing her."

"Whist!" said Jims. "What is that?"

He went to the window, which was opened, his wife following. Outside the night was dark, though there was a pale green light over the western horizon. A few stars were visible, and behind Waldon Hill a crescent moon was helping to lend a faint radiance to the eastern skies.

Lilian's room was just over that in which they stood; and as they listened they heard a sound as of a girl sobbing bitterly.

"She is at the window," whispered Mrs Lawson. "I will go up to her room."

When the old woman went upstairs and opened the door gently, she was greatly surprised by what she saw before her. The girl was sitting at the window, her long hair falling in dishevelled masses about her shoulders—her hands clasped over a small prayer-book—while she sobbed wildly, and uttered incoherent murmurings of affection, in which the listener caught the name of Philip. Beyond this figure, which seemed dressed all in white, the open window showed an expanse of dark sea, with a pallid green sky overhead, and the white crescent of the moon.

Lilian started up pale and terrified, to confront the intruder. It seemed to Mrs Lawson that there was something wild in the girl's face, and that the white dress made her look ghastly and spectral.

"You are so unhappy?" she said. "Why did you never tell us?"

"I could not tell you," said the girl, in accents of strange excitement; "I cannot tell you now. I have been praying to God that I might die; and He will not let me—He will not let me."

"Lilian!"

"I would rather die—I should like to die—and here, at Torquay. I never knew what life was until the time that Philip and I were here—and then it was only a month—only a month!"

"Lilian, think of the harm you are doing yourself by exciting yourself like this. See how you tremble and your face is white."

"And you think I am going to die, then?" said the girl, with an expression of joy that seemed like madness. "I dreamed last night that I was coming down here to die—that I met Death, like an old man with white hair, down by the sea; and he took my hand, and I was not afraid. Do you think I should be afraid if I were to die now? I should only be going to meet my mother; and Philip would come—after I am dead—to my grave, and think kindly of me. I never did anything to him that he could think unkind, did I?"

"Lilian, you are breaking my heart," said the old woman, with the tears running fast down her withered gray cheeks. "We have brought you down here to cure you of your white face and your sadness, and to make you well and cheerful again, and you talk of dying. You are not the brave girl you used to be. If your mother were here now, what would she say to this wicked notion of yours?"

"I have asked her," said the girl, turning to the open window, where the stars were visible—"I have asked her; but she will not speak."

"Do you know what will happen to you if you indulge these fancies? You will not die—you will grow mad. And I won't have anything of the kind. I am going to bring back the smile to your face, as sure as I am an old woman, who would be very miserable if anything happened to you. And I will sleep with you to-night, to see that there is no more of this sitting up and dreaming at an open window. It seems to me that there has been a good deal of it lately."

"I once asked you to sleep with me, Mrs. Lawson," she

said, "because I was afraid I might die, if my heart went on beating so. Now I am not afraid; but if that were to happen in the night, I should want you to telegraph to Philip; and he might come in time."

"Now, now," said the old woman, "no more. Get off your things, and get to bed; to-morrow morning you will find the sea-air putting new blood into your veins. You must pick up your spirits, my bairn; for we canna afford to lose ye, and that's the truth. Ye have become a pairt o' our ain lives, and it would maist kill us puir auld bodies if anything were to happen, to ye. And it winna happen, if ye will only be sensible and show some courage. Take my word for it my lassie, ye will find plenty in the world worth living for yet."

Next morning Lilian went out with Alec to show him the neighborhood. The day was bright and clear, with a warm south wind blowing over the bad laden with saline fragrance. They rambled about together in the sunlight and the fresh air —round by the lofty eastern cliffs, with the clear green water far below them—back behind the town and on to the wooded lanes and leafy nooks lying southwest of the old abbey—and then returning to the Livermead rocks, and so home by the sunset. When they got into the house, Alec's face was red with the sunlight, his eyes full of joy, and his speech almost incoherent in praise of all that he had seen. Lilian on the contrary, had been very grave and silent during this long walk; and now she merely sat down by the window and looked out at the sea. She had no adventures to tell, as in the olden times. She did not insist on everybody praising her beloved Devonshire. She did not beg them to declare there was no bay in the world so blue as Tor Bay. She sat quite silent, and seemed rather tired.

But one of them proposed that next day they should go and see the Dart: and then she said, so suddenly that it sounded like a piteous cry,—

"Oh, not up the Dart! I cannot go up the Dart with you Alec!"

"Why?" said the boy, wonderingly.

His grandmother put her hand on his arm, and he did not press the question.

Next day Alec went and saw the Dart by himself. As he sat on the steamer, the drowsy heat of the day inclining him to dreams, glided up and past the green woods, the grassy hills, and the daisy banks, he saw from a distance the figure of a man who walked by himself under the shadow of some trees by the river side.

"How like he is to Philip Drem!" he said; but the alder branches presently hid this solitary stranger from sight.

CHAPTER XXXII.

"My dear fellow, how are you?" said Major Delaney to Philip. The Major had cut Mr. Philip dead several times when that young man was merely the secretary of some society or other. But now Mr. Philip was on horseback, and the Major was leaning over the railings in the Park, and the time was May, and there was much wealth and fashion abroad, of which the Major liked to be considered a part. "Where have you been this long time?" he asked, just as if he had never seen his young friend since he and Lord Cecil dined at the Major's house.

"Oh, in the country—anywhere," said Philip, good naturedly. What was the use of quarrelling with the poor Major.

"That was Miss Kingscote who went on there with her father, wasn't it?"

"Yes."

"Handsome little girl. I hear Sir James will be in the 'Gazette' shortly."

"That's all nonsense," said Philip. "He is no more likely to be in the 'Gazette' than either you or I."

"Faith, I hope he'll be never as near it as I am," said the major, with a laugh.

"How is Miss Thormanby?"

"Very well indeed. She is walking here somewhere with Mrs. Delaney. Shall I tell them you want to see them?"

"If you will take my horse for a turn or two, I will go and find them."

Mrs. Delaney and her niece were seated on two penny chairs under the cool shade of a tree. When Philip went forward to his old sweetheart, a faint color leaped to the pale face; but the next second she was talking to him with perfect composure, as if nothing had occurred. Philip began to think that there was some mistake somewhere—that it was impossible he could ever have been in love with this woman.

"We saw you riding up and down with Miss Kingscote," said Miss Thormanby. "How very pretty she is! And she knows how to keep her dark hair smooth round her forehead to suit the style of her face."

"Yes," said Philip; "she would look very different if she were to send her hair into hysterics all around her head."

"I hope Mr. Drem is better," said Mrs. Delaney. And her niece began to fear that something awkward would be said.

"Yes," replied Philip; "he has returned to town almost well. He has been all the winter down in Surrey."

"So I hear," said Mrs. Delaney, adding, with a little toss of her head, "av course we only learn by reports. Mrs. Drem thought fit to forget us the moment you left the house. Sure I am we were not so sorry; but she moight have minded her manners."

"What do you think of those fans with the green grass all round?" said Mary Thormanby, in a desperate hurry, aiming at the first object she saw.

"They are more appropriate to the season, at least," rejoined Philip, also making a wild jump at a remark, "than the white fans with the fur."

"I don't bear malice—will be glad to see you, Mr. Drem, any time it is convanient to ye."

"You're very kind Mrs. Delaney."

"As for Mrs. Drem—"

"These parasol-whips are absurd, are they not?" broke in Miss Thormanby.

"Yes, unless one can get the sun to change each way one drove. You can put the whip at the back of your head, for example."

"Will you dine with us this evening, Mr. Drem?" said Mrs. Delaney, who was determined to make hay while the sun was shining.

"I am very sorry—I am engaged for this evening," said Philip.

"You needn't make a stranger av yourself," she said, "merely because your stepmother has cut us, I hope. I'd like to know what we did—beyond being civil to you"——

"If I drove, I should drive, now in the forenoon," said Mary Thormanby, hastily. "It must be so much pleasanter to have the whole place pretty nearly to one's self."

"Why are you not riding?" he asked.

"Because I haven't a horse at present," she said frankly.

So they chatted on for a few minutes together, and Mr. Philip was quite pleased to find that he and she got on so well. He fancied that she was a good deal more complaisant to acquaintances (to which lower grade he had now evidently sunk) than to friends; but the real explanation of the matter was, that she saw plainly he did not care whether she spoke civilly to him or not. He was indepeneent of her moods. Had she practised any of her little perversities of old, he could have found an easy remedy in merely rising and bidding her goodby. They met, therefore, on quite amicable terms; for she knew that she had lost her empire over him, and might as well submit to the altered state of affairs. When the Major came up with his horse, Philip left Mary Thornanby in very good spirits, and promised to her aunt that he would see them all very soon.

In a short time Philip had established the old relations existing between his fair acquaintance and himself, and accepted the not very onerous duties of his new position. His father was now wonderfully considerate to him—that is to say, Mr. Drem tried to control his temper, and gave his son presents, and endeavored to establish some sort of harmony between them. The son responded to these advances with every show of respect, until Mrs. Drem was quite a happy woman when she saw the prosperous result of her work. She herself, it is true, did not come in for her due share of the prevailing cordiality; but Philip expoused her cause so warmly, and so quickly resented his father's exhibitions of ill-temper towards her, that Mr. Drem soon came to see that the easiest way to propitiate Philip was to be polite to his stepmother. And she, as Philip had vowed, was the very first to enter his new phaeton with him; and Mrs. Drem was proud and pleased indeed to find herself in the Park along with her stepson, and to show to her acquaintances that if there were disagreements in the family she was not the cause of them.

"They used to say I spoiled you, Philip. Perhaps it was true. But you have not proved ungrateful, as spoiled children generally do. And now there is only one thing more that I can ask of you, and then I shall be content."

"What is that?"

"Ah, don't you know?" said Mrs. Drem, her eyes wandering to where Violet Kingscote sat in conversation with Philip's father.

"I know,', said Philip, with a sigh. and then he rose and went away.

His father, too, had seen the prudence of allowing this affair to be negotiated by Mrs. Drem. He himself never mentioned it; but Philip was given to understand that it was the one project on which Mr. Drem had set his heart, and that the social life of Sir James actually hung upon it.

"Hasn't my father given Sir James that money yet?" said Philip one day, rather impatiently, to Mrs. Drem.

"Not yet," said she.

"But why? He must have the money soon."

"I think he would like to see you and Violet more like—like engaged," stammered Mrs. Drem.

"Would he like to have us kiss each other before a roomful of people? Doesn't he see that we are always together; that I pay her as much attention as I can, short of worrying the life out of her?"

"You haven't asked her to marry you yet, have you?" said Mrs. Drem timidly.

"Look here," said Philip. "Violet and I are not going to have ourselves transformed into merchandise in this fashion. You insult the girl. You are forcing her to understand that she is being sold for a sum of money. No woman of spirit would suffer such a thing; and Violet has plenty of spirit. I give you fair warning—I know what she will do. You will provoke her into open defiance; and she will declare that she will not marry me under any circumstances whatever."

Mrs. Drem got alarmed and told her husband.

"She has none of his headstrong nonsense," said he shrewdly. "She knows the value of money better than he does. She would not give up the chance of saving her father, and getting a rich husband, merely for a fanciful notion like that."

"I don't know," said Mrs. Drem dubiously. "Violet is very sensitive and wilful on some points. Oh, I wish they would marry now, and have done with it!"

"I wish they would," said Mr. Drem. It was the first time he had agreed with his wife since the day of their marriage.

Philip reported to Violet the conversation he had had with his stepmother.

"You are a very wicked person, Philip," said Violet. "They say women are so deceitful, in concealing the truth and smoothing unpleasant matters. But we cannot tell downright bold stories as gentlemen do—scowling at you all the time, and talking in a careless, loud voice, as though you dared not disbelieve them."

"Will you kindly inform me what 'story' I told?" said Philip.

"It was as good as one, then—to say you were afraid I would not marry you, if I found out about the money."

Philip laughed heartily.

"There," said he, "I think you have got yourself into as pretty a fog as I have seen for some time. I tell a 'story' when I say I am afraid you will not marry me. Am I to understand and believe that you do mean to marry me?"

"I will not be driven into a corner," she said, "with your firstlies and fifthlies. It is bad enough to be wicked; but to pretend not to know that you are wicked is far worse."

"I should advise you," said Philip, "to be a good deal more respectful to me; because, as matters stand, people are beginning to think that we are engaged; and by and by, when you have compromised yourself beyond power of recall, I might suddenly marry you. And I am by nature revengeful."

Now this was said as a jest; but both of them had cause to remember it some little time thereafter. For it was actually the case that Rumor had conferred the consecration of an engagement upon the heads of these young people. and, truth to say, Rumor had some ground for the inference. Both Philip and Violet forgot about that line of demarkation which was to separate their private and public conduct. They got so accustomed to go about as close friends, that at balls and dinners, at picnics and croquet-parties, in the Row and at church, in theatre and out of theatre, you always found them together. Could anything be plainer? Mr. Drem ceased to have any more doubts. Even Mrs. Drem was satisfied. Her last wish was about to be accomplished, and the measure of her happiness would be full.

One afternoon Violet called upon Mrs. Drem and seemed strangely distracted in manner.

"I want to see Philip," she said. "Is he at home?"

"I think so," said Mrs. Drem. "I heard him say something about his phaeton only a few minutes ago."

"Would you see if he is in?" said Violet, rather anxiously. "I wish to see him particularly and alone, please, Mrs. Drem."

Philip was sent for, and came. Mrs. Drem left the room.

"Oh, Philip, do you know what has happened?" said Violet; and she went forward and gave him a letter. Her face was quite pale.

Philip recognized the handwriting of Lord Cecil Sidmouth.

"Am I to read all this?" he asked, looking at the number of closely-written sheets that he held in his hand.

"Yes," said Violet.

The letter was a curious one. It began, in the most matter-of fact way, to say that the writer was on the point of starting for America; that he had persuaded a number of his friends to go with him; that they had determined to join a Socialist community which had just been established there; and that they meant to give at least ten years to the experiment.

"We shall encounter ridicule and opposition of every kind," continued Lord Cecil, "and we are prepared for it. We shall have all the Owen and Fourier failures brandished in our faces; that does not matter. What we have most to fear is, the physical breakdown of men who have become effete under the influences of Eastern civilization, and also the lapses of those for whom our code may become too severe. Shall I tell you the basis of our system, Violet, that you may understand what our enterprise is? We believe that the first and best principles of morality known to the world are founded on physiological facts. We go a step farther, and say that morality is the best law of life—the law which best squares humanity with the conditions surrounding it. Whatever we find necessary to the intellectual, moral, or physical welfare of our small community, that is morality; and we mean to enforce it by law. We shall feel our way gradually. We shall not divorce the intellect from the conscience, nor the claims of digestion from either. We shall look upon man as one being; and whatever we find best suited to increase the comfort and usefulness of his life, that shall be our morality, and be made incumbent on us by law. We exclude none of the virtues and graces, which may properly accompany this state of affairs. But whatever is seen to militate against the moral or physical health of our community, that is a blunder and a crime which must be expunged. We shall pass strict laws on drainage as well as on marriage——"

"Have they ladies going out with them to the backwoods?" said Philip.

"You will see farther on," said Violet, apparently anxious that he should get to the end of the document.

"—We shall punish lying as well as theft; in short, we shall have our code embrace, by degrees, every provision for our mutual safety, independence, and moral and physical health. When experience has taught us how to construct this system, we shall expect every one to conform to it, under threat of expulsion——"

"How do they propose to expel the black sheep? They must hire policemen from the Gentiles outside," said Philip.

"Pray read on," said Violet, impatiently.

Accordingly Philip merely glanced over the rest of the letter, which was, in truth, a complete exposition of the aims and principles of the new sect. Many things were spoken of in it which Violet could not be expected to understand; and it was clear that Lord Cecil, before leaving England, had left in her hands this manifesto as to his future intentions, that she might communicate it to the circle of their mutual acquaintances.

Philip returned her the letter.

"It is full of courage and hope," he was proceeding to say, when she interrupted him.

"You have not read the last few lines. Look, Philip!"

The lines which he had overlooked were these:

"I am on the eve of starting. You will forgive me for not calling and bidding you good-bye personally; I could not bear the pain, I think. I am told on every hand that you and Philip are about to marry; and I should have supposed so, if I had not been told. I wish you every happiness, Violet; and Philip knows that I shall not grudge him his good fortune. Shall you and he ever come to see us in America, I wonder? Good-bye, Violet. God bless you; you deserve to be as happy as I wish you to be."

Philip laid down the letter slowly.

"It is you who have done this," said the girl to him, almost fiercely. "It is you who have sent him away from us; perhaps never to come back any more. You have done it, in your selfishness and carelessness. Why did you not tell him that we were not engaged—nor ever likely to be?"

She spoke with a vehemence that was strangely different from her ordinary cool composure; and her face was white, and her dark eyes full of indignation and fire. This woman, who sood there passionate and scornful, with her thin nostrils dilated, her lips firm, and her gestures quick and haughty, was very different from the pretty Violet Kingscote, with the smooth black hair, the placid face, and easy demeanor. Philip regarded her for a moment with some surprise, and then said gently:

"You are unjust, Violet. If Lord Cecil has gone away through a mistake, we can easily bring him back. He does not say in the letter that he has started for America merely because he heard an absurd rumor that we were to be married."

"But I know that is the cause—I can see it all through the letter, however he may seek to conceal it," she exclaimed, hastily. "He is too generous to think that I am to blame; but I know what has caused him to go away from his people, and his home, and his friends, on this wild attempt; and I *am* to blame. I have been the cause of it all."

"Nonsense!" cried Philip. "First you blamed me: now you blame yourself. Why don't you blame Cecil, who is really in fault? For why should he have started off merely on account of a rumor? Why did he not give you a chance of explanation!"

"Philip, we have behaved very badly to him," said Violet in milder tones.

"We can write and tell him to come back," said Philip:

"Don't you see he says he has not left his address in Europe, that he may try this experiment without interference. Besides," she added, looking down to the ground, "I could not ask him to come back, except on one condition, and that has never been spoken of between us."

"You never gave him the right, then, to ask the truth about this rumored engagement?"

"No," she answered, with her eyes still cast down, and her face hot. "He was too proud; it was the old story about money, you know—that horrid money?"

Then she added, presently,—

"You must not think, Philip, that I am vexed about his going for my own sake. But I know why he has gone; and I know that I am the cause of his leaving all his friends, and seeking some wild and wretched prairie or desert, where he may die and nobody know anything about it. It makes me feel so wretched when I think of his living away out there in banishment. I do not want him back for my own sake; you must not misconstrue anything I said, Philip. I was excited, distracted when I first heard of it. Did I offend you, Philip, with what I said?"

"My dear child," he said, "you could not offend me, if you tried. There was some pretty fire under your eyelashes, and you spoke with the vehemence of a small Amazon; but I knew you meant nothing. You cannot quarrel with me, Violet, for I won't quarrel with you. And about this mad resolve of Cecil—it is very unfortunate; but you are not to blame. He ought to have declared his affection frankly, and asked you whether you were engaged."

"There," she said, with a pretty pout, "you are going on the assumption that I wished him to do so. How do I know that he had any affection to declare?"

"Violet!"

"Well, at all events," she said with a toss of her head, although she blushed all the same, "you seem to take for granted that I am vexed at losing a lover. It is too bad of you, Philip; I have already told you that I should be glad to see Lord Cecil back, if I were never to speak to him again. I feel guilty about his leaving—that is all. I liked him very well, of course; who could help it?"

"Who could help it, indeed!" said Philip honestly. "He was the best friend I have ever had—a man as true as steel, who seemed to have no idea of tampering with his conscience in the smallest trifle. But why speak of him in the past tense, Violet? To leave England is not to leave life; it is possible to meet again in the world a man who has gone to America."

"Ten years," she said rather sadly. "Where shall we all be in ten years?"

"In ten years?" said Philip more cheerfully. "Cecil will be returning to England with a bronzed face and a trunkful of wealth. He will be the owner of innumerable mines, oil-springs, farms, and what not; he will have a hardened constitution and a head cleared of all old foibles and enthusiasms. He will step ashore, and his first words will be for you."

"For me? I hope not," said Violet; "that would be worse than his going away. And you forget that he cannot acquire this wealth you speak of; the lands and property of the society are to be held in common."

"The society will break up in six months."

"It may," said Violet, thoughtfully. "But he will not return, I know. I think he wants to forget all about England in these ten years: it will be better if he can."

"Why did he not tell me he was going?" said Philip suddenly.

"Why?"

Because I should have gone with him."

"You!"

"Yes; why not? Have not I something to forget?"

Violet was silent. Philip never spoke of that bygone misfortune; and now even the brief recollection of it seemed to have disturbed him greatly, and he knew not what to say.

"Why are you not honest with me, Violet?" he said, in a moment or two. "Why do you try to conceal the affection you have for Cecil? I saw it in every line of your face, every look of your eyes; and yet you try to hide it. I should be able to console you rather better if you were to tell me honestly that the only man you cared for had gone away from England, and that you were not likely ever to see him again. Is that not true?"

"Oh, Philip," she cried, with the tears starting to her eyes, "how can I tell you? But you know it all; you know how miserable I am, in spite of myself. I try to think it is nothing; I try to shame myself into forgetting my wretchedness. I have no right to think of him; he never told me he cared for me. But it is all over now—all over."

He took her hand in his, and said, with a laugh that sounded strangely,—

"Don't you think the best thing you and I can do is to marry in real earnest? Why not humor the bent that all these events are taking? Why not let us get to the climax at once, and see what is in store for us in life?"

She drew away her hand.

"You frighten me, Philip," she said. "What do you mean? Do you mean that we are both so miserable, that we should join our ill fortunes and laugh at destiny?"

"Destiny is laughing at us," he said gloomily. "She has had the laugh on her side ever so long; but perhaps we are no worse off than other people, if we only knew."

Here Mrs. Drem entered the room.

"Surely you young people have had your confidences interchanged by this time."

She saw at once, however, that something had occurred; and instantly surmised, from the expression of Philip's face that Lilian Seaford had been mentioned between them.

"I have heard some news," she said, pretending to see nothing. "Lord Cecil Sidmouth sailed for America yesterday, without saying a word to any of his acquaintances. Did you know?"

"Yes, Mrs. Drem, I knew," said Violet, "and I came to tell Philip."

Mrs. Drem glanced from one to the other of them, and then observed the letter lying open on the table.

"What was the reason of his going so suddenly?" she asked.

"You may read his letter, if you please," said Violet calmly, giving her the closely written sheets.

"Dear me it is so long," said Mrs. Drem. "I should be detaining you. Will you take Violet out for a drive, Philip? and she may have the letter when she returns, and will you stay and dine with us this evening, my dear? We are all by ourselves."

Philip laughed; Violet blushed; Mrs. Drem looked rather uncomfortable.

"Come along, Violet," he said. "If people *will* say we are engaged, we may as well enjoy the freedom of the supposition. My phaeton is at the door. Won't you come?"

"Yes, go, my dear!" said Mrs. Drem, kissing her.

And so, before she knew what she was about, Violet was hurried downstairs and into the phaeton.

"You look rather uncomfortable," said Philip, as he took the reins in his hands; for whatever companionship they had enjoyed before, they had never gone the length of driving by themselves in the Park.

"I am getting to be resigned," said Violet.

The very first people they saw in the Park were the Delaney's and Miss Thormanby, who all stared with sufficient surprise.

"I wish we had not come," said Violet. "What will they all think?"

"Only what they thought before," said Philip. "We cannot be any worse."

"But now we give them occasion to talk."

"So we did before."

"Well, it does not matter."

"As you say, it does not matter, Violet. And as soon as my father gets Sir James out of his difficulties, then we shall find some means of getting out of this predicament, and you will be free again."

"Yes; free again," repeated Violet with a sigh.

What object had she now in being free? To be free was to be marrieageable; and she did not wish to marry any one.

"You will gain for yourself a bad reputation, Philip," she said. "They will remember your breaking off your engagement with Mary Thormanby, and now this second one with me."

"I cannot help it," said Philip. "There was no engagement in either case. Besides, engagements are only tests after all; and if a man finds it would be better for him not to marry the girl, after discovering more of her character——"

"He ought to have discovered before," said Violet.

"Then let him pay for his laziness and go."

Presently they saw Sir James Kingscote, with another gentleman crossing over from the Albert Gate.

"Oh, there is papa," cried Violet in affright, "along with Colonel Paterson! What shall we do?"

"Stop and speak to them, of course," said Philip, suiting the action to the word.

Sir James looked surprised—not displeased.

"Mrs. Drem wishes me to stay and dine with her this evening, papa," said Violet, with another stupendous blush. She felt as if the Drem family had already caught hold of her, and was dragging her from her own home.

"Very well, my dear," said Sir James; "it is an excellent arrangement; for I must dine with Colonel Paterson, it seems. I will send the brougham for you at ten."

So they drove on again.

"He too surrenders you to your fate," said Philip, with a smile.

"Yes," she said, with another sigh.

CHAPTER XXXIII.

It seemed as though they were destined on that afternoon to meet all their mutual acquaintances; and among the first of these was Mr. Stanberry, whom Philip had not seen since he had been at Torquay. Mr. Stanberry was in an excellent humor: for he had carried an important amendment in the house the night before, he had won the second prize in a pigeon-shooting match that morning, and he was to dine in the evening at a house where he expected to meet the prime-minister. Philip pulled up by the railings: and Mr. Stanberry shook hands with him, and took off his hat to Miss Violet, whom he knew slightly.

"Haven't seen you for a year," he said; "not since we were at Torquay. How is that young lady who was there with her guardian—Miss Seaford, was that her name?"

"She's very well," said Philip, curtly.

And Mr. Stanberry glanced at Violet, and held his peace on that subject.

"Look here," he said, "I took a box for this evening at Covent Garden for my daughters; but I can't go, and neither can they. Can you make use of it?"

Philip turned to Violet.

"Will you go? I can drive you home presently. You can

dress at your leisure, come up to dinner, and we shall make a party of three or four."

"We could not do better," said Violet, promptly.

So Mr. Stanberry was thanked for his box; and Violet was driven home. In due course she appeared at Mrs. Drem's dinner-table; and then it was arranged that Mrs. Drem should accompany them to the opera.

But Violet's observant eyes had already remarked some constraint in the manner of Philip and his stepmother, and suspected that something had occurred in the interval between Philip's return home and her arrival. She was right in her conjecture. Something very important had occurred. Her father, on leaving the young people in the Park, had gone straight up to Mr. Drem's house, in the gayest of moods. After what he had seen, he thought he was safe in claiming the aid which Mr. Drem had promised him; and he accordingly made arrangements to rejoin Colonel Paterson, doubting not that, when they met at dinner, he, Sir James, would be a saved and happy man.

"When they are married, Sir James," said Richard Drem, briefly, "I shall be happy to advance you the money."

"This is too much of a bargain," said the other, flushing haughtily.

"I cannot help it," said Mr. Drem. "I am a man of business. I don't lend money on bad security; neither do I give it away for nothing."

Sir James rose.

"I can understand plain speaking," he said; "but this seems to me intentional insult.

"It is nothing of the kind," said Richard Drem, doggedly; "it is only common sense. You'll be a fool if you take it in any other way than it's meant. You won't get the same chance again; and, as far as I see the young people are likely to marry independently of our affairs."

"Then why drag my daughter into it in this way?" said Sir James. "If they mean to marry, good and well; I have no objection. On the contrary, I could not wish her to get a better husband. Philip is a gentlemanly young man, thoroughly to be trusted, and certain to be an honorable man through his life!"

"Ah, you say right—you say right!" exclaimed Richard Drem. "I have spared no expense in bringing him up—none. You wouldn't believe what that boy has cost me; and I don't regret it. At present I give him £3000 a year—£3000. So that if your daughter is valuable in your eyes——"

"Mr. Drem," said Sir James, with some severity, "once for all, I will not have my daughter put into scales and weighed. If we are to transact this piece of business, it must be between ourselves. I will not have her dragged into it. Confound it!" added the tall baronet, with a flush of vexation and anger, "I would rather sell every stick and stone in my house than insult my own daughter in this fashion!"

"You are a hasty man; you are a man of hasty temper," said Richard Drem, with a gravity which at another moment would have made Sir James roar with laughter. "You are only harming yourself with your hasty temper. If you like, you can leave your daughter out of the question altogether. Call it by any name you like. I will lend you the money, or give you the money, without any reference to the marriage—*but after the marriage has taken place.*"

"I cannot wait," said Sir James.

"I can," said Mr. Drem.

"Isn't it sufficient for you to see that they are as good as engaged—that they *must* marry?"

"No; it is not sufficient. I am a cautious man. The money is at your disposal—so soon as they marry. Get your daughter to encourage Philip to marry her."

"I will not, by God!" cried Sir James. "I am not sunk so low as that. I have tampered with the honor of my family long enough. Her mother would rise out of her grave to save the child from being degraded further. I can afford to be ruined; I cannot afford to let my daughter demean herself. Good day to you."

Before Mr. Drem could recover from his surprise, Sir James had left the room and gone out of the house.

"He makes wry faces at the first spoonful; but he'll swallow the whole of it yet," said the great merchant, with a contemptuous grin.

Then he called his wife, and told her the whole story.

"You should have let him have the money, Richard," said Mrs. Drem, thoughtfully. "He will break off the marriage now."

"He will ruin himself, if he does."

"But he is too proud to care. You must have offended him by your way of putting it. He was quite cheerful when he came; he did not even stay to bid me good-evening as he went downstairs."

"If his stomach is so proud as that," said Richard Drem, "he'd better learn to starve it."

When Philip came in, his stepmother apprised him of all that had happened.

"You know the way your father has of talking," she said. "He must have insulted Sir James. And now what is to be done? Think of Sir James becoming a bankrupt; of Margery House being sold; of Violet and him having to live in obscure lodgings, perhaps in extreme want. It would break her heart to part with Margery House. She is fonder of it, and prouder of it, even than her father is. Think of their becoming beggars, Philip!"

"There is no need for anything of the kind," said Philip calmly. "I will marry her if she likes."

"You will?" cried Mrs. Drem, with sudden joy.

"Yes," said Philip; "I don't see that I can do anything better."

"You will get a charming wife—such a charming wife!" exclaimed Mrs. Drem in delight. "You will be very happy, Philip—both of you. You have known each other so long; and Violet is such a darling creature. Oh, my dear, I am quite anxious you should settle the matter at once. Would you prefer going to the opera alone?"

Philip laughed.

"Would you like to see a poor girl cabined up in a box, with no escape from the man who wants to marry her? What if she says no? Wouldn't it be a charming performance afterwards? Or shall I ask her just before the curtain falls?"

"She cannot say no; she must say yes," cried Mrs. Drem. "Do you know, Philip, you have made me as happy as both of you will be yourselves, I am sure. And I will go or not, just as you please."

"Of course you must go with us," said Philip: and she went.

The opera was *Fra Diavolo*. When Violet—who was dressed pretty nearly all in white, with pearls and a red rose in her black hair—took her seat, Zerlina was just coming forward to sing the Diavolo Song, while the gentlemanly bandit sat and listened to her. The pretty servant-maid was no other than Pauline Lucca, of the shining eyes and thrush-like voice; and the great audience applauded the song so that she had to sing it over again, and then the stage was left to the dramatic business among the brigands.

Mr. Philip chose this interval to tell Violet, in very guarded terms, what, had occurred between his father and Sir James. Mrs. Drem sat and busied herself so with the stage, that she apparently heard nothing; while Violet, whose chair was drawn back from the front of the box, listened with an expression of alarm and pain on her face.

"*Per rimirar la bella*," sang the brigand on the stage quite unheeded.

"What are we to do?" said Violet. "If papa is offended, he will sell Margery House rather than beg anything from Mr. Drem. And I know it must have been on my account that he was hurt—he would not mind for himself. And think of his giving up the old house he is so proud of, Philip. It would break his heart. What is to be done—what can we do?"

"Well, Violet," said he, "there is one easy remedy for all his trouble—and perhaps it is the best thing you and I can do now."

"She looked at him with a quick glance of inquiry and surprise, and a faint color overspread her face. Zerlina, was at this moment taking the money that was to be her wedding-portion, and her soldier-lover was crying with all his might.

"*E posso domandare la tua mano a tuo padre?*"

"Why should we not marry, Violet?" he said calmly. "We should live very happily together, I think."

"Oh, Philip!" she said, "how very generous of you! It is only for my sake you make the offer— I know it is."

"And you accept it!"

"*Vittoria! vittoria!*" sang the soldiers on the stage bringing the first act to a conclusion, and producing a dead silence in the box. For they dared not speak now, or Mrs. Drem would overhear.

"How pretty she is, and how charmingly she sings!" said Mrs. Drem.

"Yes," said Violet, rather absently.

Mrs. Drem pretended not to see any anxiety or constraint in the girl's face, and chattered on lightly until the curtain rose again and disclosed Zerlina's sleeping apartment.

"You know what I have to offer you, Violet," said Philip in an undertone. "And I know what you have to give. But people have married, and have lived very happily, who were merely drawn towards each other by great personal esteem and liking. We must both of us make the past a sealed book, and lay it by—tenderly enough, perhaps—that won't matter. We cannot do better, Violet. You will save your father's credit—you will keep the old house—and you will satisfy everybody concerned. What do you say?"

"*Si, domani, si, domani,*" sang the pretty Zerlina, as she undressed herself before the mirror, and thought of her marriage on the morrow.

"It is so kind of you, Philip, to make it appear that you are anxious for the marriage, when I know you only pretend to be, to make it easy for me to accept."

"Hush! You must not say such things!" he said, with a smile. "Do you think so little of yourself?"

"*Questa vita, ad una serva?*" sang Zerlina, as if she were lendthem a lyrical accompaniment to their whispered talk.

"Philip," said Violet, "you will see how grateful I shall be to you for your goodness. You will not regret it—if I can help it. I shall never forget what you have done for my father and myself, and I will try to repay you for your goodness."

"Then that is settled," said he: while Zerlina, on the stage, was drawing the curtains around her and singing,——

> "O Vergine santa, in cui ho fede,
> Pregate per Ini, pregate per me."

Mrs. Drem turned at this juncture to see why they paid no attention to what was going on, and so they were forced to occupy themselves with the scene. You know that after Zerlina has retired to rest, praying for her lover, and thinking of the ceremony of the following day, her happiness is rudely interrupted, Lorenzo and his soldiers return, the brigand is discovered in her chamber, and the act closes in a tempest of indignation, and anger, and grief.

"Poor Zerlina!" said Violet.

"But she will be married by and by," said Mrs. Drem, with a kindly smile.

Violet glanced to see whether there was any hint in the words of Mrs. Drem having overheard what they had been talking about; but the pretty fair face was quite calm and assured, and the gray eyes told nothing.

"Let us go and have a promenade in the saloon," said Philip, "and fancy ourselves at La Scala."

"It will take a good deal of fancy, my dear," said Mrs. Drem mildly.

They went, nevertheless, and had some ices at one of the small tables, and then returned to their box. All during the last act they paid rather more attention to the opera than they had done; and when at last, Zerlina's troubles and griefs being all over, the curtain came down on a crowd of rejoicing villagers, Philip said to his stepmother,——

"I suppose Zerlina and Lorenzo get married to-morrow."

"I suppose so," said Mrs. Drem.

"I think you may as well ask Violet now when she and I are to be married."

Mrs. Drem, instead of betraying any surprise, took Violet by both her hands and affectionately kissed her on the cheek.

CHAPTER XXXIV.

The small world of London imitates in one way that progressive movement of attraction and repulsion which reigns throughout the universe, and is either making new suns or splitting them up. For a certain time the people of these realms converge to the great centre, until it swells and bursts, and sends them flying into all corners of the globe. But there are many who cannot wait for the autumn scattering.

When the sunlight lies sleepily on the lilac trees and limes of the squares—when the parks are trodden gray and dry—when the water-carts cannot keep the streets moist—when people's houses are a turmoil of visitors during the day and a sweltering cram at night—one gasps for air, and instinctively turns to the south, where the cool sea lies far off around breezy headlands. It is impossible to wait for the great centrifugal stampede, which will, perhaps, carry one to the equally hot streets of Florence, or the burning shores of Constanz, or the stifling galleries of Dresden and Vienna. Down in the south of England there are cunning nooks where the sea is green and clear, where the shingle is cold and white, and there are light winds playing about the shadows of the rocky cliffs. These nooks are not to be found in the blank and bare monotony of the chalk-line, where the air is full of white fire reflected from the cliffs, and even bird-life seems to have been burnt out of the scant and dusty bushes. They are to be found where the coast is jagged and dark—where there are hidden coves smothered in green foliage—where the small boats, lying out in the sunlight, seem held in the air, so clear and shining is the deep water beneath.

Mr. Philip said to himself:

"I must have one last look at Torquay by myself, for I will never take Violet there."

So, with some more or less pertinent excuse, he slipped out of his town circle, and made straight down for Devonshire. He did not know that Lilian Seaford was there, or he would not have gone. He wished merely to have a farewell ramble about the old places which he knew so well, which he might never see again; for he felt that he could not bear to take his wife there.

It was an unhappy chance that brought them together; for what was the use of renewing the sharp and bitter pain that was past? Both of them were trying to forget. He had never sought to see her even, after the marriage. He had carefully avoided going near Hampstead. He had sent her no message; no token that he was alive; and, as far as he was concerned, she might have been dead. They never met once —they took every precaution to let the past die out. They did everything that a prudent and practical world would have counselled them to do; but neither of them any the more succeeded in forgetting.

Philip did not stop at Torquay on his downward journey. He went straight on to Totnes, and put up at the inn at which they had stayed, and rambled about the neighborhood, and took one walk down by the river-side.

"She said we two should never be here again together," he said to himself, "and I laughed at her anxious face. What if I were to see her now—and she were to come walking along the bank there?"

Such an encounter was more possible than he fancied; but it did not take place. On the contrary, he met no one. The spring visitors to Torquay had all left for London—at least such of them as were not detained by illness—and there were no more parties of tourists coming to see the river.

Next day he sailed down the Dart; and the woods now were heavy with foliage, and the meadows a deep velvet-green with their long grass and its white-and-yellow stars. All about Dartmouth, too, the summer flowers were in bloom; and as you passed garden-walls, there was an odor of honeysuckle or sweetbrier in the warm air. He went down to the small church at the point—that and the great blue sea that lay along the line of the sky, were the only things which had not changed. Dartmouth looked quite a different town now; but the sea was the same sea that he and Lilian had looked at together. It was here that she had turned away quickly from the great expanse of blue, and put her hands over her eyes, and found that she could carry up to London a picture of the sea that she loved.

"Does she ever look at it now?" he said, as he sat down on a bit of the old castle, overlooking the steep rocks and the water. "Does she ever think of Torquay? And is the memory of it as pleasant as she used to say it would be? If I had never seen Torquay, I should have found life more bearable."

Indeed, he scarcely dared venture thither. When he drew near, on the next day, the three hills and their white villas and trees, it was with a strange sort of apprehension. He felt that he could scarce bear to look again at the pleasant places that were once so familiar to them. Nevertheless he went to the same hotel at which they had stayed, and hired the same rooms.

The waiters thought it rather odd that a single gentleman should want a big sitting-room—which he used very seldom, and which was costly. But cost was not a matter of much consequence to him, and he kept the room. When he first entered it, he had gone straight to the window. In a corner of one of the panes—so small as scarcely to be visible—he found the letters "L. S." inscribed on the glass—he had scrawled them there in a listless fit on the evening before they left.

There now interposed between them but the breadth of a small town, and neither knew it. Two days he spent there, driving about to places in the neighborhood, or lounging on foot around the rocky shore; but he and Lilian had never met. On the third day, however, he had gone up to the top of Flagstaff Hill, and seated himself on one of the benches there. He had a book in his hand. It was a volume which Lilian had got from the library when they were down there, and which she had been wicked enough to use—as she used most books, of whatever sanctity—for the pressing of wild flowers as they walked along. Philip remembered the name of this book—sent for it to the library—purchased it from the librarian, and had now walked up here to turn over the leaves.

There, sure enough, were the faint stains that had been left by the wild flowers—a tinge of pink or purple, as the case might be, with the outline of the stalk and the blossom indicated. How well he remembered the dingy yellow leaves of this book, in which she used to deposit these treasures, despite his remonstrances! He attached a romantic interest to the dull brown cover—it had many a time been pressed by her hand.

On the top of this windy hill, with the great curve of the bay running out into the sea down there in the south, and with the far coast stretching eastward until it was lost in the white mist of the sky, he thought he was quite alone. He sat and dreamed there, with the book on his knee, of those brief sweet days of his last sojourn in this place, and then he rose to go away, sick at heart.

He saw Lilian Seaford coming towards him, and a giddiness came over him. She did not see him—she might not see him at all, if she only changed the direction of her steps somewhat and went to another seat. She was looking far out to sea as she walked along, and seemed quite unaware of his presence.

Nor did she see him. The graceful figure, dressed all in black, passed on; and the girl sat down on a seat near the edge of the rocks, and opened a book that she carried, though she gazed out on the sea, and not on its pages. How beautiful she looked, his darling of old with the sunlight on the splendor of her brown hair! But her face was dreadfully pale and there was a sunken look about the sad eyes which touched him keenly. Had it not been for that, I think he would have gone away, and spared her the pain of the meeting; but looking at the misery of her eyes, his heart yearned to go and say a kindly word to her. What harm could there be in it? Let them meet as friends merely; but he could not help going to look into the sad face of his old love once more.

She started up from her seat with a slight cry, as if it was his spectre that had approached her, and regarded him with fear and apprehension.

"Won't you speak to me Lilian?" he said. "May we not speak to each other?"

She looked at him, and the tears welled up in her eyes.

"I cannot be unkind to you, Philip; but—but you must go away. Why did you come? Have we not suffered enough? Why did you come and make it worse?"

"I did not seek you, Lilian," he said. "I did not know you were here. We have met by a pure accident—why should we go away from each other like strangers?"

"We need not do that," she said with a sad smile, for his words had reassured her. "Sit down and let us talk a little; then you will go away—from Torquay, I mean, or I will go. For we must not meet, Philip."

"You have not been well, Lilian," he said, looking at her.

He was trembling in every limb. She, on the contrary, so soon as she knew that their meeting was an accident, seemed quite calm and satisfied.

"It does not matter much now," she said, with the same strange, sad smile on her face, and a kindly light in her eyes.

"I have no one to order me about, and make me keep well, as you used to do, Philip. And so you have come down to Torquay? It is very pretty now, is it not? Are you all alone, Philip?"

"How can you talk like that, Lilian?" he cried. "You are trying to look cheerful, and your heart is breaking. My darling! my darling! you are killing yourself; and I am standing by helpless, as if I had never been your friend, and could do nothing for you. But see now, Lilian; I will take you away from this country altogether—we will go away from England, and my little girl will grow merry again and be glad! You are looking so old, Lilian—so worn! I did not know. But see now, my darling, we will go away from England altogether, and you will grow young again, and you will learn to laugh!"

The tears were running down his cheeks as he spoke, and he had caught both her hands in his. She gently released herself and rose, and stood at a little distance, quite calm.

"I cannot be angry with you, Philip—you know I never could be angry with you—but you don't know what you say. You ask me to go away with you to another country—should I be your wife there, Philip?"

He could not answer, and she continued, in the same gentle voice:

"I cannot be angry with you, Philip—I know what you suffer, my poor boy—you do not know what you say. But if I am to speak any more to you now, you must not mention that again. And perhaps we shall not have another chance of talking together '

"Sit down, Lilian," he said. "I will say no more about it—there is an angel looking out of your eyes, and you know what is right. I do not. I think the world is all wrong; and we are blundering about what is wickedness, and what is not wickedness, when our own hearts tell us that these laws are monstrous. I say there is no sin in our going away together—the sin lay in these Lawsons telling you you ought to keep a ridiculous oath——"

"Hush, Philip!" she said. "That is all past now. We must take our life as we find it. There are people far worse off than we are. We have kindly friends, and no difficult work to accomplish. Look at our being here now, in circumstances that thousands would think inconceivably fortunate and happy."

"You have grown very wise, Lilian," he said; "but all this pleasant life has not kept your cheeks from being thin and wasted, and you will have gray hair long before your time."

"I hope I shall never have gray hair," she said, rather sadly.

"You mean that you wish to die," he said; "and yet you ask me to be thankful for our lives."

"You are a man," she said. "You have an active life before you. You have plenty to occupy yourself with; and you must forget all these old dreams. Philip," she added, suddenly, "is it true that you are going to get married?"

"What would you say if I were to answer yes?"

"I would say that I was very glad," she said, with her frank honest eyes looking up into his face.

"That is like your noble and generous heart. But I must tell you all about it," he added, rather shamefacedly, "for I would not have you think that I could change so lightly, and wish to marry only for my own sake."

So he began and told her of all the complicated circumstances which surrounded the proposed marriage. Lilian listened very attentively all through.

"I am very glad, Philip," she said, with a kindly smile! "But you must not think that an apology is necessary. You must not marry her thinking you are doing anything wrong. It is what you ought to do; and many a year afterwards, if she is what you say she is, you will be glad. If you like her so well, and if you admire her so much, you will become very fond of her, I know."

She uttered a slight sigh as she finished the words. Her eyes were looking out towards the sea—towards the point of Berry Head, round which they had sailed in the old bygone time. Her thoughts had reverted to that period, and to the deams she then permitted herself to dream, that some day she might perhaps be to Philip what she now hoped Violet Kingscote would be. It was heartbreaking to him to see the patheticwistfulness of her eyes and the calm sadness of her face. It was the face of a woman now—no longer that of a girl, and he could not somehow help associating it with gray hair and the bitterness of a wasted life.

The purity and resignation of that face had its effect upon him. He dared no more propose that she should burst the bonds that held her, and fly from England with him. There was in reality " an angel looking out of her eyes ; " and he sat and wondered what the end should be—if this beautiful, frail young life were slowly to die away before his gaze, and leave the earth emptied of its rarest loveliness.

Then she rose.

" I did not think I could have met you and talked to you so calmly," she said. " But I have so often thought that we might meet, that it was scarcely a surprise. Now you will say good-bye ; and we must not see each other again for many years. Then you will let me see your wife, Philip; and perhaps there would be no harm then in my becoming her friend —if so grand a lady would care to speak to me, and if you yourself have not forgotten me."

" Forgotten you, Lilian ! "

" Ah, no, you will not forget me Philip ; I know you too well to fear that," she said. " And if anything should happen to me soon, and your wife would come with you to see me——"

" Oh, Lilian, what do you mean ? " he cried in despair. " I will not leave you like this ! I will not leave you ! I will stay and watch over you until you have got better. My darling, you are dying of this misery ! I will not go away from you any more ! "

" Hush ! " she said gently. " You must go away Philip ; and now I am not very ill. This air will make me quite strong and you must not think of me at all. You must go away up to London at once."

Then she took his hand and looked up into his face.

" I am not sorry I ever met you, Philip," she said. " You are the best man I have known ; and I have faith in you. You will be a good man all your life, and a good husband to her. Good-bye, now—and do not be too sad hearted."

She raised his hand to her lips and kissed it gently, and went away. He sat down on the bench that she had just quitted and covered his face and wept like a child.

CHAPTER XXXV.

Events were meanwhile hurrying to a climax of some sort or other with Samuel Hickes. His conduct at this time was that of a madman, marked by wild fits of passion and dissipation, which rendered him quite a picturesque object in the eyes of the small crowd of parasites whom he had attracted around him. His money was rapidly disappearing; and he seemed anxious to squander it outright. One day he would be in deep dejection; wandering around Hampstead and Highgate, as if longing merely to catch a glimpse of his wife from a distance; the next day he would be the reckless leader and prince of a band of dingy reprobates, endeavoring to madden or stupefy himself with drink, and not very often succeeding.

At last he said to one of his companions—a needy Frenchman whom he had met in a billiard room,—

"I want you to write an announcement of my death."

"*Farceur!*" said his friend.

"I am in earnest, Fourvelle; I am indeed. You know the story of my marriage?"

"You tell it to every one each day," said the Frenchman.

"But do you know the particulars? It doesn't matter. All I say is this; the longer I stay in England, the more likely I am to kill myself. I am not going to kill myself for any woman. Fourvelle, if you only saw her——"

"Ah, I know!" said his companion. "What is this about your death?"

"I am going to put matters straight. I have no chance of winning her affection—and I am getting madder about her every day; and if I stay in England, I will kill myself and her both. I want to release her. I have done her an injury; I will make it up to her. You write me now an announcement of my death.'

"I do not understand."

"Suppose that we two are in Brussels—that I die—that you write home to tell her. Don't you see? Then I go to Brussels—post the letter there—disappear anywhere; and she is free to do what she likes. Isn't that acting fairly to her?" he added, ly,d winsth something resembling a sob.

"Oh, very fair!" said the small green-cheeked, dingy person, as he rolled up a cigarette. "Very fair; only she will never have the chance to thank you, and you will not get credit for your good will to her."

"I don't care," said Hickes, doggedly. "You write the announcement."

They were in an obscure dirty little coffee house in Soho. They called for some paper and ink, and his companion began to write,—

"*Madame, jai la douleur de vous faire part de la mort de monsieur votre mari.*"

"That is too formal," said Hickes, angrily, as the Frenchman read out line by line in English. "You must make it appear that you are in the room with the corpse, and describe what you see."

"What a ferocious comedy!" said the other, with a baboon-like grin.

In due time they had concocted between them a dramatic and pathetic letter descriptive of Hickes's death. The professional skill of the quondam playwright was brought into supply the most truth-like details, while Fourvelle translated the whole into lofty and emotional French sentences.

"You laugh not at the joke," said he to Hickes, who was sitting very gloomy and silent.

"I wish it was no joke; I wish it was true."

"My faith!" said the other. "I did not think an Englishman able to conceive such a grand passion. But you do not go right about it. She is your wife; you should go up to the house, and if she behave bad to you—if she will not see you nor speak—then you kill yourself and her, and make a story for the newspapers."

"I don't want to kill anybody," said Hickes, impatiently. "I wish you Frenchmen had some sense."

"I think it is the English who want that," said Hickes's friend, with a polite smile. "You English never get into a passion about anything but your wives. You care nothing for politics, for art, for nothing, but your wives."

"And you French care for nothing but revolutions," said Hickes, scornfully, "and barricades—revolutions and barricades. If a Frenchman were to be dropped into a desert, the first thing he'd do would be to look round for stuff to make a barricade with, just as if he was an animal going to build its nest. Have you finished that letter?"

"You need not talk so loud—yes, there is the letter. Now, what is the address?"

"I won't have you address it," said Hickes. "You'd go and tell her all about it for sixpence."

The small Frenchman started from his seat, and, with a face that was greener than usual with passion, demanded to know what Hickes meant. The keeper of the coffee house, hearing their raised voices, accompanied by a good many oaths in both languages, rushed forward to pacify them; and at length Fourvelle consented to believe that his companion did not know what he had been saying. Hickes, nevertheless, was in no very good temper when he left the place in order to go to Hampstead.

"I will have it out with the whole of them!" he said, clenching his teeth. "They think I'm a feeble, weak-minded wretch whom they can twist round their finger. They'll see! She is my wife. Any other man would have knocked the house about their ears, and blackened her eyes by this time. I have been too gentle with them. I am too simple; but now they will see if I haven't as much determination as anybody else."

"Why you make such a fuss about a woman?" said Fourvelle, who had walked out with him. "There are lots more."

"You don't understand a man raving about his own wife in your country," said Hickes, bitterly. "If it was anybody else's wife, I suppose you would."

"I have a good story about that," said Fourvelle, who let his country shift for itself. "There was a Chinaman——"

"I don't want to hear it," said Hickes sulkily; "I want to go on alone."

The small Frenchman stopped and stared; then lifted his hat and turned away. Presently, however, he came back to Hickes, and said, stiffly,—

"You promised to lend me half a crown."

"There's half a sovereign. Are you satisfied?"

"Mr. Hickes, I take my oath I will pay you like a man of honor; I will pay you before Monday next."

"You won't; nor after Monday next," said Hickes contemptuously. "What's the use of telling lies?"

Again the Frenchman lifted his hat, said nothing in reply, and walked away, having put the half-sovereign into his waistcoat pocket.

"These are the sort of men I have got among," said Hickes to himself, as he got on the outside of the Hampstead omnibus. "Leeches! It is all the polite society I can get for my money."

So he fell to reviewing his position, from the moment that he had consented to adopt Arthur Drem's suggestion until the present time. He came to the conclusion that he was an ill-used man—the sport of circumstances which were unusually cruel; and, most of all, the victim of her who ought to have helped him along in life.

"If she had liked, she might have made a very different man of me. I don't complain. I have never said a word about her selfishness; her going on from day to day thinking of that old sweetheart of hers who is as good as dead—and forgetting me, who ought to be uppermost in her thoughts. It isn't my fault that I have got among these people—that I have spent three-fourths of the money—that I have been drinking in that way. I have never been encouraged. Other people had friends and relatives to back them and help them; I have been alone. She who ought to have helped me won't look at me; and yet I dare say she'd pretend to be precious shocked if she knew how I've been going on. But that was nothing to what will be, if she won't listen to me. If she does turn me away from her door like a beggar, I'll enjoy myself my own way. I'll have a merry life while it lasts. God knows, it hasn't been very merry of late."

This he said with a sigh, which was followed by a careless laugh.

"Conductor," said he, "When you stop at Chalk Farm, you and I'll have a bottle of Champagne."

"All right, sir."

"You don't believe me? There, look at that half-sovereign! Will you believe that?"

The conductor took the half-sovereign.

"You ain't jokin', sir?"

"Either have it or do without it!" said Hickes sulkily. "I tell you to get a bottle of Champagne. I give you the money. If you're not satisfied, I'll have the half-sovereign back."

The conductor, however, was in no hurry to return the money. It was not every day he met with such a chance; and if his "fare" were an escaped lunatic—and there were several peculiarities about his appearance—at least the money was good.

Hickes drank nearly a tumblerful of Champagne, and became very red in the face. It did not improve his spirits, however, on the contrary, he became more and more morose, until, by the time he had reached Hampstead, the conductor had given up the attempt to speak to him.

"He ain't accustomed to swells' drink," the conductor remarked to the driver, as Hickes went down the road. "That 'ere stuff has soured on his stomach."

He was surprised to find a chain and padlock on the small gate leading into James Lawson's front garden. He looked up at the windows of the house—the shutters were all closed. Clearly there was no one within.

There were some people standing in the next garden, and they looked at him.

"Can you tell me where the people who stayed in this house have gone?"

"To Torquay, I think," said one of the group.

"Torquay!" said Hickes. "Thank you." And then he turned and walked down the road.

Presently he walked sharply back to the people.

"Can you tell me why they have left?"

"Miss Seaford was unwell," was the reply.

"So she still calls herself Miss Seaford," Hickes muttered to himself as he left; "and so do these people—just as if she never was married, and as if I wasn't alive. Ill, too, and gone out of London without a word. This is how I am placed. Last year everything was to be so fine and pleasant. We were to live in a house near the river about Twickenham or Kingston; I was to write my plays in peace and security, independent of managers, and doing my best in spite of them; I was to have a pretty young wife that everybody was to rave about; and the Drems were all to be very much obliged to me. Now it turns out that I am left by myself in London. I have spent nearly all my money, and insulted the manager into the bargain; so that he won't look at anything I might send him. She won't even let me see her, and is off with her own people into the country. Here am I, turned out without a human being to speak to, and it's going to rain. It's all her fault; and if the worst comes to the worst, it is she who is to blame, not I."

In his present reckless mood he would have been glad of the society of any tramp or vagabond who would have gone into a public-house with him—he had picked up a good many of these acquaintances of late—but it suddenly occurred to him that he would go down to Arthur Drem, and ask him what was the meaning of the Lawsons leaving London.

"He is sure to know; he is like the devil, and knows everything," said Hickes, as he made his way down to the station of the North-London Railway. How well he remembered going down that road one Sunday evening long ago!

"And has it all come to this!" he complained to himself. "Nobody has got any good out of it except these Drems. I daresay they are all laughing at me now, confound them!"

After he had got into the carriage, he drew out the letter that Fourvelle had written, and read it with a look of imbecile melancholy on his face. He did not understand French very well, although he was a dramatic author; and it was only here and there that he caught the sense of the rhetorical periods descriptive of his own deathbed.

"*In a land of strangers, madam, he died with your name on his lips, true to the last to the woman whom he adored above all the rest of her sex.*"

"There's more truth in that than Fourvelle, or any of these fellows, would believe," said Hickes.

"*With his eyes directed upon a crucifix on the wall opposite him, and with your portrait, madam, pressed to his lips, he breathed his last; and there is now on his face a placid smile, which tells me he died thinking of you, and blessing you for the light you threw on his worldly path.*"

"What will she think of that I wonder?" thought Hickes. "Will she be sorry at last? Who knows but that my wretched fate might at last touch her hard heart, and make her pity me! Then I might suddenly present myself, when she was in a contrite mood—no, it is impossible. She would never forgive me for having deceived her; and she will never know what I have done for her sake. I will shave off my mustache and crop my hair close; I will go away to the end of the earth and die in some fever station—she will be just as if I had never seen her. Surely that will satisfy them all; and God knows I shall not be loth to get out of this world. It's only a happy world for some people; and I'm sure I ain't one of them."

His general grievance against the world gradually shaped itself, as it had often done before, into an indictment against Arthur Drem; and after he had drunk some brandy on the way, he was in no pleasant humor when he entered the Mincing Lane office, and rather loudly demanded to see his former companion and friend. Nor indeed, was he a very respectable looking person as he stood there; and the young gentlemen clerks stared at this dingy and apparently tipsy young man, with the shabby clothes, and bleared blue eyes, and excited look, who insolently returned their stare, and seemed rather inclined to have a free fight with the whole of them.

Arthur Drem came quickly down the office—red and uncomfortable.

"What do you want?" he said angrily. "I cannot see you now; I will see you by and by."

"You will see me now—this minute, if I choose," said Hickes, who had summoned up a vast amount of spurious courage.

Just at this juncture Richard Drem came downstairs with his hat on, apparently about to go out. He heard the last words that were spoken, and was naturally astounded to hear such language in his office and in his presence.

"Who is this person?" he said severely; and all the clerks (who had turned their heads to their desks) were now in the full glow of expectation. Never in the memory of man had the serene atmosphere of Richard Drem's office trembled with such indications of a coming storm.

"If you don't know me, I know you," said Hickes, directing his attack upon the head of the house. "I am no more a 'person' than you are. My name is Hickes—do you know me now?"

"I don't know you, sir," said Richard Drem, in a towering passion. "Get out of this office!"

"Don't you provoke me," said Hickes, warming up in proportion. "I came here peaceably disposed. I don't want to quarrel with anybody. But if I'm driven to it, I'll tell these gentlemen—servants of yours—what you are, and what I did for you; and I'll give you a punch on the head, to follow!"

"Mr. Mowbray!" shouted Mr. Drem, making a desperate effort to control himself, and looking as if an apoplectic stroke would have relieved him much, "go at once for a constable."

"Don't be such a fool, Mowbray," said Hickes.

Mr. Mowbray—the gentleman who, at the beginning of this story, was found sketching the profile of an actress on his blotting paper—turned round from his desk and paused, looking very pale. He was a young man of no great stature, of slight frame; and he wore a very tight and prim costume, his tall and starched collar being particularly stiff, and lending a certain automatic precision to his motions.

He timidly ventured to open the swinging-door in the low partition, and tried to get past Hickes.

"You are an ass, Mowbray!" said Hickes, catching him suddenly by the back of his stiff collar, and shoving him through the swinging-door again, by which means he was thrown somewhat forcibly against Richard Drem.

The disorganization of Mr. Mowbray's collar and tie so upset that young gentleman that he was completely helpless; but there now ensued a general movement on the part of the office to rush at Hickes and avenge their insulted companion. Mr. Drem himself was the leader; and Hickes had already put himself into fighting artitude, and dared him to come on, when Arthur Drem threw himself between them.

"Uncle," he said, "let me pacify this maniac."

"I'll fight you both!" cried Hickes. "I'll smash you both! I'll smash the whole of you!"

"Let me get at him, sir," said one of the young men, who had the reputation for his pugilistic skill, and had taken several lessons from a professor who keeps a public-house in Windmill street.

With that he aimed a blow at Hickes over the partition, which was much more nearly catching Arthur Drem on the eye. For Arthur was now hustling and dragging his excited acquaintance out of the place; and no sooner had he succeeded in doing so, than he warmly remonstrated with him on the insanity of his conduct.

"Don't you see what you've done! My uncle would have given you anything you wanted, if you had approached him reasonably——"

"I don't want anything from you or him," said Hickes. "I've had enough of your money—and much good it has done! I want none of your money. I'm going abroad; and before I go I'll have a flare-up with some of you."

"Did you come to have a flare-up just now?"

No, I didn't. I was peaceably enough disposed; but I won't be insulted by any counter-jumper among you!"

"Why, what a baby you are!" said Arthur. "Are you inclined to be reasonable now? Will you stand me a dinner at the Green Dragon?"

"Yes, if you like," said Hickes, indifferently. "I want to talk to you."

Arthur went inside for his hat, and came out again. The two of them departed for the hostelry mentioned as if they were the best friends in the world, Hickes being merely a trifle sulky and gloomy. Arthur had really taken the surest means of subduing his temper, by talking as if nothing was the matter; and Hickes, who was pliable even in his most ferocious moods, had easily submitted, and was led like a captive lion round to Bishopsgate Street.

Here Hickes recovered some of his cheerfulness; and in a

fit of bravado to show that he had no commercial notions about money, ordered an extravagant dinner, and conducted himself generally as a weak person does who wishes to appear defiant and careless. He had fits of boastful braggadocio, followed by corresponding bursts of pathetic despondency, in which he was almost moved to tears over the hard way in which the world had treated him.

"I wish I was selfish" he said. "Other people are happy because they are selfish, and only look after themselves. They can't get unhappy, because they don't care about anybody else. It's all because I can't help thinking about this girl, Drem, that makes me wretched. Anybody else would have let her go to the devil, if she wanted; I can't."

"You're too tender-hearted—that's a fact," said Arthur, without the least smile, although he looked at Hickes.

"It has come to this at last," said Hickes, taking out the letter and throwing it to his companion.

Arthur saw in a moment what it meant, and said briefly, "No, this won't do."

"Why?"

"Because it won't suit me."

"What have you to do with it?" said Hickes, bridling up.

"Plenty," returned Arthur, coolly.

"I will go abroad, if I like, and send her that letter, if I like."

"And I will go up to her house and tell her it is a lie, if I like. It's no use Hickes. Don't you see what you would do! Do you want to set her free in order to let her marry my cousin?"

"I'd see them both in——first!" said Hickes in great excitement.

"The moment they fancied you were dead they'd go and marry—depend on it. The marriage would be invalid; but what of that, so long as you kept away and they fancied they were all right? Now listen to me. Philip is going to marry that Miss Kingscote, whom you have heard of. So soon as his marriage is over you go and murder yourself in this fashion, if you choose."

"There is some sense in that," said Hickes.

"Yes, I should think there was. Do you know that Philip only came up from Torquay yesterday?"

With an oath Hickes dashed the glass he held on the table, and smashed it into a hundred fragments.

"*That* is the reason of their escaping from London, then—

to connive at his seeing her without my knowing anything about it."

"Nothing of the kind," said Arthur. "He only went down there three days ago—perhaps to see her, because she is ill. If it is any consolation to you to know that you are absolutely in the way of their happiness, you may have it. But as I tell you, if you go and persuade these people that you are dead before Philip has married Miss Kingscote, he never will marry her; he will marry somebody else. But once this marriage comes off, then you can go and do what you like. By the way, how do you propose to live abroad?"

"I don't know—I don't care. What I'm sick of is, living here in this wretched way. I want to put things as they were before I ever went near the girl—only she shall not marry Philip Drem. I will relieve her from my presence; only she must not marry him."

"You strike the balance of justice with an admirable fairness," said Arthur. "Only to leave matters as you found them, you should put Miss Seaford—I beg your pardon, your wife—in the way of marrying my cousin. They would have married but for you."

"You are asking too much," said Hickes, with a jealous frown.

"I don't ask it!"

"You only want to make me uncomfortable," said Hickes, peevishly. "But you needn't remind me that I owe the whole of my present condition to you. Sometimes, when I think of it, I feel that I should like to choke you. I may do that yet, so you needn't laugh?"

"I hope you won't," said Arthur. "You take very absurd views of things. I look on myself as your benefactor. If you have bungled your relations with your wife, it is your affair, not mine. I told you how to secure for yourself a pretty wife and a tolerable sum of money. You got both; and you come and blame me because you have not made a good use of either. It is very unfair, very unreasonable. With any other man I should get angry; but I feel that you've done me a good turn at the same time."

"You're precious clever," said Hickes, gloomily; "but don't come near me when I'm mad with drink, or there'll be an awkward settling of accounts. After all," he added, with some vehemence, "I am not sorry for what is done. If I had not meddled in the affair, she would have married Philip Drem.

And I would sooner cut myself to pieces than see her marry that man."

As he spoke the irresolute mobile features became clouded with a concentrated jealous hate, which produced the most singular expression; and Arthur, regarding his companion, began to think that Hickes might be a more dangerous enemy, when moved by evil passion, than he had fancied. He had not credited him with the capacity for this intensity of feeling, which for the moment made the weak face almost fierce.

CHAPTER XXXVI.

Mr. Philip returned to London and to his duties as Violet's affianced bridegroom. She noticed that he was rather more constrained in his manner towards her after his visit to Torquay; that was all. He still paid her every attention; they went about continually; and although Philip was a trifle more grave and listless than was his wont, nothing interfered with the frank friendship which existed between them.

All their most intimate friends who knew of the engagement congratulated them, of course; and nothing could exceed the exuberant pleasure which Mr. Drem manifested. He took to petting Violet even as Mrs. Drem had done; but he evinced his interest in a much more practical way. He made her presents which astonished everybody, and which Violet was almost frightened to accept.

"They don't go out of the family," said Mr. Drem, merrily, to his wife.

It seemed at last, that the measure of Mrs. Drem's happiness was full. She was so pleased with the successful result of all her schemes, that her daily life was now a perpetual smile. She had nothing to do but reap the delicious results of all her manifold labors; and she saw herself recognized as the good genius of both families.

Of course the little matter with Sir James was soon arranged. He no sooner learned that Violet of her own accord had accepted Philip, then he went to her and said,—

"Is this true that Mrs. Drem tells me?"

Yes, papa," said she, looking down.

"Now, tell me, Violet—is it of your own free will that you

accepted him? You remember what I said to you about our money affairs—you haven't allowed that to influence you? You know, Violet, I would rather be a beggar to-morrow than see you making yourself unhappy in order to please me. Are you sure you accepted him of your own free choice?"

"Why, of course, papa," she said, looking up, but still somewhat red in the face. "I would not marry a man whom I did not like."

"I hope not—I hope not," said Sir James, hastily.

"If you have any objection to Philip——" she suggested, demurely.

"Objection? Pooh, nonsense! You know I haven't. I only wanted to make sure you had not resolved upon this serious step under a false impression that I particularly wished it. I do wish it, of course; but not at the expense of your happiness."

"My dear papa," she said, going up to him, "pray don't make yourself uneasy about me. Do you think, big as you are, that you could compel me to marry a man whom I did not wish to marry?"

"I shouldn't try," he said, gayly; and then, in a moment, he added, rather dubiously. "You know I fancied, Violet, when this was spoken of some time ago, you were not so well inclined towards Philip."

"But that is ages ago," said Violet; "and I have learned sense since then."

Sir James went to Mr. Drem, and made up his quarrel with him.

"You understand, then," he said, rather stiffly, "that my daughter gave her consent of her own choice? that, so far from persuading her to it, I questioned her closely as to whether she had not been under a wrong impression."

"My dear friend," said Richard Drem. "I understand all that. You will forgive my saying that I don't think it any great matter of wonder that a young lady should accept my son without being pressed to it by her father."

"Certainly not—certainly not," said Sir James. "I meant nothing of that kind. Philip is a most exemplary young man; I have said before that I could not wish for a better son-in-law."

"Quite right," said Richard Drem; "you are quite right, Sir James. He and I have had our little family disputes, but nothing of any consequence. Your daughter will find him an excellent husband."

"I hope they will be happy," said Sir James.

"So do I," said Mr. Drem; adding decisively, "and whatever money can do for them, that they will have, or my name isn't Richard Drem."

It was at this time there came to London an Anglo-Indian family, who drew much attention to themselves on account of their appearance, and their regular attendance at all places of public resort. At the Opera or at the theatres, in Hyde-Park or in Kensington Gardens of a Sunday afternoon, the *habitues* remarked this peculiar family, consisting of a tall, sallow-faced, sad-looking Englishman, a short, stout, olive-brown woman who was apparently his wife, a taller and thiner woman of similar complexion and features, six children and a black Ayah. It soon became noised around that the tall man was a Mr. Borromead, who had been in commerce in India and China, and who had sold himself to the devil in marrying the daughter of a rich Calcutta Baboo. The appearance of this woman was sufficiently singular. Her squat and swarthy person was adorned in rich stuffs of the most gorgeous colors, and her bare muscular dark-brown arms were adorned with pendulous masses of jewels which she wore on every occasion. She had a sleepy, dull powerful face, with indolent eyes shaded by long eyelashes; and she betrayed no interest in anything around her, except when the Ayah sought to restrain or correct the younger of the children; and then the dull eyes woke up into a sudden fire, and she assumed the aggressive attitude of an animal defending her young. She never spoke to the tall, gray-whiskered, sallow-faced man who was her husband; he, on the other hand, rarely spoke to her, and seemed to keep separate both from her and the children. These latter she had generally collected around her—sometimes laying a bare brown arm round one of them, with a look of satisfaction, but no smile, on the stolid face. They were of a much lighter brown than she was, and manifested much curiosity in the theatrical performances. She, on the contrary, scarcely paid heed to the stage, but regarded her children with a steady animal-like stare. The taller and thinner woman was her sister. She had a more intelligent look; but she had the same olive-brown skin, the same sleepy eyes, the same dry and jet-black hair; and she wore the same brilliant colors and massive jewellery.

Violet, Mrs. Drem, and Philip were at one of the theatres one evening, and had been noticing the strange party in an opposite box, when Mr. St. John—Philip's elderly bachelor friend in the days when he was secretary to the Analytical Society—came up from the stalls, and said that Mr. Borromead would be glad to be introduced to Richard Drem's son.

"I think he knew your father in China," said Mr. St. John.

Philip went round to the box with his friend, and the introduction took place. He was also introduced to the dusky lady in the fiery garments and diamonds; and she was good enough to bestow upon him for a second or two an indolent and sleepy look of inquiry. Then she turned to the stage, or, rather, she laid her arm on the front of the box, and regarded indifferently the heavy band of plain gold at her wrist, and the mass of rings with which her fingers were incrusted.

"The piece is not very entertaining," said Mr. Borromead, with a look of weariness. "Shall we take a turn up and down the lobby?"

"If you like," said Philip.

The tall man seemed to breathe more freely when he got outside the box. They went into the refreshment-room and sat down, and then he said,—

"I have often wished to have a few minutes' conversation with you. I have seen you often. I recognized you before hearing your name, from your likeness to your mother."

"You knew her?" said Philip, with sudden interest.

"I was engaged to be married to her," he said briefly; and there was more weariness than sadness in his face. Then he added quite suddenly, "Can I do anything for you?"

"Well—no," said Philip with a smile.

"Perhaps my offer was too blunt. I should like to become acquainted with you. Mr. St. John says you were recently not on good terms with your father, and rather wanted money. I wish I had been in London then."

"I am much obliged to you, I am sure," said Philip. "But one is not always in the mood to take money that is offered by——"

"You would have accepted my help," said Mr. Borromead curtly. "Your mother was my best friend; I was her best friend. Don't imagine I am going to say anything against your father. She married with her own free consent. Old Esturiz was ill off; I could not assist them; I was a new arrival, scarcely earning my own living. She would not have married your father but for the sake of her own father; and she had the mortification of finding that her sacrifice was of no avail. Her husband grudged the little assistance she wanted to give her father. Then old Esturiz discovered how matters stood, and refused to accept that little. No woman could be very fond of her husband after that; but she was a good and honorable wife to him to the last. When I think of that time—and I look at it as plainly as I look at this room—I hope I shall never again see any woman whom I know marrying a man whom she does not care for for the sake of his money. Better to be drowned a hundred times over."

Philip could not help thinking that part of the emphasis of this exclamation was derived from Borromead's own experiences; and, oddly enough, his new companion said directly:

"I have seen more of the world than most people, and have seen it in its most prosaic aspects; and I believe that the greatest blunder in life that any man or woman can commit, is to marry for money alone. It is fatal. Once you do that, it is all over with you."

Here Mr. St. John nodded significantly to Philip, as much as to say: "This is his constant complaint. Get him away from it."

"I suppose you have seen a good deal of English commercial life abroad?" said Philip.

The sallow-faced man said nothing for a second or two, and then he said apparently to himself,—

"Good God, how like that voice is to hers! It is so singular. The eyes are the same, naturally; but how can he imitate her voice so, when she died while he was young? You have exactly the voice of your mother," he said, looking up and addressing Philip. "You cannot remember her voice?"

"Not at all. I can remember something of her appearance —a tall, dark-eyed young creature she must have been, I think —very quiet and gentle, and perhaps a little sad."

"You do remember her," said Borromead. "That is her portrait exactly. "I will show you a picture of her, if you like."

"I have never seen one," said Philip. "The one that belonged to my father was lost somewhere in being sent to England."

"Will you come and dine with me to-morrow evening?" he said eagerly. "I'd sooner give you a dinner at my club—you'd find it more lively than my home—but I could not show you the picture. Old Esturiz gave it to me before he died—a year after your mother died. He was in great wretchedness at the time."

"Did not my father help him?"

"I tell you, Esturiz was a proud man; and they did not agree. He would not accept anything. I had but little then;

but I was getting on; and I did what I could for the unhappy old man, who was in extreme want. A few of the residents had to subscribe to bury him."

"I should like to hear all about him and about my mother," said Philip. "When shall I see you again?"

"Dine with me to-morrow evening. But no," he added gloomily, "the dulness would kill you. Lunch with us to-morrow at two; and then I can show you the portrait, and let you get out of the house. And if you can think between now and then of anything I have it in my power to do for you, you will let me know. Your father is a rich man; but rich men's sons are not always independent. You understand?"

So Philip went back to the box.

"What did the Indian say to you, Philip?" said Violet.

"The Indian is an Englishman," he said, "and he knew my mother in China."

Mrs. Drem's pale sweet face was overshadowed by a frown. Heaven knows the small and gentle woman was not devoured by jealousy, and was probably far from grudging Richard Drem's former wife whatever affection he may have bestowed on her; but the meekest of women will begin to hate the member of her own sex who is continually being held up to her as an exemplar to point out her own deficiencies. Mrs. Drem bore ill-will to her predecessor merely because she was being continually taunted with the shining beauties and perfections of her husband's former wife. At odd moments she even expressed a sort of sympathy for Philip's mother, and regarded her as the previous victim; but no sooner did Richard Drem begin to talk of his first wife having been a lady, and so on, than the present Mrs. Drem felt inclined to wish that she and her rival could change places.

"You speak as if I were better off than she is," Mrs. Drem would say bitterly to her husband. "I wish I could change places with her."

Even now, when Richard Drem's manner to his wife had much improved, and he scarcely ever referred to the young Spanish girl who had died abroad, Mrs. Drem could not bear to have her name mentioned; and consequently Philip said nothing farther to her about what Mr. Borromead had told him.

Next day, therefore, Philip went up to Mr. Borromead's house, which was on the north side of Ladbroke Square. The dusky lady of the house was more resplendent in colors, and more sleepy in face, than he had ever seen her before; and she sat at a window and looked over into the square, where her children were playing croquet under the superintendence of the Ayah. Mr. Philip, as in duty bound, began to talk to her and soon found that the only European language in which she could talk with any fluency was French. Accordingly French prevailed at luncheon; and that may have been one of the causes of Mr. Borromead's taciturnity.

There were a number of portraits among the pictures on the dining-room walls; and directly he went into the room Philip recognized the portrait of his mother, guided thereto chiefly by the likeness to himself. All during luncheon he sat and looked at it in a kind of dream, for it seemed to be bringing back to him innumerable sights and sounds of a forgotten time. Even Mrs. Borromead perceived the attention he paid to this picture, and demanded the reason.

"It is a striking picture, is it not?" said the host hastily. "A historical portrait, we believe, although we do not know the original."

"Yes, it is a very striking portrait," said Philip absently.

"Mais on dirait vraiment," said the swarthy woman, "que ce portrait vous ressemble. Les yeux ont absolument la meme expression; on dirait que ce portrait vous reconnait, et voudrait vous parler."

Philip thought so too. He fancied that the face up there, with the soft dark eyes and the tender expression, recognized him, and wished to speak to him. So powerful was this feeling, that he could scarce prevent himself going nearer and speaking to that calm, beautiful face.

"It is a wonderful picture," he said. "Do you know who is the artist?"

"Not I," said Mr. Borromead, glancing anxiously at his wife, whose languid curiosity was aroused. "I got it in China, along with a lot of lumber, in payment of a bad debt."

"Il vous ressemble," said Mrs. Borromeade to Philip; "tellement que nous devrions le donner; vous le feriez passer alors pour le portrait d'une de vos parentes."

"I will give it to you with pleasure," said Mr. Borromead, "if you will care to have it. You *might* make it pass for one of your relatives."

Philip looked at him. He seemed really to mean what he said.

"It is robbing you," said he, "of the best portrait you have. Yet I should greatly like to have it."

"And you shall have it." said Mr. Borromeade. "I will

send it to you to-morrow, if you will give me your address now."

So it was that a man drove down to Mr. Drem's Park Lane house the next day, and left a large covered picture for Mr. Philip.

"What is this you have sent home?" said Mrs. Drem to him when he came in.

"A picture?"

"Yes—I believe so."

"Oh, it is one that a friend gave me; I admired it so much."

"May I see it?"

"Certainly. But it is only a portrait."

"It is so strange that you should have taken a fancy to a portrait," said Mrs. Drem.

Two of the servants carried the picture up to Mr. Philip's study, and there it was uncovered. He was so intent upon looking at it, that he did not notice the curious way in which Mrs. Drem hastily glanced from the portrait to himself, and back again at the portrait.

"It is a fine head," she said, calmly.

"Yes," he said, rather relieved to see that she did not guess who the original was.

"Did you ever see a woman with so tender an expression of the face as that one?" he asked, still gazing wistfully at the picture.

"Violet has a pretty face," said Mrs. Drem with a calm smile.

They both left the room together, and he had no notion whatever that this pale, placid little stepmother had immediately recognized the portrait as that of the woman who had been so often used to mortify her small share of vanity.

Philip never told his father that he had got this portrait; but one day when he entered the study, Richard Drem was standing before the picture. He stared guiltily when Philip opened the door.

"Where did you get that, Philip?" he said gently, yet with wonder on his face.

"Mr. Borromead gave it to me, sir."

"Borromead!" thundered Richard Drem, his manner changing instantly, "How dare that man have a portrait of my wife?"

"I believe he got it, sir, from my grandfather," said Philip calmly.

"Your grandfather, sir, was a drunken old idiot," cried Richard Drem with a red face, "who probably sold the picture for a couple of teals."

"I don't believe it," said Philip. "Mr. Borromead has told me a good deal about him; and he was with him when he died—in deep distress and misery."

"So he has been poisoning you against your father?" cried Richard Drem. "Do you know that he is the man who sold himself to a hideous Indian woman for her money?"

"I believe he did," said Philip. "And I believe he regrets it considerably at this moment."

'You shall not speak to that man. I say, I forbid you to go near him or speak to him. I forbid you to utter a single word to him."

"Pray reflect, sir," said Philip respectfully, "whether I am likely to obey your commands or not, before you announce them. I will speak to Mr. Borromead when I choose to do so."

"Then you had better ask him to support you in idleness!" said Richard Drem hotly. "If I am to support my son, I will exact obedience from him."

"So that if I speak to Mr. Borromead, I must again leave your house—this time being the last, as I told you before. Is that what you mean?"

"No, no, Philip," cried the father in desperation—"I did not mean that. You must not go away from me again—from your old father, who has no other comfort in the world but you. Why will you provoke me? Why will you speak to a man who is my greatest enemy?"

"This is talk for children—not for men," said Philip impatiently. "I am sick of it."

With that he walked out of the house, leaving Richard Drem to consider whether, in his present fit of passion, he should not cut the picture of his dead wife to pieces, merely because it had belonged to his ancient rival.

Singularly enough, Philip had not gone ten yards from the door when he saw Mr. Borromead driving past in a brougham. The carriage was at once stopped.

"I was coming for you. Mr. St. John is very ill, and wants to see you," stammered Mr. Borromead.

They drove to the station, and went down to Wimbledon directly. The old man with the white hair and blue eyes had been suddenly struck down, and scarcely expected to live till the morning. All his thoughts ran upon his collection of beetles, which he was anxious should be given to some institution where they should be properly displayed.

"I have asked you in my will to take care of that," he said to Philip in a weak voice.

"I will do my best," said Philip. "Pray, don't think any more about them."

"You may incur some expense in removing them, and you may have to provide new cases for them."

"That is of no consequence," said Philip.

"No," said St. John with a sigh of satisfaction; "for I have left you what little money I had. Everything I have is yours now—or will be before the morning."

"But have you no relations?" said Philip with some surprise. "I have plenty of money, you know."

"I have not a single relation alive. The money you have you get from your father. You will be none the worse for having some of your own. I wish it was more. I always had a liking for you; and I am sorry I cannot give you what is of more value to you, and let you marry that girl whom you used to speak of."

The words were coming less and less distinct, until they ended in a little sharp sigh. Then the stillness of death.

"His soul went past us just now," said Mr. Borromead with a sort of fear.

Philip remained down at Wimbledon until the time of the funeral. The interval he spent in arranging the dead man's affairs, and getting the beetle-cases into order. After some correspondence, he discovered a public institution anxious to have the collection, and thither it was sent.

All these things being done—the funeral over, the housekeeper and servants paid and dismissed with presents, the house transferred to the landlord, and the furniture bought by him at a valuation—Mr. Philip returned to town. There remained to him out of the St. John estate a sum of £23,000. What was he to do with it? He wished for no better cigars than those he smoked.

CHAPTER XXXVII.

"You and I have not been quite so frank with each other of late as we used to be," said Violet to Philip one forenoon.

They were in the Horticultural Gardens, seated on two gray little chairs in the shadow of a cool lime-tree. Violet, in a light morning costume, was indolently engaged with some graceful fancy-work; Mr. Philip was reading, and occasionally talking to her. Beyond them and all around them a hot June sun fell on the almost empty gardens—on the still ponds, and the gravelled paths, the poplar avenues, and geranium beds.

He laid down the book on his knee, and looked at her.

"I don't think we have," he said. "Because we have both had to pretend that we were anxious about this marriage; and neither of us is. I don't think," he added with a smile, "that we shall be any the worse off for that."

"I am beginning to be afraid," she said.

"Why?" he asked. "You see plenty of people marrying merely for considerations of money and position—women of refined taste linking themselves to men of bad temper and coarse habits. Yet they seem to live well enough on a system of mutual toleration. In our case there is more than that. You and I are never likely to alter our opinion of each other—we shall be sure, at least, never to be on less amicable terms than we are at present. Now, suppose that we are married now—suppose that you and I have come down after breakfast to amuse ourselves in these gardens. I am quite satisfied, for one. I think you are very pretty, you know that nobody could be more amiable—that a pleasanter companion could not be found within these islands—what more do I want? And I shall never think otherwise. I shall always like your frankness, your cheerfulness, your shrewdness, and the bright look of your eyes; and I shall always be thankful to you for marrying me; and we shall get on very well."

"Your frankness frightens me," she said seriously. "When I try to hide from myself the real state of matters, you crush all my self-deception with a few horribly true words. What you say is quite true, Philip," she added sadly. "We can hope for nothing more than that."

"Is it not enough? Why did you and I come here this

morning? Was it not because we like to be together, and talk together?—that we enjoy each other's society?"

"Do you think it is enough?" she said, looking him straight in the face. "Or do you only say so to give me a little comfort? I think you dread what is coming more than I do—only you are too generous to show it. You are not in love with me, Philip, and you never will be."

"I am not," he said. "But whereas, if I were madly in love with you, you might have some natural fear about what may follow our marriage, you cannot as matters stand. A love of that kind might change, and the falling away of it leave you wretched; and my great esteem and liking for you will not change, and we shall always continue on good terms."

"Philip," she cried, with a sudden impulse, "do you believe that? or are you only talking to comfort me? Are you deceiving me? Do you believe what you say? Ought we to marry at all, with this dreadful clear conciousness about us?"

"Shall we be any better if we do not marry?" he said; and then he saw by the expression of her eyes that her thoughts were far away—across a great ocean, in the wild heart of an unknown continent, where a small body of enthusiasts were trying to work out in a new way the problem of life.

"Sometimes I wish we did not know each other so well," she said, "that we were not so hideously frank. I wish we could deceive ourselves just a little bit, to make the future a little bright, if only in the way of possibility. Don't you think we might come to love each other by and by—perhaps years after our marriage? If we could only believe it would come at any time, however late, it would be something to hope for. Philip, what do you think? When you and I are growing old —when these present years will be gone by and forgotten, and we shall have learned to help each other and be kind to each other—will it come then that we shall have the love for each other that we want now, and be really like husband and wife?"

The anxious dark eyes were fixed upon him with so much entreaty, that he was almost ready to swear that he loved her there and then. He avoided the question, however, by saying lightly,—

"Do you want us to be like husband and wife—as we see most husbands and wives? Must I be courteous to all women except you, and browbeat you whenever I have the chance? Must I be glad of an excuse for getting out of your society, to leave you in the house by yourself? Must you become mercenary, narrow-minded, and fretful towards me? I think we will do something better than all that, Violet."

She sat silent for some little time, and then she said,—

"I am very much afraid, Philip. It seems to me we are both persuading each other, giving each other false courage; and that we shall both find, when it is too late, that we have made a desperate blunder."

"Shall we have as much satisfaction in each other's society as we are having now?"

"Perhaps so," she said. "But we shall be miserable because there is nothing more. We shall go on living day after day in a sort of half-listless disatisfaction, always thinking what our marriage should be, and what it is not."

"Violet, you are unreasonable," he said. "You erect an ideal standard beforehand, and are prepared to call our married life a mistake. People would be far more satisfied with their life, if they systematically compared it with less fortunate lives rather than with more fortunate lives. After we are married, you must not think of what our life might be under impossible conditions; you must think what it would have been, had we never married at all."

"You are right, I dare say," she said; "but yet I am afraid."

From the date of this conversation, Violet observed a change in Philip's manner towards her. Was it not strange that her eyes, once so full of gay light and cheerfulness, should have become anxious and apprehensive—should have grown morbidly sensitive to such faint alterations in the people around her? Philip was more attentive to her than ever; in place of the uncompromising honesty of speech that usually existed between them, he strove to place a certain courtesy and restraint, which prevented her asking the real meaning of his attentions. He wanted to comfort Violet by making her believe that he was really falling in love with her, and at the same time to prevent her destroying the illusion by putting direct questions to him. So long as they talked to each other with what she had called "hideous frankness," such an illusion was impossible. She would have found out the truth in half a dozen seconds. He did not love her—would never love her till the end of time; but he liked the girl so much, that he strove to give her the gratification of supposing that he was acquiring a greater tenderness for her than he had hitherto possessed.

The task was not an easy one; and sometimes he sickened of it. Sometimes he felt inclined to go to her and say,—

"Violet, you are right. We shall be miserable if we marry. Better continue good friends as we are."

On the other hand, was it not better to secure the perpetuity of his pleasant friendship by the ceremony of marriage?—and was it not likely to do a great deal of good in other directions? Margery House must not be brought to the hammer.

The possession of the £23,000 rendered Philip more independent of these considerations; and he was inclined at first to hand over the money to Sir James. He decided, however, that he would leave to his father the opportunity of being generous, reserving for Violet's disposal the sum which he had inherited from old St. John.

The state of affairs generally was not a very stable one. It wanted a good deal of argument to show that the course events were taking was the best for all parties; and even when the argument was proved, there remained a lot of lurking suspicions and doubts which were not calculated to give any one concerned a sense of security. The engine was on the rails, and it actually moved; but there was such a vast deal of complicated and delicate machinery, that one became afraid of its meeting with any slight obstacle, which would infallibly produce a collapse and catastrophe.

"Philip," said Violet one evening, "why have you never told me anything about Miss Seaford? You never speak of her at all."

"You forget she is married," he said coldly.

"Do they live happily?" she asked gently.

"They do not live together," said Philip hastily. "They never have lived together."

"Why?"

"I do not know," he said, rather impatiently. "I believe he was sorry for what he did, and went away—and why did you talk about that?"

He rose and abruptly left the room.

On another occasion she entered a room where he was sitting alone. He was so profoundly absorbed, that he did not hear the sound of her approach.

"What are you thinking so deeply about?" she said, putting her hand on his shoulder.

"Shall I tell you?" he said quite absently and dreamily.

"Yes—I want to know."

"I was thinking that there is a man alive whom I may have to murder yet. I think it will come to that."

CHAPTER XXXVIII.

THE collapse of this unnatural condition of affairs arrived at last; and it was sudden and decisive. The atmosphere had been becoming daily more sultry and unwholesome, until there came such a flash of white fire, and such a crackling peal of thunder, as made those concerned jump. When the sky cleared, the relations of these people were found curiously altered; and one not unimportant member was found wanting from the circle.

It had soon become apparent to Philip, that the more he tried to make himself and Violet lovers, the less did they become friends. There was now no need for him to less ententionally the confidence which had of old prevailed between them; it had gradually been supplanted by a certain restraint, which marked each of their meetings. And these had become fewer and less frequent. Mr. Philip discovered that the charming companionship of Violet on all occasions—in the Park, at Opera, ball, and rout, and all the divers places which London offers to young people desirous of meeting each other—was getting less satisfactory than formerly; and chiefly for the reason that the poor girl was evidently in great tribulation as to how this state of matters was to end. She no longer told him so; but he saw that her anxiety had almost become misery, and he was unable to offer her any consolation. As for himself, he was perfectly haunted by a refrain that came to him from out of the half-forgotten past: and the words that were ringing in his ears were Violet's own: "*Whatever you do, Philip, don't marry a woman with whom you are not very deeply in love.*"

This is what it had come to. Mrs. Drem's scheme for the securing of everybody's happiness had been followed out to the letter, and the end of the play was fast approaching, at which all the people were to find themselves in proper combinations and in happiness. Everything had been so assorted, that there was not a single character who had not been properly compensated and settled in life—except, perhaps, poor Cecil; and he had gone off on his own account, and could not be brought on the stage. Mrs. Drem stood by to ring down the curtain, and allow her various *proteges* to retire into that private happiness with which the public had nothing to do.

One day Philip caught Violet in tears.

"What are you crying about?" he said; for he had scarcely ever seen her cry.

"I don't know," she said.

"That is a very good thing," he replied.

"You have not been kind to me of late," she confessed at last.

"I?"

"You are not to blame. You try to be kind, but you are only making both of us hypocrites; and I, for one, am wretched."

"So I have been thinking for some time," he said, gently, "and have been devising a means to alter this unbearable condition of things. The fact is, Violet, you and I must not marry, whatever comes of it."

"We must now," she said, almost with a shudder. "How are we to escape it? My father will be so vexed; both Mr. and Mrs. Drem will be so angry with me and angry against you too; how can we escape it now?"

"You would like to escape?"

She looked at him with a timidity which was not frequently seen on the clear, round, bright face.

"Will you think me unkind if——"

"If you say you would rather not marry me?" he asked with a smile. "Not at all. The fact is, Violet, just as we fancied we were getting everything right, everything was going farther and farther wrong. A week or two more of this, and I should have asked you the same question. As it is, it is better you should ask me to be released from this compact. I had begun to fear it too."

"We were fast ceasing to be friends," she said.

"I was beginning to think you rather a nuisance, Violet."

"I should have hated you, if you had married me."

"It is singular, is it not, how we find out all these reasons for separation the moment we resolve to separate."

"But how can you do it?" she asked. "You will have to do it all; and I am afraid I cannot help you. If I were to say that I won't marry you, because I have changed my mind, they would not believe me. But shall I say that Philip?—I don't want you to have all their anger."

"You leave the matter in my hands," said he, "and don't trouble your head about it."

"Are you quite sure you can get us both out of this terrible situation, Philip?" she said.

"You are so anxious not to marry me! Yes; I can get you out of it in a very definite and irrevocable way."

"What will you do?" she said, in the tone of a small girl to whom a schoolboy proposes some deed of robbery in a neighbor's garden.

"I will make them stop forever trying to make you marry me by marrying you to somebody else."

She scarcely comprehended him.

"Look here, Violet. I have fallen of late into my old useless life—useless to myself and to everybody. Within the last week I have determined to make one final effort to put all these things straight that have been going so confoundedly wrong with you and with one other person. I made one trial a year or two ago, and missed it; this time I *must* succeed, or else get myself abolished off the face of the earth as a blunder. I shall have one more fling at it; and if I fail, you will not hear much more of me. So far as you are concerned, the thing is simple enough. I will start at once for America, and I will hunt out Cecil, and bring him back to you, and make him marry you."

First she turned pale, and then she began to sob hysterically.

"Why was it I could not love you, Philip! You deserved it."

"That would have made matters worse," said he with a smile. "Now listen: I shall merely send a brief letter of explanation to my father and Sir James, telling them both that I will not marry you, and that I have gone abroad. My father will be furious——"

"And Margery House!" said Violet, with a sigh. She saw it going now, and knew that it was partly her doing.

"Your father need not sell Margery House," said Philip, coolly. "I will transfer £15,000 out of my £23,000 to his account at the bank. That will let him get over his present difficulties."

"Oh, Philip," she cried, "you burden me with your goodness! How can I show you how grateful I am!"

"You may have an opportunity some day," he said, seriously, almost sadly. "After I come back—after I have brought Cecil to you—I have something else to do. I may get into trouble, Violet—into disgrace that would frighten you if I spoke of it now. And you are the only one in England whom I shall ask to remain my friend then. And you will?"

"You know I will, whatever it is," she said, bravely giving

him her hand, and looking him in the face, although her eyes were full of tears.

"Whatever comes of it, Violet, you believe the best of me.'

"I will never believe anything but what I know of you now."

These were almost the last words he spoke to her in England. A few days afterwards he had all his preparations ready for leaving and just before he drove to the station whence he was to go down by a night train to Liverpool, he wrote the following letter to Violet's father :

My dear Sir James—I have judged it better for Violet's sake, as well as my own, that the proposed marriage should not take place. If you ask her, she will tell you that it is out of no disrespect to her that I have come to this resolution. I know you would not willingly do anything to interfere with your daughter's future happiness ; and this marriage, we have both of us decided, would not have been a happy one. She is aware of my resolve. She is also aware that—being about to start for America—I have taken the liberty of transferring to your bank account a sum of £15,000, which I now beg you to make use of. You can repay me at any time—I have no particular use for the money; and I ask you to take it merely that Violet should not have to part with Margery House—a catastrophe which she, rightly or wrongly, fears might happen. I must leave her to make my peace with you, and to persuade you to use the money which I have placed in the —— bank under your name."

"There," said Philip, as he put the letter in his pocket, " I hope he will not go off into a passion, and make a vow never to touch the money. But Sir James has a good deal of common sense, like his daughter."

He also wrote a brief note to his father, saying that, in order to avoid the unpleasant scenes which might arise from his having broken off the marriage with Violet Kingscote, he had gone off for a trip to America.

"About *his* going into a passion there is not much doubt," he said, putting the one letter beside the other.

Mrs. Drem was surprised that he shook her hand and bade her good-by when he left that evening to go down to his club. But she thought it was perhaps some bit of serio-comic extravagance, and said nothing.

His outfit and small stock of luggage had been previously sent down to Liverpool ; and now, as he walked into the station, he had nothing but an umbrella in his hand. He was a quarter of an hour early ; and so he got his ticket and was lounging about, when he saw a hansom drive up, from which there descended a young lady, alone, and deeply veiled.

"Violet!" he said in amazement; "why did you think of such an imprudent thing?"

"I could not help coming to see you off—to thank you, Philip—oh, I don't know what to say to thank you!"

"Nonsense!" said he; "get into a cab and drive home before anybody discovers your absence. You must not go driving about London alone like this. And in a hansom too!"

"I thought I should be late," she said.

"I suppose I must see you home," he said, "and take my chance of an early morning train."

"Don't be unkind, Philip," she said. "Let me go on to the platform with you."

So they went on to the platform together, and Violet stood by his side trembling a little with excitement amidst all the bustle of passengers and porters.

"Westward, ho!" said Philip, "to bring back the lover to his own true love! It is a quest worthy of ancient times, is it not?"

He saw that she blushed, because—with the most natural motion in the world—she had lifted her veil, and had raised the pretty round face a little bit. "Take your seats, please!" She gave him two kisses instead of one this time, and said, "God bless you, Philip!" with a sort of sob; and then the train slowly left the platform, and she caught a last glimpse of his face through a mist of tears.

CHAPTER XXXIX.

To go to America to find out a particular man without knowing his address, is rather a bold enterprise; but Philip, once in New York, found, to his surprise and delight, very little difficulty in discovering the whereabouts of Lord Cecil. Public attention had been drawn to the new band of social regenerators, who, undeterred by the numerous failures of the Owen Communities and the Fourier Phalanxes, were making still one more experiment. The constitution of the Washoota Convention, its habitat, and its principal members, were well known in New York; and special prominence in all the articles descriptive of the new association was given to Lord Cecil Sidmouth, who was taken to represent the up-springing of a new feeling among the English aristocracy, and as a pioneer for others of his class.

Mr. Philip immediately left New York, and went down into Pennsylvania. It took him a day to get down to the station nearest the Washoota Convention ; and next morning he got a horse and proceeded to ride over to the farm. It was a hot and bright July day ; and as he trotted along the heavy and sandy road in the glare of the sunlight, the clusters of chestnuts that appeared every where along the watercourse offered a tempting shade ; while here and there he saw a grove of walnut-trees the shadows of which underneath their dark green, were even deeper. The rough and sandy road followed the windings of the river along a picturesque and fertile valley sparsely inhabited ; and when at last he came in sight of Washoota, he regarded it at first as merely one of the ordinary farms of somewhat unusual size.

As he drew nearer, however, he perceived his mistake. First he came to a tolerably-sized sawmill down by the riverside ; and he could hear the whirring of the bands and wheels within. Two or three rudely constructed carts, or rather drays, stood outside, with a couple of good horses yoked in one of them. There was no human being about, however—probably the men were inside.

A minute or two thereafter, however, he came in sight of the new community, Down in some meadows near the river he saw a number of people busy in tossing hay about. Above these meadows, on a level plateau, were a number of plain-looking buildings, which, for the most part being built of new wood, and having vines trained up the front, had a bright and pleasing look in the sunshine. The central building was a two-storied erection, about two hundred feet in length. There was little ornament about it except a projecting porch over the door, and a wooden balcony along the end. The square in front of this large house was prettily planted with plots of flowers. Behind it was a deep grove of walnut trees with a number of wooden seats dimly visible ; and adjoining that a spacious kitchen garden, in which one or two ladies were engaged in gathering vegetables—presumably for the midday meal.

"Cecil's red hair, for a thousand pounds !" cried Philip to himself, as he watched a short square-built young man, in rough trousers and shirtsleeves, busily handling a rake. He rode his horse down to the river side, and hallooed across. Cecil looked up, but did not recognize him.

"Where is your bridge?" cried Philip.

"Come across where you are, if you want anything. It isn't deep."

He forced his horse into the current, and gained the opposite bank; then, so soon as he was clear of the tall weeds, he jumped to the ground and went forward, leading his horse by the reins.

"Cecil, old man, don't you know me?"

"Philip Drem!" said the other, looking as if a ghost had appeared. "What brought you here?" Then he added quickly, "Is she ill?"

"Violet? No. Never was better."

"What is the matter, then? Why have you left her?"

"Leave her? I am not bound to her."

"You are not married, then?"

"No, nor likely to be. Put down your rake, and come and get me something to drink; then I will tell you all the story. I am frightfully thirsty."

"I can't give you anything better than milk," said Lord Cecil, with a laugh. "We have neither wine nor spirits, although, as you see, we have plenty of vines."

"Anything that is fluid will do. So this is your model farm? It is wonderfully pretty; and you seem to live an enjoyable life. What is that in the field beyond the houses?"

"Tomatoes. Did you never see a field of tomatoes? We get eight dollars a bushel for them by sending them to New York."

"But your Convention has not had time to cultivate all this place?"

"Bless you, no! We bought the six hundred acres and the sawmill pretty much as you see them; only we have had to build the small schoolhouse there, and that big building; and we are about to try the making of bricks, when we may still further improve our premises. And how are you, Phil? And how are they all in the old country? By Jove, it's a pleasure to hear your voice again!"

By this time they had left the meadows, and were strolling up by the side of a melon field (very picturesque this was to look at just then) towards the central house. Lord Cecil took his friend into the dairy, and there obtained a tumblerful of new milk from a smart young dairymaid, who blushed a good deal. Mr. Philip wondered whether the blush meant that this was a young lady who was amused at being caught in a masquerade dress. Lord Cecil paid with perfect gravity the sum of one cent for the milk, and then they went outside. Philip's horse had now been brought up by a lad; and Cecil himself took it into the stables and attended to its comfort.

"Now tell me what has brought you here," said he, when they had got into the open air again.

"I came on a mission of search for you," said Philip. "I have been sent to bring you back to England."

"Who sent you," said Lord Cecil, with much astonishment.

"I am not going to compromise anybody; but you ought to guess. Your coming away here was all owing to a blunder. You thought I was going to get married. I had no such intention. It is true that your leaving England, and some other matters which I need not explain now, made Violet and me enter into a foolish and impossible compact. We found it could not be kept. The fact is, we were nearly being goaded into marrying each other; and it was only when the thing became imminent that we saw it would not do. Accordingly I am here. I will not say who sent me; perhaps nobody sent me. But I mean to carry you back to England with me."

"And leave the Washoota?" said Lord Cecil.

"You are a profound impostor, Cecil. As I told you my story I saw your face gradually lay aside its normal scowl, until you very nearly reached the catastrophe of a smile. Then presently you say, with the voice of a sick infant, 'Leave the Washoota?' Why, yes, of course; leave the Washoota—before it leaves you. It is sure to be a failure. Where is the Havershaw Community? Where is the Kendal Community? Where is New Harmony? Where is Yellow Spring Community? Where are all the Phalanxes, and Brook Farm, and Hopedale?"

"You are quite wrong; you are all wrong," said Lord Cecil, anxiously. "The Washoota is different from all these. We are bound to succeed. We have no communion of property; it is an impossible theory. We have no coercive laws about religion; every man may please himself in that, as in everything else, so long as he does not interfere with his neighbor's freedom. We do not invite all the idle and incompetent and swindling populations of the large towns to join us, and share the profits of our labors. We are a joint-stock company, each man being paid for his particular kind of work on a scale of relative values; and the profits will be divided equally among the members at the end of the year."

"How do your shares stand?" asked Philip, with the scant courtesy of a sceptic.

"At par," replied Lord Cecil, boldly. "But we don't aim at making money. We aim at living a wholesome, honest, agreeable, and invigorating life; and all conditions, moral and otherwise, which produce that result we elevate into fixed laws. Moses was the first promulgator of our system. We want to do for modern society what Moses did for the Israelites. Only we shall not frighten our people from eating pig by brandishing thaumaturgic wonders in their eyes. We shall appeal to their reason in raising this or that natural provision into the law.

"And if there are dissentients?"

"We will expel them."

"And if they refuse to go?"

"They must starve."

"And if they steal?"

"We will duck them in the river."

"The fact is, you mean to save the heavy expense of government—which we at home pay in the shape of taxes—by governing yourselves. But amateur governments and amateur farming at the same time, want a deal of attention. How if a lot of you fall sick?"

"We have already instituted a fund for the support of the sick or aged; and the fund is stopped out of the profits. I tell you, we don't want to make money; and our scale of relative values is merely nominal. Breakfast costs three cents, dinner five, supper four. Our wages vary from seven to twelve cents per hour—the latter is the maximum. We guarantee a market for everything that a man does—provided he tells us first what he is going to do—and we give him value-checks for his work; which checks are good against food, and also against the yearly division of profits. If a man likes to save, good and well; but the scale will not permit of any man swallowing up the money of the community."

"The upshot of the matter," said Philip, "seems to me to be this: that your scheme will work well if all your companions are as disinterested as you in their aims. But it will never be applicable to the world at large, until the world at large is peopled exclusively by Cecils. Now, is it fair that you people, who could live honorably and comfortably in any sphere, should withdraw the leaven of your influence from the world, which wants it badly? You are not laboring for the world; the world is not perfect enough to benefit by your scheme.

Your only chance of success is to keep out the black sheep; but if you mean to benefit the world, you must invent something that will include the black sheep. Your farm is a pretty plaything; but it preaches no sort of gospel whatever. It is an amiable association of intelligent persons, who might have got it up in England as well as in America. If you were to offer its shelter and assistance to people in general, you would soon have to construct the same cumbrous system of repressive law and punishment which society has had to get up for its protection elsewhere."

"But, don't you see," retorted Cecil, who looked rather disgusted at having his scheme of general social reformation so ignominiously narrowed in its possibilities, "that even if we can't do the world any good, we can at least retire from the corruptions and affectations of society, and live a sweeter and wholesomer life by ourselves."

"Yes, certainly. But if we have got down to this lower platform, Cecil, what do you say to my mission? You are only pleasing yourself here—you are not working for the good of society. And so I tell you that I have been sent to summon you to England, and I can see something in store for you there better than hay-making and the division of annual profits."

"Get thee behind me, Satan!" said Lord Cecil.

At this moment there rang a bell which was heard all over the farm; and presently there were seen to gather from all sorts of corners and nooks the inhabitants of the small colony, who had laid aside their implements.

"They are coming in to dinner," said Lord Cecil. "You must dine with us. That is the dressing-bell—or rather the washing-bell—and in ten minutes another bell will bring them into the dining-hall."

Philip and his companion entered the hall as the people assembled—men and women, mostly in the prime of life, plainly dressed, very happy-looking and healthy. There were a few young people also, of both sexes; and some children, who were accommodated at a side table. The general table extended down nearly the whole length of the large room; and the windows fronting the balcony being open, a light wind came in and stirred coolly around the place. The dinner was excellent—plenty of plain and wholesome food, in considerable variety, and thoroughly clean and well cooked. There was nothing drank but water.

"What do you do with your grapes?" said Philip.

"Sell them," said Cecil.

"Suppose one were to be sick, and wanted wine?"

"The doctor has wine in his store," was the answer.

"I wish I was ill," said Philip.

"I am not going to break the laws for your sake," said Lord Cecil, sturdily; "so you must content yourself with water."

After dinner there was half an hour's rest, most of the members going into the walnut grove, and sitting down to chat, or read, and smoke. Smoking was nearly universal among the men, so that it was clear the Washoota Convention had been considerate to one of vices. Lord Cecil introduced Philip to several of his friends: and also to a tall, lean, and brown person, who called himself Joshua J. Smith. Mr. Smith condescended—nay, eagerly, consented to take one of Mr. Philip's cigars; and while rolling the same about in his teeth, delivered an extempore harangue on the prospects of the Convention, which he regarded chiefly in their pecuniary aspect. Mr. Philip feebly endeavored to follow his calculations as to the growing of okra and the production of hominy, and finally gave a lazy assent to everything that he said. When he had gone away, Lord Cecil said,—

"We are all afraid of that man. He has got too much power. He owns three-fourths of the stock, and we are beginning to see that he has come into the scheme merely to make money. Any day he might compel us to sell out in order to pay him, and he has used this power to enforce his own notions about various things. He alone was able to abolish the conscience clause we had in the little school here, merely by threatening to burst up the whole concern."

"Ah, then, you are not quite in so flourishing a condition as you had led me to believe," said Philip.

"We are flourishing enough," said Lord Cecil, warmly. "Nothing could be more prosperous: only we want time. In ordinary hands we should have no fear whatever; but this mercenary brute is a dangerous fellow; and several are deeply disgusted, and a few have already left. They say he wants to get the whole place into his hands, and that he would like to get us into trouble, in order to force us to sell the estate, the mill, and the houses to him. Lots of us, on coming here, expended whatever ready money we had in building and improving, without keeping any particular account; but this fellow came with a different purpose; we wanted more money; he lent it to us on the security of stock; the stock became his; in short, he is the principal owner of the place."

"And you are his day-laborers."

"That is an ugly way of putting it."

"It may prove to be the true one when he clears you out."

"To tell you the truth, this man's insolence and intermeddling have nearly made me resolve, on one or two occasions, to quit the place for good."

"Quit it now for good," said Philip. "I thought you would jump at the invitation I offered you."

"If I leave here, it will be a confession of failure."

"Never mind what it is. Suppose the scheme were ever so successful, it would work in no way towards the benefit of mankind. It would set the example of withdrawing from our mixed imperfect society those very elements which it can least spare. On the other hand, don't you understand my message? Anybody less given to theorizing than you would not require a moment to decide."

"I suppose I must go with you," said the red-headed young man, with a sigh, as he looked down on the sunny meadows and the stream. He had really become attached to the spot, and to his dreams of what the Convention was to accomplish. He still believed in it. With a fresh incoming of money, might not Joshua J. Smith—the Old Man of the Sea—be removed from his place?

"You are not very grateful to—to the person whose messenger I am," said Philip.

"I am grateful," he said. "When I get to New York—when I find myself actually on the way to England—I shall be filled with joy. I shall not be able to say how much I thank you and her for a happiness I had given up forever. But just at present, don't you see, Philip——"

And again his eyes wandered over the pleasant valley, until at the corner of the melon field, they lighted upon the lanky figure of Mr. Joshua J. smith.

"If you wait here two days, I will go with you," he said, decisively.

"Can you put me up here?"

"Of course. You may have a bed and such food as you saw; and you can take a turn at something, if you like, to amuse you. Smith wants us to pay for strangers' accommodation, not in the nominal currency of the Convention, but according to the prices which the accommodation would fetch in New York. That is only a bit of his sharp practice; and I suppose he will force it on them by and by."

"Suppose we drown Joshua J. Smith before we go; you

have got no punishment for murder here, have you, beyond expulsion?"

"I wish we could put him through a sausage-machine, or get rid of him somehow."

After all, Lord Cecil was not the foundation-stone of the Convention, and the Washoota people made less fuss about his going than Philip had expected. Two days thereafter, Philip and he were riding along the sandy road to the nearest village, whither Lord Cecil's small stock of luggage had been already sent.

"It was very generous of you, Phil, to come all this way to oblige two unhappy young people."

"I owed Violet a good turn," he said. "But don't suppose she was pining for you. On the contrary, she disguised her affections admirably, and you must not go back with the notion that you are conferring a favor on her. She is rather an exacting young woman, you know."

"Violet and I will understand each other perfectly," said Lord Cecil, who had resumed his eyeglass on quitting his bucolic life. "What I am mostly concerned about is, the extent to which my small income will go in providing her with a suitable house."

"Take a small house in the country, or by the sea," said Philip; "have it prettily and neatly furnished, and keep a good cook, and Violet will be happy. You forget, however, that I was not commissioned to come out here with an offer of her hand to you. Perhaps she won't have you at all. Marriage, in fact, was never mentioned between us—at least *your* marriage was not."

"If Violet has brought me back to Europe for nothing——" said Lord Cecil, speaking as if he were already there.

"You will dog her steps until she repents? Very well; but don't say that I said she would marry you."

Philip never having been in America before, the two friends stopped a day or two in New York, went up to Boston, had a look at one or two of the lakes, and finally sailed from Quebec. Philip, indeed, spent nearly three weeks in America; but he did not write a book about it.

The day after his return, Mr. Philip met Miss Violet by appointment, in Regent Street.

"I am going to take you to see a friend," he said. And she blushed and said nothing, although she had spent the morning in inventing pretty speeches of gratitude for him.

The trysting place was the National Gallery, which on the

student-days may be regarded as the most notorious flirting-spot of London. A good number of the gentler students are accomplished men-slayers themselves, and the policemen in charge of the rooms preserve an excellent gravity when they come upon couples in corners who have been staring at one picture for an hour. Toward four o'clock many gentlemen call, and inquire for their sisters, and the doorkeeper is obliging. From that hour most of the easels are deserted; and fairies in light attire, with green bands through their flaxen hair, consort with grave persons who pretend to have a sympathy with high art; and these walk about in isolated pairs, and become æsthetic in their conversation. Sometimes the flirt is not content with one visitor; and the story goes that there was lately a promising young performer who used to carry about with her three photographs, all fitting one brooch, into which receptacle she placed the picture of him whose afternoon it happened to be. Philip asked for a certain Miss St. Quentin, and he and his companion were permitted to walk up into the rooms. Violet strove to retain her composure, and only partially succeeded. Philip saw that the hand which held a flower he had given her trembled much. In the second room they saw Miss St. Quentin at her easel; a young gentleman was talking to her. All at once this gentleman started from his chair, and came hurriedly forward.

"Oh, Cecil," said Violet, with a pretty look of wonder, " are you here?"

Miss St. Quentin, a tall young lady, with large eyes and artistically-disarranged fair hair, asked Mr. Philip if he had seen the head of Andrea del Sarto, and he went with her to see it. She began to tell him that she had been painting her own face from a looking-glass, and that she had found out that she could see her soul. After gazing for four or five minutes, her soul came into her eyes, and then she tried to catch the expression of it. She went on to touch upon pre-Raphaelitism, and the propriety of girls dressing always in white, and always bearing white lillies in their hands as they sat in their homes. She talked rapidly, vaguely, and prettily for a length of time, until she suddenly found that her companion was not listening, and seemed to be unconscious of her presence.

CHAPTER XL.

ONE evening Hickes sat down and wrote the following letter, which he addressed to "Miss Seaford." He was in the reading-room of an obscure club which he had joined, and which held its midnight meetings in the neighborhood of Charing Cross. It was towards ten o'clock at night, and the place was empty.

"DEAR LILIAN," he wrote—"I have seen you very often of late, although you have not seen me once. I have watched for you, sometimes for a whole day together, and I have been satisfied if I could only catch a glimpse of your face. And then again, when you went away, I have felt more miserable than ever; for you looked so ill and careworn and sad, and I know that I have helped to make you so. Perhaps you will misapprehend me to the last—I cannot help it—but I implore you to give me one last chance to clear myself, and tell you what I cannot tell you now. I have made you afraid of me, I know; and I am not sure you will grant my request. Even then it will not much matter, for I cannot live like this. Do not be afraid; I will never seek to compel you to speak to me; but if you do not, one resource is left me. I will ask to see you to-morrow morning about ten o'clock. If the love I have for you, and the wretchedness I feel, could only plead for me, you would not refuse me an interview of a few minutes."

He went out and posted this letter; then returned to the club. He could not drink anything, and he was quite pale.

Men came in from the theatres, had some supper, talked in the smoking-room, and went home. Hickes sat still, and spoke to none; but as the time went on, he grew more and more restles. He kept turning over newspapers and magazines, but he read not a line.

"Why has everybody gone so soon?" he said impatiently to the waiter.

"It is half-past one, sir," said the man.

"But they are often here until three."

"Sometimes, sir," said the other with a sigh of resignation.

The waiter went downstairs and fell fast asleep. Hickes continued to walk about the room in a restless way. He had been drinking wildly until the day before; then he had suddenly stopped; and now he felt a strange lightness in the head that seemed ready to form itself into odd aerial shapes. There was a newspaper in particular which had fallen beneath a chair; and this newspaper, without the least noise, seemed to have the power of rising and lifting the chair with it, and would then, as gently subside into its former position. He had a general and feverish apprehension that phantasms and hideous things might appear if he suddenly turned his head in any one direction; but this motion of the newspaper was the only abnormal thing that he actually saw.

By and by, however, the newspaper under the chair grew smaller and whiter, and at last had the appearance of the head of a corpse. The corpse was that of a woman, and the face was fixed and blanched, with the eyeballs staring blankly upward. He could not move but only look. He had never seen this woman—the dead face was that of a stranger. All at once, however, the eyes began to move and to look at him, and the face began to laugh.

He sprang upon the table nearest him with a shriek that rang through the empty house. The waiter came running up stairs and into the room; and then Hickes, with the prespiration standing on his pale face, jumped down from the table, and in a hurried and excited way apologized for the noise he had made.

"When will the daylight be here?"

"Presently," said the man, looking to the window, where there was a blue tinge appearing through the blinds.

"I will go now, then," said Hickes.

He walked down the empty street to Charing Cross, and here a strange sight presented itself. All round the gray-stone square the tall buildings were dark and ghostly, and the lamps burned brightly in the violet-hued twilight of their shadows. But overhead the transparent blue had lightened, and behind St. Martin's church there came up from the east a pale clear glow that was faintly tinted with yellow. The new light in the eastern sky glimmered down on the square; but all around the silent buildings were a deep lilac in color, with the shining points of the gas-lamps growing redder as the dawn above cleared and became silver-gray. Far down in the south the clock-tower of the Parliament-houses caught a tinge of the morning on its eastern front; and Big Ben boomed out the hour of three with a slow distinctness that increased the profound stillness that reigned around. There a cab came rattling along from Pall Mall under the dusky blue shadow of the National Gallery; some workmen appeared down in Parliament Street carrying bags of tools in their hands; the white fire above St. Martin's church crept farther over the violet transparency of the sky; the stars in the west sank farther and farther out of sight; and the coming day seemed to bring a breezy freshness with it up out of the east. Hickes shivered slightly, and then turned listlessly to walk up the empty Haymarket, and so northward.

It was still early morning when he arrived at Hampstead. He saw the postman go up to James Lawson's door, and he knew that his message was now being taken in to Lilian. He had got two hours to idle away—how should he pass the time?

He went up to the Heath and lay down, turning his face from the glare of the sun. But sleep was impossible. He felt languid and physically wretched; but he could not sleep. A restless impatience had taken possession of him; and he tossed about on the bare grass, and moaned to himself, and tried in vain to collect his thoughts. Sick and exhausted as he was, there was a fire as of fever in his veins; and all he hoped for was, that he would have enough strength left to carry him over the crisis that was approaching.

As he staggered up to James Lawson's door, few would have recognized in this broken-down, trembling wretch the methodical and contented young man who used to live an easy and uneventful life in Sloane Street. He shook in every limb; his eyes were bleared, and yet restless and wild; his face was pallid and sunken; his gait the gait of a man who has just come out of a fever. He was so weak that, after knocking at the door, he had to steady himself by placing his hand on the wall until the maid-servant came.

"Ask Miss Seaford if I may speak to her for a few minutes."

"Will you come in, sir?"

"No. Go and ask her first—and be quick."

"She said, if you called, you were to come in."

"She said that?"—and the pallid face lit up somewhat.

"Yes, sir; Miss Seaford is waiting for you now."

He entered the house with the air of a delirious man. He was shown into a room; and there before him stood Lilian Seaford quite calm and pale. He started and shook violently when thus confronted with her; then he regarded her for a moment with a strange expression of face; and finally he sank helplessly into a chair, crying,—

"Oh, my darling—I have killed you—I have killed you!"

"Are you ill?" she said. "Can I get something for you?"

He was still trembling violently, and looked, indeed, like a dying man.

"Yes; get me some brandy. No!" he suddenly added, with impetuous vehemence; "I will not take brandy, or anything. I have tasted not a drop of brandy for two days—I will not touch it again."

"I am glad to hear it," said Lilian.

"How cruel you are!" he said. "You speak as if I were a complete stranger to you—as if I were a dog. How cruel and hard-hearted you are, in spite of your pretty face and your soft eyes! You have the face of an angel—something I have never seen in the face of a woman—something that I dream about—and yet you have not the kindness of a woman."

"I am very sorry for you," she said, looking down. "You are ill; what can I do?"

He started to his feet.

"Do you know that, in spite of your cruelty, I love you better than ever a man loved a woman? It is passion within me—a burning thing that is killing me. I do not care whether you are cruel; if you were a devil, I should be quite as hopelessly lost. And sometimes I think you are a devil in guise of a woman; and I make up my mind to tear the mask off, and expose you, and punish you."

She retreated a step or two, frightened by his excited manner.

"Do not be afraid," he said, "I made a mistake just now. I determined not to frighten you—not to threaten—but to beseech from you. I forgot myself that was all; sometimes I lose control of myself like that, when I think over all I suffer. If you only knew what I suffer—the hours of agony night after night, the horrible waking, the weary watching up here to see you, and then to look at the door being shut, and find myself out here alone. Lilian, if you knew how wretched I am, you would pity me. You cannot be so hard-hearted as you seem. I can see in your eyes now that you are not proud and implacable—that you are a little sorry for me. And if you have given me a little pity, why not a little love!—only a little—I beg it from you!"

He stretched out his hands to her; and she was so moved by his entreaty. that it was almost in despair she cried,—

"I cannot—I cannot! Anything but that! for that I cannot

give you. I am sorry—I am distressed, when I hear what you say. There is almost nothing I wouldn't do to make you less wretched than you are. I am deeply sorry; but I cannot do what you ask."

"Will you not try," he said, bitterly. "You are so calm and satisfied, that you do not need the affection of others. You will not try to be affectionate—to think kindly of me, who would be so grateful to you."

"I have tried," she said with a sigh. "If I had thought that it was possible for us to live together on the only terms on which a husband and wife should live together, I would not have been so obdurate as you think I have been. I thought it was possible at one time; I thought I might become affectionate towards you, and that I might forget what led to the marriage. But when it came to the last moment, I knew it was impossible. I should have preferred death. You say I am hard-hearted. Perhaps I am. But I cannot help it—I cannot help it; and I am very sorry. I have tried to like you much, deeming that was my duty. It has all been to no purpose."

"The Lawsons have set you against me." he said.

"Certainly not," she replied. "And I have tried to think only of your better qualities, and to bring myself to like you. I think you might have been very happy with some other woman. Perhaps I have done you more harm than you have done me. If so, I am deeply grieved for it."

"How good you are?" he said suddenly; "how tender, and kind, and thoughtful! You have no selfishness; you say nothing of yourself—of what I have done to you. You are all this; and it makes me the more desperate that I cannot reach your love. Oh, Lilian, is it quite impossible?"

She was silent.

"Is there no hope for me at all—none?"

"I need not tell you what is untrue," she said—and there was a tender pity shining in the dark blue eyes as she looked at him—"I shall never love you as a wife ought to love her husband."

He seemed scarcely to comprehend her words for a little while; and then he murmured to himself, with his eyes turned vacantly towards the carpet:

"None—no hope—none at all! This is the end—I have come to it at last. I thought it was coming. Long ago I seemed to know that I would sit here this morning—is it not strange?— and ask you this very question. I can remember it all as if you and I had lived hundreds of years ago, and had met as we met this morning, and spoken as we have spoken. I remember to have heard you say these things. That is why I am not surprised. This morning I had forgotten. I thought there was a chance. I lay upon the Heath there, and I made myself believe you might have some pity on me. There is no chance now, you say; it is all over and gone."

He moved a few steps nearer the door.

"I have not spoken harshly to you?" he said. "There is nothing of this morning you will remember afterwards and wish it had been otherwise?"

"You must not go away like that," she cried. "You tremble —you are ill. Sit down, and I will get you some water."

"The water you would bring is not strong enough," he said, with a bitter smile. "The water I want to drink is some that will kill in a second."

She shuddered, in spite of herself, as she regarded him; and this he perceived at once, and a shadow of vexation passed over his face.

"What a fool I am!" he said. "I swore I wouldn't frighten you any more. I did not mean what I said. We are parting very good friends, are we not?"

He offered her his hand as he said good-bye; and she strove to conceal the reluctance with which she had to approach him. But when she touched his hand, she started. It was burning.

"I am sure you are ill," she said. "Shall I ask Mr. Lawson to come and see you?"

"No," he said, looking at her with a strange wistfulness. "If I am ill, there is a cure for me. There is none for you. Will you ever be what you once were—what I can remember you— when you were so young and happy, and I could hear you singing in the house when I passed it? It is not a long time since then; but there has been a great change in you—a great change. Can anything alter you back now, and make you what you were? Can we bring back these two years, and take away from your face all they have put there? If I could do that, it would be something; and then you would say, with your kindness, that if I was bad, I was not altogether bad—that I did my best to undo what I had done—that I had tried to make you happy at last. Good-bye: I shall not trouble you much more. You have been far kinder to me than I deserved; but you will never know— my God! you will never know—how much I loved you!"

He tottered rather than walked out of the house, and as he stepped into the sunlight, the fresh breeze touched his cheeks and stirred him. Upon the Heath the trees were green, and overhead the sky was pure and blue; there was a sound of laughter from some children playing in the white dust of the road; and a young woman going past was singing blithely to a baby she carried in her arms.

"The world is a fine world for some people," he said, "but it has been against me. If I only could begin over again! It would be something now to have a holiday, and be at rest with all people, and to come up here and lie on the Heath, and drink in the sunlight and the fresh air. That is all over now. There is sickness and fire in my blood, and I cannot rest. Brandy—brandy!—I must have brandy, or I shall die before I get home."

Some copious libations that he drank at a public-house produced the most extraordinary effect upon him. Going directly to his brain, the spirit produced a sort of delirium; and Hickes got on the top of the omnibus in a wild exuberance of mirth. He laughed and sang as the heavy vehicle rumbled into London; he shouted and tossed his hands into the air; and challenged the conductor to drink some more at the next halting-place.

"You've been 'avin' a drop already, sir," said the man with a laugh; although there were some symptoms of the stranger's hilarity which did not all suggest drunkenness.

When they had got into town, Hickes went to a gunsmith's, and said he wanted a saloon-pistol for rat-shooting.

"I have a rare stock of them," he said merrily. "They have bred plentifully this year, and I want to thin the coveys a bit. May I try the range of these pistols?"

"Certainly," said the gunsmith, taking Hickes into a long chamber behind the shop which was fitted up for the purpose.

Hickes's manner of handling the weapon was dangerous; and once or twice the gunsmith had to put aside the muzzle when it was too directly staring at him.

Hickes fired a number of shots out of various pistols, revolvers included.

"If you fire in that careless fashion," said the gunsmith, good humoredly, "you will kill somebody some day."

"That is precisely what I mean to do," said Hickes, gayly.

"That kind of sport costs too much in this country," observed the other, grimly.

"Tell me, now," said Hickes. "This saloon-pistol looks rather toyish. Are you sure it would kill a rat?"

"You see," said the gun-maker, "that the ball will go through an inch-thick deal board at twenty-yards."

"Is the bone in a man's chest as hard as a deal board?"

"The bone? What bone?"

"Well, the ribs—the plate that covers the chest—whatever it is. Do the ribs go up all the way?"

The gunsmith began to think that his new customer was mad, and hoped he would buy some weapon or other and get out.

At last Hickes chose one of the pistols, and the parcel was made up for him.

"Two pounds, you said, and half a crown for the box of caps? I find I have here two pounds three shillings and sixpence: would you mind taking the whole sum? It is only a whim of mine."

The man looked astonished; but Hickes gave him no time to reply. He put the money on the counter and went out into the open air, saying gayly to himself:

"The last sixpence! the last sxipence! See how I have timed my exit!"

His appearance and the manner of his walking made a good many people turn and look at him. He did not heed them much. He sang snatches of songs—most of them old theatrical favorites, like "The Green Bushes," or "When a Little Farm we Keep"—and recited bits of plays, waving the little brown parcel in the air. Sometimes he laughed aloud; and a startled passer-by would look with dismay on this pale and haggard wretch, whose ghastly hilarity seemed so strange beside his enfeebled frame and sunken cheeks. At length he reached his lodgings, and went singing upstairs.

As he entered his room, his manner suddenly changed. Arthur Drem was there.

"I don't want to see you just at present," said Hickes, gloomily.

"But I want to see you," said Arthur Drem, with some show of anger. "Do you know that Philip Drem has come back from America, and that he knows all about that money transaction between his father and you? He must have got the story from you. Nobody but yourself would be such an ass as to tell him."

"I have not seen him for a year," said Hickes sulkily.

"But you have told some one who knows him. You must have done so. And don't you understand what you have done By heavens, he will murder you!"

"He won't," said Hickes.

"You seem not to care; that's because you don't know him. Mind you, there's no bluster about him, as there is about his father. When he sets about a thing he means business; and if he comes down here to pay you out, he will make it a caution to you."

"Did you come down to tell me all that?"

"I came down to warn you that he is very likely to find you out; and you may be fool enough to tell him more than he knows. I don't know how much that is; but there has been a furious scene between his father and him over it. He is out of the house now, for good and all; and I tell you you had better look out."

"I think you had better look out," said Hickes, with composure. "You came to ask me not to tell your share in the matter. Perhaps I will, perhaps I won't."

"He will throw you out of the window before you have the chance of uttering a word. My advice to you is, to get out of London."

"I am going."

"Where?"

"I don't know, nor you either."

"You are mad—or drunk. You *have* been drinking I see."

"I tell you I don't want to hear any more of your insolence!" cried Hickes, in an excess of fury. "I have business to transact. I am pressed for time. I was in capital spirits till I saw you; and I don't want any more of you. Get out!—if you don't I have got here a pistol for shooting rats, and you'll be the first."

"None of this nonsense," said Arthur.

Hickes untied the parcel, took out the pistol, and put a bullet-cap in it.

Then he went to the farther end of the room.

"One," he said.

Arthur moved towards the door, his face white with rage He did not know how far this madman would go.

"Two," said Hickes.

Arthur caught hold of the door and opened it.

"Four!" shouted Hickes; and the next moment there was a sharp click—not a report—and Arthur heard the crash of the bullet through the panel of the door some dozen or so of inches from his face. He darted on to the landing at once, and heard Hickes lauging merrily inside.

Arthur stood for some time irresolutely on the stairs. He

was vexed to have received this ignominious expulsion; but at the same time the joke that Hickes had just played was a very awkward one, and he did not much relish the notion of facing this devil-may-care wretch again. He heard Hickes shutting and locking the door, and then all was silent in the room.

He descended the stairs, and met the landlady.

"Has Mr. Hickes been drinking?" asked Arthur.

"He have been going on awful," said the frank landlady. "Pore young man, he seems much distressed, and in consequence has drunk hisself as drunk as ever was, night after night. And in the morning he is 'elpless and crying, and wishes he could kill hisself, and is as ill as ill can be and worse."

"I shan't disturb him; I will write to him," said Arthur, who had still a lively recollection of the whistle and crack of the pistol-bullet.

He was just stepping out into the street, when he was confronted by a man who was about to ring the bell. Arthur, looking up, saw before him his cousin Philip, and involuntarily receded a step.

"Don't go away, Arthur," said Philip; "I want you. Is Hickes in this house?"

"Yes," said Arthur, rather timidly. It seemed to him that his cousin had grown graver, sterner, older, since he saw him last; and he noticed that he held in his hand a small wooden case.

"You must go inside with me, to be a witness to an act of justice. You know what Hickes has done,—it's only of late that I discovered the real infamy of it. The law does not punish a crime like that; and so——"

"I told him you would kill him!" cried Arthur, beginning to tremble violently. "I won't go into the house with you; I won't be a party to it. You are going to murder him, and he is so weak he can scarcely stand, and you are strong. It isn't fair——"

"He will have the same chance for his life that I shall have. I shall not lay a finger on him."

"I know what you mean," cried Arthur, who was more green than white with fear, "and I won't be a party to it."

"I think you will," said Philip, calmly looking at him. "I know everything about the hand you had in that business. I may settle with you afterwards; perhaps I shall never have the chance. But I should advise you to come with me just now, for your own safety."

The door was still open; Arthur stood aside to let Philip pass.

"No," said he; "you go on first, and show me the room."

Arthur, trembling in every limb, went up the stairs, and paused before Hickes' door. He was speechless with terror; and when Philip bade him enter the room, he clung to the railing as if determined not to budge a foot. Philip went to the door himself, and tried to open it. It was locked. He rapped on the splintered panel; there was no reply. Then he went back a step, lifted his foot and drove the door in.

The spectacle that then met their eyes made Philip drop the box that was in his hand, while Arthur uttered a cry of horror. On the floor before them lay Hickes, with his mouth open, dead. There was no trace of blood about; but there lay by his side the saloon-pistol with which he had shot at Arthur. Arthur stood at the door, with a complexion as ghastly as that of the prostrate man, and saw Philip go forward and lift Hickes's arm.

"He is dead," said Philip.

At length Arthur, still trembling, ventured forward and the landlady, who had been alarmed by the smashing in of the door, came running upstairs and entered the room, where she broke into a series of hysterical cries.

"Be quiet, woman!" said Philip. "We must carry this unhappy wretch to his bed; where is the room?"

She opened a folding-door; and she and Philip—Arthur would not go near the corpse—lifted the body and put it on the bed. Presently Arthur followed, carrying in his hand a paper which he had picked off the table. He handed it to Philip, who read these words, written in a straggling and tremulous hand,—

"This is the last time, Lilian, I shall ever speak to you. When they show you this paper, you will know that I have tried to make what reparation I could for all that I have done to you. I hope it is not too late. I hope you will get well and strong; I hope you will get the old color and light back to your face. In a minute or two I shall set you free; and you will be able to do what you like. Don't think too hardly of me. I have acted badly by you; but I did not know that I was going to be so desperately in love with you—so wretched and broken down. If I have done wrong, I have had my punishment, and this is the end. You don't know what I suffered in wandering about, trying to get a glimpse at you, and never received a word or a look from you. Since there is no hope for me, I don't care to live; and in any case, I am determined to do my best by you now. Good-bye; and don't think I was so bad as I seemed to be. Forgive me for all that I have done——"

The letter was not finished, nor was there any signature. Philip turned to Arthur, who was looking at the corpse, and said,—

"Are you pleased with the result of your work? You ruined this miserable man's life, and you have murdered him. I came to punish him—that duty has been taken out of my hands. But you, who are a greater scoundrel than he ever was, remained unpunished——"

"But you should be satisfied—you should be satisfied," cried Arthur. "Isn't this enough? There is no harm done to you, or to her, that can't be set right now. Why should you want to hurt me? I will do anything you like by way of reparation. What can I do, Philip—what can I do?"

"We will see," said his cousin.

CHAPTER XLI.

PHILIP went abroad, wandered about from town to town for about a month. At the expiry of that time he could no longer control his impatience. Finding himself in Paris, he suddenly started one evening by the express-train, and found himself next morning in London. He rested for a few hours at one of the large railway hotels, and then took the train up to Hampstead.

As he drew near to James Lawson's house, it seemed to him that the blinds on the windows were all drawn down. What was the reason of it? Hastening his steps, he approached the house, and saw with dismay that his eyes had not deceived him.

"Have I come too late?" he groaned aloud. "Is it all too late now—while I have been idling abroad, and keeping back from her?"

He went up to the house—the door had inadvertently been left open an inch or so—he entered, and hurriedly walked into the small parlor where the family generally sat. The first thing that he saw was the figure of Lilian bent over the table her face resting down on her hands. He uttered a cry of joy, and she started up.

" You are not ill ! " he cried, taking her hand.

" Hush ! " she said, and he saw that her eyes were full of tears.

" What is the matter ? " he said, too overjoyed to think of her possible answer. " I thought you were ill, or dying, my love, my darling; and now I hear you speaking to me—and I know you are mine now—forever. But, Lilian, what is the matter ? Why are you so silent ? Are you vexed with me for not coming sooner ? Did you think I was not coming ? "

" Not that—not that," she said ; and she crept closer to him, and hid her face on his breast. " Of course I knew you would come, Philip. But don't you know what has happened —why the blinds are down ? "

" Alec ? "

" Yes," she said. " And the last words he said to me— only this morning—were, ' *Why doesn't Philip come to you—why doesn't he come ?* ' He has been asking for you during all these three days, since ever he knew he would not recover. And I tried to make him believe that you would come; and he was very wretched about it. We sent for you repeatedly—no one had your address. It was for my sake that he was so anxious you should come. I could not convince him."

" And I was forcing myself to stay away," said Philip, " lest you should think me indecorous in my haste to see you. I wish I had come sooner. It was with difficulty that I remained abroad so long. What was his ailment ? "

" He died of fever; but he had been very weak and ill of late. Mr. and Mrs. Lawson are beside themselves with grief; you must not ask to see them now."

" You look very worn, Lilian, and tired. You have been sitting up all these nights."

" Sometimes for a little while," she said.

" Will you go out now and breathe the fresh air ? "

" Ought I ? " she said, looking up to him with her simple obedience of old.

" Yes," he said. " You can do no more good at present. And you must consider yourself a little—it will be quite a new experience for you."

" I mean to take very great care of myself now," she said. And he kissed her and she left the room.

In a few minutes they left the house together; and Philip turned, according to old habit, towards the East Heath Road.

" Not that way—not that way," she said, with a slight shudder. " I wish never to see that road again. You must take me away, Philip, where I shall forget all that time, and what has happened since."

"What is the time you remember with most pleasure?" he asked.

"Why, you know," she said.

"Yes, I know," he said. "And I shall take you down to Devonshire; and we will live there if you like, and take up the threads of our past life there, just as if nothing had occurred since. When we go down, you will begin to think it was quite lately you and I walked down by the Dart that evening—you remember?"

"Have I ever forgotten it? And we shall go down to Paignton—shall we not?—and walk on the sands; and we shall see Brixham, and Berry Head, and the sea; and we shall go again to the old church out on the Point. But I was all wrong, Philip, about bringing away a picture of it. Do you remember, I told you to shut your eyes, and you would carry away a clear memory of it? I have never been able to bring the picture before me; for whenever I thought of the place and of you, I could not see anything for tears."

"The time of tears is all over," he said.

"Is it ever over?" she asked with wistful eyes.

Her brief experience of life had not been a very joyful one.

"You have a great balance of happiness to receive, my darling," he said. "You have had all your griefs at the outset of your life. Providence owes you a deep debt of happiness. And the very first thing I shall do will be to prove you a false prophet out of your own lips. I will carry you off to Tor Bay; and you and I shall see the Dart together once more; and I shall laugh at your prediction."

"You must never laugh at it, Philip," she said, gravely, "or at anything that has happened since then. We cannot forget these things; we shall never forget them. Perhaps, if we are to have happiness now, it will be all the sweeter when we think of what is bygone. And oh, my darling, the delight of talking to you, and being with you again, is almost more than I can bear."

So they wandered on, not heeding very much where they went; and their speech, somehow or other, came back and back again to Tor Bay. In imagination they seemed to hover around the pleasant shores that had once been so beautiful to them: and all their brighter schemes for the future had the sea and the sunlight and the green hills of these Devonshire scenes mixed up with them.

"You will have to grow younger now," he said. "You are scarcely twenty but you look twenty-five. So next year, when you are twenty-one, you must look twenty-four; and when you are twenty-two, you must look twenty-three; and when you are twenty-three, people will think you are twenty-two; until, when you are twenty-five, you will be back again to twenty—and less than twenty; and we shall have you running and laughing and singing, as you did at Torquay. Do you remember when you ran back all the way from Paignton, only because you feared to be late for breakfast?"

"You had no flowers, for your table that morning," she said.

"Only one—a rose," he answered. "And until you have grown young again, I think I must give up petting and patronizing you. You have lost all your childish ways; you must get them back them again before I begin to spoil you. You are too much of a woman now, Lilian—your eyes have been so sad of late."

"But I am going to take great care of myself now, I told you," she said. "I will think of nothing but happy things; and I will get strong—for you would not care for me if I were poor, and haggard and weak."

"My darling," he said, "if your hair were white, and yourself grown quite old, I would pray to have white hair and to grow old for your sake. But it is youth, not age, the next years will bring you. I will take you out into the sunlight, and get back your color, until you are like a wild rose. Who was the Wild Rose of the Dart in the old times?"

"In the old times!" she said with a sigh. "I daresay the Dart is as beautiful now as it was then; and has gone on since, not caring for us or remembering us; and has sung quiet songs in the evening for all sorts of people except us."

"And now it will sing a song for us—not quiet, but brisk and cheerful—in the morning; and if it doesn't, we will appeal to the sea, and you shall hear the laugh and the splash of the waves all around the coast from Berry Head to the Thatcher!"

"But there is no singing like the singing of the Dart," she said. "It is so still in the evening, like the stirring wind in the woods."

Then she said,—

"You are not on good terms with your father?"

"No," he said; "nor can I ever hope to be. It is only quite recently that I learned a story which I shall never tell you, because it would make you believe that the world was full of devils. But what I discovered then has almost made it impossible that my father and I can ever meet again. When I look at your face, and think of how he and others were implicated in producing the suffering that is written there, I declare to you that forgiveness seems impossible. It is too much to ask of any man. It is enough charity if I keep my hands off them; and I don't mean to have any settling of old scores with either my father or my cousin. I cannot forgive them. If forgiveness ever becomes possible, it must come from you."

"If I thought it would please you to be friends with your father," she said "I would go to him to-morrow and make my intercession."

"You go to him?" he cried in alarm; "you must never go to him without my knowledge and presence. Do you understand, Lilian! I will never risk a repetition of all that is bygone."

"But how are you and he ever to become friends?"

"I am in no hurry."

"I did not think you so unforgiving."

"You don't know what you ask," he said, hastily. "You know nothing of what he and others have done; and I will not tell you—it would do you no good to know. When I see you getting young and blithe again, I may think differently; but just at present—just at present—when I look at you——"

"Ah, don't talk like that, Philip?" she cried. "You make me afraid. I have never seen you like that before. They must have done you some terrible wrong."

"It is you whom they have wronged, and I have kept an account of it; yes, I have kept an account of it. I have put it aside at present; but I have not drawn my pen across it."

"But some day," she said, with a smile, "when I am rummaging among your things, with the curiosity of—of——"

"Why don't you say it?" he said.

"Suppose that I said it," she said with a blush—"and I come across the book that holds the account, I will take it out into the garden—we shall have a garden, shall we not?—and I will light a small fire of dried leaves and sticks, and put the book on it, and you will see it burn quite away."

"And we will get somebody to gather up the ashes very carefully so as not to leave a speck, and carry them down to the sea-shore. No; I wouldn't have the sea polluted with the remains of such a story; we shall have a hole dug for them in the sand, and bury them out of sight."

"Tell me now, what are you going to do, Philip," she said. "What is your work going to be?"

"To make you strong and cheerful, in the first place," he said. "Don't you know that I have a small sum of money that might keep us very well? Only I must have some occupation besides; and we shall settle all that afterwards. When once we get down to Tor Bay, we shall construct schemes by the dozen. And all the time the sea-air will be making your cheeks pink and your eyes bright again."

"Now let us go back to Mr and Mrs. Lawson's," she said, with some sudden compunction for they had almost forgotten the trouble of these poor people in their own joy, and so they returned to the house, and gave such comfort and assistance as they could. They had been out for something less than an hour; Lilian had grown a year younger in the time, and the difference in her look was apparent to every one.

About three months after that Philip and she, one calm afternoon, stood by a grave.

"To-morrow we go away," she said, "and yet I don't feel as though we were leaving those that are buried here behind us. They follow us as the moon follows us, wherever we go, and we have only to look up and we find their faces there. Did I ever tell you, Philip, how vexed I was that poor Alec should die and not know that you had come back? For I thought he would go to mamma, and tell her that he had left me miserable, and she would be very sad. But now she must know that you came, and Alec must know, also, and my father; and they will all be happy to see how happy I am."

"Are you so very happy already?" he asked.

"I could not be more happy," she said, as she stood there with her head on his arm.

Then she said,—

"I think the more friends we have up there the less we can tell the difference between that world and this. It seems an easy thing to go and join them—except for leaving you, Philip. Oh, my darling! I hope we shall live together and die together—always together until the end; and then it does not much matter how short or how long life may be."

That is the cry of many souls that scarce know whether to hope or fear—that find life a mystery around them, unsettling, uncertain; while the seasons come and go, and the dead are at peace.

www.ingramcontent.com/pod-product-compliance
Lightning Source LLC
Chambersburg PA
CBHW030309240426
43673CB00040B/1113